Born in Sussex, **Douglas Streatfeild-James** grew up in Malta, Britain and Canada. After graduating from Oxford University in 1989, he spent six years in the army where he honed his map-reading skills to 'adequate' and learned that being cold, wet or hungry was definitely to be avoided. Since a pre-university spell spent wandering around India and Nepal he has been travelling at every available opportunity. During periods of extended vagrancy, he has trekked in South America, canoed across France and motorcycled across Europe.

Douglas is the author of *China by Rail* and he has contributed to *Silk Route by Rail*, both also from Trailblazer. He wrote Lonely Planet's *Goa* guide and is co-author of LP's *South India* guide.

Trekking in the Pyrenees
First edition: 1998; this second edition: 2001

Publisher
Trailblazer Publications
The Old Manse, Tower Rd, Hindhead, Surrey GU26 6SU, UK
Fax (+44) 01428-607571
info@trailblazer-guides.com
www.trailblazer-guides.com

British Library Cataloguing in Publication Data
A catalogue record for this book is available from the British Library

ISBN 1-873756-50-X

© **Douglas Streatfeild-James 2001**
Text, maps and photographs unless otherwise credited

© **Sarah Jane Riley 2001**
Cover photograph and photographs opposite p161 and p225

© **Nick Hill 2001**
Illustrations on pp61-4

The right of Douglas Streatfeild-James to be identified as the author
of this work has been asserted by him in accordance with
the Copyright, Designs and Patents Act 1988

Editor: Patricia Major
Typesetting: Henry Stedman
Layout: Bryn Thomas
Maps and index: Jane Thomas

The quotation from *A Moment of War* (Laurie Lee) on p291 is reproduced
by permission of Penguin Books

Warning: mountain walking can be dangerous.
Please read the notes on when to go (pp20-2) and on mountain safety (pp36-9).
Every effort has been made by the author and publisher to ensure that the information contained herein is as accurate and up to date as possible. However, they are
unable to accept responsibility for any inconvenience, loss or injury sustained by
anyone as a result of the advice and information given in this guide.

Printed on chlorine-free paper from farmed forests by
Star Standard (☎ +65-8613866), Singapore

TREKKING
IN THE
PYRENEES

DOUGLAS
STREATFEILD-JAMES

WITH ADDITIONAL MATERIAL AND RESEARCH BY
GREG & JANE KNOTT, ED ELTON,
SARAH NEWBY, DEAN SEWELL,
PETE HAWKINS AND GILL HARRINGTON

TRAILBLAZER PUBLICATIONS

Acknowledgements

There are lots of people to thank for helping with the second edition of this book.

Firstly, a big thank you to the people who helped to update the guide. Thanks are due to Pete Hawkins and Gill Harrington for their work on the GR10 section between Bagnères de Luchon and Aulus Les Bains; to Ed Elton and Luke Southwell for covering all of the GR10 to the east of Aulus (and a few sections to the west of it); to Greg, Jane and Freddie Knott for an extremely thorough coverage of the GR10 through the Pays Basque, and to Sarah Newby and Dean Sewell for their detailed research of the GR11 route through the Aran Valley. There is no way that I could have covered the entire route by myself, this time around, so without their help this book would not literally not have been possible.

Secondly thanks are due to Simon Mills who walked with me for two and a half weeks along of the GR11 and to Sarah Jane Riley who set the pace during a fortnight in the Central Pyrenees.

On the trail I was grateful for the company and advice of those I met along the way, including among others John Critchley, Richard Friend, Alison Gould and John Darley. Thanks also to the users of the first edition of the book who wrote in with their comments: Heather Ann Jilks, Trevor Crippin, EJ Neather, Wim Busschers, Paul Ellis, Robert Turner, Jeremy Smallwood, Vicens Olmos i Blanch, Richard Mattey and Richard Bell. Thanks, too, to Neil and Rossella Hardy for helping out (twice!) with missing information on Ax-les-Thermes.

Finally, special thanks are due to the people who put the guide together: Bryn Thomas for seeing it through, Patricia Major for editing it, Corinne Sinclair for euro conversions, and Jane Thomas for drawing and editing more brilliant maps.

A request

The author and publisher have tried to ensure that this guide is as accurate and up to date as possible. Nevertheless things change: prices rise, new hotels are built and trails are rerouted. If you notice any changes or omissions that should be included in the next edition of this book, please write to Douglas Streatfeild-James at Trailblazer (address on p2) or email him on dougsj@trailblazer-guides.com. A free copy of the next edition will be sent to persons making a significant contribution.

Updated information will shortly be available on the Internet at
www.trailblazer-guides.com

Cover photo: The Brèche de Roland, from Refuge des Sarradets
© Sarah Jane Riley

CONTENTS

PART 4: CENTRAL PYRENEES

Hautes Pyrénées, Haute Garonne, Ariège, Aragon, Catalonia – Facts about the region

General description 155– Hautes Pyrénées, Haute Garonne & Ariège 155 – Aragón and Catalonia 156 – Getting there 157

INTRODUCTION

From the rolling foothills of the Basque Country to the bare rocky peaks of the Maladetta Massif, the Pyrenees have something for everyone. Deep green valleys characterize the western end of the range, while dusty brown slopes speckled with vineyards are distinctive in the east. The harsh, empty landscape of the Central Pyrenees can be forbidding and beautiful by turns, with its passes, gorges, caverns and waterfalls.

The Pyrenees offer all that's best in walking: fantastic scenery, great places to stay, good weather and, above all, variety. Serious trekkers will relish the chance to seek out the untouched valleys of the high mountains. Those who prefer an easier pace can stay closer to civilization, enjoying the culture of the area through which they are walking. The region can provide the best of both worlds. Stay high in the mountains for days on end if you like, either camping or using the excellent mountain refuges that are available on both sides of the border. When you decide to venture down, the hills are scattered with beautiful villages, ideal places for an overnight stop. Try the local wine and cuisine, relax and regain strength for the next day on the trail.

There's a wide variety of other activities, too. If you like to break the day's trek for an hour or two, there are literally hundreds of perfect lakes in which to cool your feet or, if you're hardy enough, to swim. The clear mountain tarns are ideal for a day's fishing, and the ancient churches are worth a visit in their own right. For the adventurous there's everything from mountain biking and paragliding to rafting and rock climbing.

Traditionally the Pyrenees have been compared to their nearest neighbours, the Alps, and because of their inferior height have somehow remained off the walker's 'wish' list. The result is an area of mountains which has, for the most part, escaped the commercialization that has occurred elsewhere; a place where there is still scope to explore an area of untouched natural beauty.

USING THIS GUIDE

In this guide the region is split into three sections: Western, Central and Eastern Pyrenees. The introductory chapters cover getting to the mountains and what to expect when you get there. Thereafter, the information about each area is to be found at the start of the appropriate section. If, for example, you are planning to go to the Basque country (Western Pyrenees) you will find information on trains, planes and buses in Part 1. Information about local bus services once you arrive is to be found at the beginning of the section itself or in the relevant village section in the trail guide.

Trail maps

The sketch maps in this book are designed to be used in conjunction with large-scale contour maps, not to replace them. The maps are drawn to make route planning easier by showing the detail which other maps do not: **walking times**, **accommodation**, **viewing areas**, **water points**, **accommodation**, difficult **route junctions** and other useful observations. Everywhere to stay that is within easy reach of the trail is marked – be it a top hotel or an empty shack. Further details about each place can be found in the text.

Routes and walking times

The routes are described from west to east, the direction in which most walkers tend to tackle longer treks through the Pyrenees. A good reason to follow the trend if you're walking the GR10 is that it involves a long uphill stretch on most mornings and with an early start you can complete much of it in the shade. If you plan to walk from east to west allow for the fact that the timings on the maps may vary slightly in the opposite direction.

Note that the time given along the side of the map refers only to the time spent walking, so you will need to **add 30-40% to allow for rest stops**. Remember that these are **my timings** for the section; every walker has his or her own speed. With the first edition of this book, several readers commented that they found these timings on the fast side. The times are, however, consistent so you should err on the side of caution for a day or two until you see how your speed relates to my timings on the maps. When planning the day's trekking, count on between five and seven hours actual walking, and allow for an occasional rest day.

Spelling and vocabulary

Consistency becomes very difficult in a book like this where three languages (French, Spanish and Catalan) are involved as well as anglicanizations. Well-known place names presented no problem but the situation became confusing when, for example, on a single map sheet Orbaiceta was also spelt Orbaitza and Orbaizeta. Words used only in a small region, *gave* (stream) for example, were simple, but others commonly used throughout the Pyrenees are often spelt differently in different places. The word *étang*, for example, is used for many lakes in the French Pyrenees; in Spanish it's *estany* and in Catalan *estanh*. Likewise the word refuge: in French *refuge*; in Spanish *refugio* and in Catalan *refugi*.

Accordingly I have spelt everything exactly as it appears on the maps that walkers are most likely to be using, with no attempt at standardization, and I have, as far as possible, used the French and Spanish word or phrase appropriate to the region.

With a group or on your own?

INDEPENDENT TREKKING: OFF THE BEATEN TRACK

If you're an experienced mountain trekker, and enjoy long days through deserted valleys, you'll find plenty of memorable treks in the Pyrenees. In order to get away from the crowds, you'll have to venture a little off the beaten track but within a relatively short distance there are some wonderful places to discover. Miles into the mountains, you can pitch your tent amidst magnificent scenery and if you are lucky have the place all to yourself in the morning. There can be disadvantages: camping can be miserable in poor weather, and what with food, cooking gear and a tent, you'll have to carry much more in your rucksack. For most trekkers, however, the effort is amply repaid.

INDEPENDENT TREKKING VIA GÎTES D'ÉTAPE & REFUGES

If the thought of spending your holiday hauling a huge backpack around the mountains doesn't appeal, fear not. There are enough facilities along the major paths to bring independent trekking within the reach of everyone. From early June to late September the main routes through the Pyrenees are well served by *gîtes d'étape* (lodges) and *refuges* (mountain huts), where food and accommodation are available. If you use these throughout your trip, you can cut down substantially on the amount of kit you need to carry – a light sleeping bag is all that is needed for overnight gear. Quite apart from lightening the load, there are other perks: a hot shower at the end of the day, delicious local food, and even cold beer.

Staying in lodges is obviously more costly than camping, and it's less flexible, too. There may be occasions in peak season when you have to adjust your plans in order to be sure of having somewhere to stay. In two or three areas along the GR10 and several sections of the GR11 where no accommodation is available, walkers are forced either to camp or make use of *cabanes* (shepherds' huts). These areas, almost entirely towards the eastern end of the range, are clearly marked in the book.

GROUP TOURS AND GUIDED WALKS

The decision of whether or not to trek with an organized group may rest on several factors, but if you enjoy the company of other people and would prefer to leave the route planning to someone else, a group walking holiday may be for you. There can be great advantages in joining a group: you may, for example, have specialist guides who can point out local flora and fauna. These are often local people who can tell you about the area you are passing through, and groups that are led by professional mountain guides may be able to follow a mixed itinerary of trekking and other adventurous activities such as rafting or climbing. On the mundane side, if you are going with friends whose stamina and trekking skills vary, the provision of transport ensures that the slower ones can take a break while the rest enjoy a full itinerary. Trekking companies offer various permutations: you can be part of a large or small group; you may be accompanied by a guide throughout the day or simply pointed in the right direction to enjoy the walk by yourself.

The drawback in taking a guided walking holiday is that you may find yourself tied to a fixed itinerary and to a large group of other people. An alternative to being part of a group is to get a trekking company to tailor an itinerary just for you. Several companies do this and will make bookings for all transport and accommodation in advance of your arrival.

TREKKING AGENCIES

Many specialist agencies offer guided treks. While most of them have standard walking tours, several also cater for special interests or abilities.

Trekking agencies in the UK
● **HF Holidays** (☎ 020-8905 9388, 🖹 020-8205 0506, 🖳 info@hfholidays.co.uk, www.classicwalking.co.uk) Imperial House, Edgeware Rd, London NW9 5AL. HF Holidays use Barèges in the central Pyrenees as a base for one- and two-week guided walking holidays, with a choice of an easier or harder walk each day. In addition to their Classic Walking holidays, they also offer a Natural World trip specializing in flora and fauna, and an Alpine Rambles trip for those who like taking things more easily.
● **Exodus Walking Holidays** (☎ 020-8673 0859, 🖹 020-8673 0779, 🖳 www.exodus.co.uk) 9 Weir Rd, London SW12 0LT. Exodus run small group guided treks of one or two weeks' duration, particularly in the Central Pyrenees. They also have groups which specialize in other activities including mountain biking, canyoning, paragliding, rafting and winter walking.
● **Naturetrek** (☎ 01962-733051, 🖹 01962-736426, 🖳 www.naturetrek.co.uk) Cheriton Mill, Cheriton, Nr Arlesford, Hampshire, SO24 0NG. Naturetrek run guided birding and botany tours to both the Spanish and French Pyrenees. Groups of 10-16 people are accompanied by an expert naturalist.
● **Pyrenean Mountain Tours** (☎/🖹 01635-297209, 🖳 pmtuk@aol.com & pmtfrance@aol.com, www.pyrenees.co.uk) No 2 Rectory Cottages,

Rectory Lane, Wolverton, Tadley, Hampshire, RG26 5RS. This small company runs summer and winter mountain walking trips from its base in Luz-St-Sauveur. They organize both guided and non-guided walks and can plan an itinerary to individual requirements.
● **Ramblers Holidays** (☎ 01707-331133, ▤ 01707-333276,🖳 info@ram blersholidays.co.uk), Box 43, Welwyn Garden, Herts AL8 6PQ. Ramblers Holidays run walking holidays in Andorra.
● **Headwater Holidays** (☎ 01606-813333, ▤ 01606 813334, 🖳 info @headwater.com, www.headwater-holidays.co.uk) 146 London Rd, Northwich, CW9 5HH; Headwater offer one-week walking holidays in the central Pyrenees, based at Argèles-Gazost in the Val d'Azun, and at Ax-les-Thermes.
● **Pyrenees Adventures** (☎ 01433-621498, ▤ 01433-620135 🖳 www.pyr adv.demon.co.uk) Clifton House, Hill Head, Bradwell, Hope Valley, S33 9HY. Pyrenees Adventures specialize in guided walking trips in the Basque country from a base in a traditional farmhouse. In addition to their standard walking tours in the Basque country, they also organize a Spanish Border Trails trip, following the GR10 and GR11, which is designed for the fitter and more adventurous.
● **Cox & Kings** (☎ 020-7873 5000, ▤ 020-7630 6038, 🖳 www.coxand kings.co.uk) Gordon House, 10 Greencoat Place, London SW1P 1PH. Cox & Kings run a two-week botanical tour to the eastern Pyrenees.

Trekking agencies in Continental Europe
● **France La Balaguère** (☎ 05.62.97.20.21, ▤ 05.62.97.43.01, 🖳 bala guere@wanadoo.fr, 🖳 www.balaguere.com) Route d'Argeles-Gazost, 64500. La Balaguère is probably the biggest of the trekking companies operating in the western and central Pyrenees.

● **Germany STB-reisen GmbH** (☎ 06128-982513, ▤ 06128-982515, 🖳 stb-reisen@t-online.de 🖳 www.stb-reisen.com) Platter Str.87, 65232 Taunusstein. This company specializes in all aspects of French tourism, including walking holidays.
● **Wikinger Reisen GmbH** (☎ 02331-9046, ▤ 02331-904704, 🖳 www .wikinger.de) Kölner Str. 20, D-58135 Hagen. Wikinger offer walking tours to the Eastern Pyrenees.

● **Netherlands SNP Travel** (☎ 024-3277 000, ▤ 024-3277-099, 🖳 ww w.snp.nl) PO Box 1270, 6501 BG Nijmegen. SNP offer individual walking and cycling tours all over Europe.

● **France Individuelle** (☎ 020 688 0066, ▤ 020 686 9359, 🖳 www .france-individuelle.com) Danzigerkade 10, NL 1013 AP Amsterdam. France Individuelle offer walking tours in the French Pyrenees and give you the option of hiring a donkey to help transport your kit.

Trekking agencies in the USA
● **Cox & Kings Travel** (☎ 800-999-1758, 🖹 813-258-3852, 💻 www
.coxandkings.com) 25 Davis Boulevard, Tampa, Florida 33606. Cox &
Kings run a two-week botanical tour to the eastern Pyrenees.

Trekking agencies in Canada
● **Butterfield & Robinson** (☎ 416-864-1354, 🖹 416-864-0541, 💻 www
.butterfield.com) 70 Bond St, Suite 300, Toronto, Ontario, M5B 1X3.
Butterfield organize a couple of eight-day walking trips, both of which are
based in the Western Pyrenees.
● **World Expeditions** (☎ 613-241-2700, 🖹 613-241-4189, 💻 worldexpe
ditions.com) 78 George St, Ottawa, Ontario, K1N 5W1. World expeditions offer a week-long walking tour of the Cathar castles and another
week on the pilgrim trail to Santiago de Compostela.

Trekking agencies in Australasia
● **In the French Pyrenees** (☎ 0500-500301, 🖹 0500-500302, 💻 pyre
nees@acenet.com.au, www.acenet.com.au/~pyrenees), PO Box 469,
Bowral, NSW 2576. Patrick Arrieula, a native of Béarn, offers walking and
gourmet tours in the French Pyrenees around the Béarn and Basque areas.
The tours are run in May and October, usually over nine days. Patrick can
also offer tours for private groups with a tailor-made itinerary.
● **Pyrenees Adventures** (☎ 02-9929 5347, 🖹 02-9922 4765, 💻 pyr
adv@ozemail.com.au, web: www.pyradv.demon.co.uk) 82 Bellevue St,
Cammeray, NSW2 2062. Pyrenees Adventures specialize in guided walking trips in the Basque country from a base in a traditional farmhouse.

Getting to the Pyrenees

The Pyrenees are accessible by road, rail and air: you can reach the mountains from almost anywhere in Europe in a matter of hours. A good public transport network facilitates getting right into the mountains.

BY AIR

For the Basque country, the closest airport is Biarritz, although Bordeaux
is much better served and is only three or four hours by train from the
mountains. Pau airport is useful for access to the western part of the central Pyrenees, as is Lourdes, although direct flights to either of these from
outside France are almost non-existent; you'll have to go to Paris and get
a connection. The best-served airport near the French Pyrenees is
Toulouse, which also has excellent connections into the mountains themselves. Perpignan airport gives best access to the Mediterranean coast.

In Spain, Bilbao is a good option if you intend to start walking from the Atlantic coast, and Barcelona is worth considering for access to Andorra, Ax-les-Thermes and the Catalan Pyrenees.

From the UK

Prices Scheduled flights direct from the UK to one of the Pyrenean airports, using a major airline such as Air France (☎ 08450-845 111), British Airways (☎ 08457-733 377) or Iberia (☎ 0845-601 2854), all tend to cost around £200 (although flights to Barcelona are slightly cheaper). Fares on the 'no-frills' airlines – Go (☎ 0870-607 6543), Easyjet (☎ 0870-600 0000), Buzz (☎ 0870-240 7070) and Ryan Air (☎ 0870-333 1242) – can be much cheaper, and it's quite possible to get a return ticket for under £100 if you book far enough in advance and take advantage of special offers. Note that these airlines positively encourage you to book online; an extra charge may be made if you book by phone. See p16 for web sites.

● **Bordeaux** British Airways has two direct flights every day from Gatwick. Air France has several daily flights between Paris and Bordeaux, but currently has no direct flights from the UK to Bordeaux. At the time of writing, Buzz had yet to confirm whether they would be running a flight from Stansted to Bordeaux, and the frequency of any service.

● **Biarritz** Ryan Air has a daily flight from Stansted to Biarritz. Air France has no direct flights from the UK, but has eight daily flights between Biarritz and Paris.

● **Pau** There are no direct flights from the UK, but Air France has several daily flights from Paris to Pau.

● **Lourdes** There are no direct flights from the UK, but Air France has a daily flight from Paris to Lourdes.

● **Toulouse** British Airways has three flights every day from Gatwick. Air France operates three flights per day from Heathrow, and also offers a service from Manchester via Paris. At the time of writing the frequency of Buzz services between Stansted and Toulouse was still to be confirmed.

● **Perpignan** Ryan Air has a direct daily service from Stansted. None of the major airlines has direct flights from the UK to Perpignan, but Air France and AOM French Airlines (UK ☎ 01293-596663) have regular flights from Paris to Perpignan.

● **Barcelona** BA has four flights every day from Heathrow and Gatwick, and one flight a day from Birmingham. Iberia operates two flights a day from Heathrow. British Midland has a daily flight from Heathrow. Easyjet has daily flights from Luton. Go operates a daily flight from Stansted.

● **Bilbao** British Airways has two daily flights from Gatwick, and Iberia operates a daily service from Heathrow. Go has a daily service from Stansted.

 Airline websites
Booking direct from an airline's website can sometimes be cheaper than booking through a travel agent and with the UK-based 'no-frills' airlines (Go, Easyjet, Ryanair, Buzz) it may be the preferred method of booking. Some no-frills airlines make an extra charge for telephone bookings.

No-frills airlines
www.easyjet.com
www.ryanair.co.uk
www.buzzaway.com
www.go-fly.com

Other airlines
www.britishairways.com
www.iberia.com
www.airfrance.com

The **Flight Centre** has a useful website where you can check schedules and prices for all scheduled flights (apart from those of the 'low cost airlines') departing from that particular country. There are currently five local websites:

Australia www.flightcentre.com.au
Canada www.flightcentre.com/canada
New Zealand www.flightcentre.com/nz
UK www.flightcentre.co.uk
USA www.usa.flightcentre.net

From Continental Europe

There are direct flights from some of the major European cities into Toulouse but to get to any of the other Pyrenean airports, you will almost certainly have to go to Paris and change. The best people to try for information (apart from your local travel agent) are Air France and the national airline of the country from which you are flying.

From the USA, Canada and Australasia

There are no direct flights from the USA, Canada or Australasia into the Pyrenean airports, so you'll have to go to Paris or another European airport. Check with a travel agent to see which airlines are offering the best connections.

BY RAIL

The French rail network is excellent, providing fast services to the major cities in the foothills of the Pyrenees and regular connections, either by train or by bus, to some of the towns and villages in the mountains. Combined with the 300km/h Eurostar service from London to Paris, rail travel from the UK to the Pyrenees is an attractive option. With an early start from London, and a good connection, you can be in Hendaye by mid evening.

TGV

Although there are a large number of daily trains, the most convenient method of rail travel to the Pyrenees is by TGV (*train à grande vitesse*) –

Rail information
Rail Europe (a subsidiary of SNCF) provides a quick and efficient service by which you can order rail tickets and have them mailed to you at no extra charge. Contact details in the UK are: **Rail Europe UK** (☎ 08705-848 848, 🖷 08705-717 273) 179 Piccadilly, London W1V 0BA. The website (www.raileurope.co.uk) has excellent information and also gives details of service agents worldwide. Insurance and car hire can also be arranged through this organization and there's an associated company which books accommodation.

the French high-speed rail network. Travel by TGV costs a bit more than a ticket on a slow train, and reservations are required, but the comfort and speed more than make up for this.

Bayonne, Biarritz, St-Jean-de-Luz, Hendaye, Pau, Lourdes, Tarbes and Toulouse, are all served by the TGV. From Paris to any of these cities takes around six hours.

Other services
Although only the stations listed above are served by the TGV, there's a range of normal services too, including some direct trains from Paris and elsewhere that go right into the heart of the mountains. St-Jean-Pied-de-Port, Bagnères de Luchon, Ax-les-Thermes and Banyuls-sur-Mer are the main stations involved. Details of services from main railheads into the mountains are given at the beginning of each relevant section of the book. Fares are cheaper on normal trains than on the TGV.

Discounts
Passengers on all services can save money by travelling off peak (*periode bleue*) or by buying tickets well in advance. There are numerous money saving schemes and the offers seem to change from month to month, so it's worth asking when you enquire about or book your ticket. Recent offers have included:
● Children aged 4-12: 25% discount
● Young people aged 12-25: 25% discount (50% if travelling off peak)
● Senior travellers (over 60 years of age): 25% off for off-peak travel
● Découvert Séjour: 25% off fares as long as you stay for a Saturday
● Tickets booked eight days in advance: 25% discount
● Tickets booked 30 days in advance: 40% discount
● Discovery 2: 25% discount for two people travelling together

BY CAR

Travelling by car to the Pyrenees can be cost effective if there are two or more of you and may be an attractive option if you've got a lot of gear.

TOULOUSE – PRACTICAL INFORMATION

Toulouse is the most frequently used access point for those flying to the Pyrenees. The reasons for this are twofold: the city's airport is served by regular flights from around Europe, and public transport connections into the mountains are very good. Because of inconvenient flight timings, however, many trekkers are forced to stop over in Toulouse for at least one night. This is no great hardship. Toulouse is a lovely city with plenty of good restaurants, shops, and museums; a couple of days here at the end of a walking trip may be just the way to relax after some strenuous trekking. If you do need to stop in Toulouse, the following information may assist:

Where to stay
● **Near the airport** The area around the airport is like a gigantic business park, with no shops and, apart from the airport itself, only one place to eat. Cheap accommodation is available within 10-15 minutes' walk of the terminus at the hotel *Formule 1* (central reservations ☎ 08.36.68.56.85) which is next to the autoroute. It's a rather soulless establishment, and the only place to eat is at another hotel on the far side of a bridge over the motorway, but the price isn't bad: €24/155F for a room. You could get a taxi from the airport to the hotel, but it's also possible to walk. If you ask around for directions, there is a route along the service roads next to the airport which leads to the hotel, (thereby avoiding the need to walk along the hard shoulder of the motorway).
● **In the city** Despite the temptation to book into the nearest hotel to the bus or train station, it's worth going further afield to find a good place to stay. I'd recommend the *Hôtel du Taur* (☎ 05.61.21.17.54, 🖃 05.61.13.78.41) 2, rue du Taur, which is literally just off the Place du Capitole, the main square in the city. The hotel is very comfortable and the location is excellent. Double rooms cost from €36.60/240F.

Local transport
Toulouse airport is some 10-15km from the city centre, in a suburb called Blagnac. The cheapest way to get to and from the airport is by the airport shuttle service, which runs to and from the main bus station which is next to the main railway station in the centre of Toulouse. Buses run approximately every 20 minutes, the first bus heading out to the airport at around 05.20 and the last bus running at about 20.20. Going from the airport into the city, the first bus goes at about 07.50 and the last bus at about 23.30. At weekends the first and last buses are respectively later and earlier. For more information on timings, contact the bus company (☎ 05.34.60.64.00, 🖳 www.navetteviatoulouse.com). A one-way ticket costs €3.50/23F; a return €5.50/36F.

Tourist office
The tourist office (☎ 05.61.11.02.22, 🖃 05.61.22.03.63, 🖳 ottoulouse@mipnet.fr) is in the Donjon du Capitole, just to the east of the Place du Capitole.

Moving on
From Toulouse it's easy to get trains to Perpignan, Bagnères-de-Luchon, Ax-les-Thermes, Lourdes, Pau, Bayonne or Hendaye. Each of these places is a transport hub from which local transport links can be used to get into the mountains. By way of example of fares, a one way train ticket from Toulouse to Bayonne is €30/197F.

Having your own transport also gives you the flexibility to explore the region more widely. Travelling from the UK, you have a choice of cross-Channel ferries to the ports of northern France (Calais, Le Havre etc), although you're then faced with a long drive southwards. A convenient way of avoiding this marathon is to take a direct ferry to northern Spain. **Brittany Ferries** (UK ☎ 08705-360 360, 🖥 www.brittanyferries.com) operate twice weekly services from Plymouth to Santander, and **P&O Ferries** (UK ☎ 08702-424 999, 🖥 www.poportsmouth.com) have twice weekly sailings from Portsmouth to Bilbao. It takes about three hours to drive from either port up to the area of Irún and Hendaye.

BY COACH

It's a long haul from the UK to the Pyrenees by coach, and the bargain fares available from some low cost airlines make coach travel seem an unnecessarily masochistic choice. One advantage, however, of taking the bus is that there's usually last minute availability, which may not be the case with flights, and the coach company is sometimes prepared to be flexible with return dates if you decide you want to stay a little longer. Eurolines (☎ 0870-514 3219; 🖥 www.eurolines.co.uk) 52 Grosvenor Gardens, Victoria, London SW1, have summer services to Perpignan (20 hours, £109 return), Bayonne (19 hours, £116 return), Lourdes (via Pau and Tarbes) (21 hours, £116 return) and Toulouse (20 hours, £116 return).

Visas

Visas are not required by members of other EU countries or by US or Canadian nationals who plan to be in either France or Spain for less than 90 days. All other nationalities require a visa.

Note that in the Pyrenees the 90 day rule becomes superfluous; since there are no border controls you could easily claim that you've just come across the mountains for a few days and will be returning shortly.

Budgeting

Budgets for trips to the Pyrenees can vary widely. If you head off into the wilderness on arrival, and come back to civilization only to catch the train home, the costs will be very low. If, on the other hand, you make a point of trying some of the local restaurants and of having a couple of beers in the evening, your expenditure will be considerably higher.

CAMPING

If you plan to camp in the hills every night, you can get by on as little as £5/US$8 per day – all you will need to buy is food. Realistically, though, assuming that you might want to eat at a local café occasionally, and every now and again stay in a campsite where there's a shower, you would be wise to bank on £10/US$16 per person per day.

GÎTES

Staying in *gîtes d'étape* (lodges) and *refuges* (mountain huts) en route is more expensive. If you buy food every night and cook for yourself using the facilities provided in most gîtes, you should make do on about £12-15/US$19-24 per day. If, however, you eat the meals provided by the guardian and possibly splash out on a glass or two of wine to go with your supper, your costs are likely to come to £20-25/US$32-40 per day. You can stay below this if you really try hard but a drink or two in the evening soon puts the price back up.

EXTRAS

Although there are few additional expenses on a walking holiday, set aside some cash for the inevitable extras – postcards, snacks, and a few really good meals along the way.

When to go

The walking season in the Pyrenees starts in mid June and ends in late September. It is quite possible to walk outside this period but the weather may be unpredictable and you cannot guarantee that all the normal summer walking facilities will be available. Note that if you are walking in mid June and are relying on lodges for overnight accommodation, it will be necessary to ring ahead to check whether each place is open. See p41 for more on climate and temperatures in the Pyrenees.

SNOW-FREE PERIOD

In late May many of the lower routes (ie much of the GR10) should be fine but there's always the risk of a late snowfall which would cause problems. It's not so much that the routes would be impassable but that the route markers, many of which are painted on the rocks, become invisible under even a light layer of snow. Note that higher passes (ie over 2000 metres) may not be free from snow until early or even mid July. The routes that involve crossing particularly high passes are marked in this

FURTHER INFORMATION

Useful Web sites

Sites which can be helpful for planning a trip include the following:

● The **French Tourist Department** site, at **www.franceguide.com** is a good place to start, and has an updated list of events as well as a variety of other background information.

● For an insight into the **Pays Basque**, look at **www.infobasque.com** where you'll find full details of Basque news and events, as well as some tourist information.

● The **Spanish Tourist Office** has a site at **www.spaintour.com**. There's little specific detail about the Pyrenees, but it does have information about general subjects such as exchange rates and travel around Spain. There's also a link to another useful site: **www.tourspain.es**.

● **Catalonia's** own site, **www.publintur.es**, is well designed, and offers a guided tour of the region, complete with insights into culture and history, and what's on offer to visitors.

● For information about **Eurostar services**, see **www.eurostar.com**.

● Other info about European **rail services** is at **www.raileurope.com**.

● **SNCF** (the French railway company) have a site at **www.sncf.fr**. The timetable section is particularly useful.

National tourist offices

● **Australia** French: (☎ 02-9231 5244, 🖷 02-9221 8682, 💻 frencht@ozemail.com.au) 25 Bligh St, Sydney, NSW 2000.

● **Belgium** French: (☎ 02-505 3813, 🖷 02-514 3375) 21 avenue de la Toison d'Or, B-1060 Brussels. Spanish: (☎ 02-280 1926, 🖷 02-230 2147) avenue des Arts 21, B-1040 Brussels

● **Canada** French: (☎ 514-288-4264, 🖷 514-845-4868) 1981 avenue McGill College, Suite 490, Montreal, Quebec H3A 2W9. Spanish: (☎ 416-961-3131, 🖷 416-961-1992) 2 Bloor St West, 34th Floor, Toronto, Ontario M4W 3E2.

● **Denmark** French: (☎ 33 11 49 12, 🖷 33 14 20 48) NY Ostergade 3,3, DK-1101 Copenhagen K. Spanish: (☎ 33 15 11 65, 🖷 33 15 83 65) Store Kogensgade 1-3, 1264 Copenhagen

● **Germany** French: (☎ 069-97 58 01 21, 🖷 069-74-55-56) Westendstrasse 47, Postfach 100 128, 60001 Frankurt Main. Spanish: (☎ 069-72 50 33, 🖷 069 72 53 13) Myliusstrasse 14, 60325 Frankfurt Main. There is also a Spanish tourist office in Dusseldorf (☎ 0211-680 3980).

● **Ireland** French: (☎ 01-679 0813, 🖷: 01-679 0814) 10 Suffolk St, Dublin.

● **Netherlands** French: (☎ 020-623 43 61, 🖷 020-620 33 39) Prinsengracht 670, NL-1017 KX Amsterdam. Spanish: (☎ 070-346 5900, 🖷 070-364 9859) Laan Van Meerdervoort 8-8, 2517 AJ, The Hague.

● **UK** French: (☎ 020-7399 3500, 🖷 020-7399 3540), 178 Piccadilly, London W1V 0AL; Spanish: (☎ 020-7486 8077, 🖷 020-7486 8034) 22-23 Manchester Square, London W1M 5AP.

● **USA** French: (☎ 212-838-7800, 🖷 212-838-7855) 444 Madison Avenue, 16th Floor, New York NY 10022; Spanish: (☎ 212-265-8822, 🖷 212-265-8864) 666 Fifth Avenue, New York, NY 10103. There are also Spanish tourist offices in Chicago (☎ 312-642-1992); Los Angeles (☎ 213-658-7188); Miami (☎ 305-358-1992).

book. If you're planning to try them in June/early July you'll need to check with a tourist office or, better still, with the guardian of a nearby refuge, as to whether the route is passable before setting out. Ensure when you ask that you get clear advice as to whether the route is passable to walkers *without special equipment*, as some guardians may make the assumption that you have climbing gear. The alternative is to equip yourself with an ice axe, crampons etc to enable you to make the crossing safely. (For more details, see the section on mountain safety, on p36).

GÎTES AND REFUGES

Gîtes and refuges tend to have wardens in permanent residence only from mid June to late September. If you plan to be walking outside this period, you should phone in advance before relying on using them.

NATIONAL HOLIDAYS

Summer holidays in both France and Spain tend to fall between mid July and mid August, and make a considerable difference to the availability of accommodation. This can work both to your advantage and disadvantage: you can guarantee that all facilities will be open during the period, and that transport services such as local buses into the mountains will be running at maximum capacity; equally, you may find that the most popular lodges will be very full. If you're planning to get off the beaten track and camp rough, this will be less of a hassle.

Route options

The route that you choose will depend on your level of experience, the time available, and what you particularly want to see. There are a variety of footpaths through the mountains but worthy of special mention are the three trans-Pyrenean routes. For an overall **route map** see p320.

GRANDE RANDONNÉE (GR) 10

The GR10 is one of the network of French long distance paths which cover much of the country. Generally, these routes are well marked and maintained by local volunteers, and the GR10 is no exception. Throughout its 700km course from the Atlantic to the Mediterranean there are only a few places where route-finding causes any real difficulty. Likewise in all but a few areas, the GR10 is well supplied with facilities en route. Day stages tend to start with a climb out of a valley and end with a descent into another valley in order to reach a gîte d'étape or guest house where walkers can stay the night. For many, this may sound unlike what they had in mind, and indeed, during the mid summer holiday there can be a lot of people following the same path. There are, however, benefits: route finding is scarcely ever a problem, leaving plenty of time to enjoy the scenery. If you're walking by yourself and concerned about the safety aspects, it can be reassuring to know that the path you are following is relatively well trodden, and that if you encounter a problem you will most probably be able to get help from fellow walkers. Finally, since there are good facilities along the way, there's no need to carry your life on your back. You can really keep the weight to the minimum and know that you've got somewhere to stay in the evening.

GRAN RECORRIDO (GR) 11

The GR11 is the Spanish coast to coast path which runs through the mountains of Navarra, Aragón and Catalonia. It's much newer than the GR10, and passes through countryside which is far wilder and more remote. There are fewer villages and practically no lodges on the way, so camping and carrying several days' worth of provisions are necessary. The route is, by and large, well marked but route-finding is made trickier by the inaccuracy of the Spanish maps. Nonetheless, the GR11 passes through some incredibly beautiful areas and has much to recommend it.

HAUTE RANDONNÉE PYRÉNÉENNE (HRP)

The HRP is the classic high-level coast to coast route. It attempts to follow the ridge of the mountain range from Atlantic to Mediterranean, crossing between France and Spain as the land dictates. Trekkers on the HRP may still find snow in the high passes in early to mid-June, and an ice axe is necessary in certain places in early summer. There are few places where the route descends to the valleys, so that food and a tent must be carried throughout. The HRP should be attempted only by experienced mountain trekkers.

High-route walkers tend to be rather dismissive of the GR10 (*tranquille* is the word they use) and there's no doubt that the scenery is much wilder and more mountainous along the HRP than on the lower paths. In some ways, ironically, the GR10 is harder work; the HRP tends to stay on the ridge of the mountains, only coming down where necessary, whereas the GR10 literally climbs and descends into every valley in order to stay much closer to civilization.

OVERALL

Walkers intent on trekking from coast to coast tend to decide on one or other of the three options above and to follow the route religiously. This is as much for practical reasons as for others: there are separate guide-books for each of the routes, and few maps show all three routes in rela-

ROUTE MARKINGS
Regular way marking along the GR10 and GR11 generally means that route-finding is simple. The fact that much of the way is so well marked can, however, sometimes cause a problem: when walkers encounter a stretch of path with no markings, they assume that they must be in the wrong!

GR10/GR11

The route of the GR10 is indicated with red and white way-marks, which may be painted on trees, rocks or buildings. A white line next to a red line marks the way. If the pair of lines has a stem beneath it so that it seems to form a 'flag', there is a turning ahead (in the direction of the flag). **GR10/GR11 ROUTE**

A red and white cross indicates that you have come the wrong way. There are variations but these are usually fairly self-evident: a pair of lines which clearly bend left or right may indicate that you should follow the path around a corner.

GR11 markings are also in red and white and are very similar to those on the GR10.

 WRONG WAY

OR

TURN LEFT AHEAD

HRP

HRP markings, usually dark red, are not so formalized; in some areas they're clear and in others they are non-existent.

---

tion to each other. There's no reason why, with a little planning, you shouldn't take the best of each route. I met a group of walkers who had hired a guide to take them on an individual route across the Pyrenees, combining elements of the GR10, GR11 and HRP as seemed most interesting at the time.

This book gives a complete description of the GR10 (ie all the stages from the Atlantic to the Mediterranean) and also describes about two-thirds of the GR11. In addition, connections with some of the best sections of the HRP are included, as are a few interesting variants and suggested itineraries. Of course it's impossible to cover all the options, and the most interesting way to travel is also to do a bit of exploring for yourself off the beaten track.

What to take

The basic essentials

What you decide to pack in your rucksack will depend largely on the sort of walk that you intend to do. If you plan to camp, you will need a tent, cooking gear and all the other bits and pieces, whereas if you're going to be staying in refuges and gîtes, you can make do with much less. The overriding principle, however, is to keep your baggage as light as possible. Be brutally objective about which items you really need and which ones you can do without. Remember that if your pack feels heavy when you try it on at home, it will feel a great deal heavier after you've hauled it up a couple of steep hills. There is a standard procedure amongst all but the best organized GR10 walkers: within the first week most people make for a post office in order to send home large bundles of surplus items.

What to pack it all in

Unless you're going on an organized trek where the company is going to move your baggage for you, you'll need a good **rucksack**. A compromise needs to be struck between getting one big enough to hold all your gear, and one so big that you end up filling it with unnecessary items; a rucksack of about 65 litres' capacity should be ample. It's a good idea to get one with a couple of external zip-up pockets; being able to put a few essential items (waterbottle, snacks, waterproof jacket etc) in pockets separate from the rest of your gear means that you can get to them quickly and easily. You don't need a state-of-the-art backpack with loads of adjustment straps but whatever you buy should be robust and feel comfortable.

A **small day sack**, a little rucksack of, say, 20 litres' capacity, can also be invaluable for carrying camera, film and other essentials if you go off sightseeing or for a day walk. This smaller bag should be frameless so that it can be squashed up in the top of your rucksack when you don't need it.

Sleeping bag

Even if you plan to stay in gîtes every night, you'll need a sleeping bag of some sort, as gîte owners insist on the use of a bag to keep the mattresses from getting dirty. At the most basic level, since almost all gîtes provide blankets, you could probably make do with just a **sheet sleeping bag**. On the other hand, if you take only a sheet bag you'll have a chilly night if you ever come across a place without blankets or have to spend a night in a cabane, let alone outdoors. The best compromise, if you plan to stay in gîtes, is a light (one- or two-season) **sleeping bag**. If you're going to be camping, you'll probably need a three-season bag. Whatever bag you end up with, ensure that you have a 'compression sack' into which it can be packed, so that it takes up a minimum of space. A **liner** of some sort is a good idea to protect the bag itself.

A **sleeping mat** is essential if you're planning to camp but is a waste of space if you're going to be using gîtes or refuges. If you're heading for a part of the GR10 where there's a lack of accommodation, you have a dilemma: do you carry a sleeping mat which will be used only on two or three occasions, or rough it out for a couple of nights? A compromise would be to buy a small 'thermarest' style inflatable mattress; alternatively, cut down a foam sleeping mat so that you have a section just big enough to cushion your hips and shoulders.

Footwear and foot care

A good pair of walking boots is essential. Pyrenean foot paths are made up of sharp, loose stones, so ensure that your boots have good ankle support and sturdy soles, with enough protection so that you don't feel every pebble. There are many areas, too, where paths pass over large areas of rocks, requiring a certain amount of boulder hopping; boots with good grip on the soles inspire a lot more confidence and are safer.

Choosing boots The choice of boot is a matter of personal preference: whatever is most comfortable for you is best. Make sure that the boots fit well; they should not be so loose as to allow rubbing on the heel but there should be enough room at the front so that on long downhill sections you don't get battered toes. If you plan to wear gaiters (not necessary but useful in some cases) ensure that the boots will take them, and if you're going to wear crampons (these shouldn't be necessary but see Mountain Safety, p36) again check that they will fit.

Socks Some people swear that wearing two pairs of socks, a thin inner pair and a thick outer pair, is the best way to avoid blisters; others simply go for a single pair of thick socks. Whatever you choose, ensure that they are natural fibre or at least a good ratio mixed fibre as they are better for your feet and are easier to keep clean.

Foot care There are many ways to protect your feet, but unfortunately none of them is foolproof. Some people prepare for a walking holiday by rubbing white spirit into their feet; over three or four weeks, this hardens the skin and thus helps to prevent blisters. Another good way to avoid blisters is to put zinc oxide tape/plaster (available at any chemist) on the patches that are likely to cause problems – heels and toes in particular. The tape, rather than your skin, then takes the friction of the boot. There are numerous other products on the market, including 'moleskin', 'foot cushions' and special blister treatment packs available from sports stores.

The best way of looking after your feet is to wash and dry them thoroughly and give them every opportunity to breathe, wearing sandals or flip-flops in the evening. Ensure that your socks are clean and dry, and that your boots fit well. Lace them firmly particularly towards the ankle to give good support.

Extra footwear It's a good idea to carry a second pair of shoes, to allow your walking boots time to air in the evenings. Whatever you choose, ensure that they're light. Flip-flops or 'trekking sandals' allow your feet to breathe; trainers take up more space but are more practical if you're going to be wearing them to go sightseeing.

Packing your kit
Everyone has their own way of packing a rucksack, but a few general pointers may be helpful.

● **Waterproof it!** Almost inevitably there will be times when you and your rucksack get soaked. If the clothing and sleeping bag inside the rucksack get wet too, the results will be at least uncomfortable and at worst dangerous. Spending a night in damp clothes and a wet sleeping bag could easily lead to hypothermia. Ensure that your gear is thoroughly waterproofed. Rucksack liners (large heavy duty plastic bags) can be bought from camping stores. Put everything inside the bag and fold or tie the top; if there's not enough room to get the sleeping bag and clothes into the same liner, get two, or even three.

● **Have a system** Develop a system so that you know where your stuff is inside the rucksack. For easy access, keep items that you want to get to quickly (guidebook, waterproof etc) near the top of the bag. Put all items in separate plastic bags if they're going to be packed outside the main liner.

● **Food** Fresh food goes off quickly in the heat; chocolate melts. To avoid this bury your edibles deep inside your rucksack. If you're going to be carrying a lot of food, put it all in a large container (eg a plastic biscuit box) and pack this halfway down your rucksack. Try to put the rucksack in the shade when you're resting.

Clothes

In general, the summer months in the Pyrenees are warm, so you don't need to bring lots of kit and, unless you're planning to camp at altitude, you won't need too much warm clothing. For everyday walking in the Pyrenees, the standard gear for most people is shorts, T-shirt, and sun hat.

Shorts/trousers Most people wear shorts but if you're prone to sunburn then loose cotton trousers are more sensible. Whatever you choose to wear, ensure that they're robust, and light enough to dry quickly after washing or if you get wet.

Shirts Although T-shirts are good for trekking, you should pack at least one long-sleeved shirt. This is useful for wearing in the evening when the temperature drops, and also during the day if your arms and neck get sunburnt.

Warm gear You need to carry at least one item of warm gear: a fleece jacket or a jumper is ideal. A set of thermal underwear takes up very little space in a rucksack and, if you're camping or staying in a cabane, can make all the difference between a comfortable night and an uncomfortable one. For those camping at altitude, or in the very early or late season, other warm gear is necessary – a woolly hat and gloves are essential.

Underwear Three changes of whatever you usually wear is fine.

Lightening your load
One method, which lots of GR10 walkers hit upon to lessen the load they have to carry, is to post parcels ahead to strategic points, where they can be picked up en route. The early stages of the GR10, for example, have plenty of accommodation, whereas the later sections do not. Why carry a camping stove for the first three weeks when you can pick it up from a post office near the spot where you're actually going to need it? If you plan to walk the whole of the GR10 you will have to use at least ten maps. Take three or four at a time, and pick up the rest along the way, at the same time posting the used maps home. A trekker I met while researching this book, wrote:

'I learnt much about the French postal system along the way. The posting of my most valuable tramping equipment by ordinary post from Bidarray to Luchon was successful, even if it did take them a little time (10 minutes) to find the parcel. However, I then posted substantially the same parcel contents on to Banyuls, again by ordinary post. A postal employee apparently carefully removed the label from my parcel and stuck it to a fake parcel, the contents of which were useless. My tip to your readers is that, when posting valuable items in France, be sure that you register and insure the parcel. It is only by this means that you can be reasonably certain of it being delivered correctly. It is not unreasonably expensive to do so.

I also posted several parcels from various places back to Australia. They contained mostly used guidebooks, exposed photographic film and literature on local detail. Three out of six of these have not arrived...again the lesson is don't use ordinary post.' **Andrew Craig** (Australia)

Sun hat This really is a must. The sun can be bakingly hot, particularly when it is reflected off the rocks on all sides. A broad brim protects the vulnerable nose and the back of the neck. It doesn't matter if the hat looks silly as long as it does the job.

Socks Three changes of socks should be enough; if you're planning to wear an inner and outer pair this obviously means six pairs of socks in total.

Swimsuit Not essential though it could be a good idea to have one. The lakes are very cold but some people brave them, and some towns have swimming pools, which are very welcome after a hot day's trekking.

Towel Make this a small towel, preferably quite thin, so that it takes up as little space as possible and dries quickly.

Waterproof A waterproof is essential if you're going to be trekking through the Basque country, where it can be very wet. Even in the rest of the Pyrenees, although it really doesn't rain too much, when the skies open they do so in a serious way. Some walkers also go for a pair of waterproof trousers though for the time that you use them it's debatable whether it's worth carrying the extra weight. The alternative to a waterproof jacket is a poncho which covers you and your rucksack. This is certainly much cheaper; a poncho only costs a few pounds and it packs up very small. Most French walkers use them.

Gaiters Gaiters are not essential. For those walking in the Basque country in particular, there are likely to be rainy days when they will come in handy, or mornings when they will protect against rain-soaked undergrowth.

Toiletries
Keep these to a minimum. You'll need to bring soap and a small bottle of shampoo. Loo paper is provided in most gîtes but not in many refuges; bring a roll just in case. If you're going to be camping, bring a lighter too, so that you can burn the used paper. Ensure that you pack a tube of high factor sun lotion (factor 15) to protect your face and neck, in particular. Lip balm is also useful.

Some sort of travel detergent is essential for washing clothes. Camping stores stock biodegradable clothes washing liquid which will not pollute natural water sources.

While biting insects are not much of a problem in the Pyrenees, repellent can still be useful as some areas are inhabited by horseflies, which have a painful sting.

Medical kit
There are excellent medical facilities available in France and Spain, so you're not trying to pack a complete operating theatre but just enough remedies to sort out minor problems. You should be able to fit all of this in a small waterproof box. Take along paracetamol for headaches and aspirin for inflammation of the joints; both can be used as general pain killers. Plasters/bandaids are useful for small cuts, and antiseptic cream or wipes will help to prevent infection. A small bandage can have a number of uses, and if you think that your knees might give you trouble, elastic knee supports are invaluable. Imodium is useful if you have diarrhoea. Water purification tablets are necessary – see p40 for details. Bring ample supplies of any prescription drugs which you need; if you have contact lenses pack plenty of cleaning solution.

General items
● **Essential** No one should go out in the mountains without a compass. Other essential items include: sunglasses; a torch (most walkers choose to carry a head torch) and a spare set of batteries; a loud whistle to summon assistance in an emergency; a small sewing kit; a penknife; two one-litre water bottles; a map case.

● **Useful** A long-burning candle is a good idea if you plan to spend much time camping or in cabanes as you'll save battery power that way; matches or a lighter; a few metres of string for use as a clothes line; a universal bathplug (many washrooms in gîtes don't have plugs, which can make clothes washing tricky); a small pair of binoculars; a diary; an address book; a pack of cards.

Extra walking gear
A walking stick or pole is extremely useful, mainly for taking some of the shock off your knees when you're going down hill, but also for keeping unfriendly dogs at bay and helping you keep your balance when you're fording streams. You can buy wooden walking poles in many of the small villages throughout the mountains; alternatively you can go for the modern approach and get one or two extendible ski-style poles.

From mid-June to late September an ice axe is not necessary on most of the routes described here. Note, however, the point made on p20 ('Snow Free Period') that some of the higher passes may not be free from snow until as late as early-mid July. If you're planning on following a route that includes high passes (ie over 2000m) before early-mid July, either bring an ice axe and crampons or be prepared to alter your itinerary if it turns out that there is still snow on your route.

Some people buy a waterproof rucksack cover, which fits over the outside of the pack and keeps it dry during showers; it's no substitute for waterproofing gear inside the bag itself. If you're going to be walking off the beaten track, and if you're not carrying a tent, you might also choose to take a survival bag. If you get into trouble, this can be guaranteed to give protection against the elements and, being brightly coloured, will be visible to searching helicopter crews.

Finally, even if you're not planning to camp at all, take a small amount of food with you for emergencies. Keep this separate from your daily snacks and open it only if you really need it; make sure that the food you choose to carry will keep for several weeks.

Cooking gear
In France, the blue Camping Gaz cylinders, both the old type and the new resealable version, are available just about everywhere. Methylated spirits (*alcool à brûler*) is sold in hardware stores and supermarkets. Coleman/ Epigas cylinders are less easy to obtain. You can buy a suitable gas bottle with the right screw thread in some French hardware stores; the French use them for blowtorches. Although these cylinders work OK, the bottles are very tall, so they're not particularly practical. Special mention is made in this book of stores where Epigas (or the French equivalent) is available.

In Spain there are long sections of the GR11 where it's hard to get hold of any fuel at all. Some campsites and refuges sell the old style (puncture type) Camping Gaz cylinders, but few if any sell the new style cylinders and Coleman/ Epigas refills are equally rare. There are several villages where supplies of all types of camping fuel are available (eg Torla and Benasque) but these are few and far between. A possible solution to this problem is to use a multi-fuel stove which can burn petrol.

Provisions

If you're going from gîte to gîte you'll need very few provisions – just snacks for the day. You can stock up on these at each small village that you come to. Apples, chocolate, peanuts and raisins are all good choices. You can also ask the owners of the gîte or refuge if they can provide sand-wiches or a packed lunch.

Keen campers all have their favourite foods. In general you want the burden to be as light as possible, so dried foods are best: instant soups, pasta and mashed potato all make for a filling meal; rice is good too, but it takes quite a long time to cook. A little tin of meat or a few spices add flavour. Most people also carry coffee or tea, and some bring powdered milk which can be made up and used on breakfast cereal. Dried sausage (*saucisson*) is obtainable everywhere and is tasty as well as easy to carry. Excellent ewes' milk cheese (*fromage de brebis*) can often be bought at shepherds' huts high up in the mountains.

Money – see also p57

Most lodges and refuges do not accept credit cards or travellers' cheques. **Cash** is always a safe option for paying your bills so carry plenty of local currency to avoid frequent trips down from the mountains to find a bank. At most banks there's usually an **ATM** (cash dispenser), enabling Visa, MasterCard, Cirrus, Maestro, Eurocard and EuroCheque cardholders to withdraw local currency directly from their home bank account. Visa (Carte Bleue), is the most widely recognized **credit card** in France and MasterCard comes a close second. Rather than using a credit card in the ATM, use your **bank card** (debit/cheque guarantee card) which will prob-ably have one of the electronic money symbols (Cirrus, Maestro etc.) shown on it; with a credit card you'll get a cash advance on your credit card account and you may have to pay interest on this money. The loca-tion of ATMs and banks is noted in the guide section of this book.

Travellers' cheques (American Express, Thomas Cook or any of the other well-known brands) can also be useful. If you cannot get to a bank, remember that in France all but the smallest post offices will change money. Note that you will not find anywhere to change money on Saturday afternoons and Sundays. **Eurocheques** are accepted in a few places but are not commonly recognized, even by French banks.

Photographic equipment

Film is easily available in both France and Spain but you should bring enough to ensure that you don't get caught short when the perfect shot presents itself. There is generally plenty of light, so 100ASA film should be fast enough. Ensure that you bring a spare set of batteries for your camera as many cameras stop functioning completely when the power goes.

RECOMMENDED READING

The Pyrenean classics

Some of the most famous books about the Pyrenees date from the last century or early years of this one. If you can find any of these you'll be doing very well indeed; but they're fun to look out for and would make fascinating reading (quite apart from the fact that they're very valuable).

The classic text is *Souvenirs d'un Montagnard* by Count Henry Russell, but Charles Packe's *Guide to the Pyrénées*, published by Longmans in 1880 comes a close second. Only slightly less rare is Hilaire Belloc's *The Pyrénées*, published initially by Methuen in 1909. The Pyrenees were the subject of a vast number of travelogues published around the turn of the century, many by otherwise unknown authors. Most of these accounts tend to be fairly repetitive but they can be quite fun reading, at times.

General guidebooks

There are a number of good guidebooks on the market if you intend to go exploring away from the mountain trails. Cadogan Guides' *Gascony and the Pyrenees* is detailed for the French Pyrenees as far east as Ax-les-Thermes, while Rough Guides' *The Pyrenees* gives equal coverage on both sides of the border and along the length of the range. *Discover Pyrenees* by Berlitz is a good general guide if you've got your own transport and the time to explore.

Walking guidebooks

Cicerone Guidebooks have published guides to the both the GR10 (*The Pyrenean Trail GR10* by Alan Castle) and the GR11 (*Through the Spanish Pyrenees GR11: A Long Distance Footpath* by Paul Lucia). The former is rather dated in its information, but the latter is good, and is the only complete description to date of the GR11 published in English. Also from Cicerone is *Walks and Climbs in the Pyrenees* by Kev Reynolds, which contains little background information but has descriptions of a large number of routes. The classic book about the HRP High Level Route is Georges Véron's *Pyrenees High Level Route*. There are several other books but avoid older publications such as *Walking the Pyrenees*, published by Robertson McCarta, which is now completely out of date.

There are loads of guide books in French, but the classic guides are the *Topoguides* which are published by the Fédération Française de la

---

(Opposite) The Basque country may not have the highest mountains in the range but the scenery can be just as spectacular as anything in the Central Pyrenees. (Photo © Greg and Jane Knott).

Randonnée Pédestre. Four guides cover the entire GR10, but they're quite expensive – averaging about 90F per booklet.

In Spanish, the most comprehensive guide to the GR11 is the *GR11 Senda Pirenaica*, produced by the Comité Nacional de Senderas de Gran Recorrido. The fourth edition (published in April 2000, ISBN: 84-8321-066-5) is in two parts: a guide book with lots of information about the routes/wildlife/history of the region etc, and a separate folder containing 47 route maps, one for each day stage. The maps are far better than any others available, so even if you don't speak Spanish, the guide is worth buying for the maps alone.

Flora and fauna

There are a number of well illustrated guides on the market; what you buy will depend largely on how heavy a manual you are prepared to carry in your rucksack! Collins do several suitable books: the *Collins Field Guide – Birds of Britain and Europe* is comprehensive, but may be a little too weighty for most walkers; the *Collins Nature Guide* of the same title is handier. Of a similar size and weight, the *Collins Pocket Guide – Alpine Flowers*, is good news.

Other books

Fiction   There's not a lot here to choose from! Ernest Hemingway's novel *Fiesta* is largely set in Pamplona, in the foothills of the Navarrese Pyrenees, and his characters briefly visit Burguete (near Roncesvalles). The description of Pamplona during the festival of San Fermin (the bull running) is classic. If your command of the French language is good, pick up a copy of the novel *Ramuntcho* by Pierre Loti; the fictional village of Etchezar is modelled on Sare in the Basque Country.

Non fiction   Laurie Lee's *A Moment of War* contains a brief description of his passage across the Pyrenees to join the Republican forces during the Spanish Civil War, and an absorbing account of what he found when he got to Spain. Of a completely different genre, speliologist Norbert Casteret's book *Ten Years Under the Earth* details his incredible exploits in the 1920's and 1930's. Casteret was responsible for, among other things, proving that the Garonne had its source in the Maladetta, discovering the highest ice cave in the world (in the Ordesa National Park) and finding the oldest statues in the world, in a prehistoric cave dwelling. The fact that his equipment often consisted of no more that a handful of candles and his bathing costume somehow makes his story all the more fascinating!

Travelogues include Roger Higham's *Road to the Pyrenees*, published in 1971, which details his exploration of the Pays Basque and Béarn. JM

(Opposite)   The ancient game of pelote (see p82) is ingrained in the Basque way of life and no Basque village is without its court, which may be an outdoor court (*fronton*) as shown here or an indoor one (*trinquet*). (Photos © Greg and Jane Knott).

Scott's *From Sea to Ocean, Walking along the Pyrenees*, published in 1969, makes most coast to coast walks nowadays seem rather tame; the author sets off with little clear idea of his exact route but makes plenty of interesting discoveries along the way. *Clear Waters Rising* by Nicholas Crane is justifiably one of the best known of recent walking books. One chapter deals with the Pyrenean section of the author's epic walk across Europe.

There are numerous books in French, most of which seem to be aimed at the tourist market. Editions Sud Ouest have published well-written books about everything from Pyrenean legends to the French Resistance, and local cuisine. There are lots of books, too, about the Cathars.

MAPS

France

The Institut Géographique Nationale (IGN) produce excellent maps. If you intend to stay in the French Pyrenees you need only decide whether you want to carry 1:50,000 scale maps or 1:25,000.

● **1:50,000** IGN produce a special **Éditions Randonnées Pyrénéennes** – ten sheets that cover the entire length of the range, with footpaths, gîtes, refuges and cabanes marked. The sheets are numbered 1-11, but No 9 is not required if you're sticking to the GR10. These maps are more than sufficient if you plan to stick to the main paths but you should bear in mind that they are not always entirely accurate. New forest and mountain trails are constantly being built, gîtes and refuges open and close, and the GR10 occasionally changes course. Each map sheet also has a list of useful telephone numbers on the bottom.

● **1:25,000** The IGN **Serie Bleue** of 1:25,000 maps covers the whole of France, and has much greater detail than the 1:50,000 series. If you're hoping to go exploring these may be the maps you need but, unless you plan to spend a long time off the beaten track, don't bother. You will need a minimum of 18 maps to cover the whole of the Pyrenees, and quite apart from having to carry them, this is likely to make a large dent in your budget.

Spain

If you're only planning to nip across into Spain for a quick excursion, you may be pleasantly surprised to find that some of the French IGN maps actually give coverage across the border. The Aigüe Tortes National Park, for instance, is largely covered by the Éditions Randonnées Pyrénéenes map No 6. The process of extending IGN coverage across the border, which seems to have been started because Spanish mapping was so poor, is to be continued. A plan has been afoot for quite a long time now for a special edition of walking maps which cover areas of particular interest; for example one sheet will include the whole of the Aran Valley and the border crossings to the north of it. Nothing, however, has come of this yet.

In the meantime, if you plan to do a lot of walking in the Spanish Pyrenees there are three main choices.

● **Comité Nacional de Senderas de Gran Recorrido** The guidebook *GR11 Senda Pirenaica*, produced by the Comité Nacional de Senderas de Gran Recorrido, comes complete with a pack of 47 maps, one for each day stage of the GR11, with a few extra sheets detailing some route variants. These are by far the most accurate maps available of the GR11, as well as being the most convenient to carry. They don't, however, show much apart from the route itself, so they're no use if you want to go exploring. In 2000, the guidebook was up to its fourth edition (published in April 2000, ISBN: 84-8321-066-5)

● **Editorial Alpina** Editorial Alpina produce a series of booklets and maps which cover almost the whole of the Spanish Pyrenees. The booklets, which are in Spanish, give useful local information and contain a walking map for the area. The maps are notably hazy on detail (containing, for example, no depiction of vegetation) and there are occasional glaring inaccuracies (on one map the scale bar is the wrong size for the particular scale of map!). Almost as confusing is the fact that they are produced in different scales – a 1:25,000 map may abut a 1:40,000 map. If you've come across the border from France and have been using the 1:50,000 series, you may well find yourself using three different maps, all with different scales, in quick succession.

Having said this, the Editorial Alpina maps are widely used, and once you get used to them they are generally adequate. At least 18 maps are required to cover the Pyrenees, although the series does not have a sheet covering the western end of the mountains – the first map is of the Roncesvalles area.

● **Spanish Military Survey Maps** Very few people carry these but they are worth considering if you are planning to do a lot of walking in the Spanish mountains. Although they are sometimes very dated, they give accurate contour, building and vegetation detail, which is lacking in the Editorial Alpina series. Whereas Editorial Alpina maps can be bought locally in the Pyrenees, the Military Survey maps cannot, and they're not easy to get hold of in the UK either, so order them well before you leave. Because the map sheets are small, you'll need 20 or more of the 1:50,000 maps to get from coast to coast. 1:25,000 scale military survey maps are also available but are unsuitable for walking because they contain less footpath information.

● **Institut Cartographic Catalunya** Also worth looking out for are the excellent 1:50,000 maps produced by the Institut Cartographic Catalunya. The 11 sheets cover only the area from Andorra to the Mediterranean but are far better than the Editorial Alpina maps for the same area. In the UK they can be ordered through bookshops from Cordee.

Where to buy maps

IGN maps should be available at any large travel bookstore and are on sale throughout France. Spanish maps are harder to obtain, and even in the Pyrenees you may find that the shops have sold out of the very map sheet you need so get them before you travel.

Stanfords (☎ 020-7836 1321, 📄 020-7836 0189, 🖥 www.stan fords.co.uk) 12-14 Long Acre, London, WC2E 9LP, is the best place in London to buy maps. They have all of the above in stock, although they need advance warning to get the 1:25,000 Spanish Military Survey Maps.

The Map Shop (☎ 01684 593146, 📄 01684 594559, 🖥 Themap shop@btinternet.com, web: www.themapshop.co.uk), 15 High Street, Upton upon Severn, Worcestershire, WR8 0HJ provides an excellent service if you're short of time. For a small fee they'll mail any map to you, first class.

Mountain safety

GENERAL

Mountain walking is potentially a hazardous activity. Even straightforward sections walked in mid summer can become difficult or dangerous if you encounter unexpected problems such as poor weather, tiredness or injury. While this book is designed to cover summer trekking routes which are within the ability of most people, any walker must always be aware of the possibility that conditions may change unexpectedly. The following paragraphs highlight some areas which should be considered before starting your trek.

WEATHER AND EQUIPMENT

The weather can change extremely quickly in any mountain region, and the Pyrenees are no exception. While a well-planned trek making use of gîtes along the way can allow you to travel light, you should still be prepared for problems, should they arise. Ensure that you have warm clothing in case the weather turns bad, and take great care to keep your set of warm clothes dry. If this means that, first thing in the morning, you have to get back into the damp clothes you were wearing the day before, do so.

TREKKING ALONE

One of the golden rules of mountain walking is that you always walk in company if at all possible. Sometimes it just doesn't work out that way but there are still things you can do to minimize the risks. Carry a bright-

WEATHER FORECAST SERVICES
There are telephone numbers that you can call in any area to get the latest weather forecast. Bear in mind, however, that the service for, say, Haute Garonne is trying to predict the weather for a wide area of which your corner of the mountains is only a small part. The problem is exacerbated because the weather in the mountains is much less predictable than that lower down.

Often the guardian of a refuge or gîte is a better source of information about local conditions than any recorded message. The latest forecast is often written up in gîtes or in campsites. For forecasts in the following areas telephone:

Western Pyrenees
- **France** Pyrénées Atlantiques (☎ 08.36.68.02.64); mountains (☎ 08.36.68.04.04)
- **Spain** Pays Basque (☎ 906-36.53.20); Navarre (☎ 906-36.53.31)

Central Pyrenees
- **France** Hautes Pyrénées (☎ 08.36.68.02.65); Haute Garonne (☎ 08.36.68.02.31); Ariège (☎ 08.36.68.04.04)
- **Spain** Aragón (☎ 906-36.53.50); Catalonia (☎ 906-36.53.25)

Eastern Pyrenees
- **France** Pyrénées Orientales (☎ 08.36.68.02.66)

ly coloured piece of clothing or a bright plastic survival bag that can attract attention to your position if necessary. Carry a whistle and remember the international distress signal (six sharp blasts from a whistle, followed by a minute's silence).

Lastly, if at all possible, tell someone where you are planning to go. This is not so important if you're sticking to the GR10 or any one of the large mountain trails, but if you're going to go exploring by yourself it's essential.

EXPERIENCE

No great level of experience is required to walk the GR10 – it's well marked and there's plenty of shelter along the way. If you're thinking of doing the HRP or of going off the beaten track, you will definitely need to be a confident map reader with a sound knowledge of high-level trekking. Remember that although the route ahead may look simple in bright sunshine, in rain and mist it's very easy to get lost even on a relatively straightforward section.

Do make sure that you are fit. The GR10 may not be technically difficult but there's an awful lot of climbing and descending and, if your body isn't used to it, the first few days will be painful. Knee and ankle strains can often be avoided by ensuring that you've done some training before you set out on your trek.

EMERGENCY HELP
Several different organizations are involved in mountain rescue. In France responsibility in a particular area may fall upon the **Peloton de Gendarmerie de Haute Montagne** (PGHM), the **Compagnie Republicaine de la Securité** (CRS), or the local **pompiers** (fire brigade). Emergency medical assistance is from the **Service d'Assistance Medicale Urbain** (SAMU). In Spain, groups range from specialist mountain rescue organizations to the local **bombers** (fire service). Key telephone numbers are given below, but if you're carrying a map in the Éditions Randonnées Pyrénéenes series, you will find extra numbers for local services listed next to the map key.

Western Pyrenees
● **France** PGHM Oloron-Ste-Marie (☎ 05.59.39.86.22); SAMU (☎ 15); Gendarmerie (☎ 17); Pompiers (☎ 18)
● **Spain** Bombers de Navarra (☎ 112); SOS Aragón (☎ 112)

Central Pyrenees
● **France** CRS Gavarnie (☎ 05.62.92.48.24); PHGM Pierrefitte-Nestalas (☎ 05.62.92.75.07); PHGM Luchon (☎ 05.61.79.28.36); CRS Luchon (☎ 05 61.79.83.79); PHGM Savignac (Ariège) (☎ 05.61.64.22.58); SAMU (☎ 15); Gendarmerie (☎ 17); Pompiers (☎ 18)
● **Spain** Bombers de Aragón (☎ 062); Bombers de la Generalitat de Catalunya (☎ 085); Bombers de Andorra (☎ 112) SOS Aragón (☎ 112)

Eastern Pyrenees
● **France** PGHM Osséja (☎ 04.68.04.51.03); CRS Perpignan 04.68 61.79.20; SAMU (☎ 15); Gendarmerie (☎ 17); Pompiers (☎ 18)
● **Spain** Bombers de la Generalitat de Catalunya (☎ 085)

SNOW

As already mentioned above (see **When to go** p20), although the walking season in the Pyrenees starts in mid June, there may well still be snow on the high passes until early or even mid July. While it's often possible to cross snow and ice safely with the right equipment and with a proper knowledge of how to use it correctly, if you're equipped only for summer walking attempting such crossings could be dangerous. In particular, two hazards stand out:

● Residual areas of snow may start to melt from the underneath. As the rocks on the mountain side warm up they can melt the snow in contact with them. In this way, a gap can open up between the rocks and the snow/ice above. Melt water running down the slope may enlarge any cavity, until there is a substantial gap between the crust of snow on the surface, and the rocks below. If the crust of snow gets too thin a walker could fall through. At best this would be extremely disconcerting. At worst it could result in serious injury.

● Stopping yourself from sliding on a steep snow slope is likely to be impossible if you do not have an ice axe. The last sections of snow to melt are those on slopes which receive the least sunshine. Often these slopes are steep and there are inevitably rocks at the bottom of the slope. Should you slip while crossing such a snow slope there will be little chance of stopping yourself sliding at great speed and hitting the rocks below, again with chances of serious injury.

Having highlighted these two particular hazards, it has to be said that many trekkers do walk across sections of snow in the early summer, and few experience problems. The difficulty comes in gauging what's safe and what isn't. This guidebook is about summer trekking only, and it would be inappropriate to try to offer further guidance, beyond the following points:
● Before starting in early or mid summer on a route that involves crossing a high section (ie over 2000m) ask for local advice about conditions. Possible sources of information include the guardian at a refuge, staff at a tourist office (or Bureau des Guides), or other walkers. Make it clear (if such is the case) that you are not equipped with anything beyond walking gear – in case anyone assumes that you're carrying mountaineering equipment.
● Although an ice axe is essential for crossing very steep sections of snow and ice, walking poles are extremely useful for stabilizing yourself on less steep sections of snow. Note that walking poles will not help in stopping you if you fall and start to slide.
● If you're trekking very early in the season, take appropriate equipment and know how to use it.
● If in doubt about the safety of a particular section, or your ability to cross it, turn back.

MOUNTAIN RESCUE SERVICES

There are mountain rescue services on both sides of the border. Remember, if you are involved in an accident and need to summon the rescue services that they will need an exact location of where to find the casualty. **See Emergency Help, opposite, for emergency contact numbers.**

Mountain rescue helicopters serve the most popular areas of the Pyrenees. The sign for a person on the ground to alert a helicopter that they need assistance is to hold both arms above their head in a 'Y' shape; so **never** wave both your arms at a passing helicopter unless you need help.

Health precautions

POSSIBLE PROBLEMS

The Pyrenees are not high enough to cause altitude sickness but they are plenty high enough to cause problems if you have not prepared physically for your trek. As long as you are in good health when you start there are likely to be few problems. Sunburn is a potential danger.

Water purification

Water from the taps of any lodge or gîte in Spain or France will be of drinking quality, and all refuges have a tap or pipe (usually outside) where drinking water is freely available. The only question, therefore, is whether or not to purify water taken from mountain streams; some trekkers do and some don't. The generally received wisdom is that if there may be live-stock grazing further upstream it's best not to drink the water without purifying it. Since flocks of sheep can be found grazing well above 2000m in the Pyrenees this effectively means that you have to purify almost all except spring water which is taken directly from the side of the mountain.

Water may be purified either by boiling or by using chemical meth-ods. If you're going to boil it, technically you should do so for around five minutes in order to kill all bugs. For chemical purification there are gen-erally two types of products available: chlorine or iodine based. Although both are pretty effective against bacteria, iodine is more reliable in getting rid of other pathogens and is the better option. Either get hold of a prod-uct such as Potable Aqua – where you simply add tablets to your water, or buy some 2% Tincture of Iodine from a chemist. Add five drops of the tincture to each litre of water and allow it to stand for twenty minutes. It's not particularly good for you to drink large quantities of iodized water, so try to use chemical purification only as a last resort.

TREATMENT UNDER EU REGULATIONS

Members of EU countries should complete a form E111, which entitles them to treatment by the health services of other EU countries.

In the UK the form is available from any post office. Take the form with you on your travels, and take a photocopy as well; a hospital or clin-ic may demand to keep a copy of a patient's E111 when they are treated. The form does not mean that you will get free treatment on the spot, and you may find that you are expected to pay. Theoretically, however, you should be able to claim most of the costs back when you get home although reports indicate that it can be a very slow and complicated process.

TRAVEL INSURANCE

An E111 form is no substitute for proper medical cover on your travel insurance. Should you need to be brought home for treatment, or if you call out the mountain rescue services, you may find yourself faced with a large bill. Many travel insurance policies make an extra charge to cover sporting activities, and trekking often comes into this category. If you don't tell them that you're going to be trekking, your insurance could well be invalid when you come to make a claim.

PART 2: THE PYRENEES

Facts about the Pyrenees

GEOGRAPHICAL BACKGROUND

Stretching from the Atlantic to the Mediterranean, the Pyrenees form a natural barrier some 450km long between Continental Europe and the Iberian Peninsula. At the eastern and western ends of the range, the mountains descend to the coastal plains in a series of foothills, while the central area of the Pyrenees boasts a number of impressive peaks – the highest of which is the Pico de Aneto (3404m). The tiny principality of Andorra lies in the middle of the mountains, near the eastern end.

CLIMATE

The summer climate of the Pyrenees is warmer than many people imagine. The mountains are, however, subject to a number of climatic factors, which make for marked regional variations in weather along the range.

The east-west factor

Although the range is only 450km long, there is great contrast in climate at each end. In the western Pyrenees, the weather is governed by systems coming in from the Atlantic, often bringing rain and cloud. While this means that you're more likely to get wet at some stage, it also contributes to a fabulously green landscape.

 The legend of Pyrène

According to legend, the Pyrenees are named after Pyrène, the daughter of a king who ruled the area. His court, it is said, was in the cave at Lombrives, near Tarascon-sur-Ariège, the largest and most spectacular cavern in the region.

Hercules, engaged in the Twelve Labours imposed on him by jealous Juno, noticed the young and beautiful Pyrène, and they fell in love. He stayed for a while in the royal household promising to return for Pyrène after accomplishing his next task. Soon afterwards, however, Pyrène discovered that she was pregnant, and fled into the woods to escape her father's anger. As she wandered through the trees, she was attacked by a lion, and cried out to Hercules to help her. Although he was far away across the world, he heard her cry and came as fast as he could. He arrived too late, however, and found her dead. In anguish he threw up a range of mountains as her tombstone, and named them after her – the Pyrenees.

The eastern end of the range gets much of its weather from the more stable Mediterranean climate; good conditions are pretty much guaranteed but trekking can be hot and dusty work.

The north-south divide

The Pyrenees form a divide between the weather systems of Continental Europe and the Iberian peninsula; in summer, conditions are notably more stable and sunnier in the Spanish mountains than in their French counterparts. If you are caught up in a spell of bad weather in France, it's worth considering going south. Travelling only a few kilometres across the border can take you from rainy, misty France to bright sunshine in Spain.

Altitude

The other major factor governing the climate is altitude. With mountains of over 3000 metres in height, wind and weather conditions can vary greatly.

Typical summertime temperatures are given below but note that these are figures for the whole of the *département*, and thus will not account for reduced temperatures in the high mountains. Note too that, as in all mountain ranges, conditions can be very unpredictable; you can easily go from extreme heat to extreme cold in just a short space of time.

❏ **Typical temperatures in South-West France (May to October)**

Aquitaine (western Pyrenees): May 18°C, June 23.7°C, July 27.2°C, August 25.7°C, September 24.2°C, October 19.7°C

Midi-Pyrénées (central Pyrenees): May 19.1°C, June 26.4°C, July 27.6°C, August 27.2°C, September 25°C, October 19.3°C

Languedoc Roussillon (eastern Pyrenees): May 20.1°C, June 26.5°C, July 28.4°C, August 28.1°C, September 26.1°C, October 21.1°C

Storms

The Pyrenees, particularly on the French side, are prone to rain storms in the late afternoons, and thus most people try to make an early start and complete the day's walking by the early afternoon. If the skies are clear you have plenty of time to dawdle, but it is comforting to be within easy reach of your destination should the weather start to change.

HISTORICAL OUTLINE

For centuries, the Pyrenees have been a natural and cultural watershed, and the history of the region is every bit as complex and intricate as its topography. While great empires and cultural movements lapped at the base of the mountains, small pockets could remain unaffected. Individual kingdoms constantly altered shape and influence through local alliances. The border as we see it today did not become fixed until 1659, with the signing of the Treaty of the Pyrenees.

Because specific areas often have a story all of their own, a synopsis of the local history is given at the beginning of each section of the book. This historical overview aims only to give an outline of important events in France and Spain which had their inevitable effect on the kingdoms of the Pyrenees.

Prehistory

Some of the oldest remains in Europe have been found at the foot of the Pyrenees. Bones uncovered in a cave at Tautavel, near Perpignan, are believed to be those of an ancestor of homo sapiens, who lived around 450,000 years ago. The significance of the find can be appreciated when you consider that the next nearest remains so far unearthed in the area, belonged to a cave culture which lived over 400,000 years later. Even this is pretty early, though, and the cave paintings which have been found at, among other places, Niaux, near Tarascon-sur-Ariège, are immensely significant. The people who painted these images lived somewhere between 10,000 and 30,000 years ago.

To put all of this in perspective, Neolithic culture, during which man began to grow crops and to keep animals, reached the mountains about 7000 years ago, and little is known about the people who lived here at the time. There are few remains of the Neolithic Pyreneans, although a scattering of dolmens and stone circles suggests the area was widely settled.

Pre Roman

Coming into surer territory, it seems likely that from about 1000BC onwards, the Celts drifted through the Pyrenees from central and northern Europe. It's possible that the ancestors of the Basques arrived at about this time, too; Roman historians, writing several centuries later, speak of a tribe called the Vascones who were settled in the Pyrenees. At the same time as the Celts were spreading down from Central Europe, the coastline provided access for trading nations. The Greeks, Phoenicians and Carthaginians all set up bases along the Mediterranean coast.

The Romans

In 238BC the Carthaginians invaded Spain, and twenty years later Hannibal used the peninsula as a springboard for his forces, during the Second Punic War. He lost, and the Romans began the long process of incorporating 'Hispania' into their empire. In all, it took them nearly a century to bring the warlike people to some sort of peace, and even then, pockets of the North-West remained effectively out of their influence. It has been suggested that the Basque country was one of these 'independent' areas and thus, while the language of the rest of Spain became Romanized, the Basque language remained unchanged.

At the same time as the Romans were bringing the peninsula to heel, they were also at work to the north of the Pyrenees. By around 50BC the northern slopes were safely under control and incorporated in the Roman province of Aquitania. This was about as near as the Pyrenees have ever got to being united under one rule. The high mountains were still the preserve of the local tribes but the land on both sides and all along the range was firmly Roman.

As Roman power began to wane, however, both Hispania and Gaul suffered a gradual disintegration. The Romans, struggling to protect their homeland from invasion, gradually withdrew their garrisons from the west, leaving the area vulnerable to attacks from the north. In 409AD a huge force passed through the western Pyrenees, and Roman control of the area effectively came to an end. The Romans called for assistance from the Visigoths, who managed to quell the other tribes and became the de facto rulers of the peninsula.

To the north of the Pyrenees, the Visigoths held power for half a century or so, before being pushed back over the mountains by the Franks. The loose-knit collection of tribes in France was brought into some sort of order, towards the end of the fifth century, by the Frankish chief, Clovis, who founded the Merovingian line. Despite this nominal centralization of power, however, the local rulers in the Pyrenees retained almost total autonomy.

The Moors and Charlemagne

While France was slowly descending into chaos, Spain, under the Visigoths, wasn't doing much better. The new rulers inherited what was left of the Roman infrastructure and basked in their good fortune. Consequently when the Moors invaded from North Africa in 711, the Visigoth armies were chronically unprepared. In the space of less than five years, the Moors came to control almost all of the peninsula. A brief attempt to push beyond the Pyrenees, met with defeat at Poitiers in 732, and thenceforth the Muslim sphere of influence remained to the south of the mountains. The Pyrenees became the centre of the Christian resistance to the Moorish occupation, and the unique culture that we can still find in many parts of the mountains is partly attributable to this. Romanesque architecture, which began to flourish in about the 11th century, has some of its finest and earliest examples in the Spanish Pyrenees.

At the same time as the Moors were seizing the peninsula, power was changing hands in France. In 750, Pepin the Short became king of the Franks and founded the Carolingian Dynasty. In 771, following the deaths of both his father (Pepin) and his brother (Carloman), Charles the Great – Charlemagne – became the king. In the 43 years of his rule, Charlemagne extended the French empire to include most of Europe. In doing so he almost succeeded in bringing the Pyrenees back under central control with the formation of the Spanish Marches, a buffer zone to the south of the mountains. Notably Charlemagne also suffered his most famous defeat in the Pyrenees. Answering the request of a Moorish emir for assistance, in 777 Charlemagne crossed the mountains and campaigned on his behalf. While returning to France in 778, however, the rearguard of his army was ambushed and slaughtered by the Basques, near Roncesvalles. The tragedy was immortalized in the medieval lay, the *Chanson de Roland*.

The Early Middle Ages

By the start of the eleventh century the scene had changed dramatically. South of the Pyrenees, the Moors were weakened by the collapse of the Umayyad Caliphate, which had been the central power in Muslim Spain. Although it was not until the Battle of Las Navas de Tolosa in 1212 that the tide really turned in favour of the Christian monarchs, fledgling states such as Navarre now had much greater freedom, and began to develop.

Central control had weakened in France too, as Charlemagne's heirs gradually lost their grip over his vast empire. The break-up of the established order on both sides of the Pyrenees allowed the ambitions of local rulers to take flight. Catalonia, which had been part of the Spanish March formed by Charlemagne, now came into its own, and Aragón, under a powerful local lord, became a distinct state. On the northern side of the mountains, Foix and Béarn were but two of the regions which were effectively self-governing.

The High Middle Ages

The Capetian dynasty came to power in France in 987 but initially little was achieved to bring the autonomous states together under central rule. Things looked promising in 1137, when Eleanor of Aquitaine, the heir to the largest of the provinces, became the wife of the French monarch, Louis VII. Fifteen years later, however, the marriage was annulled and she married Henry, Count of Anjou, who became Henry II of England in 1154. This effectively put a whole new twist into the plot, as it brought the whole of Aquitaine under English control.

It should not be supposed that this put all the land north of the Pyrenees into English hands, for much of it was already held by the Spanish. Navarre stretched over today's border and included what we now know as Basse-Navarre, and much of Rousillon and Cerdenya were also in Spanish hands. In 1137 the kingdom of Aragón and the county of Barcelona were united, and James I of Aragón subsequently ruled over a huge chunk of the southern and eastern Pyrenees.

One other event is worthy of special mention from this time: the brutal suppression of the Cathars. The Cathars were a non-violent Christian sect, with a strong following in the eastern Pyrenees. Both for their nonconformist doctrine, and because they posed a threat to the power of the Catholic Church, the movement was branded heretical. After failing to persuade Raymond of Toulouse to do the dirty work, Pope Innocent III declared a crusade against the Cathars. The armies employed were those of professional treasure seekers, such as Simon de Montfort (see p281), father of the Simon who initiated the first English parliament. For 30 years the Languedoc region was ravaged by these armies, and terrorized by the clandestine operations of the Inquisition. The last Cathar stronghold, at Montségur, fell in 1244; 225 Cathar *parfaits* (priests) were burnt to death.

Late Middle Ages

The late Middle Ages were characterized throughout Europe by the establishment of the state, and the slow move towards central government. In a gradual succession of victories, which started with Las Navas de Tolosa in 1212, the Christian monarchs of Spain succeeded in pushing the Moors southwards. Despite almost incessant struggles between the individual states, the marriage in 1469 of Isabella I of Castille and Ferdinand II of Aragón effectively joined the two largest kingdoms in the land. By the end of the century, they had ejected the Muslims from southern Spain, and had managed to bring all of the other kingdoms under their control. The arrangement was a loose one, however, and individual kingdoms such as Navarre and Catalonia retained a large degree of autonomy for centuries. The founding of the nation, however, coupled with the discovery of the New World, set the scene for Spain's growth to become the most powerful nation on earth.

In France, the Hundred Years War (1337-1453) was fought to expel the English from the Continent. Although individual rulers in Aquitaine and Gascony remained powerful during this period, Charles VII's eventual success in expelling the English, signalled the beginnings of a recognized monarchy.

The 16th-18th centuries

The French state grew stronger throughout the sixteenth century but continued to be racked by problems. In the South-West this took the form in particular of religious dissent, and the Protestant courts of Bordeaux and Béarn resisted the influence of the Catholic monarchy. Béarn eventually provided the answer: Henry of Navarre (at this stage Basse-Navarre was in French hands). By Salic Law, Marguerite de Valois, sister of the late Henry III, could not inherit the throne which was offered to Henry of Navarre provided he became a Catholic. 'Paris is worth a Mass' he observed of his conversion and he was crowned Henry IV in 1589. To end the religious wars still ravaging the country he introduced, under the Edict of Nantes (1598), laws confirming the rights of Protestants (mainly Huguenots) and religious toleration towards them throughout Catholic France. He is still remembered by the French as one of the best monarchs in the country's history. In 1610, he was assassinated by a religious fanatic but by this time central control of the nation was well and truly established.

Meanwhile Spain reached the height of her power during the sixteenth century, with the addition of enormous wealth from her empire in the New World. By the close of the century, however, the golden age was already coming to an end, and the defeat of the Spanish Armada in 1588 effectively marked the downturn in Spanish fortunes. During the first half of the seventeenth century there were regular border disputes with France, resolved only with the signing of the Treaty of the Pyrenees in 1659. The treaty, which finalized the border as we see it today, was consolidated by the marriage of Maria Theresa, the daughter of Philip IV, to Louis XIV, in 1660.

Forty years later, a much simpler solution to Louis's territorial ambitions presented itself. In 1700, following the demise of the last of the Spanish royal line, Louis accepted the Spanish throne on behalf of his grandson, Philip V. Louis's comment at the time, 'Il n'y a plus de Pyrénées', proved to be prematurely optimistic. Unable to countenance the prospect of the French and Spanish united under one royal household, the other major European nations took up arms; the War of the Spanish Succession (1701-14) ended in defeat for France and Spain. In the aftermath of the war, Philip V abolished the individual parliaments of all of the Spanish states apart from Navarre and the Basque Provinces.

The French Revolution and the Napoleonic Wars

The turmoil of the French Revolution (1789-1799) inevitably spread south across of the Pyrenees with the influx of refugees. Events took a more direct turn in 1795, when the French Army crossed the border and took several towns, including Bilbao and Figueras. Their withdrawal was negotiated with the concession of a part of Spain's overseas territories, and from this time an alliance was maintained between the two countries. While France under Bonaparte went from strength to strength, Spain suffered a number of humiliating defeats, including the ending of its naval power at Trafalgar in 1805.

In 1808, under the pretence of a joint operation against Portugal, French forces entered Spain, and promptly occupied a number of cities. While the Spanish people rose against the French invaders, the royal family were relieved of the throne, which Napoleon gave to his brother, Joseph. The Peninsular War (1808-1814) which followed, saw French and British forces competing for control of Spain and Portugal. In 1813 Wellington's victory at Vittoria forced the the French to retreat northwards through the Pyrenees, hotly pursued by the allied forces.

The 19th and early 20th centuries

For the French, the period following the end of the Napoleonic wars was one of confusion, with the reintroduction of the monarchy, followed by the founding of both the second and third republics. In the Pyrenees, far from the politics of the capital, the spa towns became fashionable, and

Pyrenéisme began, with the first real interest in the mountains themselves. Towards the end of the nineteenth century all the major peaks were climbed, and colourful characters such as Henry Russell wrote some of the most famous literature about the mountains.

Spain suffered a much more turbulent fate during this period. From 1833-1839 the First Carlist War was fought over the succession to the throne, and between 1868 and 1874 the monarchy was suspended after a rising of army officers. In 1874, after another brief Carlist uprising, a monarch was restored to the throne, and a government was formed. This rather shaky system lasted until 1917, when it collapsed. Spain remained neutral throughout the First World War, experiencing its own internal violence and confusion.

The Spanish Civil War

The 1920's and 1930's failed to produce any suitable solutions to Spain's internal conflict and, following elections in 1936, the army under General Franco seized power. The Spanish Civil War (1936-1939) racked the country and ended in the deaths of tens of thousands, and the flight into France of tens of thousands more. In the early part of the war, idealistic young foreigners passed through the Pyrenees to join the Republican forces; by the end of the war, shattered Republicans crossed the mountains seeking refuge in France. This last dash to safety was made, by many in mid-winter, across the high passes of the central Pyrenees. Thousands died in the attempt.

The Second World War

Spain remained neutral throughout the Second World War, and consequently the Pyrenees were a natural escape route for allied personnel and those who wished to join the Free French forces. The French Resistance was particularly strong in the South-West, and escape routes were operated at great risk by guides all along the length of the mountain range. Some of the best *passeurs* were Spanish farmers and shepherds who had fled from their homes during the Spanish Civil War.

Since the War

The period since the end of the war has seen fundamental changes, particularly to the south of the mountains. In the wake of the Nationalist victory, thousands of former Republicans were put on trial and whole regions that had supported the Republican cause were penalized. In the Basque country, for example, speaking Basque in public was no longer allowed. In this adverse political climate, and with the economy so badly mishandled that Spain spent most of the next two decades in recession, many refugees opted to remain in France rather than return to their homes. On Franco's death in 1975, the nation voted overwhelmingly for democracy and in 1978 the Basque country and Catalonia were given a large degree of autonomy.

ECONOMY

Despite the fact that a succession of writers over the last century described life in the mountains as a rural idyll, the truth is that the *montagnards* (mountain people) of the Pyrenees endured a hard lot with little reward. The economy was, until recently, almost entirely based on farming. Transhumance, the custom of following livestock up or down the mountain according to the season, was a way of life well into this century.

Things have changed radically but not without cost to local life. In the Spanish Pyrenees hamlets have been deserted, and many mountain villages now have only a handful of inhabitants. With the growth of industry, jobs in the factories provided more money and an easier living, attracting most young people away from the rural economy. The abundance of hydroelectric power on both sides of the mountains has made the foothills of the Pyrenees a good place for energy intensive industries, such as aluminium smelting. Related industries have flourished too, and Toulouse is a major centre for aircraft construction.

In the mountains themselves, farming is still a way of life but tourism is now a major earner. You can instantly tell a village which has captured the tourist trade in some way; unlike the others nearby, there is building work in progress and a sense of rejuvenation.

THE PEOPLE

The range of mountains that has separated Spain from the rest of Europe throughout history has thrown up many strange affiliations. In some cases villages to the north and south of the Pyrenees share common language and culture, while there is rivalry between valleys on the same side of the mountains. However high the passes, there has been considerable intermingling between communities ever since the area was settled.

Place names emphasize the links: Marcadau (meaning market) was on one of the main trading routes; the Hospice de France and Hospital de Venásque were set up to shelter travellers on either side of the high Venásque Pass, and St-Jean-Pied-de-Port is named after the pass to which it provides access.

The montagnards all along the Pyrenees are a tough and independent lot to whom borders have never been particularly important. Smuggling has been a way of life for centuries and, according to recent reports, is still big business with the movement of duty-free cigarettes from Andorra. There are concessions, of course, to the government and to tourists but you still get the feeling that die-hard Pyreneans will do exactly what they want, regardless.

Separatism

With this tradition of toughness and independence it's not all that surprising that there are calls from some parts of the community for self rule. The most vociferous group calling for independence are the Basques, some of whom, under the guise of the organization ETA have resorted to terrorism to achieve their aims. Most of the Spanish Basque community were perfectly satisfied when, in 1978, the Pais Vasco was granted autonomous status, effectively being allowed to govern itself. A small tearaway group, however, opted to continue the violence and since then have shot and bombed their way into the news. There is no equivalent of ETA among the French Basques.

Demands for greater autonomy can also be heard from the Catalans, and there is a common bond between the inhabitants of Spanish Catalonia and the villagers who live on the French side of the mountains.

LANGUAGES

Obviously most people speak either **Spanish** or **French** (many villagers speak both – which is handy if you plan to be walking on either side of the border and don't speak both languages yourself). There are two other main languages: Basque and Catalan.

Basque is unique and is the oldest language still in use in Europe. Basques on both sides of the border speak the same language, which they call Euskara. During Franco's time, the use of Basque was forbidden but following his death it was granted equal status under the 1978 constitution; nevertheless, despite concerted attempts to keep the language alive, it appears to be losing ground. A recent survey in Spain showed that only 26% of the two million Spanish Basques speak Euskara as their first language, and in 1997 only one school in Hendaye was teaching Basque as a first language.

Like Basque, **Catalan** was banned by Franco but was given equal status with Castilian after 1978. Although the Catalan movement for greater autonomy seldom gets into the news, being overshadowed by the violence of the Basque separatists, it is still a force in local politics. Recent moves to force offices and government departments in Catalonia to use Catalan are meeting with resistance from many people.

GEOLOGY

The formation of the Pyrenees was not a single incident but the culmination of several; hence the geology of the area is complex. In outline, however, the mountains were caused by a huge, slow-motion crash between the Iberian Peninsula and rest of Europe. This collision of the continental plates began around 200 million years ago and is still continuing today.

Formation

The oldest rocks located in the Pyrenees date from around 500 million years ago when a range of mountains, known to geologists as the

Hercynian Range, was formed. The range covered much of Central Europe, and the Massif Central is one remnant of it.

With the constant movement of the earth's crust, part of the mountain range was torn down over the next two hundred million years, and the rocks that had formed the centre of the range were covered by a shallow sea. Gradually layers of sediment were laid down on the sea bed over the top of the Hercynian rock.

Around 220 million years ago, the direction of movement of the earth's crust (the so-called 'tectonic plates') changed, and they began to be forced inwards. It is thought that this change in direction may have been caused by the collision of the continent of Africa with the land mass of Europe. Between about 58 million years ago and 24 million years ago, the inward movement caused a number of sections of land to be crushed up against Europe. Among these were the Italian peninsula, causing the formation of the Swiss Austrian Alps, and the Iberian peninsula, causing the formation of the Pyrenees – thus the Alps and the Pyrenees are contemporaneous.

The rocks in the Pyrenees are much older than their Alpine counterparts, for, as the Iberian peninsula squeezed up against Europe, it was the old Hercynian rock covered with its layer of newer sedimentary rock that was forced upwards. In some areas, the new covering of sedimentary rocks proved malleable and bent with the movement, thereby remaining above the older rock. At the point of greatest pressure, however, along the central axis of the range, the sedimentary rocks often did not bend but shattered, exposing the older, Hercynian, rocks beneath.

Erosion

The fact that all this occurred 24 to 58 million years ago means that the mountains we see today must be looked at with an understanding of the erosion which has occurred since. In many places the younger, softer rocks, even if they remained on top, have been eroded, partially or entirely.

The Quaternary Period, which is the period of the last 1.6 million years up to the present day, has seen a series of ice ages. Glaciers hundreds of metres thick fundamentally altered the shape of the landscape to leave it pretty much as it is today. U-shaped valleys, arêtes (sharp, mountain ridges), cirques (deep, bowl-shaped hollows at valley heads), moraines (deposits of rocks and debris) and hanging valleys are all legacies of glaciation, and are clearly seen throughout the Pyrenees.

NATIONAL PARKS

For information on **Pyrenean flora and fauna** see p60.

Parc National des Pyrénées

The park, which was created on 23 March 1967, has a central zone of 457 square kilometres and an outer zone of 2063 square kilometres. It contains a wealth of flora and fauna including, apparently, 571 species of algae! Of more interest to most visitors are the spectacular birdlife and other wildlife. In 1997 there were estimated to be 14 pairs of bearded vultures, 18 pairs of royal eagles and 200 pairs of Griffon vultures. Among the park's other occupants are izards, marmots and even bears.

● **Rules** Dogs are not allowed in the park (even on a lead), and mountain biking is forbidden. Strictly speaking, **camping** is not allowed in the park but it is generally tolerated as long as certain rules are followed. Pitching a tent is permitted for one night only, as long as the location is more than one hour's walk from the park boundaries and from any paved road. Tents are not supposed to be put up before the early evening (ie 6-7pm) and are to be down by 9am. Obviously no litter or damage to the surrounding area is tolerated, and fires are not allowed. Refuges in the park generally have a small area near the building where camping is permitted. **Fishing** is allowed in the park (as elsewhere in the Pyrenees) as long as you have a fishing permit, which can be bought from any tabac. The fishing season runs from March to September.

● **Information** For more information contact the **park office** (☎ 05.62 .44.36.60, 🖳 www.parc-pyrenees.com), 59 route de Pau, 65000 Tarbes.

Parque Nacional de Ordesa y Monte Perdido

From its tentative beginnings in 1918, when an area of around 20 square kilometres was designated a protected zone, the park now covers 156 square kilometres with a peripheral zone of a further 190 square kilometres. Included within this area is the spectacular Ordesa Canyon and its smaller neighbour, the Añisclo Canyon. To the north, Ordesa shares a border with the Parc National des Pyrénées.

● **Rules** Fires are not allowed, and **camping** is permitted only in certain areas – near the Refugio de Goriz, around Refugio San Vicenda and in the area of Ermita de Pineta. As long as you are sensible, you can probably get away with putting up a tent elsewhere just for a night. Leave no litter.

● **Information** For further information contact the **park office** (☎ 974-48 62 12 or 24 33 61).

Parque Nacional d'Aigües Tortes i Sant Maurici

The park was designated on 21 October 1995 and has a total area of 488 square kilometres of which 141 square kilometres is the inner area. Sant Maurici lake is near its centre.

● **Rules** Fires are not allowed, and camping is permitted only near refuges. Bathing in the lakes and rivers is against the rules.

● **Information** The park office is in Espot (☎ 973-62.40.36)

Réserve Naturelle de Néouvielle

The reserve is a protected area rather than a designated national park, but it's subject to most of the rules already listed above for other places. Camping is limited to one site near the Lac d'Aubert.

Practical information for the visitor

LOCAL TRANSPORT

France
Public transport in the French Pyrenees is good, although bus services tend to run only to the larger villages. If you're planning to travel to or from the mountains by public transport, it makes sense to use, as a start or finish point, one of the following towns and villages which are served by buses or trains.
- **Western Pyrenees** Hendaye, Bidarray, St-Jean-Pied-de-Port, Borce/Etsaut, Arrens-Marsous.
- **Central Pyrenees** Arrens-Marsous, Cauterets, Luz-St-Sauveur, Gavarnie, Barèges, Vielle Aure, Bagnères-de-Luchon, Seix, Aulus-les-Bains, Mérens-les-Vals.
- **Eastern Pyrenees** Mérens-les-Vals, Mont Louis, Arles-sur-Tech, Banyuls-sur-Mer.

Spain
Public transport in Spain is less regular than that in France and there tends to be only one or possibly two buses a day into the mountains.
- **Western Pyrenees** Roncesvalles, Ochagavia, Sallent de Gallego
- **Central Pyrenees** Torla, Bénasque

ACCOMMODATION

There is a wide variety of accommodation available, and this book attempts to give a selection of the best of each sort. While the larger villages generally have some very pleasant hotels and *chambres d'hôte* (guest houses), the choice of accommodation in the mountains, as you would expect, is much more limited: gîtes d'étape (lodges) and refuges (mountain huts) are the two main options. In mid summer, try to ring in advance and reserve a place at any of the above. Not only will this ensure that you have accommodation at the end of a full day's walking but you may also find that you get preferential treatment if you can give a couple of days' notice (ie a better bed, or even a room to yourself). There are a few areas along the GR10 where no accommodation is available, and where the only option other than camping is to stay in a cabane (shepherd's hut).

Hotels
Spending the occasional night in a hotel is well worth it. After the dormitory conditions of the gîtes d'étape, you can enjoy privacy, a proper bed,

and no snoring neighbours – guaranteed! Moreover, almost all Pyrenean hotels have a restaurant where you can try excellent local food, and a glass or two of good wine, which should, after all, be part of the general experience of travelling through France or Spain. The great thing about all this is that small hotels are often not all that much more expensive than the gîtes. Treat yourself!

Chambres d'hôte and casas rurales

Another option is staying in a local house. In France, staying in a chambre d'hôte is often no cheaper than a night in a small hotel, and since food is usually not available, they don't represent any great bargain. In Spain, *casas rurales* (called *casas de pagès* in Catalonia) can be much better value and are definitely worth checking out – although, again, you are often expected to bring your own food.

Even if staying in a local house does cost you a little more, you may judge it to be money well spent. It's an interesting experience and allows plenty of opportunity to chat to the owners about the area through which you are passing.

Gîtes d'étape

The name says it all: these are lodging houses which have been set up along the routes of major footpaths, and which tend to form the start and end point of the day stages. They vary in quality, facilities and efficiency. Some are run as full time businesses in the summer, in which case you can expect everything to be in good shape. In other places the gîte is not much more than a camping barn.

Accommodation is almost always in a dormitory, often with one or two large platforms, on which mattresses have been laid side by side. Try to get the space near the window, as in mid-summer with a full complement of walkers, it can get a bit stuffy at night. Food is usually available but again it pays to ring in advance and confirm this. There are almost invariably kitchen facilities though the standard can vary greatly. A night's accommodation (*la nuitée*) in a gîte costs around €11.50/75F; breakfast generally costs €3.80-4.60/25-30F, and an evening meal (*repas*) normally costs about €12.20/80F. Half board (*demi-pension*), therefore, costs around €27.50/180F.

While the gîtes can be crowded in mid summer (they tend to open only from early June to the late September), and they are by no means cheap, there are certain obvious advantages. Showers, a bed, and shelter from the elements are some of them; in addition, you get to meet other walkers, try local cuisine, and get information from the gîte owner.

Refuges

Refuges in the Pyrenees may either be staffed (ie with a guardian) or unstaffed.

> **Discounts at refuges**
> If you intend to use refuges regularly during your trek, you can save
> money by joining one of the large mountaineering organizations. Most
> of the French refuges are owned by the **Club Alpin Français** (CAF), mem-
> bership of which gives an instant 50% discount. In addition, there is an agree-
> ment of réciprocité between the CAF and many other mountaineering groups.
> The details of the agreement are renegotiated every year. Proof of membership
> of any of the clubs included in the agreement, along with a valid Reciprocal
> Rights card, should secure at least a 20% discount. The agreement also
> includes most refuges in the Spanish Pyrenees.
>
> To find out more, contact your national mountaineering association. In the
> UK this is the **British Mountaineering Council** (☎ 0161-445 4747 web:
> www.thebmc.co.uk) 177-179 Burton Rd, Manchester, M20 2BB. You could
> also try contacting the Club Alpin Français (☎ 01 53 72 87 00) Commission de
> Gestion des Refuges et Chalets, 24 avenue de la Laumière, 75019 Paris.

Staffed refuges Staffed refuges are to be found along the most popular walking trails. Some of these places are quite large – Wallon can take
a hundred people in peak season, and there are many others which can
accommodate 50-60 people. Conditions are rather like those in a gîte but
because of the remoteness of the refuges, (supplies must be brought up
either by helicopter or by mule), prices are slightly higher and facilities
rather more basic. A night in a refuge costs around €11.50/75F, breakfast
about €4.60/30F, and supper €14/90F; thus demi-pension is usually in
the order of €30/190F. Prices in Spanish refuges (*refugios*) are similar.
Very few refuges have a shower, and in many the loo is a draughty lean-
to shelter away from the main building. Bring your own loo paper – it
isn't provided.

Although the largest refuges have a guardian (and sometimes staff) to
handle the large numbers of visitors, they are only there during peak season. Guardians are in residence from early June to late September and, if
feasible, Christmas, Easter and a few weekends in between. When the
guardian is not in residence, a small section of the refuge is generally left
open for passing walkers.

Even in peak season, it is perfectly acceptable to pay for accommodation only and to provide your own meals; cooking areas are often set
aside, where you can use camping stoves safely. Unlike gîtes, however,
there are no kitchen facilities provided.

Unstaffed refuges A number of smaller refuges throughout the
Pyrenees do not merit a guardian – even in peak season. They have basic
facilities and a conscience box; place your donation in the box before you
depart, and ensure you leave everything clean for the next users.

Cabanes

The last sort of shelter available in the mountains are the cabanes. These are marked on IGN maps (as are gîtes and refuges), and in the later stages of the GR10 they occasionally offer the only accommodation available. Cabanes are generally shepherds' huts which are available for use by walkers. There is no charge for using them but it is expected that walkers will leave them clean.

There is always the risk that others may want to use the same cabane as you do, and if you arrive to find that there are already trekkers, shepherds or hunters in residence, you'll just have to go elsewhere, or sleep outside. Try to ensure, therefore, that you arrive at your chosen cabane with plenty of time and energy to go elsewhere if necessary.

Cabanes vary greatly in quality, and brief remarks on each are given in this book. At the most basic, a cabane may be a dark, dirty and smelly shelter for no more than two or three people. There are, however, a few cabanes which are kept in very good condition, and which occupy excellent positions in otherwise deserted countryside. The best of these can be great places to spend a night.

Camping

French and Spanish campsites are generally excellent, with good facilities and a pleasant atmosphere. Prices vary considerably according to the standard of the site (they are rated by stars) and the popularity of the area. Tariffs are worked out in one of two ways: some charge separately for the tent site (*emplacement*) and for the occupants, whereas others have a flat rate for a couple of walkers with a small tent. Pretty much all campsites have showers and proper toilets.

Rough camping is feasible in the mountains themselves but, if you're near anyone's land, ask first. For details on camping in the national parks, see p51.

LANGUAGE

Many of the locals speak both French and Spanish, but English speakers are rather less common. Getting by in English is easy enough, but don't expect to find out a lot about what you're eating, or whether the path is clear ahead. Learning a little French or Spanish before you go will considerably enhance your trip, and it's well worth carrying a small phrase book. If all else fails, head for the nearest tourist office, where you'll find someone who can speak English. See p304 for phrase lists.

ELECTRICITY

Electricity on both sides of the border is 220V, and the plugs are of the two round-pin variety.

HOLIDAYS AND FESTIVALS

There are numerous holidays and festivals throughout the Pyrenees. It's best to get more information from the tourist office of either country before you travel. Some of the larger festivals are as follows:

Festivals – Western Pyrenees
● **13 July – Celebration of the Tribute of the Three Cows**, Ronçal. This treaty, which allows the neighbours from the Ronçal and Barétous valleys to graze their animals on each other's land, is one of the oldest in the world. See p104.
● **Mid-July – Bull running** The most famous festival in Spain takes place in Pamplona, Navarre.
● **Early August – International Pyrenean Folk Festival**, Oloron-Ste-Marie.

Festivals – Central Pyrenees
● **July – Jazz Festival,** Germ.
● **Mid-July – Jazz-Altitude**, Luz-Saint-Sauveur.
● **Late July – Theatre Festival**, Gavarnie.
● **Mid-July – Tour de France** This famous cycle race passes through the central Pyrenees.
● **Late August – Floral Festival**, Bagnères-de-Luchon.

Office hours
● **France** In France, working hours are much the same as in the UK, except that shopkeepers usually take a long break from midday until about 3.30pm, then shops stay open until about 7pm. Banks also take a short mid-day break and tend to close completely over the weekend. Post offices are open from around 9am to 6pm, and are also open on Saturday mornings.
● **Spain** The Spanish have a much more relaxed attitude to life. Shops come to life at around 9am and work stops for a longish siesta from mid-day onwards. Around mid-afternoon there are signs of activity, and shops then stay open late into the evening.

Public holidays
● **France** There are two major holidays during the walking season: Bastille Day on 14 July, and the Feast of the Assumption on 15 August.
● **Spain** In the walking season there are public holidays in mid June (Corpus Christi), 24 June, 25 July, 15 August (Assumption), and 12 October.

MONEY

Currencies
France and Spain are among the first group of European countries committed to using the **euro (€)**, and currently all shops are compelled to give prices in euros as well as in the local currency. Euro currency will become

❏ Rates of exchange

	France	Spain	Euro
Aus$1	3.96F	100pta	€0.60
Can$1	4.95F	125pta	€0.75
Euro €1	6.56F	166pta	–
FF1	–	25pta	€0.15
DM1	3.35F	85pta	€0.51
NLG1	2.97F	75pta	€0.45
NZ$1	3.24F	82pta	€0.49
Ptas100	3.94F	–	€0.60
UK£1	10.83F	275pta	€1.65
US$	7.63F	193pta	€1.16

For up-to-the-minute rates of exchange check the Internet on **www.oanda.com**

available in January 2002; the franc and the peseta will cease to be legal tender in July 2002.

● **France** The French franc (F) comes in notes of 500, 200, 100, 50 and 20. There are coins for 20, 10, 5, 2, 1, and $1/_2$ franc. The franc is divided into 100 centimes; there are coins for 20, 10 and 5 centimes.

● **Spain** The Spanish peseta (pta) is issued in banknotes of 10,000, 5000, 2000, and 1000. There are bronze-coloured coins for 500, 100, 25 and 5 pesetas, and silver-coloured coins for 50 and 1 pesetas.

Tipping

● **France** A service charge is included in restaurant bills so a tip is not expected. Taxi drivers expect a tip of around 3F, whatever the length of the journey.

● **Spain** For waiters and taxi drivers 5-10% is about right, or the small change in a café or cheap restaurant.

POST AND TELECOMMUNICATIONS

Postal services

Postal services in France and Spain are efficient. You can save time, however, by buying stamps in tabacs.

Having poste restante sent to any of the large French post offices is easy. Letters or parcels should be clearly addressed with the surname in capitals and underlined, then sent to Poste Restante, Bureau de Poste, Name of town, Post code (given in the guide section of this book). You will need to produce some proof of identity to be able to pick up your mail. Along the GR10, good places to collect poste restante are:

● **Western Pyrenees** Hendaye, St-Jean-Pied-de-Port, Lescun, Arrens Marsous.

● **Central Pyrenees** Cauterets, Luz-Saint-Sauveur, Vielle Aure, Bagnères-de-Luchon, Seix, Ax-les-Thermes.

● **Eastern Pyrenees** Arles-sur-Tech, Banyuls-sur-Mer.

Phone, fax and email

Most though not all public telephones in France and Spain use phone cards. In France, *télécartes* are available at tabacs and at post offices. In Spain *tarjetas telefónicas* can be bought at small shops and post offices. To make a domestic call within France, note that you should always dial the full ten-digit number even when calling within the same area.

To make an international call from France dial 00 and then the country code (44 for the UK, 1 for USA & Canada) followed by the area code (minus the 0) and the number you require. French phone boxes which have the symbol of a blue bell on the side will receive incoming calls. From Spain dial 07 before the country code.

Most post offices have a **fax** machine available for a small charge, but otherwise try a hotel or bookshop (*librairie*).

There are few, if any, places from which to send and receive **email** apart from cities such as Toulouse, Lourdes, Tarbes and Pau.

FOOD

One of the greatest pleasures of walking in the Pyrenees is the chance to sample a variety of French and Spanish food. Pyrenean cuisine is generally simple, delicious and very filling – preparing people for the strenuous mountain lifestyle.

Throughout the Pyrenees, meals often start with a thick and filling soup, with huge hunks of potato and other vegetables. In France this soup is known as *garbure*. A plate of *charcuterie* (cold meats, usually served with some salad) is another excellent way to start a meal and to taste some of the delicious locally made *saucisson* (sausage). Main courses are generally meat or fish. In France, *poulet Basquaise*, chicken in a thick dark sauce, is a favourite in the western Pyrenees. *Piperade*, a tangy mixture of tomatoes, onions, peppers and garlic may be served with pork or chicken, or in an omelette. Another traditional dish is *boudin* – black pudding sausages which are often served with cooked apple chips.

In Spain, sausages are also common; in the Valle d'Aran, spicy *butifarra* sausage is a speciality. The Spanish are also keen on stews, – huge filling dishes generally made with lamb or chicken. In the same area, one of the more unusual opportunities is to try izard (a relative of the chamois); the dark, strong-tasting meat is served up in a thick wine sauce. Mountain trout is very popular on both sides of the Pyrenees and is guaranteed absolutely fresh from the nearest river or lake.

The other food trekkers are likely to eat frequently is cheese. *Fromage de brebis*, made from ewe's milk, can often be bought from shepherds themselves, who make it in their huts, high on the mountain side.

DRINK

The quality of Pyrenean wine varies greatly – try them all in order to discover one you like. From the table wines of Irrouleguy in the Basque country to the sweet aperitif wine produced in Banyuls on the Mediterranean coast, there should be something here to satisfy everybody. Beer is reasonably priced and just the thing after a hot day's walking. The

French tend to stick to beers such as Pelforth, Amstel and Kronenbourg – try Pelforth Brune if you like dark beer. The Spanish have several brews worth trying from the ubiquitous San Miguel to Estrella Damm and others.

There is an array of local aperitifs and digestifs, from Izarra in the Basque country to Ratafia in the Valle d'Aran.

THINGS TO BUY

The best things to bring away from the Pyrenees as souvenirs are the local foods and wines. A whole cheese makes an excellent gift, although there may be a strong temptation to keep it for yourself. Wine is another good option, as are locally produced honey and liqueurs.

SECURITY

Travelling in the Pyrenees is very safe, and generally you can leave your belongings in a gîte or refuge without worrying. It's common sense, however, to take some standard precautions. Don't leave valuables lying around, and keep your passport and money with you at all times.

Flora and fauna

FAUNA

Mammals

The most famous inhabitants of the mountains are the **brown bears**. Up to the late nineteenth century there were plenty of bears in the Pyrenees but chronic overhunting, coupled with deforestation made them all but extinct by the middle of this century. In an effort to reintroduce the species, several Slovenian brown bears have been released into the mountains over the last couple of years. Reports suggest that there are now around 6-8 bears living in the Pyrenees. See p188.

Other well-known mammals in the mountains include **marmots**, beaver lookalikes which make their home in the rocks and have a high-pitched cry that sounds similar to a bird call. They're inquisitive creatures, and it's not unusual in the less well-walked valleys to find one or two of them perched on the rocks checking you out as you pass by. Marmots were actually hunted to extinction in the Pyrenees during the last century but were reintroduced, and large colonies are now flourishing on many of the rocky slopes.

Another creature native to the Pyrenees is the **izard**, a relative of the chamois. It is found on high mountainsides through the range, and has distinctive narrow upright horns with backward pointing tips. Izards are hunted in late September each year, but recently a greater threat to the species has been an unknown disease which has affected the eyesight of many of the animals. Not to be confused with the izard, the **mouflon** is a type of wild sheep which was originally an inhabitant of these mountains but had to be reintroduced from Sardinia. Although they stand about the same height as izards, mouflon are easily distinguishable by their large curved horns and because they tend to be found in herds on the lower slopes.

Perhaps the most peculiar inhabitant of the mountains is the **desman**, a small aquatic mammal belonging to the mole family. It has webbed feet and a long snout which it uses like a snorkel while hunting for its food. The desman eats fish and makes its home in a burrow in the bank of a stream on the lower slopes of the mountains (below about 1800m).

Other common mammals of the Pyrenees include deer, foxes, squirrels, badgers and wild boar.

Reptiles

Just about the only animal you should avoid (apart from the bear, of course) is the **Pyrenean viper**. There's no particular danger of getting bitten, and I saw only one (alive) in five months, but watch your step on the likely sections of the route. There was also great excitement in 1992 when a new species of frog, **Rana pyrenaica**, was discovered living in the high mountain streams.

Birds

The Pyrenees are home to a wide variety of birds including many that you'd be lucky to see elsewhere in Europe. Most interesting of these are the raptors.

LAMMERGEIER

Probably the best known is the **Lammergeier (Bearded Vulture)**, which can grow up to a metre in length, with a three-metre wing-span. Loners by nature, they nest in the high crags and cliffs of mountain ranges, producing only one or two young each year. Lammergeiers have a peculiar way of feeding: they scavenge the bones carrying them to a great height, before dropping them to break open as they hit the ground. They then swoop down to eat the bone marrow. The adult lammergeier's shape and colouring are distinctive. The wings are long, pointed and slightly swept back, and the tail is diamond-shaped and tapering to a point. The adult bird has black wings and tail, with a golden-coloured underside, legs and hood. Particularly apparent on the head is a band of black which covers the eyes and runs to the front of the head where it ends in a 'beard' – hence the name. Young lammergeiers are much harder to identify, as they remain a dark buff colour with only a pale grey underside until full adulthood. Lammergeiers are now very rare in Europe, existing only in Spain, the Alps and SE Europe. There are estimated to be very few pairs left in the Pyrenees.

The **Griffon Vulture** is much the same size as the lammergeier but is

GRIFFON VULTURE

far more common. It, too, nests on crags and cliff faces, using any available ledge or crevice. The bird's in-flight silhouette is notable for the broad parallel-sided wings, the feathered 'fingertips', and the short, almost square tail. In colouring, the body of the adult is pale fawn as is the forward part of its wings. The tips and trailing edges of the wings and the tail are black. Seen from below, this bar of pale colour formed by the body and the front edge of the wings is distinctive. The head is white with a cream ruff around the neck. The griffon vulture often soars at great height and in the company of others.

The **Egyptian Vulture** is one of the smallest in the vulture family with an average length of 60-65 cm and average wing-span of 1.5 metres. When at rest the visible plumage of the adult is almost all white, with a large white ruff. The face is yellow and the beak long and curving, giving the head the appearance of being long and thin. In flight, the body, tail, and forward edges of the wings are white, while the trailing edges of the

EGYPTIAN VULTURE

wings and the wing-tips are black. In silhouette, the wings are slightly pointed, and the tail is diamond-shaped. The immature Egyptian Vulture is dark brown with a mottled body and forward edges of the wings.

Like the others of their family, Egyptian Vultures nest on cliff faces though usually in a hole in the cliff where both adults look after a single egg. The Egyptian Vulture feeds off carrion but only after its larger brothers have fed first.

The majestic **Golden Eagle** is one of the rarer birds in the Pyrenees but can still be seen. Adults grow up to 90cm long with a wing-span of around two metres. The adult colouring is almost entirely dark brown with golden tinges on the forward parts of the wings and the head. The tips and trailing edges of the wings, as well as the tail, are brown. In flight, the wings, which broaden perceptibly towards the wing-tips, are canted slightly forwards and upwards, and the tail is long, broad and almost square at the end. Immature Golden Eagles are also dark brown in the main

GOLDEN EAGLE

but have a very distinctive white panel on the under side of the wings and a white base of the tail. They can soar for long periods and are adept hunters, eating smaller birds, rabbits and other small mammals. They nest on cliffs or in trees, building a huge eyrie to which they return year after year.

The **Black Kite** is a migratory bird that is versatile in its ability to adjust to a number of habitats including river estuaries and towns. Adults grow to around 55cm in length with a wing-span of around 160cm. The adult bird is actually dark brown in colour rather than pure black. In flight it has slightly bowed wings and a long tail with a shallow fork. The Black Kite has

BLACK KITE

a regular high-pitched cry. It feeds on small animals and carrion and will also scavenge from rubbish tips.

Bonnelli's Eagle grows to a length of around 70cm with a wing-span of 160-170cm. The adult bird has grey-brown upper plumage, with a mottled white neck and underbelly. Seen in flight, the undersides of the wings are predominantly greyish white with a prominent band of black, and black edging at the trailing edge and wing-tips. In silhouette the wings are slender, and the tail is long and

BONELLI'S EAGLE

square-ended with a black tip. The immature bird is generally light brown in colour. Like the Golden Eagle, the Bonnelli's Eagle is becoming increasingly rare.

Among the many other species of birds to be found in the mountains, two are particularly notable. The **Ptarmigan**, which grows to around 35cm in length, makes its home on the mountain tops. It is notable for its

dual appearance, cunningly swapping its brown and white summertime costume for a winter plumage of pure white wings and body with a black tail. In summer the female is distinguishable from the male by her slightly darker colour, and in the winter the male has a black stripe across the eye, while the female does not. The Ptarmigan nests on the ground and typically lays 10-12 eggs.

PTARMIGAN

The largest member of the grouse family, the **Capercaillie** is found much lower down the slopes, below the treeline. These large turkey-sized

birds live in pine forests and feed on shoots and berries. Capercaillies can fly (often noisily), and they will rest in trees but nest on the ground.

Females are reddish-brown in colour and grow to around 60cm in length, whereas males grow up to 90cm and have a dark plumage with a red comb.

CAPERCAILLIE

The males are highly territorial and have a ritual to deter intruders which includes puffing themselves up, spreading their tails and going through an elaborate series of calls. If this fails, the male will attack energetically. One handbook of birds notes: '…the male gives out his curious love-notes in early spring; at this time he shows off somewhat like a Turkey-cock, and becomes so excited that at a certain phase of the 'song' he is temporarily deaf and blind. His encounters at this season with his rivals are fierce and bloody; and on the continent savage old birds have been known to attack persons…'

FLORA

The Pyrenees are well known for their spectacular flora. The huge number of species (160 of which are indigenous) is due in part to the range of climates experienced in the mountains.

Highland (lower levels)

At the lower levels (below about 1800m) there is great variety. Rosebay Willow Herb, Valerian and White Cloud adorn the banks of streams; the hillsides are visited by Trumpet Gentians and the woods are good places to find bright pink Martagon Lilies, purple Foxglove and Granny's Bonnets.

Gentiana acaulis
Trumpet Gentian (closed)

Lactuca perennis
Mountain Lettuce

Succisa pratensis
Devil's Bit

Saxifrage

Gentiana acaulis
Trumpet Gentian (open)

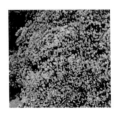

Genista hispanica
Spanish Broom

Allium schoenoprasum
Chives

Epilobium angustifolium
Rosebay Willow Herb

Dianthus monspessulanus
Fringed Pink

Salvia pratensis
Meadow Clary/Wild Sage

Wild Rose

Armeria alliacea
Garlic Thrift

Iris latifolia
Pyrenean Iris

Erinus alpinus
Fairy Foxglove

Malva moschata
Musk Mallow

Dianthus deltoides
Maiden Pink

Silene

Stachys alopecuros
Yellow Betony

Cirsium
Thistle

Sedum reflexum
Reflex Stonecrop

Aster alpinus
Alpine Aster

Sub-alpine

At the 'Sub-alpine' level (between about 1800m and about 2400m), one of the commonest flowers is the dark blue Pyrenean Iris, but there are many others. Look out for Saxifrages, Sedums and the highly distinctive Mountain Houseleek. Sometimes it's the smallest flowers that are the most colourful: they include the purple-fringed Alpine Aster, the dayglo Maiden Pink, and deep blue Spring Gentian.

Lotus alpinus
Alpine Birdsfoot Trefoil

Merendera montana
Merendera

Geranium cinerium

Silene vulgaris
Bladder Campion

Gentiana verna
Spring Gentian

Horminum pyrenaicum
Dragonmouth

Saxifrage

Sempervivum montanum
Mountain Houseleek

Eryngium bourgatti
Pyrenean Eryngo

Hieracium
Hawkweed

Rhododendron ferrugineum
Alpenrose

Trifolium alpinum
Alpine Clover

Phyteuma hemisphericum
Hemispherical-headed Rampion

Alpine

Above 2400m it really is a case of survival of the hardiest, as these tiny flowers spend at least half the year buried under the snow. They are small, wiry and surprisingly colourful: Alpine Clover, Hawkweed and Alpenrose are all common sights.

TREES

Some of the most extensive beech woods in Europe are in the Pyrenees. Oak, birch and hazel also grow in abundance, as well as several varieties of pine trees. Most notable of the pines is the Pinus Uncinata, which grows up to 30 metres in height and can survive at altitudes to up to 2600m. It is one of the longest-living trees in the world; some are 600-800 years old, some even older. Keep an eye open for scarring on the trunks of the older trees; the shepherds used to tap the trees for sap, which was used to fuel the lanterns in their huts at night.

MINIMUM IMPACT TREKKING

With areas of outstanding natural beauty throughout the world under attack, the onus is on every visitor to the Pyrenees to do their own bit in helping to preserve the landscape.

There are a number of ways in which you can assist without creating any great difficulties for yourself – it's just a matter of following a few simple rules.

Don't leave litter

The following sign had been pinned up on a notice board in Mérens-les-Vals:

'A bit of orange peel lasts six months before decomposing. Silver foil lasts eighteen months, textiles last 15 years, and a plastic bag ten to twelve years. An aluminium drinks can will last for 85 years on the ground, or 75 years in the sea. Scrap iron takes more than two centuries to be broken down. It takes the soil five years to recover from unauthorized dumping. Think about it.'

Some people persist in leaving rubbish along the main trails and near the refuges. Everything that you take up into the mountains should either be eaten, buried if it's biodegradable, or carried with you to the nearest village where you can find a bin. It is not possible to dump your litter at refuges as they have to deal with their own rubbish. Guardians, however, have supplies of plastic bin bags which they give away free to encourage walkers to take their litter with them.

Don't pick the flowers

However tempting it may be, leave the flora completely intact for the next people to enjoy.

Stay on the main trail

Increasing numbers of visitors are travelling to the Pyrenees in the summer – particularly to the busiest areas of the Central Pyrenees. This is causing severe erosion along the paths. The staff of the national parks and the local population elsewhere can cope with carrying out erosion control on one path but not on several where walkers have made separate ways up or down the hillsides.

Burn used lavatory paper

Used lavatory paper is an unsightly health risk. If you're camping rough or just have to answer the call of nature along the way, burn the paper rather than leaving it to rot in the open air. Bury the faeces.

Don't pollute water sources

If there's a latrine available, use it. Don't defecate within 20 metres of a water source.

When washing yourself or your clothes using detergents, don't pollute streams or lakes. Carry the water well away from the water source, and after using it dispose of it at least 20 metres from the original source.

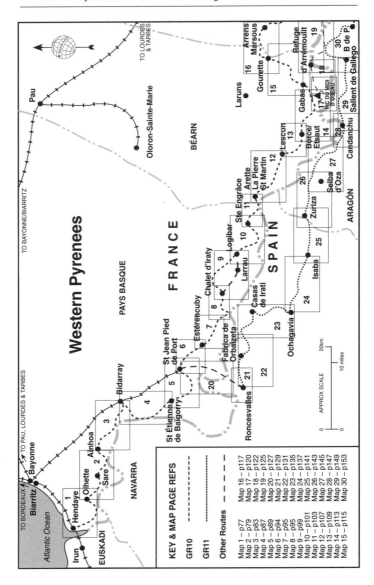

Western Pyrenees

FRANCE

PAYS BASQUE

BÉARN

SPAIN

ARAGÓN

NAVARRA

EUSKADI

Atlantic Ocean

TO BORDEAUX
TO PAU, LOURDES & TARBES
Biarritz
Bayonne
Irun
Hendaye
Olhette
Sare
Ainhoa
Bidarray
St Étienne de Baïgorry
St Jean Pied de Port
Estérençuby
Fabrica de Orbaizeta
Roncesvalles
Chalet d'Iraty
Larrau
Casas de Irati
Logibar
Ste Engrâce
Arette
La Pierre St Martin
Lescun
Borce
Etsaut
Gabas
Candanchu
Selba d'Oza
Zuriza
Isaba
Ochagavia
Sallent de Gallego
B de P.
Refuge d'Arrémoulit
Gourette
Laruns
Arrens
Marsous
Oloron-Sainte-Marie
Pau

TO BAYONNE/BIARRITZ
TO LOURDES & TARBES

PIC DU MIDI D'OSSAU

20km
10 miles
APPROX SCALE
0
0

KEY & MAP PAGE REFS

GR10 ——————
GR11 ——————
Other Routes — — — —

Map 1 – p77
Map 2 – p79
Map 3 – p83
Map 4 – p87
Map 5 – p89
Map 6 – p94
Map 7 – p95
Map 8 – p95
Map 9 – p99
Map 10 – p101
Map 11 – p103
Map 12 – p107
Map 13 – p109
Map 14 – p113
Map 15 – p115
Map 16 – p117
Map 17 – p120
Map 18 – p122
Map 19 – p125
Map 20 – p127
Map 21 – p129
Map 22 – p131
Map 23 – p135
Map 24 – p137
Map 25 – p141
Map 26 – p143
Map 27 – p145
Map 28 – p147
Map 29 – p149
Map 30 – p153

PART 3: WESTERN PYRENEES

Facts about the region

GENERAL DESCRIPTION

The Western Pyrenees are defined here as the area from the Atlantic coast, inland as far as the eastern edge of the French département of Pyrénées Atlantiques. The département, which comprises the provinces of **Pays Basque** and **Béarn**, is mirrored to the south of the border by the Spanish Basque country, the autonomous region of **Navarra** and the western part of the region of **Aragón**.

Although the extent of the area is easy to sum up in a few words, its history and culture are impossible to pigeonhole. Unlike the Central Pyrenees, where high mountain ridges have defined areas much more clearly, this region of low hills and confused topography has allowed a mixing of communities. The border between France and Spain, finally settled by the Treaty of the Pyrenees in 1659, may have made a formal

---

 Trekking in the Western Pyrenees – Highlights
● **France** On the French side of the Western Pyrenees, the GR10 is particularly memorable for passing through a succession of beautiful villages. **Biriatou**, **Aïnhoa** and **Sare** are examples of typical Basque villages, with their ancient churches, *frontons* (pelote courts) and colourful old houses. Further to the east, in Béarn, the mountainside hamlet of **Lescun** is considered by many to be one of the most beautiful spots in the Pyrenees. All visitors should make a point of seeing **St-Jean-Pied-de-Port**, the capital town of Basse-Navarre, with its fifteenth-century walls, and imposing citadel. Also worthy of a special mention is the 11th century church in **Sainte-Engrâce**, which is held to be one of the best examples of early Romanesque church architecture in the Pyrenees. The western sections of the GR10 aren't just notable for the villages through which they pass: there are stunning views of the **Kakoueta and Holzarté gorges**, and the **Chemin de la Mâture** is one of the most memorable sections of the whole GR10.
● **Spain** On the Spanish side of the border, although the villages are not particularly exciting, special mention must be made of the monastery at **Roncesvalles** and of **Ochagavia**, a lovely little village of red-roofed houses. Several sections of the GR11 through the Western Pyrenees are also particularly impressive. Notably, the following stages: Isaba–Zuriza; Selba d'Oza–Candanchú; Candanchú–Sallent de Gallego; and Sallent de Gallego–Balneario de Panticosa provide some challenging walking through quite amazing natural scenery.

definition of nationality but local affiliations have never lost their importance. Nowhere is this clearer than in the case of the Basques – one of the most fiercely nationalistic communities in the world.

The Western Pyrenees, watered amply by weather systems from the Atlantic, are an area of incredible greenness and fertility. While the hills here in no way approach the dramatic presence of the mountains in the Central Pyrenees, they've a grandeur of their own. The deep valleys, beautiful villages, and slow, friendly way of life are perfect for anyone who isn't too worried about going very far, or very high but would rather explore and enjoy an area of natural beauty and unique culture.

THE BASQUE COUNTRY

Politics and history

The **Basque Country** (Euskalleria in Basque) spreads out on both sides of the French-Spanish border. The ancient divisions of Labourd, Basse-Navarre and Soule, with a population of around 250,000, make up the French **Pays Basque**; Guipúzcoa, Vizcaya and Alava provinces, with a population of around $2^1/_2$ million make up the Spanish **Pais Vasco**. While each area has its own character (the coastal provinces, for example, have a proud maritime history) much cultural heritage is shared.

Basque identity is tied up in a question of origins. The Basque language, Euskara, which has no known related tongue, is claimed by linguists to be the earliest of European languages. No one is quite sure where the ancestors of the Basques came from; some historians suggest that they were the earliest Celtic settlers, others that they came from north Africa, still others that they may have been a lost tribe of Israel. Whatever the answer, it is clear that Spanish and French Basques can trace their ancestry back to some of the earliest settlers of the Iberian peninsula.

The Basques are a proud and independent people who have asserted their individuality from the earliest times, their bloody revenge on Charlemagne in 778 being only one example. The French Basques formally became part of France when, in 1790 the Pays Basque and Béarn were brought together into a new département – the Basses Pyrénées. In 1970, despite local attempts to get departmental status for the Pays Basque, the département was renamed the Pyrénées Atlantiques; attempts to gain a level of self-government through a departmental administration are still continuing. In Spain, the Basque provinces enjoyed some autonomy until the Spanish Civil War, when Franco plotted the devastating bombing of Guernica, and thereafter removed their independence. In 1979 they were granted autonomy by the Spanish government, and although the majority of Spanish Basques are quite happy with the arrangement, it has proved insufficient to pacify a tiny minority who have resorted to terrorism, under the banner of ETA.

For the walker

The Basque Country is a region of deep, emerald-green valleys and squat farmhouses tucked into the folds of the hills. The half-timbered houses have remained in the same families for generations, and on the lintel over the front door of each is recorded the year in which it was built and the name of the family. Huge, rough-cut corner stones and thick wooden shutters give an air of indestructibility, while fresh whitewash and brightly painted woodwork lend a sense of house-proud homeliness.

Food and drink

The local cuisine consists largely of huge, nourishing dishes with plenty of calories to see you through a tough day in the hills. *Jambon de Bayonne* (cured Bayonne ham) is the most famous speciality, and may be served with *piperade*, a sauce made from peppers and tomatoes. *Poulet Basquaise* is also very popular. *Fromage de brebis* (ewes' milk cheese) is made by farmers and shepherds throughout the region. *Gâteaux Basques* are a popular dessert to take up any space which might be left. *Irouleguy* is the most famous of the local wines, while *izarra* is the local liquor. Beer drinkers trekking through the Pays Basque should try the local brews which, although not widely advertised, are often available if you ask for them by name. Some caution is required if you're planning an early start the following morning; *Akerbeltz* and *Oldarki*, the two most widely available brews, both weigh in at about 6% alcohol by volume.

BÉARN

Politics and history

Although Béarn may be less well known by name than the Pays Basque, it too has a proud history. Nowhere in the Pyrenees is the cross-border tradition more clearly seen than here. On 13 July each year, at the Col de La Pierre St-Martin, the communities of the Roncal valley (Spain) and Barétous valley (France) celebrate the Tribute of the Three Cows. The tradition goes back to 1375, and is thought to be the earliest peace treaty still in force in Europe.

For many years Béarn existed as a semi-independent and powerful statelet. Its proud boast is having been the birthplace of King Henry IV (1553-1610), who was born in Pau, son of Antoine de Bourbon and Jeanne d'Albret, Queen of Navarre. Henry acceded to the throne in 1589 and is remembered as one of the best rulers in French history. Although Béarn was quite clearly a part of the French state from this time, it maintained a surprising level of autonomy for years to come.

For the walker

Beyond the village of Sainte-Engrâce, which stands at the eastern extent of the Pays Basque, Béarn is a transitional zone between the hills of the coastal belt and the high mountains of the Central Pyrenees. There is a striking contrast between the rich greenness of the Basque country and the limestone moonscape that surrounds the Pic d'Anie (2504m). This area of karst (limestone) formations boasts some of most memorable views in the Pyrenees – the Aspe and Ossau valleys, the Cirque de Lescun, the Chemin de la Mâture and the Pic du Midi d'Ossau (2884m).

NAVARRA

Politics and history
In its day, Navarra was one of the most important kingdoms in the Pyrenees, and stretched across the mountains to include what is today the French district of Basse Navarre. The rise of Navarra as an independent kingdom started with its first king, Iñigo Arista (824-852), and the kingdom reached its peak around the 11th century during the reign of Sancho el Mayor (1004-1035).

Navarra was a springboard for efforts to push the Moors out of Spain, and in 1212 it was the king Sancho el Fuerte who led the charge in the Battle of Las Navas de Tolosa, where the Moors were routed. The power of the kingdom began to wane in the fifteenth century, the decline accelerated by a dispute between two leading families.

In 1479, Navarra became divided; the Spanish lands were annexed by Ferdinand of Aragón, while the northern half of the territory went to Catherine of Foix. Catherine's grandson was Henry of Navarre, who subsequently became Henry IV of France. In 1512, Spanish Navarra was formally annexed by Castille/Aragón, although it remained semi-independent until 1841, when it finally became a province of Spain.

For the walker
Navarra is largely undeveloped and consequently this is an area to consider if you like the idea of getting away from things – including other walkers, and most facilities. The sections of the GR11 (the Spanish long distance path) which pass through Navarra are hardly exciting; there are lengthy stretches along rough forestry roads and in places the route is poorly marked. They do, however, provide a logical itinerary across this part of the Pyrenees with far fewer walkers than on the French side of the border, and occasional highlights – such at the monastery at Roncesvalles, and the pretty villages of Ochagavia and Isaba.

ARAGÓN

Politics and history
The Romans started mining activities in several places in the Pyrenees but the high valleys remained largely untouched by them or, later, by the Moors. Christianity appears to have reached the mountains in the seventh

and eighth centuries, and at the end of the eighth century the region came under the control of the Franks when Charlemagne created the Spanish March.

With the slow disintegration of Charlemagne's empire, and the gradual retreat southwards of the Moors, the kingdoms of northern Spain began to sort themselves out. Aragón, initially an area of the March under a nominated governor, began to emerge as a separate entity from the eighth century onwards, and from the ninth century became linked by marriage to neighbouring Navarra.

Even after the union of Aragón and Castille in 1479, the kingdoms of Aragón, Catalonia and Navarra retained a large degree of self-rule, and it was not for some time that border questions were settled.

Walking in Western Aragón

In comparison to Navarra, the sections of the GR11 through western Aragón begin to feel truly mountainous. Although the scenery is not as dramatic as that to be found to the east, in the central area of the Spanish Pyrenees, there are several spectacular day stages. In some ways you get the best of all worlds here: great scenery and fewer other walkers than you'll encounter on the sections through the Ordesa region, which follow.

GETTING THERE

Getting to the Western Pyrenees
● **Air** There are airports in Bordeaux, Biarritz and Pau.
● **Train** TGV services from Paris run to Bayonne, Biarritz, Hendaye, Pau and Tarbes.
● **Coach** A summertime coach service to Bayonne is operated by Eurolines from London. See p19 for more information.

Getting to the walking
● **Western end** Starting the GR10 from its western end is easy. For those flying to Bordeaux or Biarritz there are numerous daily trains from both places to Bayonne, Hendaye and Irun. Those flying into Pau can also easily get a train west to Bayonne and Hendaye, although there's also easy access to the mountains by catching a bus south. Alternatively you can catch a direct TGV from Paris to Hendaye.
● To get into the hills further eastwards there are various possibilities:
● **Bidarray** (p84), **St-Étienne-de-Baïgorry** (p86), **St-Jean-Pied-de-Port** (p92). There are three or four daily trains from Bayonne along the branch line, via Bidarray (NB the name of the station is actually Pont Noblia) and St-Martin-d'Arossa to St-Jean-Pied-de-Port. The journey takes an hour, and a one-way ticket costs €7/47F. The first train from Bayonne to St-Jean currently departs at 9.03; the last train departs, during July and August at 21.05 and for the rest of the year at 19.25. From St-Martin-

d'Arossa there is an SNCF bus service to St-Étienne-de-Baïgorry. If you miss the train, a taxi from Bayonne to St-Jean-Pied-de Port will cost about €60/400F. Europcar has an office in Rue Hugues, opposite Bayonne railway station

● **Borce/Etsaut** (p110) From Pau there are regular trains to Oloron-Ste-Marie, from where there's an SNCF bus service to Borce and Etsaut.

● **Gabas/Bious Oumette/Lac de Bious Artigues** (p112) There are few **buses** passing through Gabas. In July and August the Pic Bus runs twice daily (excluding weekends and holidays) between Laruns, to the north, and the Col du Portalet, to the south. Currently the morning service leaves Laruns at 08.55, calling at Gabas and at Bious-Oumette on its way south; on the return journey (depart Portalet at 10.20) it stops only at Gabas. The afternoon service departs Laruns at 15.20 calling at Gabas (not Bious-Oumette) and returns via both Gabas and Bious-Oumette (depart Portalet at 16.25). More information on the service can be sought from the operators, SARL Canonge (☎ 05.59.05.30.31, 🗎 05.59.05.32.98).

In summer there may be one additional daily service running from Pau via Laruns to Fabrèges (just south of Gabas) in the morning, and running back to Pau in mid afternoon.

The company that runs the Pic Bus also operates **taxis**; a taxi from Laruns to the Lac de Bious-Artigues costs around €26/170F.

● **Gourette** (p116) Buses operate to and from Gourette during the peak season (ie July and August). They are operated by Citram Pyrénées (☎ 05 59.27.22.22) and there are currently three services each way every day, stopping at Laruns en route.

● **Arrens Marsous** (p118) There are two buses a day between Tarbes and Arrens Marsous (every day except Sundays and holidays). The buses go via Lourdes (bus station) and Pierrefitte Nestalas (from where there are connections to Cauterets, Luz-St-Sauveur and, indirectly, Gavarnie). From Tarbes to Arrens takes one and a half hours; from Lourdes to Arrens takes just over one hour. The buses are operated by Salt (☎ 05.62 34.76.69, 🗎 05.62.34.76.61).

Car hire

This will obviously not be ideal for most people, as it's very expensive to hire a car and then go walking for several days. If you want to have a very flexible itinerary it may, however, be suitable. There are car hire services in the following towns:

● **Lourdes** Avis (☎ 05.62.42.12.97) has an office at the railway station

● **Pau** Avis (☎ 05.59.13.31.33), avenue Didier Daurat, Budget (☎ 05.59.62.72.54), avenue Jean Mermoz, Europcar (☎ 05.59.92.09.09), 115 avenue Jean Mermoz

Western Pyrenees – GR10

The starting point for both the GR10 and the HRP is the quiet resort town of Hendaye on the border between France and Spain.

HENDAYE

✉ code 64700

Hendaye sits on the northern bank of the Bidassoa River, the waterway which marks the border between France and Spain. Across the river, the tenement buildings of Fontarabie and Irún do little to tempt the visitor further southwards and it has to be said that Hendaye is hardly exciting. Stock up on provisions, have a good meal and possibly a quick swim – and then go.

Orientation and services

The town is divided into two parts: Hendaye Ville, which is the area around the railway station and near to the border bridge, and Hendaye-Plage, which is 2km to the north. As its name suggests, the latter of these is the area to find the beach as well as a multitude of small hotels and the nearest of the campsites. Although there are several shops around the seafront, the large stores, including two supermarkets, are to be found nearer the ville. There's a daytime bus service running to and from Fontarabie across the border. It goes every half hour from the traffic circle behind the beach, past the railway station and on to Fontarabie. **Taxis** wait outside the railway station or can be booked: try Tino Taxis (☎ 05.59.20.56.79 / 06.09.72.86.67) or Agur Chingudy Radio Taxis (☎ 05.59 20.85.82).

The **post office** is on rue des Aubepines, just to the south-east of the traffic circle in Hendaye-Plage. Next to it is the **tourist office** (☎ 05.59.20 00.34, 🖹 05.59.20.79.17, 💻 tourisme.hendaye @wanadoo.fr), where they provide a useful free map of the town. A few metres to the north of the traffic circle are two **launderettes** – more useful if you're ending your walk in Hendaye than if you're just starting. There is a row of **banks** and bureaux de change opposite the railway station, and there are also a couple of branches with cash dispensers near the Place de la République. Many, if not all, banks in Hendaye are closed on Mondays. **Europcar** have an agent in a garage just to the east of the railway station (☎ 05.59.20.70.86) and **Avis** have an office opposite the station (☎ 05.59.20.79.04).

For supplies before starting your walk, the best place is the enormous Champion supermarket on rue Iran-datz. They sell the blue camping gaz here (both the old and new style cylinders) but do not stock Coleman Epigas. If you need Epigas, try the Bricotruc branch on the upper level (ie above the supermarket). They sell large bottles of gas designed for use with blowtorches, although the thread size should be suitable for Epigas stoves.

Where to stay

As one would expect in a resort town, there is no shortage of accommodation.

● **Hendaye-Plage** The undisputed top place in Hendaye-Plage is the *Hôtel Ibaia* ☆☆☆☆ (☎ 05.59.48.88.88, 🖹 05.59.48.88.89), though its four-star rating seems rather over the top. Double rooms start at €99/650F. Close by, and actually on the sea front, is the *Hôtel Restaurant Lafon* ☆☆ (☎ 05.59.20 04.67, 🖹 05.59.48.06.85), a large, friendly boarding house where double rooms start at €49/320F. Better value is the *Hôtel de Paris* ☆☆ (☎ 05.59.20 05.06, 🖹 05.59.48.02 82), which is on the traffic circle just back from the seafront. Rooms start at €34/220F and there's a pleasant shady terrace where you can sip your beer and mentally prepare yourself for the walk ahead.

Other hotels of a similar standard and price in Hendaye-Plage, include the *Hôtel Uhainak* ☆☆ (☎ 05.59.20.33.63, 🖹 05.59.48.13.72); *Hôtel Les Buisso-*

nets ☆☆ (☎ 05.59.20.04.75, 🖹 05.59 20.79.72); *Hôtel Valencia* ☆☆ (☎ 05.59 20.01.62, 🖹 05 59.20.17.92) and *Hôtel Bergeret Sport* ☆☆ (☎ 05.59 20.00.78, 🖹 05.59.20.67.30).

● **Hendaye Ville** In Hendaye Ville the nicest place is *Chez Antoinette* ☆☆ (☎ 05.59.20.08.47, 🖹 05.59.48.11.64), where doubles start at €38/250F during high season. There are several places that are conveniently close to the railway station. *Hôtel La Palombe Bleue* (☎

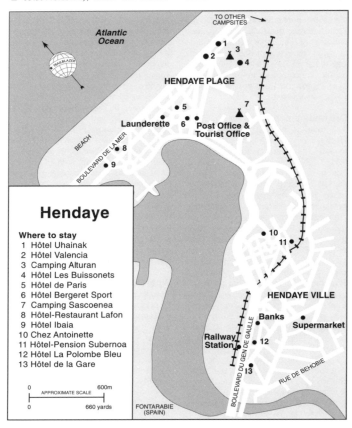

Atlantic Ocean

TO OTHER CAMPSITES

HENDAYE PLAGE

BEACH

BOULEVARD DE LA MER

Launderette

Post Office & Tourist Office

Hendaye

Where to stay
1 Hôtel Uhainak
2 Hôtel Valencia
3 Camping Alturan
4 Hôtel Les Buissonets
5 Hôtel de Paris
6 Hôtel Bergeret Sport
7 Camping Sascoenea
8 Hôtel-Restaurant Lafon
9 Hôtel Ibaia
10 Chez Antoinette
11 Hôtel-Pension Subernoa
12 Hôtel La Polombe Bleu
13 Hôtel de la Gare

HENDAYE VILLE

Banks

Supermarket

Railway Station

BOULEVARD DU GEN DE GAULLE

RUE DE BEHOBIE

| 0 | | 600m |
APPROXIMATE SCALE
| 0 | | 660 yards |

FONTARABIE (SPAIN)

05.59 20.43.80) used to be the cheapest of these, but prices have risen recently: single rooms now start at €29/190F and doubles start at €44/290F. Directly opposite is the *Hôtel de la Gare* ☆☆ (☎ 05.59.20.81.90), where double rooms start at €38/250F. If you're looking for something cheaper, you could try *Hôtel/Pension Subernoa* (☎ 05.59.20.08.33), on rue Subernoa. It's a fair way from the station and is a bit dingy but has basic double rooms from €35/230F during high season.

There are several campsites but they are all a fair way from the railway station. The nearest to the station is *Camping Sascoenea* ☆☆☆ (☎ 05.59.20 05.44, 🖹 05.59.20.55.77) where it costs, in high season, €18/120F for two people and a tent. There is a restaurant on site. *Camping Alturan* ☆☆☆ (☎ 05 59.20.04.56) is the next nearest to the town centre and is located just behind the beach on Hendaye-Plage; again, it costs €18/120F for two people and a tent. Although there are several other campsites around Hendaye, they are all much further out and the prices only minimally lower. The following are pleasant enough: *Camping des 2 Jumeaux* ☆☆ (☎ 05.59.20.01.65) – one person with a tent can get in here for €14/91F; *Camping Ametza* ☆☆☆ (☎ 05.59.20.07.05) – more expensive but it has a swimming pool; *Camping du Moulin* ☆☆ (☎ 05.59.20.76.35) – almost the entire clientele are in camper trailers – very residential; *Camping Les Acacias* ☆☆☆ (☎ 05.59.20.78.76) – again they're rather surprised to see a real live backpacker – most people here have brought the kids' bikes, the barbecue etc and are well settled in.

Where to eat
Nearly all the hotel restaurants have reasonable food but particularly worth a try are the restaurants of the *Hôtel Bergeret Sport*, and of *Chez Antoinette*. For Chinese and Thai food, try *Le Jardin de Jade*, on Boulevard de la Baie de Chingudy.

Route maps
● **Scale and walking times** All the following trail maps are drawn to a scale of 1:100,000 (10mm = 1km/0.625miles). Walking times are given along the side of each map, and the arrow shows the direction to which the time refers. Black triangles indicate the points between which the times have been taken. Note that the time given refers only to the time spent walking, so you will need to **add 30-40%** to allow for rest stops. Remember that these are **my timings** for the section; every walker has his or her own speed. With the first edition of this book, several readers commented that they found these timings on the fast side. The times are, however, consistent so you should err on the side of caution for a day or two until you see how your speed relates to my timings on the maps. When planning the day's trekking, count on between five and seven hours actual walking, and allow for an occasional rest day.

● **Up or down?** The trail is shown as a dotted line. An arrow across the trail indicates the slope; two arrows show that it is steep. Note that the arrow points towards the higher part of the trail. If, for example, you're walking from A (at 900m) to B (at 1100m) and the trail between the two is short and steep it would be shown thus: A—>>—B.

● **Refuges, gîtes and cabanes** Everywhere to stay that is within easy reach of the trail is marked. See the text for more details about each place.

● **Other information and symbols** Altitudes are given on the map in metres. Places where you can get water are shown by a 'W' within a circle.

HENDAYE → OLHETTE   [MAP 1]

Officially the GR10 starts on the sea front by the casino building, and weaves its way through the streets passing eventually along rue Subernoa, chemin Biantena and rue Errondenia. The red and white GR markings (see p24) first appear on rue Biantena, and by the time the path leaves the outskirts of the town they are well established.

At the top of rue Errondenia the GR 10 turns right, following the lane past a farmhouse on top of a small hill and down to a point where it is crossed by a track. Turn left and follow the track over a knoll and down an access lane to the main road (N10). Turn left along the road and, after 20-30 metres, head off to the right on an overgrown footpath. Stay on this path until it comes to the crest of a hill where it crosses a vehicle track, and begins to descend steeply through bracken. At the bottom, follow the tarmac lane to an underpass below the autoroute, beyond which the lanes lead towards **Biriatou**, which you reach about two hours after starting from the sea front. A signpost on the edge of the village, OLHETTE 4H 15, directs you left to continue the GR10 towards Olhette or right to enter the village itself, where accommodation is available in two *hotels*. *Hôtel Baskea* ☆☆ (☎ 05.59.20.76.36, ▤ 05.59.20.58.21) has only seven rooms and charges €40/260F for a double room. *Hôtel Larretcheko Borda* ☆ (☎ 05.59.20.20.32; ▤ 05.59.20.03.38) has double rooms from €33/220F.

Beyond Biriatou, the GR10 climbs steeply up a rough footpath to just below the Rochers des Perdrix, and then contours around the hillside to the **Col d'Osin (370m)**. At the col there's a yellow sign, OLHETTE 3H 20, and there are good views over the next section of the walk. Descend to the Col de Poiriers, before climbing steeply again along the side of a wood, and then towards the summit of Mandalé (573m). The path skirts north around the top of this hill and then descends to meet a tarmac road, beside which is a large and busy *venta*. Follow the road downhill to the **Col d'Ibardin (317m)**, which you'll get to about four hours after starting from Hendaye.

The Venta

At the Col d'Ibardin is a large *venta*, a traditional market area straddling the border, which in days gone by offered bargains for shoppers from both France and Spain. These days, with the advent of the European Community, there's little to attract people here in the way of duty-free savings, so the sales pitch has turned to discounted items and bulk selling. You may find anything here from a cheap leather jacket to tacky souvenirs, discount alcohol, or cartons of cigarettes. The mass of cars and concrete make this a far from attractive spot, and most walkers will hasten to get through it. There are, however, two or three places to eat if you need a snack or shelter from the Basque weather.

Map 1 – Hendaye to Olhette 77

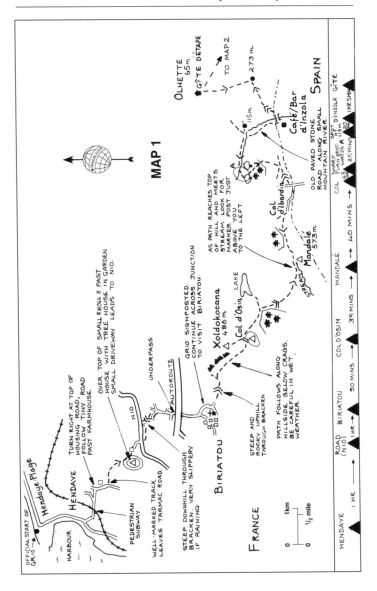

MAP 1

OLHETTE
65m
GÎTE D'ÉTAPE
TO MAP 2

273 m

115m

Café/Bar
d'Inzola

SPAIN

OLD PAVED STONE
ROAD ALONG SMALL
MOUNTAIN RIVER.

AS PATH REACHES TOP
OF HILL AND MEETS
STREAM LOOK FOR
MARKER POST JUST
ABOVE YOU
TO THE LEFT.

Col
d'Ibardin

Mandalé
573m.

STREAM

Col d'Osin
LAKE

Xoldokoaña
486m.

GR10 SIGNPOSTED.
CONTINUE ACROSS JUNCTION
TO VISIT BIRIATOU.

PATH FOLLOWS ALONG
HILLSIDE BELOW CRAGS.
BE CAREFUL IN WET
WEATHER.

UNDERPASS

NIO

AUTOROUTE

BIRIATOU

STEEP AND
ROCKY UPHILL
THROUGH BRACKEN

OVER TOP OF SMALL KNOLL & PAST
HOUSE WITH TREE HOUSE IN GARDEN.
SMALL DRIVEWAY LEADS TO NIO.

TURN RIGHT AT TOP OF
HOUSING ROAD. FOLLOW
FOLLOW TINY ROAD
PAST FARMHOUSE.

Hendaye-Plage

HENDAYE

OFFICIAL START OF
GR.10

HARBOUR

PEDESTRIAN
SUBWAY

WELL-MARKED TRACK
LEAVES TARMAC ROAD.

STEEP DOWNHILL THROUGH
BRACKEN. VERY SLIPPERY
IF RAINING.

FRANCE

0   1km

0   ½ mile

HENDAYE   1 HR.   ROAD BIRIATOU 50 MINS   COL D'OSIN 35 MINS   MANDALÉ 40 MINS   COL SHARP SPOT D'INZOLA GÎTE   HERE 5MIN
(NIO)   TURN LEFT. 45 WARDS A 115m
                                                                   25 MINS 20

From the Col (the road junction at the bottom of the slope), walk north for 50 metres along the tarmac, before turning right near a signpost: OLHETTE 2H 10. After a short but steep climb the GR10 joins a track which turns sharply to the left and descends along the valley side. Just before meeting a minor road (at point A on Map 1), the path cuts down into a dip and, turning eastwards, continues downhill through the trees on the north side of the little valley.

At the eastern end of the valley (near spot height 115m on the map) the path meets an old paved way leading south-eastwards to the Spanish border. Turn right and follow the old road alongside a rushing stream; just before arriving at **Inzola** there are four or five stepping stones which can be precarious if the watercourse is in spate. About 200m beyond the stones, you'll see the *Café-Bar d'Inzola*, where food and drink are available but there's no accommodation.

From the café, cross a tiny footbridge and climb north-eastwards, following narrow paths up the gullied hillside, to a pleasant grassy col (spot height 273m). From here the GR10 makes a gradual descent northwards along the valley side to the gîte d'étape at Olhette. The *gîte* (☎ 05.59 54.00.98) is open all year and can take 14 people. Conditions are basic but quite adequate, with a hot shower and a small kitchen area. It costs €9/60F for the night, or €28/180F for demi-pension. The nearest village of any size is Ascain, which is four km away.

OLHETTE → AÏNHOA   [MAP 2]

A sign, SARE 3H 05, outside the gîte points the walker across the stream and up the opposite hillside. The initial climb is hard-going, particularly in hot weather, and takes nearly an hour as you struggle south-eastwards towards the dominating shape of La Rhune (900m – see p80). The path is easy to follow, although the variety of painted markers can be a little confusing; there are blue and yellow marks as well as the normal red and white. The consolation in the rather hard first hour is that when you reach the **Col des Trois Fontaines (563m)**, just below the summit of La Rhune, you've pretty much done the day's climbing. At the col, a signpost, SARE 1H 35, indicates the way around the edge of a wood, on the far side of which is a large track leading south-eastwards.

After about ten minutes the GR10 crosses the **rack railway**, a miniature railway running to the summit of the hill and a popular tourist attraction, and then starts to descend along a small footpath towards Sare. About halfway down the hill the footpath doubles back on itself to join a rock-strewn track which eventually leads down to a tarmac lane. Follow the lane to within the last kilometre or so of Sare. From here the GR10 cuts across the fields for 10-15 minutes on two overgrown footpaths before emerging on a tarmac lane leading into the village.

Map 2 – Olhette to Aïnoa 79

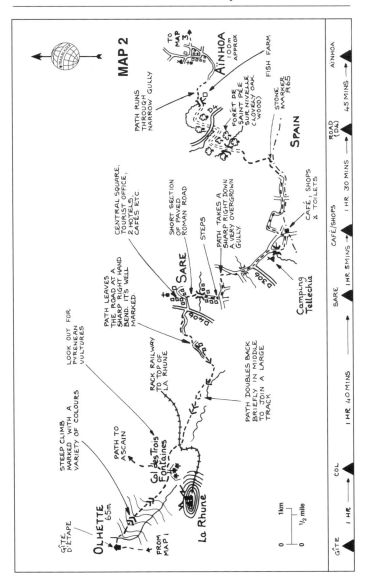

MAP 2

TO MAP 3

AÏNHOA
100m APPROX

PATH RUNS THROUGH NARROW GULLY

FORÊT DE SAINT PÉE

SURNIVELLE (LOVELY OAK WOOD)

FISH FARM

STONE MARKER R65

SPAIN

CENTRAL SQUARE, TOURIST OFFICE, 2 HOTELS, CAFÉS ETC.

SHORT SECTION OF PAVED ROMAN ROAD

STEPS

PATH TAKES A SHARP RIGHT DOWN A VERY OVERGROWN GULLY.

CAFÉ, SHOPS & TOILETS

SARE

Camping Tellechia

PATH LEAVES THE ROAD AT A SHARP RIGHT HAND BEND. IT'S WELL MARKED.

LOOK OUT FOR PYRENEAN VULTURES

STEEP CLIMB MARKED WITH A VARIETY OF COLOURS

PATH TO ASCAIN

RACK RAILWAY TO TOP OF LA RHUNE

PATH DOUBLES BACK BRIEFLY IN MIDDLE TO JOIN A LARGE TRACK

Col des Trois Fontaines

La Rhune

GÎTE D'ETAPE

OLHETTE 65m

FROM MAP 1

0   1km
0   ½ mile

GÎTE ◄ 1 HR ► COL ◄ 1 HR 40 MINS ► SARE ◄ 1 HR 5 MINS ► CAFÉ/SHOPS ◄ 1 HR 30 MINS ► ROAD (D4) ◄ 45 MINS ► AÏNHOA

The Storming of La Petite Rhune

The ridge just to the west of La Rhune was the scene of one of the last engagements of the Peninsular War when, on 10 November 1813, Wellington's forces carried the Heights of the Nive. Among the units taking part were the Rifle Brigade ('the bloody fighting 95th') who formed part of the formidable Light Division. In his autobiography, Harry Smith (later Lt Gen Sir Harry Smith), describes the capture of La Petite Rhune:

'As we started for our position before the great, the important day, the night was very dark. We had no road, and positively nothing to guide us but knowing the bushes and stones over a mountain ridge. Colborne stayed near the Brigade, and sent me on from spot to spot which we both knew, when he would come up to me and satisfy himself that I was right. I then went on again. In this manner we crept up with our Brigade to our advanced picquet within a hundred and fifty yards of the enemy...The anxious moment of appearing day arrived. We fell in, and our attack was made on the enemy's position in seven columns, nor did we ever meet a check, but carried the enemy's works, the tents all standing, by one fell swoop of irresistible victory...Ours was the most beautiful attack ever made in the history of war.'

SARE

Sare is a lovely little place – acclaimed as one of the most beautiful of the Basque villages. While this means that in summer its streets are crowded with tourists, it also means that there are several places to stay and to eat, and Sare is an ideal place to break the day's walk for a leisurely lunch.

There are a couple of small **shops**, useful for stocking up. More information can be had from the **tourist office** (☎ 05.59.54.20.14; 🖷 05.59.54.29.15) which is open from 10.00-12.30 and 14.00-18.00.

On weekdays during July and August there's a regular **bus service** (☎ 05.59.26.30.74; 🖷 05.59.26.01.43) between Sare and St Jean de Luz (just north of Hendaye), from which it's possible to pick up onward transport by bus or train. The service operates only three days a week during the rest of the period between April and October.

There are a couple of local **taxi** operators: try Taxi Ederko (☎ 05.59 54.26.92) or Transport de Personnes (☎ 05.59.54.27.23).

Where to stay

Top of the pile is the **Hôtel Arraya** ☆☆☆ (☎ 05.59.54.20.46, 🖷 05.59.54 27.04, 🖳 www.arraya.com), which has a lovely terrace restaurant and a rather exclusive atmosphere; double rooms start at €60/395F. On the other side of the street, the **Hôtel de la Poste** (☎ 05.59.54.20.06) is rather more basic; it's open from mid June to mid September and has rooms from €26/170F. The tourist office also lists a number of *chambres chez l'habitant* (chambres d'hôte) which might be worth a try, though you should check where they actually are, before booking. Among those on offer are: **Maison Etxola** (☎ 05.59.54.28.09) from €41/270F for a double room, breakfast included; **Maison Argi-Alde** (☎ 05.59 54.20.93) doubles from €30/200F; **Maison Mendian** (☎ 05.59.54.25.96) doubles from €40/260F.

The nearest campsite to Sare is the **Camping de la Petite Rhune** ☆☆☆ (☎ 05.59.54.23.97, 🖷 05.59.54.23.42), which is 1¹/₂ km south of Sare. It's €11/73F for two people and a tent.

The GR10 leaves Sare via an old paved lane, next to which is a sign: AÏN-HOA 3H 20. The lane passes over a tiny bridge and ends at a set of steps beside a small wayside shrine. At the top of the steps, turn left and continue eastwards for several hundred metres; at the end of this access lane, go right for 300-400m down an overgrown pathway, to meet a larger road (D306). Turn right and follow the road for about half a km before turning left down a small lane leading south-eastwards towards the border. A short way down here is **Camping Tellechea** (☎ 05.59.54.26.01) a fairly basic campsite which is open only during July and August; emplacement is €3/20F and it's €2/14F per person.

Just past the campsite the GR10 turns right along another lane, passes through a farmyard, and rejoins a short stretch of road leading to the border, where there's a **venta**. Facilities here include a shop, toilets and a café; it's not a very attractive area but it could be a good place to stop for a snack. From the venta, the GR10 continues towards Aïnhoa almost entirely on country lanes or large farm tracks which are well marked. An initial loop is made to the north before the path heads back to the border near marker stone 63. As the path finally swings northwards towards the D4 road, it passes through an area of attractive oak forest before crossing the main road and heading into Aïnhoa village.

AÏNHOA
✉ code 64250

Aïnhoa is a pretty village centred around a short main street. Sadly, apart from places to stay and eat there are few facilities here which are of much use to walkers. There are several shops selling trinkets, but none of them sells food. There's no bank (the nearest bank is in Espelette, some five kilometres to the north west) and there's no public transport (the best bet is to hitch a lift or get a taxi to Cambo-les-Bains, and pick up public transport there). The **tourist office** (☎ 05.59.29.92.60; 🖹 05.59.29 86.31) is in the Mairie on the main street; they should be able to help with queries about transport. There's also a **post office**. From a sight-seeing point of view, Aïnhoa has an open air pelote court, and a lovely old church.

Where to stay
The top place in town is undoubtedly the **Hôtel Argi Eder** ☆☆☆ (☎ 05.59 93.72.00, 🖹 05.59.93.72.13). It's rather over priced, with rooms starting at €91/ 600F, but the facilities include a swimming pool and two tennis courts. Although staying here will be well out of most walkers' price range, if you're after a really good meal try the restaurant – set menus range in price from €19/125F to €29/190F, and the food is excellent. The **Hôtel Ithurria** ☆☆☆ (☎ 05.59.29.92.11, 🖹 05.59.29.81.28) almost manages to match Argi Eder on price: rooms here start at €84/550F. The restaurant looks very good but is expensive; the 'Menu Basque' at €28/180F might be interesting, though. Luckily there are a couple of cheaper places to stay in the village: **Hôtel Oppoca** ☆☆ (☎ 05.59.29.90.72, 🖹 05.59.29.81.03) has double rooms from €35/230F, and **Hôtel Ohantzea** ☆☆ (☎ 05.59.29.90.50) is a friendly place with doubles starting at €46/300F.

Finally **Camping Harazpy** (☎ 05.59.29.89.38; 05.59.29.90.26) is conveniently close to the centre of the village and is relatively cheap – €3/19F for emplacement, and €3.75/18F per person. The camping is open from mid June to mid September.

❑ **Pelote**
Undoubtedly the most famous of Basque games is pelote (*pelota*). Despite the fact that we glibly give it a single name, there are around 20 versions of the game. Its classic form, which is descended from the game of *paume*, is known as *main nue*; as the name suggests, players use their bare hands to serve and return the ball. In other versions, the players use varying forms of *palas* (wooden bats), *pasakas* (leather gloves) or *chisteras*, basket-shaped contraptions made of chestnut and willow, which are attached to the hand with a glove. No Basque village is without its pelote court (see photos opposite p33); this may be an outdoor court (*fronton*) or an indoor court (*trinquet*). The extent to which Basque life rotates around pelote is revealed in the way in which the courts have become central landmarks in towns and villages. You may be told that your hotel is near the *trinquet municipal* or be directed to the avenue du Fronton.

The fastest version of pelote is played using huge basket-shaped gloves called *grand chisteras*. This game, *cesta punta*, is the fastest ball game in the world. Often known by the name of the court in which it is played, *jäi alai*, the game has become popular in Florida, and the many of the best Basque players now pursue their sporting careers in the United States.

AÏNHOA → BIDARRAY [MAP 3]

The GR10 leaves Aïnhoa along the lane running eastwards from the centre of the village and past the Argi Eder hotel. A sign at the start of the lane indicates the route and some likely timings: COL DES VEAUX 3H 30; BIDARRAY 7H. The tarmac road soon gives way to a loose-surfaced track which winds up the steep hillside to the **Chapelle de l'Aubepine**, and the **three crosses** which can be seen from the village. From the chapel, follow a good vehicle track which runs north-east around the side of Ereby (583m). On the north side of the hill look out for a **small sheep shelter**; the GR10 passes next to the building before joining another track heading south-east. Some 1¼ hours after starting from Aïnhoa you'll reach the **Col des Trois Croix (510m)**.

Although the IGN 1:50,000 map shows the route skirting to the north of Atxulegi (617m), the sign (COL DES VEAUX 2H) and the route markers actually direct walkers along the vehicle track which passes to the south of the hill top. The rough road descends to a track junction and then climbs to a col (spot height 566m on the map). Keep an eye out for vultures to the east of the col; they are often to be seen circling above. From here the route is well marked; a vehicle track leads initially along the side of the valley, but it soon narrows to a footpath that descends to the **Col des Veaux (574m)**.

Just to the west of the col itself, the path passes some farm buildings and the *gîte d'étape* (☎ 05.59.29.82.72), which is open all year and can take 14 people: it costs €8/50F for the night and €9/60F for the evening

Map 3 – Aïnhoa to Bidarray 83

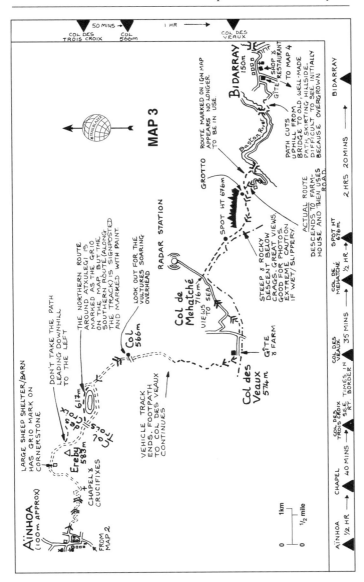

MAP 3

Aïnhoa
(100m APPROX)

FROM MAP 2

LARGE SHEEP SHELTER/BARN
HAS GRID MARK ON
CORNERSTONE

DON'T TAKE THE PATH
LEADING DOWNHILL
TO THE LEFT

Ereby 583m

CHAPEL &
CRUCIFIXES

Col des Trois Croix 617m

THE NORTHERN ROUTE
AROUND ATXULEGI IS
MARKED AS THE GR10
ON THE MAP, BUT THE
SOUTHERN ROUTE (ALONG
THE TRACK) IS SIGNPOSTED
AND MARKED WITH PAINT.

LOOK OUT FOR THE
VULTURES SOARING
OVERHEAD

Col 566m

VEHICLE TRACK
ENDS. FOOTPATH
TO COL DES VEAUX
CONTINUES

RADAR STATION

Col de Mehatché 716m

VIEWS TO SEA

Col des Veaux 574m

GÎTE & FARM

STEEP & ROCKY
DESCENT BELOW
CRAGS. GREAT VIEWS.
GOOD FOR PHOTOS.
EXTREME CAUTION
IF WET/SLIPPERY.

ACTUAL ROUTE
DESCENDS TO FARM-
HOUSE AND THEN USES
ROAD

SPOT HT 676m

GROTTO

ROUTE MARKED ON IGN MAP
APPEARS NO LONGER
TO BE IN USE.

Bastan River

PATH CUTS
UPHILL FROM
BRIDGE TO OLD, WELL-MADE
PATH SKIRTING HILLSIDE.
DIFFICULT TO SEE INITIALLY
BECAUSE OVERGROWN

Bidarray 150m

SHOP &
RESTAURANT

GÎTE

TO MAP 4

HIMALAYA

1km

½ mile

0

0

COL DES
TROIS CROIX

COL 566m

50 MINS

1 HR

COL DES
VEAUX

BIDARRAY

AÏNHOA — ½ HR → CHAPEL — 40 MINS → COL DES TROIS CROIX — SEE TIMES IN RT. BORDER → COL DES VEAUX — 35 MINS → COL DE MEHATCHÉ — ½ HR → SPOT HT 676m — 2 HRS 20MINS → BIDARRAY

meal. There's also a restaurant here, an ideal place to stop for lunch and to fill up with water.

From the Col des Veaux, the path heads eastwards, and soon joins the tarmac road leading up to the **Col de Mehatché (716m)**. At the col, which marks the border between the provinces of Labourd and Basse Navarre, the GR10 swings south-eastwards. The ensuing $1^1/_2$ km are easy, until the path reaches the top of the crags (spot height 676m on the map). From here the GR10 drops steeply towards Bidarray – a descent which many remember as one of the narrowest and most vertigo-inspiring on the GR10. The views are magnificent, but ensure that you leave plenty of time for this section and take it slowly; only three days after starting from the Atlantic, your knees may not have adjusted to the stresses and strains of mountain walking, and this particular section has caused more than its fair share of injuries. Near the bottom of the descent a brief diversion (only a few metres) is possible to visit the **Grotte du Saint qui Sue**, a small cave with an iron cross and a couple of tiny icons.

Just below the cave, the path cuts down through bracken to join a tarmac lane. Follow the lane downhill to a bridge over the river, and then east along the valley bottom. After 2km along the river, you come to an old stone bridge; the GR10 does not cross the bridge but cuts uphill to the right, just before it joins a footpath leading directly to Bidarray. Unfortunately route marking here is poor, and some exploration in the undergrowth is required to find the way. The footpath eventually joins another lane which leads to a road junction and the *gîte*.

BIDARRAY
✉ code 64780
Arriving in Bidarray on foot, it would be easy to think that the village consisted only of the buildings near the gîte d'é-tape. In fact, Bidarray is split into two parts: the gîte, shop, restaurant, tourist office, post office, church and one hotel are in the upper part of the village, while the lower part, near the River Nive and the D918, boasts a couple more hotels, a campsite and the railway station. Three or four daily trains running each way between Bayonne and St-Jean-Pied-de-Port stop at the small station, which is shown on timetables as 'Pont Noblia'. If you're heading for Saint-Étienne-de-Baïgorry it's possible to catch a train to Ossès-St-Martin-d'Arrossa (one stop to the south-east) and then get an SNCF bus service to Saint-Étienne.

The old church in the upper part of the village is well worth looking into. It has massive stone walls, dark wooden pews, and prayer books in unpronounceable Basque.

Where to stay
The *Hôtel du Pont d'Enfer* ☆☆ (☎ 05.59.37.70.88, 🖹 05.59.37.76.60), which takes its name from the ancient bridge in front of it, is very pleasant and has rooms from €23/150F. The restaurant is the best place to eat in Bidarray; the 'Assiette Express' (€11/70F) is good value. Directly across the river is the *Hôtel Noblia* ☆☆ (☎ 05.59.37.70.89) where rooms start at €23/150F; the restaurant has menus from €9/62F upwards.

Also worth a try is the *Hôtel Barberaenea* ☆☆ (☎ 05.59.37.74.86, 🖹

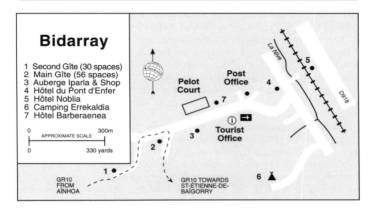

Bidarray

1 Second Gîte (30 spaces)
2 Main Gîte (56 spaces)
3 Auberge Iparla & Shop
4 Hôtel du Pont d'Enfer
5 Hôtel Noblia
6 Camping Errekaldia
7 Hôtel Barberaenea

```
0              300m
  APPROXIMATE SCALE
0              330 yards
```

Pelot
Court

Post
Office

Tourist
Office

La Nive

D 918

GR10
FROM
AINHOA

GR10 TOWARDS
ST-ÉTIENNE-DE-
BAÏGORRY

05.59.37.77.55), just behind the pelote court, where rooms start at €28/180F.

Signposted from the bottom of the hill, and about 1 km down the lanes to the south, is the *Camping Errekaldia* (☎ 05.59.37.72.56) where chambres d'hôte are also available. The (double) rooms are €28/180F (breakfast included), and it costs €3/20F per person in the campsite.

In the upper part of the village the only place to stay is the *gîte d'étape* (☎ 05.59.37.71.34). The main building sleeps 50 but is occasionally booked out by large groups, so they've opened a second building which takes 30, some 200m to the west. A night in the gîte costs €8/50F.

BIDARRAY → SAINT-ÉTIENNE-DE-BAÏGORRY   [MAP 4, p87]

The section from Bidarray to Saint Étienne is a long one, and as there is only one possible place to fill up with water all day it's essential that you carry plenty to drink.

From the gîte, head south along the small lane. After $^3/_4$ km the GR10 leaves the tarmac and winds up the hillside on a footpath. There is a brief pause in the climbing when the path reaches a grassy shoulder (just north of spot height 602m on the map), but the ascent soon resumes towards the craggy ridge ahead. Care is required in a couple of places where the path becomes narrow but there are no real difficulties apart from the route marking, which becomes rather uncertain as you approach the crag. Avoid the path which can be seen heading off to the right and zigzagging up the steep hillside, and look instead for a route around to the east of the crag, and into a grassy bowl beside it. The path climbs the side of the bowl, past the ruins of a sheep shelter, to the top of the ridge.

If the weather is fine, the next section is excellent, as the GR10 runs along the top of the **Crête d'Iparla**, with spectacular views to the east.

About an hour and a half to the south of the **Pic d'Iparla (1044m)**, the path makes a rocky descent to the **Col d'Harrieta (808m)**.

A signpost (BAÏGORRI 4H) directs the way onwards for the GR10. Climb through the beech woods on the far side of the col, and continue south along the ridge, going over the tops of Astaté (1022m) and **Buztanzelhay (1029m)**, before descending to the Col de Buztanzelhay (843m). From here, cut downhill along a stream, and then head south-eastwards along a ridge, before joining a loose-surfaced vehicle track which winds down the hillside.

After about a kilometre, the GR10 leaves the vehicle track and continues down the ridge on a footpath, which runs through trees to a tarmac lane below. Follow the lane for about $^3/_4$km to a sharp right-hand bend. If you are planning to continue along the GR10, follow the road southwards towards the centre of **St-Étienne-de-Baïgorry**.

If you're heading for the gîte, follow the old cart track which descends to the left from near the sharp bend in the road. The track leads to another tarmac lane, which crosses a stream and meets a main road (D948). About 100 metres to the north of the junction are the gîte d'étape and campsite.

SAINT-ÉTIENNE-DE-BAÏGORRY

✉ code 64430

The main part of village of St-Étienne is actually about a kilometre to the south-west of the gîte d'étape, but there are buildings spread out along the road between the two.

St-Étienne's wonderful church is to the south, and a visit is highly recommended. If it looks plain and unassuming from the outside, wait until you get through the door: literally every inch of wall and ceiling is decorated, and the three tiers of galleries add to its unique atmosphere.

Where to stay

By far the best (and most expensive) place to stay in St-Étienne is the *Hôtel Arcé* ☆☆☆ (☎ 05.59.37.40.14, 🖹 05.59 37.40.27), which has double rooms from €53/350F. The shady terrace restaurant overlooking the river could be difficult to prise yourself away from, if you once settle in; there are menus from €17/110F and an extensive à la carte menu. Just to the south-west of the

church, on the main road, the *Hôtel Restaurant Juantorena* ☆☆ (☎ 05.59 37.40.78) is much more reasonable: rooms cost €28-37/185-240F. Further to the north-east, the *Hôtel Hargain* ☆ (☎ 05.59.37.41.46) is a small and friendly place; rooms are from €26/170F and the restaurant looks good too. Near the gîte d'étape, the *Hôtel Restaurant Izarra* (☎ 05.59.37.41.77, 🖹 05.59.37.48.76) is a rather battered old building with rooms from €28/180F. It's not great value for its accommodation, but it's the best place to eat if you're staying in the gîte. The Menu Randonneur is good value at €9/60F, and the €12/80F menu is worth trying, if only for the Salade Navarraise.

The cheapest place to stay is inevitably the *gîte d'étape* (☎ 05.59 37.42.39) where it costs €8/50F per night. The gîte sleeps 48 people and has a small but well equipped kitchen. No meals are available. The owner of the gîte also runs the campsite beside the building, which is good value at €3/20F per person. The *Camping Municipal d'Irouleguy* (☎ 05.59.37.43.96), a short

Map 4 – Bidarray to St-Étienne-de-Baïgorry 87

Water sources near the Col d'Harrieta
According to a walker I met some days later, there is a very good water source near the col. Take the horizontal path (not the GR10) leading south-west from the col, and the spring is within five minutes' walk. Another option, useful in bad weather, is to take the path leading down to the east from the col, which provides the quickest way down from the ridge, and leads to the village of Urdos.

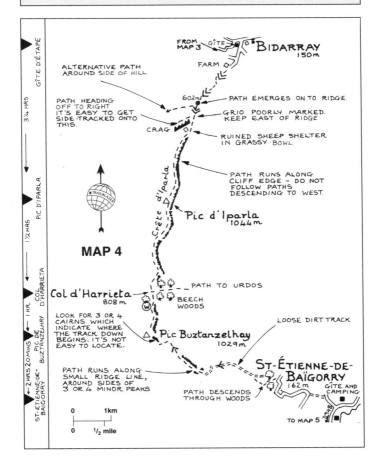

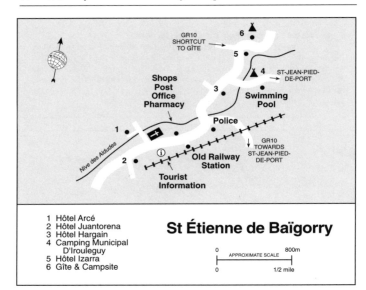

1 Hôtel Arcé
2 Hôtel Juantorena
3 Hôtel Hargain
4 Camping Municipal
    D'Irouleguy
5 Hôtel Izarra
6 Gîte & Campsite

St Étienne de Baïgorry

0   800m
       APPROXIMATE SCALE
0   1/2 mile

way to the south-west, charges €2/13F per person.

Services

Most of the **shops** (including food shops, pharmacy and a tabac) are in the main part of the village, but there's a large **supermarket** opposite the municipal campsite. A public **swimming pool** is near the supermarket. The **tourist office** (☎ 05.59.37.47.28, 05.59.37 74.60) is opposite the church.

The railway station has been closed for some years, but there are SNCF **buses** which run the 7km north-east to St-Martin-d'Arrossa, where there's a railway station. There is also usually a daily bus to St-Jean-Pied-de-Port, leaving early in the morning and returning in the evening.

ST-ÉTIENNE-DE-BAÏGORRY →ST-JEAN-PIED-DE-PORT [MAP 5]

A sign (ST JEAN PIED DE PORT 6H 15; MONHOA 4H) points the way out of St-Étienne along the lane heading east from the police station. The lane runs under the railway line, and from here the GR10 begins to climb along footpaths and after a while along a farm track. It joins a tarmac lane briefly (near spot height 521m), before heading off to the south-west on a loose-surfaced road which climbs around the west side of **Oylandaroy (933m)**. It's a rather tedious walk up this track to the **Col d'Aharza (734m)**, and a more interesting option, which is marked on the IGN maps, might be to take the old path which climbs straight over Oylandaroy, passing the chapel which sits on the top.

Map 5 – St-Étienne-de-Baigorry to St-Jean-Pied-de-Port 89

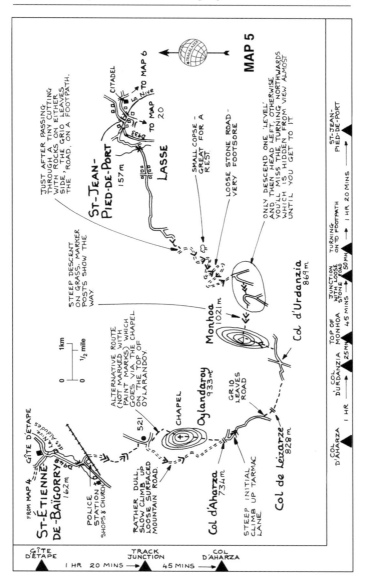

MAP 5

JUST AFTER PASSING THROUGH A TINY CUTTING WITH ROCKS ON EITHER SIDE, THE GRIO LEAVES THE ROAD, ON A FOOTPATH.

CITADEL

La Nive

TO MAP 20

ST-JEAN-PIED-DE-PORT 157m

LASSE

SMALL COPSE – GREAT FOR A REST

LOOSE STONE ROAD – VERY FOOTSORE

ONLY DESCEND ONE 'LEVEL' AND THEN HEAD LEFT. OTHERWISE YOU'LL MISS THE TURNING NORTHWARDS WHICH IS HIDDEN FROM VIEW ALMOST UNTIL YOU GET TO IT.

STEEP DESCENT ON GRASS. MARKER POSTS SHOW THE WAY.

d'Urdanzia 869m

Munhoa 1021m

Col d'Urdanzia

ALTERNATIVE ROUTE (NOT MARKED WITH PAINT MARKS) WHICH GOES VIA THE CHAPEL ON THE TOP OF OYLARANDOY.

1km

½ mile

0

0

CHAPEL

Oylandaroy 933m

521

GRIO LEAVES ROAD

GÎTE D'ÉTAPE

FROM MAP 4

des Aldudes

La Nive

ST-ÉTIENNE DE-BAIGORRY 162m

POLICE STATION
SHOPS & CHURCH

RATHER DULL SLOW CLIMB UP LOOSE SURFACED MOUNTAIN ROAD.

Col d'Aharza 734m

Col de Leizarze 828m

STEEP INITIAL CLIMB UP TARMAC LANE.

COL D'AHARZA — 1 HR → COL D'URDANZIA — 25 MINS → TOP OF MUNHOA — 45 MINS → JUNCTION WITH LOOSE STONE ROAD — 50 MINS → TURNING ON TO FOOTPATH — 1 HR 20 MINS → ST-JEAN-PIED-DE-PORT

GÎTE D'ÉTAPE — 1 HR 20 MINS → TRACK JUNCTION — 45 MINS → COL D'AHARZA

Go straight over the Col d'Aharza, and about 100m downhill on the far side turn right up a tarmac lane. The lane climbs steeply to start with and then levels out, skirting around the eastern side of Munhogain. After a little more than a kilometre, near the Col de Leizarze, follow a footpath to the left. It leads around the hillside to the **Col d'Urdanzia (869m)**, which is marked by a simple iron cross and a tiny shepherds' hut that is usually kept locked.

Follow the small tarmac road north-eastwards from the col for a few hundred metres, before heading left across the grassy slopes, to the top of **Monhoa (1021m)**, from where there are excellent views. The path goes straight down the eastern spur of the hill and briefly joins the road, before short-cutting down the hillside, and meeting the road again lower down the slope. Don't be misled by the well worn footpath continuing straight down the hill; you should turn left along the road at the first place where you meet it again. At the next sharp bend there's a junction, and the GR10 heads north-eastwards, continuing down a track to the right of the stony mountain road.

One and a half kilometres down this road and just after passing through a tiny cutting, the GR10 leaves the track and heads downhill to the right on a footpath. Soon the footpath widens to a track, and within a few minutes you join a tarmac lane. Two km along the lane, you come to the village of **Lasse**, and 1¹/₂km further down the road is **St-Jean-Pied-de-Port**.

SAINT-JEAN-PIED-DE-PORT
✉ code 64220

St-Jean-Pied-de Port is an ideal place to take a day's rest at the end of the first five days' walking. It's a lovely and historic old town with plenty to see, and some excellent places both to stay and to eat.

Services

There are several **banks and cash dispensers**. In particular there's a large branch of the Crédit Agricole behind the Hôtel Continental. Opening hours are Monday to Friday 09.00-12.15 and 14.00-17.00, and the cash dispenser outside gives out both francs and pesetas. Just to the north-west of the Crédit Agricole is the **post office**, which is open Monday to Friday from 09.00-12.00 and 14.00-17.00, and on Saturdays from 09.00-12.00. Post restante is easy to claim (ID required), and you can also send and receive faxes here (📱 05.59.37.90.09). To the north of the post office is the **railway station**. St-Jean is at the end of a branch line from Bayonne, and there are 3 to 4 trains a day going in either direction. A ticket one way costs €7/47F and the journey takes an hour.

Due east of the train station, the **Stoc** supermarket has every type of food you could possibly want. At the other end of the town, almost opposite the *gîte d'étape,* the new **LiDL** supermarket is similarly well stocked. Probably more convenient than either of these, however, are the two small general stores on the rue d'Espagne in the centre of town. Just a few yards from the *gîte d'étape* is a **laundry** (there's no launderette in St-Jean) which is open Monday to Saturday (halfday closing on Saturday). They charge €3/18F per kg of washing.

For camping equipment there's a good **sports store** on the avenue de Jaï-

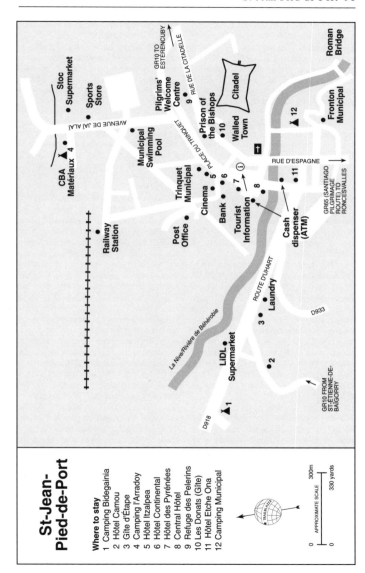

St-Jean-Pied-de-Port

Where to stay
1 Camping Bidegainia
2 Hôtel Camou
3 Gîte d'Étape
4 Camping l'Arradoy
5 Hôtel Itzalpea
6 Hôtel Continental
7 Hôtel des Pyrénées
8 Central Hôtel
9 Refuge des Pelerins
10 Les Donats (Gîte)
11 Hôtel Etche Ona
12 Camping Municipal

0   300m
0   330 yards
APPROXIMATE SCALE

TRAILBLAZER

Roman Bridge

Stoc Supermarket
Sports Store

AVENUE DE JAI ALAI

CBA Matériaux ▲ 4

Municipal Swimming Pool

PLACE DU TRINQUET

Pilgrims' Welcome Centre

RUE DE LA CITADELLE

GR10 TO ESTERENCUBY

Citadel

Prison of the Bishops
9
10

Walled Town

Fronton Municipal

▲ 12

Trinquet Municipal

Cinema
Bank
5
6
7
8
ⓘ
11

RUE D'ESPAGNE →

Post Office

Tourist Information

Cash dispenser (ATM)

GR65 (SANTIAGO PILGRIMAGE ROUTE) TO RONCESVALLES

Railway Station

La Nive/Rivière de Béhérobie

ROUTE D'UHART

Laundry

D933

3

LiDL Supermarket

2

▲ 1

D918

GR10 FROM ST-ÉTIENNE-DE-BAIGORRY

Alaï. They sell both the old (puncture) and new (resealable) type blue Camping Gaz cylinders. The only place to get gas cylinders suitable for Epigas stoves is the hardware store, CBA Matériaux, next to Camping de l'Arradoy, where they sell the very large gas bottles designed to be used on blowtorches.

The **tourist office** (☎ 05.59.37.03 57, 🖷 05.59.37.34.91) have plenty of information about various activities in the area. Finally, for those who are walking the pilgrimage route to Santiago (see p126ff), the **Pilgrims Welcome Centre** (☎ 05.59.37.05.09) is at 39 rue de la Citadelle and is open from mid May until the end of September.

Where to stay
St-Jean draws a large number of tourists during summer, so there are plenty of places to choose from.

The most upmarket place in town is the *Hôtel des Pyrénées* ☆☆☆ (☎ 05.59 37.01.01, 🖷 05.59.37.18.97) where prices start at €85 / 560F for a double room. Of much the same standard but rather more relaxed and friendly is the nearby *Hôtel Continental* ☆☆☆ (☎ 05 59.37.00.25, 🖷 05.59.37.27.81), where rooms start at €61/398F. The *Central Hôtel* ☆☆ (☎ 05.59.37.00.22, 🖷 05.59 37.27.79) is another fairly smart but relaxed place, with rooms starting at €50/330F.

Coming down to earth slightly, the *Hôtel Etche Ona* ☆☆ (☎ 05.59.37 01.14) is pleasant, with rooms from €38/250F, and the *Hôtel Itzalpea* ☆☆ (☎ 05.59.37.03.66, 🖷 05.59.37.33.18) is also good news, with rooms starting at €34/220F, and a restaurant serving very reasonably priced food.

If you're dying of heat exhaustion as you enter St-Jean, you could do far worse than to stay at the *Hôtel Camou* (☎ 05.59.37.02.78) which is the first hotel that you pass as you enter the town. It's peaceful and friendly and has the added attraction of a small swim-

ming pool. Rooms range in price from €29/190F to €36/235F.

There are three budget places to stay. A couple of hundred metres further down the road from the Hôtel Camou is the *gîte d'étape* (☎ 05.59.37.12.08), which is run by Mme Etchegoin, a friendly and helpful woman. It's €8/50F per night here, and breakfast is available for an extra €3/20F. The gîte takes only 12 people, so ring in advance if possible. Mme Etchegoin also has a few chambres d'hôte available. *Les Donats* (☎ 05 59.37.15.64) is a more recently opened gîte at 40 rue de la Citadelle, in the old walled part of the town. It takes 14 people, is supposedly only for walkers, and charges much the same prices as the main gîte. The cheapest place in St-Jean is the *Refuge des Pélerins* (☎ 05.59.37.05.09) at 55 rue de la Citadelle. It's only for pilgrims who are walking the Santiago route (pilgrims must show their 'pilgrim passport'; those who are starting in St-Jean can buy one from the Pilgrims' office for €1.50/10F). There are 16 beds in the refuge, showers and a kitchen. On proof of 'pilgrim status', it costs €6/40F per night.

There are three campsites close to the town centre. To the west of the gîte d'étape is the *Camping Bidegainia* ☆☆ (☎ 05.59.37.03.75), which is remarkably good value, charging only €1/7F for emplacement and €1/7F per person. Near the fronton municipal is the *Camping Municipal* (☎ 05.59.37.11.19) which is popular because of its location close to the shops and cafés. The tariff here is €2/13F per person and €1.50/8F for emplacement; the office is open only from 08.00-10.00 and 17.00-20.00.

To the north is the *Camping de l'Arradoy* ☆☆ (☎ 05.59.37.11.75), which charges €1.50/10F for emplacement, and €1.50/ 10F per person.

What to see – St-Jean-Pied-de-Port
The paved streets of the walled town are well worth exploring. Popular places to

visit within the walls include the **Citadel** on top of the hill (you can't get in, but there are good views from the outer walls), the imposing **south gate** of the town, and the **church** which stands just inside it.

The **Prison of the Bishops**, half-way up the hill between the gate and the citadel, isn't especially interesting but the upper floors of the building house a display of photographs which give the visitor an insight into the Basque way of life. Entry to the prison and display is €1.50/10F.

The weekly **market**, which takes place on Mondays on the Place du Trinquet, is well worth looking out for. It's a focal point for farmers and artisans selling local produce – cheeses, wines, honey, linen and more.

Also thoroughly recommended is the chance to see a game of **pelote**. During the summer there are fairly regular games, which are well advertised around town, and which take place either at the trinquet municipal (the indoor court) or at the fronton municipal (the outdoor court). Entry can be reasonably costly (€8/50F to get in to see a game in the trinquet municipal) but it's well worth it.

ST-JEAN-PIED-DE-PORT → RONCESVALLES   [MAP 20, p128]

For a description of the pilgrimage route to Roncesvalles, the **Chemin St Jacques**, see p128.

ST-JEAN-PIED-DE-PORT → ESTÉRENCUBY   [MAP 6, p94]

From the centre of St-Jean, go straight up the rue de la Citadelle, and leave the old walled town through the gate of St Jacques at the top of the hill. After 400m, at a road junction, there's a blue sign pointing south-east down the D401 (ESTÉRENCUBY 4H 00; CARO 0H 45). A kilometre up the road, follow a brief detour to the right on a footpath, before the GR10 descends into **Caro** along a tiny lane. There's a water point beside the road in the village, though there's no indication of whether it's potable. It would be wise to purify it.

Beyond the village the GR10 remains on lanes for a further 1¹/₂km, until, having skirted around the side of a small hill (spot height 305m on the map), it cuts down through trees to a stream. The path climbs again on the far side of the stream, and enters the tiny hamlet of **Ahadoa**. From here two possible routes present themselves to the walker. Purists will opt to follow the GR10, as it climbs over the top of **Handiamendi (642m)**, and descends on the far side. Those who are feeling lazier may choose to head south down the lanes which contour around the base of the hill – a flatter and quicker route to Estérencuby. The 'proper' route over the top of the hills involves a relatively short but steep climb. From the lane junction in Ahadoa a signpost (ESTÉRENCUBY 2H 45) points the way up a clear footpath. At the top of the hill, the footpath goes over a small col, and soon joins a rough vehicle track, where there's a further sign (ESTÉRENCUBY 1H 30). Follow the track as it winds down the hillside into the village below.

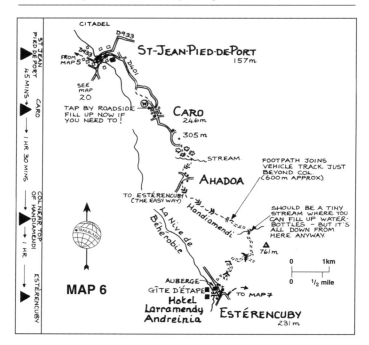

MAP 6

ESTÉRENCUBY
✉ code 64220

Estérencuby is a quiet, pretty village with a choice of places to stay.

The largest hotel is the *Hôtel Larramendy Andreinia* ☆☆ (☎ 05.59 37.09.70, 🖨 05.59.37.36.05) where there are rooms available from €28/180F. The restaurant serves good food and the Menu Randonneur is solid value at €9/58F. The *Auberge Etchegoyen* (☎ 05.59.37 09.77) is next to the pelote court and has rooms for €23/150F to €26/170F; the restaurant has fixed menus starting from €10/65F and it also looks worth trying.

The *gîte d'étape* is run by the Hôtel Larramendy Andreinia (use the telephone number above). It's a small, modern place, which sleeps only 12, so book in advance if possible. It costs €9/60F per night.

ESTÉRENCUBY → CHALET D'IRATY (COL BAGARGIAK) [MAPS 7-8]

Beside the church, a yellow sign, COL D'IRAU 4H 00 & COL BAGARGIAK 8H 30, points the way eastwards up a small lane. Follow the lane uphill for two kilometres, before leaving it, and cutting up the hillside on a narrow, thorny path. At the top of the path, join another tarmac lane which leads across a plateau past the tiny settlement of **Phagalcette**. Beyond this

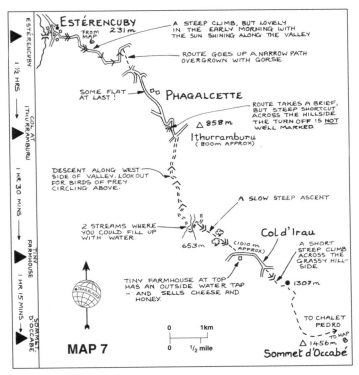

ESTÉRENCUBY 231m FROM MAP 6

A STEEP CLIMB, BUT LOVELY IN THE EARLY MORNING WITH THE SUN SHINING ALONG THE VALLEY

ROUTE GOES UP A NARROW PATH OVERGROWN WITH GORSE.

SOME FLAT AT LAST!

PHAGALCETTE

△ 858 m

ROUTE TAKES A BRIEF, BUT STEEP SHORTCUT ACROSS THE HILLSIDE. THE TURN OFF IS <u>NOT</u> WELL MARKED

Ithurramburu (800m APPROX)

DESCENT ALONG WEST SIDE OF VALLEY. LOOK OUT FOR BIRDS OF PREY CIRCLING ABOVE.

A SLOW STEEP ASCENT

2 STREAMS WHERE YOU COULD FILL UP WITH WATER.

653m

Col d'Irau (1010m APPROX)

A SHORT STEEP CLIMB ACROSS THE GRASSY HILLSIDE.

● 1307m

TINY FARMHOUSE AT TOP HAS AN OUTSIDE WATER TAP - AND SELLS CHEESE AND HONEY.

TO CHALET PEDRO
TO MAP 8

△ 1456m
Sommet d'Occabé

0   1km
0   ½ mile

MAP 7

Left margin (vertical):
ESTÉRENCUBY
1 ½ HRS →
COL AT ITHURRAMBURU
1 HR 30 MINS →
TINY FARMHOUSE
1 HR 15 MINS →
SOMMET D'OCCABÉ

SNACK BAR
Chalet de Cize

ROAD TO LARRAU/ CHALET D'IRATY

'TRIANGULAR' CHALETS

TO MAP 9

AT WEEKENDS THIS AREA IS PACKED WITH HOLIDAY-MAKERS.

FROM MAP 7

△ **Sommet d'Occabé** (1456m)

Chalet Pedro (1000m APPROX)

SMALL LAKE

Chalet d'Iraty (COL BAGARGIAK)

GÎTE D'ÉTAPE (2 BUILDINGS) (1320m APPROX)

0   1km
0   ½ mile

MAP 8

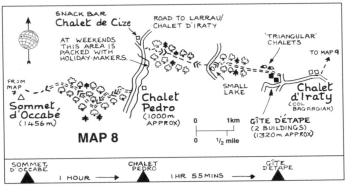

SOMMET D'OCCABÉ   CHALET PEDRO   GÎTE D'ÉTAPE
        1 HOUR →   1HR 55 MINS →

there's another brief diversion on a (poorly marked) footpath before you rejoin the road for a final climb to the col at **Ithurramburu**.

Several paths meet at the col, but route-finding is no problem as the GR10 is relatively well marked and there's also a sign: COL D'IRAU 1H 45 & COL BAGARGIAK 6H 15. Head south, descending along the side of the valley on a vehicle track. At the southern end of the valley, the track crosses two streams and turns northwards. Within 400m the GR10 turns off to the right and begins to climb up the hillside on a steep footpath. After a tiring ascent, you eventually reach the col; there's a farmhouse here where they sell cheese and honey, and there's a water point on the outside of one of the buildings. A sign here used to (it has now been removed) give the following timings: CROMLECHS D'OCCABÉ 1H 30 & COL BAGARGIAK 4H 30.

Follow the tarmac road south-eastwards to the **Col d'Irau**, and climb straight up the side of the hill beyond. There's no path as such but there are marker posts that guide you up on to the ridge. From here you follow a cart track to the south of the nearest hill (1307m) and on towards the **Sommet d'Occabé (1456m)**. Just north of the Sommet, the path swings eastwards and begins to lose height. Soon you join an extremely rutted vehicle track that descends sharply through the beech trees. The route is poorly marked in places but it's hard to go wrong; stay on the track and look out for the occasional faded paint marks. Approximately one hour after passing the Sommet d'Occabé, you come to a tarmac road, on the far side of which is **Chalet Pedro** (☎ 05.59.28.55.98, 🖹 05.59.28.74.43), a popular spot for day trippers. There's a restaurant, a handful of apartments for rent (minimum for a weekend), and numerous short, marked walks around the local hillsides. There is a sort of *gîte* here (€11/70F per night) but it has only four beds; if you haven't booked in advance you're likely to be disappointed. For most walkers, Chalet Pedro is just a great place to stop for lunch, a cold drink or an ice cream. It's also a good place to fill up the water bottles: the tap on the end of the main building dispenses spring water.

Follow the road north from Chalet Pedro for about a kilometre. Just before the road junction at Iraty-Cize, leave the tarmac and climb south-eastwards across the wooded slopes of a hill, before descending to the road on the far side, where there's a small lake. As you cross the road, you are passing from Basse Navarre into Soule, the easternmost of the Basque regions. The path immediately climbs again, zigzagging through the woods and then following a vehicle track to the top of the hill, where there are a couple of modern, wedge-shaped ski chalets. Continue eastwards past these to a road and track junction. The two large buildings just below the junction are the gîte buildings but to register you have to go some 700m east to the main office in Chalet d'Iraty.

(Opposite) Top: The Crête d'Iparla, between Bidarray and St Etienne de Baïgorry (see p85), provides spectacular views. (Photo © Greg and Jane Knott).
Bottom: The medieval town of St-Jean-Pied-de-Port (see p90).

CHALET D'IRATY
✉ code 64560

Chalet d'Iraty is primarily a ski resort, which is turned to other uses in summer. In common with most ski resorts, it's a rather drab and ugly place when there's no snow, but it's a convenient overnight stop for walkers.

The registration/booking for the *gîte* is done at the information office (☎ 05.59.28.51.29) in the main complex of buildings. A night in the gîte costs €12/80F, and with two large buildings available the capacity must be at least 50 people. Despite this, it's still worth booking in advance (especially at weekends) as they frequently hold events such as mountain-biking competitions. The buildings themselves are modern, with good washing and kitchen facilities. There's a cheap but unexciting *restaurant/bar* near the information office and also a small **épicerie**.

The nearest *campsite* is a couple of kilometres down the road; it would be easier to pick up provisions on the way past the main buildings and find somewhere to camp just to the south of the Pic des Escaliers (ie just beyond Iraty).

❑ **Iraty to Logibar – alternative route**

The GR10 from Chalet d'Iraty to Logibar takes about six and a half hours, and there are two areas where route-finding can be time-consuming in bad weather. Those who want to take a short cut could consider the alternative route that is marked on the IGN 1:50,000 map, via the village of **Larrau**. Much of this alternative route is along the road but it has some advantages, – it's much quicker (about 3½ hours) for a start. The main attraction of taking the shorter route, however, is that Larrau has campsite, restaurant, two hotels and a shop, whereas there's only the gîte and auberge in Logibar. The route described below is the main route (GR10).

CHALET D'IRATY → LOGIBAR   [MAP 9, p99]

Just east of the information office and the restaurant, turn left down a forestry road which leads to a small col. From the col, follow the footpath which climbs up the southern side of the **Pic des Escaliers**. The path is steep at first but it soon levels out and becomes a pleasant walk across the grassy hillside to the top of the ridge, from which there are excellent views to the north. After a spectacular but not particularly well marked descent you reach a rough forest road. Follow it to the right for about 500m, before a sign post, LOGIBAR 5H, directs you to go left down another track. A sign, ATTENTION PALOMBIÈRES, warns of a potential hazard: the path below this point passes in front of a number of platforms used by hunters who shoot wood pigeon (*palombe*) in the spring and autumn. Beware!

(Opposite) Top: The Basque country is full of surprises. These three crosses, near a tiny chapel on the hillside above Aïnhoa (see pp81-2), make the long climb uphill seem worthwhile. (Photo © Greg and Jane Knott). **Bottom:** The Chemin de la Mâture, near Borce (see p111), was carved out of the rock face in the 18th century to allow access to the extensive forests above the Aspe and Ossau valleys.

❏ **Walking times on trail maps**
Note that on all the trail maps in this book the times shown alongside each map refer only to time spent actually walking. Add 30-40% to allow for rest stops.

At the first sharp bend in the new track, the GR10 continues straight ahead (east-north-east) on a footpath which leads around the grassy hillside. After about an hour you come to a small locked **house** with an outbuilding; descend past the house and under the seven large trees below it, and join a track just beyond the trees. The track rises over a spur and then descends to an area of scrub which is laced with paths made by cows and sheep. It's easy to lose the markers here but if you head straight through you should emerge near a **cow trough** and a large stone with big red and white stripes. Go up past the side of the trough and then veer to the right into a small grassy dip, where you'll find the next marker. From here the path begins to climb again, emerging eventually at a track junction by a small col (just north-east of spot height 1041m on the map). A yellow sign, Logibar 3h 15, is welcome reassurance you're on the right path!

Follow the vehicle track along the top of the hill to a fenced-off field. The GR10 avoids the field by passing down a muddy cart track to the right-hand side, before taking a footpath which skirts the bottom of the enclosure. Follow this footpath south-eastwards along a spur, past two small hillocks, and eventually to an old gate, beyond which is a **croft**. Painted on the roof of the croft is Logibar ¹/₂h, but this is wishful thinking for all but fell-runners: most people still have at least an hour of walking ahead of them.

The path climbs gently, levels off for a few hundred metres, and then begins to descend along a fence line. At a metal gate, follow the course of an old cart track down the hill. After a steepish descent, you join a tarmac road lane very briefly before short-cutting down the hillside on another footpath. Rejoin the road below, and follow it down to **Logibar**.

LOGIBAR

✉ code 64440

Logibar really only consists of a single building, the *Auberge Logibar* (☎ 05.59.28.61.14), which is a combination of an inn, restaurant and gîte d'étape. The gîte takes 36 people, has reasonable kitchen facilities, and costs €9/60F per night. Double rooms in the auberge cost €23/150F. Food at the restaurant is adequate and reasonably priced. Logibar is popular with day trippers, because it is the nearest parking place for a visit to the famous Gorges d'Holzarté.

LARRAU

✉ code 64560

Larrau is the nearest place with a shop, and is 2.5km up the steep road from Logibar; try hitching a lift as it's a 40-minute walk.

The *Hôtel Etchemaite* ☆☆ (☎ 05.59.28.61.45, 🖹 05.59.28.72.71) has rooms for €34-43/220-280F, while the *Hôtel Despouey* ☆ (☎ 05.59.28.60.82.) charges €24-30/160-200F for a room.

The *campsite* in the village charges €1.50/8F for emplacement and €2/12F per person.

Map 9 – Chalet d'Iraty to Logibar 99

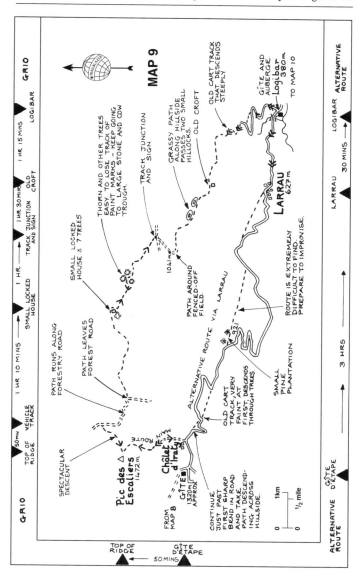

MAP 9

GR10

50min — TOP OF RIDGE / VEHICLE TRACK

1 HR 10 MINS — SMALL LOCKED HOUSE

1 HR. — TRACK JUNCTION AND SIGN

1 HR. 30 MINS — OLD CROFT

1 HR. 15 MINS — LOGIBAR

GR10

LOGIBAR ALTERNATIVE ROUTE

SPECTACULAR DESCENT

PATH RUNS ALONG FORESTRY ROAD

PATH LEAVES FOREST ROAD

SMALL LOCKED HOUSE & 7 TREES

THORN AND OTHER TREES EASY TO LOSE TRACK OF PAINT MARKS – KEEP GOING TO LARGE STONE AND COW TROUGH.

TRACK JUNCTION AND SIGN

GRASSY PATH ALONG HILLSIDE PASSES TWO SMALL HILLOCKS.

OLD CROFT

OLD CART TRACK THAT DESCENDS STEEPLY

GÎTE AND AUBERGE Logibar 380m

TO MAP 10

Pic des Escaliers 1472m

MAIN ROUTE

Chalet d'Iraty Gîte 1320m APPROX

FROM MAP 8

CONTINUE JUST PAST FIRST SHARP BEND IN ROAD AND TAKE FAINT PATH DESCENDING ACROSS HILLSIDE.

OLD CART TRACK, VERY FAINT AT FIRST, DESCENDS THROUGH TREES.

ALTERNATIVE ROUTE VIA LARRAU

PATH AROUND FENCED-OFF FIELD

1041m

921m

SMALL PINE PLANTATION

ROUTE IS EXTREMELY DIFFICULT TO FIND. PREPARE TO IMPROVISE.

LARRAU 627m

30 MINS — LARRAU / LOGIBAR

3 HRS — GÎTE D'ETAPE / ALTERNATIVE ROUTE

0 1km
0 ½ mile

50 MINS — TOP OF RIDGE / GÎTE D'ETAPE

LOGIBAR → SAINTE-ENGRÂCE   [MAP 10]

Cross the Gave de Larrau and immediately turn left to a wooden bridge, which spans the river flowing from the Gorges d'Holzarté. On the far side of the bridge, next to a clear sign (SAINTE-ENGRÂCE 7H; PASSERELLE D'HOLZARTÉ 0H 50) the path divides, with the 'real' GR10 heading direct-ly uphill, and the alternative route, via the spectacular **Gorges d'Holzarté**, going right. The alternative route, which rejoins the main path after about 2¹/₂ hours' walking, is more interesting but takes about an hour longer and can be quite wet after bad weather. Both routes are described below.

GR10

From the sign, the GR10 climbs steeply on a small footpath through a wood, before emerging from the trees to climb even more steeply through bracken. On reaching a small level area the path, which to this point has been climbing up the end of a spur, diverts along the north side of the spur. It soon begins to climb again, albeit at a much easier gradient and through trees which offer welcome shade. The footpath soon becomes a wide stony track which eventually meets a rough road. A yellow sign at this junction simply says 'SAINTE-ENGRÂCE' with an arrow pointing south-wards along the rough road. Follow the road south for over a kilometre until it emerges on to an open area of spur and bends sharply round to the left, before starting to descend. On the right here is a rounded hillock (spot height 999m on the IGN map), and there's a yellow sign beside the track: COL D'ANHAOU 1 HR 45; SAINTE-ENGRÂCE 5 H 15. This is the point at which the alternative route rejoins the GR10.

Alternative route

Turn right, following the sign pointing towards the 'PASSERELLE D'HOLZARTÉ', and climb along a rocky but well worn trail, which gains height above the gorge. After about 45 minutes it levels out, and as it swings to the left, the **suspension bridge** comes into sight. Crossing it can be a little disconcerting – many of the timbers look as though they should be replaced and the whole structure sways and bounces.

   On the far side of the bridge a tiny footpath zigzags up the hillside, and after half an hour meets a large and nearly level track heading south-east. Follow the track for approximately 2¹/₂km to the footbridge which crosses the south-east end of the valley. From here a poorly defined trail climbs north-westwards across the opposite hillside. Gradually the path becomes clearer and eventually you reach the small grassy col (just to the east of spot height 999m) where you rejoin the official GR10.

Both routes

The next part of the path is not particularly well marked and varies slight-ly from what is printed on the IGN 1:50,000 map. From the col (spot

Map 10 – Logibar to Sainte-Engrâce 101

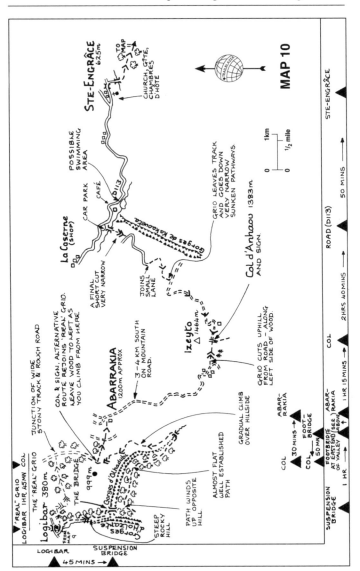

MAP 10

STE-ENGRÂCE 625m.

TO MAP

CHURCH, GÎTE, CHAMBRES D'HÔTE

POSSIBLE SWIMMING AREA

La Caserne (SHOP)

CAR PARK

CAFÉ

D113

GRIO LEAVES TRACK AND GOES DOWN VERY NARROW SUNKEN PATHWAYS

Col d'Anhaou 1383m. AND SIGN

A FINAL SHORT CUT VERY NARROW

JOINS SMALL LANE

Gorges de Kakouéta

Izeyto 1464m.

GRIO CUTS UPHILL FROM ROAD - ALONG LEFT SIDE OF WOOD.

ABARRAKIA 1200m APPROX

3-4 KM SOUTH ON MOUNTAIN ROAD.

COL & SIGN. ALTERNATIVE ROUTE REJOINS 'REAL' GRIO. LEAVE WOOD TO LEFT AS YOU CLIMB FROM HERE

JUNCTION OF WIDE STONY TRACK & ROUGH ROAD

THE 'REAL' GRIO

'REAL' GRIO LOGIBAR 1HR 45MN COL

Logibar 380m.

THE BRIDGE

999m.

Gorges d'Olhadubi

GRADUAL CLIMB OVER HILLSIDE

ALMOST FLAT WELL ESTABLISHED PATH

PATH WINDS UP OPPOSITE HILL.

STEEP ROCKY HILL

Gorges d'Holzarte

FROM MAP

LOGIBAR

SUSPENSION BRIDGE

1km

0

½ mile

0

SUSPENSION BRIDGE

1 HR.

COL

30 MIN

FOOT-BRIDGE

COL

50 MIN

ABARRAKIA

FOOTBRIDGE AT EAST END (SEE VALLEY ABOVE)

1 HR 15 MINS

ABARRAKIA

COL

2HRS 40MINS

ROAD (D113)

50 MINS

STE-ENGRÂCE

LOGIBAR

45 MINS

height 999m), the GR10 climbs south-eastwards, leaving the wood just to the left, and it passes over a couple of small hummocks to meet a loose-surface vehicle track. Go straight across the track and continue to the hut and sheepfold at **Abarrakia**. Join the vehicle track here and follow it southwards for 3¹/₂ km; it's not a very interesting walk, although there are excellent views of Chardekagagna (1893m), to the right. After passing two houses and a large animal shed, leave the rough road and climb up a small gully to the left to reach the Col d'Anhaou (1383m). At the col there are a number of tracks, and a sign: SAINTE-ENGRÂCE 3H 30.

Head down the vehicle track on the far side of the col and after a few minutes you come to a small house. There are two options from here: either you can take the path down the western side of the **Gorges de Kakoueta**, or take the longer route which circles the gorge and passes down the eastern side. When I first researched this guide in 1997 walkers were being encouraged to take the western route (apparently lack of funds had meant that the eastern path had not recently been marked) and this is the route described here. However, having followed this same route again recently, I learned (afterwards) that the eastern route had supposedly been reopened. Sadly, having passed the section already, I can't give a description of the eastern route, but it would be worth asking in Logibar (or Sainte Engrâce if you're heading westwards) about which route is currently recommended. The remainder of this route description details the path along the western side of the gorge.

Follow the vehicle track as it winds downhill below the house. After about 45 minutes the GR10 leaves the track and cuts directly down the hill on footpaths that are in a very poor state of repair; deep channels have been eroded into the hillside. Eventually you reach a road, which you follow down to another short cut, again down a 'sunken' path. At the bottom of the valley, cross the river via a small stone bridge and come to the main road (D113).

From here it's about three weary kilometres east along the tarmac to the nearest accommodation. Note that there are no shops in Sainte-Engrâce; the nearest shop is in La Caserne, 2km to the north-west, so if you need supplies you should make for La Caserne before going to the gîte.

SAINTE-ENGRÂCE
✉ code 64560

The commune of Sainte-Engrâce actually incorporates all the hamlets along several kilometres of road but, since the closure of the only other lodge, the only facilities are the gîte and auberge, which are opposite the ancient church. The *gîte d'étape*, is run by the *Auberge Elichalt* (☎ 05.59.28.61.63), next door. The gîte

takes about 30 people, costs €8/50F per night, and has good kitchen facilities. Demi-pension costs €23/150F and includes, courtesy of Mme Burguburu, probably the best evening meal you'll get in any gîte in the Pyrenees. The house next door to the auberge also advertises *chambres d'hôte*. The owners of the auberge can help out with *camping* space – €3/20F gets you a place in a nearby

Map 11 – Sainte-Engrâce to Arette La Pierre St-Martin 103

field and use of the showers in the gîte.

Before leaving Sainte-Engrâce, take a look into the **11th century church**. The interior is simple, and the bare stonework and rounded vaults are legacies of the Romanesque tradition. Of particular interest are the carvings around the tops of the pillars nearest to the altar, which depict scenes from everyday life.

SAINTE-ENGRÂCE → ARETTE LA PIERRE ST-MARTIN [MAP 11]

Continue down the lane from the gîte and, just beyond a tiny bridge, turn right. After a couple of minutes you cross another small bridge, and start to climb along a narrow and overgrown footpath. The path soon enters a small gully, which marks the border between Soule (Pays Basque) and Béarn. Follow the gully for 20-30 minutes in an easterly direction, before cutting up the gully side to the left and continuing to climb through the beech woods that cover the hillside. Route-marking in this area is not always clear; if in doubt, continue uphill and you should be able to pick up the path again after a while. After about 1^1/$_2$ hours of ascent, the path arrives at a

❏ **Weather alert**
The route from Sainte-Engrâce to Arette la Pierre St-Martin is not particularly tricky, but in poor weather route-finding on the hillsides around the Soum de Lèche can be problematic. In the event of low mist or rain, less confident walkers might be wise to wait for conditions to clear. If you decide to go ahead, ensure that you have a compass, and that you pay particular attention to the map and route markers.

distinctive cow trough; the likeness of a human head, sculpted into the rock beside the trough, wears a hat with 'Le Guardien' written around the brim.

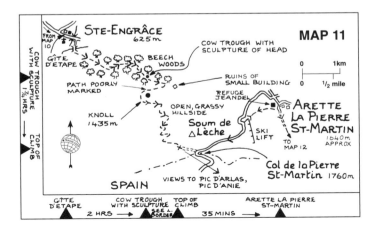

La Pierre St-Martin
In the centre of the col stands La Pierre St-Martin (St Martin's Stone), which is the site of one of the best known annual rituals in the whole of the Pyrenees.

This ritual has its origins in a 14th century squabble between the inhabitants of the Barétous valley (France) and the Roncal valley (Spain). The dispute centred on the rights to graze livestock on the high pastures around the col. The best pastures were on Roncalese territory, and hence attempts by the Barétous farmers to graze their herds there were not appreciated.

After a series of violent encounters, a settlement was reached in 1375 with the **Tribute of the Three Cows**. Every year the Barétous villagers would hand over three heifers in return for the rights to use pastures in the Roncal valley. The treaty, believed to be the oldest remaining in force in Europe, is still observed every year on 13th July. It's not like it used to be, of course. Nowadays, the three animals are taken back home after the ceremony. The number of participants has grown, too – to around 3000 people.

Above the cow trough the path leaves the woods and becomes less distinct as it climbs across the grassy slopes. Although a few posts have now been used to mark the route, many of the markers are painted on low rocks and are hard to see until you get near to them. If in doubt, stand at the edge of the wood, with the grassy bowl of hillside in front of you, and look for the small knoll on the right-hand side. The path passes just to the north of this knoll, before turning back on itself and circling around to climb in a south-easterly direction. Further up the hillside the route becomes more obvious, but keep your eyes open as it twists and turns on its way uphill.

Finally, on reaching the highest point of the climb, a bizarre spectacle is seen to the south-east. After the greenery of the Basque country, you're suddenly faced with the bare moonscape of the limestone country around the **Pic d'Anie**. The Pic itself is a sign of the changes ahead. At 2504m it is the first of the high peaks you'll encounter as you move from the coastal region into the central Pyrenees.

The GR10 descends along a rough vehicle track to the tarmac road at the **Col de la Pierre St-Martin (1760m)**.

From the col, the GR10 turns northwards and follows the road for about a kilometre before cutting across the empty ski slopes, and under a ski lift. As you cross the small ridge on the far side of the slope **Arette la Pierre St-Martin** comes into sight.

ARETTE LA PIERRE ST-MARTIN
✉ code 64570
Arette la Pierre St-Martin must be quite attractive under a layer of snow but it's pretty bleak in summer. Nevertheless, it has reasonable facilities which make it a convenient overnight stop for walkers.

The gîte d'étape is next to the GR10, as it descends into the resort. *Refuge Jeandel* (☎ 05.59.66.14.46) can accommodate 19 people and charges €8/52F per night or €22/145F for demi-pension. There are kitchen facilities for those who are self-catering. The owner also has a small store of supplies for sale (chocolate, pasta, tinned food etc) although it's worth checking that the shop in the main building of the resort isn't open before you blindly accept his prices. Be slightly wary, too, of false hospitality. Being offered a cold drink as you collapse on to the bench outside the door of the gîte isn't just a show of spontaneous generosity: you'll be charged for it when you leave.

The few facilities that exist in Arette during the summer are to be found in the ground floor of the very ugly high-rise building. There's a **cash dispenser**, **épicerie** and **launderette**, and a **tourist office** with information on activities including hang-gliding, canyoning and caving. However it should be noted that the shop appears to open only in mid summer (ie July/August) when there are likely to be enough walkers passing through to make it worthwhile.

ARETTE LA PIERRE ST-MARTIN → LESCUN   [MAP 12, p107]

Leave Arette la Pierre St-Martin along the track heading roughly southwards across the hillside. After approximately 25 minutes you come to a small grassy bowl (*pescamou* on the map). At this point, the GR10 heads off to the left across the grass, while the High Route goes straight on.

> ❑ **Weather alert**
> This section is not difficult but is best avoided in bad weather because it's not very well marked. You spend at least two hours crossing a bare limestone plateau where it's very easy to mistake the path and wander off along an imaginary line of cairns. If in doubt, wait a day in Arette la Pierre St-Martin for the weather to clear.

On the far side of the grass the GR10 strikes off across the rocks. Keep a careful eye out for the markers; it's very easy to lose them. After an hour of meandering across the limestone 'pavement', the path arrives at a large track and crosses under two ski lifts before dropping back onto the rocky terrain. For 30-40 minutes the route continues across the plateau, until you approach a large cliff on the right hand side. This is an excellent marker – the path passes literally along the base of the cliff. After 5-10 minutes the path does the seemingly impossible and cuts uphill (right) to cross the ridge itself. The last few metres to the **Pas de l'Osque (1922m)** are a scramble.

From the narrow ridge of the Pas de l'Osque, you descend along a rocky path into a dip and climb the far side to the **Pas d'Azuns (1873m)**. It's a lovely place to stop for a few minutes and take in the view: on the far side of the valley the Pic d'Anie dominates the scene, and down below you can see the roof of the tiny shepherd's cabin dwarfed by the landscape around it. The path winds down the hillside and after 20 minutes reaches the **Cabane du Cap de la Baight (1689m)**. The cabane is occupied during the summer months and fromage de brebis is for sale. There is a water point next to the cabane and a sign which points the way along the GR10

> ### Climbing the Pic d'Anie
>
> Despite its imposing size, the Pic d'Anie is a straightforward climb. To get to the peak one can either take the HRP (High Route) from Arette, which approaches from the north-west and rejoins the GR10 at the Cabane du Cap de la Baight, or follow the GR10 to the cabane and climb from there. For those walking the section from Arette to Lescun, the former is quicker by at least an hour.
>
> The HRP leaves Arette on the same path as the GR10 and splits off after 25 minutes as described above. It is not as well marked as the GR10, but there are markers nonetheless – splashes of dark-red paint indicate the way. The path heads south to the border and then south-east towards the pic across a rocky and boulder-strewn landscape. At the Col des Anies, directly to the north of the pic, directions are painted on a large boulder. From here the route across a limestone plateau is indicated with paint marks and small cairns. The path up the Pic is also visible, a clear diagonal scar on the side of the mountain. It's a steep walk to the top, which you should reach approximately $1\frac{1}{4}$hours after leaving the Col des Anies.
>
> I started from the Cabane du Cap de la Baight and returned to it, before continuing to Lescun; as a rough guide on timing, walking up from the cabane and back took me nearly five hours. Allow plenty of time for the descent: it's over 800m of rocky downhill path from the top of the Pic to the cabane, and this can be hard on the knees.

(REFUGE DE L'ABÉROUAT 1H) and to the Pic d'Anie (PIC D'ANIE 2H 15). See above for information on climbing the Pic d'Anie.

From the cabane the GR10 goes down the valley and enters a beech wood. After about an hour you come to the **Refuge l'Abérouat** (☎ 05.59.34.50.43) which is open during July and August and seems to specialize in taking groups. Individual walkers should still be able to stay here though: it costs €12/80F for the night, or €23/150F for demi-pension.

Below the refuge, the GR10 joins the tarmac road for 5-10 minutes and then diverts to the right on a cart track that can be a quagmire in wet weather. The path rejoins the road briefly before leading off cross-country at the next hairpin bend. Three to four hundred metres down the track there's an unmarked path junction. Take the lower path (don't go into the field), and the markings resume at a fallen tree some 300m further on. Soon after this the path joins a tarmac lane, where it turns left and via a couple more well-marked shortcuts, makes its way into **Lescun**.

LESCUN
✉ code 64490

Lescun is lovely little village, indeed many people remember it as the prettiest spot on the GR10. Perched on a hillside, with the imposing shape of the Pic d'Anie towering over it, it seems the quintessential Pyrenean hamlet with winding streets and old stone houses.

Services

Lescun doesn't boast much in the way of services. There's a **post office** (which doesn't change cash/traveller's cheques)

Map 12 – Arette la Pierre St-Martin to Lescun 107

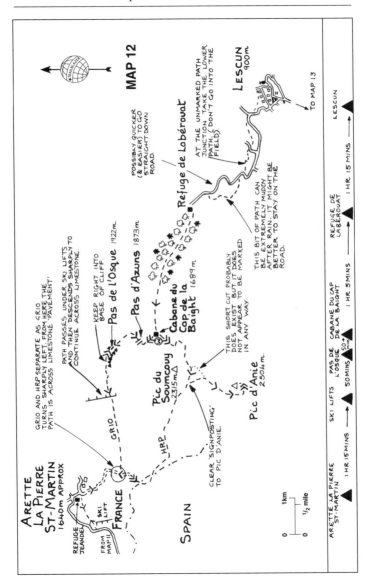

MAP 12

ARETTE LA PIERRE ST-MARTIN 1640m APPROX

REFUGE JEANDEL

FROM MAP 11

SKI LIFT

FRANCE

GRIO AND HRP SEPARATE AS GRIO TURNS SHARPLY LEFT. FROM HERE THE PATH IS ACROSS LIMESTONE 'PAVEMENT'.

PATH PASSES UNDER SKI LIFTS AND THEN DESCENDS SHARPLY TO CONTINUE ACROSS LIMESTONE.

KEEP RIGHT INTO BASE OF CLIFF

Pas de l'Osque 1922m.

Pas d'Azuns 1873m.

Cabane du Cap de la Baight 1689m.

Refuge de Labérouat

POSSIBLY QUICKER (& EASIER) TO GO STRAIGHT DOWN ROAD

AT THE UNMARKED PATH JUNCTION TAKE THE LOWER PATH (DON'T GO INTO THE FIELD).

LESCUN 900m.

TO MAP 13

THIS BIT OF PATH CAN BE EXTREMELY MUDDY AFTER RAIN. IT MIGHT BE BETTER TO STAY ON THE ROAD.

THIS SHORT CUT PROBABLY DOES EXIST BUT IT DOES NOT APPEAR TO BE MARKED IN ANY WAY.

GRIO

HRP

Pic du Soumcouy 2315m△

Pic d'Anie 2504m.

CLEAR 'SIGNPOSTING' TO PIC D'ANIE.

SPAIN

0 ___ 1km
0 ___ ½ mile

ARETTE LA PIERRE ST-MARTIN ← 1 HR 15 MINS → SKI LIFTS ← 50 MINS → PAS DE L'OSQUE ← 50 MINS → CABANE DU CAP DE LA BAIGHT ← 1 HR 5 MINS → REFUGE DE LABÉROUAT ← 1 HR 15 MINS → LESCUN

and next to the hotel is a small **épicerie** which has a limited stock. 100m down the lane is **Depann Sports** where blue Camping Gaz and Coleman/Epigas cylinders are available, as well as food, maps and guide books. The owner of the shop gives good advice on routes and weather. There is no bank in Lescun; the nearest bank/cash dispenser is in Bédous, on the way to Oloron-Ste-Marie.

There are 2-3 SNCF **buses** to Oloron every day which run along the valley below Lescun. It's a 5km walk down the hill to get to the bus stop, then 31km on the bus (€4.50/30F one way). If you need to get out of the mountains it's much better to wait a day and get to Borce and Etsaut, both of which are on the road and are served by the same bus service.

Where to stay
The *Hôtel Pic d'Anie* ☆☆ (☎ 05 59.34.71.54, 🖅 05.59.34.53.22) is recommended. It's not particularly grand but it's very comfortable and friendly; double rooms are from €40/260F. Some walkers have reported hearing 'mysterious noises' in the hotel in the middle of the night. Whether this was the ghost of a former inhabitant or simply another guest who'd had a long night in the bar is uncertain – but I'd be fascinated to hear any more reports! Those not on a shoestring budget should try the hotel restaurant; the food is delicious and portions generous – the €14/90F menu is worth every franc. The hotel accepts credit cards (Visa & MasterCard) both for hotel and restaurant bills, as well as for payment by those staying in the gîte (see below).

Just across the road is the gîte d'étape – *Refuge Pic d'Anie*, which is run by the hotel. It's clean and modern with excellent kitchen facilities, and it costs €9/60F per night. It sleeps only 14, so it's worth booking in advance.

The new *Maison de la Montagne* (☎ 05.59.34.79.14) is a recently opened and very comfortable gîte d'étape with 20 places in four-bedded rooms. It's open all year and charges €9/60F for the night or €24/155F for demi-pension. There's a Bureau des Guides here, and information on a variety of activities in the local area, including walking tours, climbing and canyoning.

The *Camping Municipal Le Lauzart* ☆☆ (☎/2 05.59.34.51.77) is about 1km south-west of the village and has a well stocked shop on site.

LESCUN → BORCE/ETSAUT   [MAP 13]

Take the road running south-west out of the village, down to the Pont du Moulin. There's a sign here (ETSAUT 6H 05 & PLATEAU DE LHERS 1H 25) pointing directly up a steep rocky footpath which shortcuts up to the road above. Since the sign was erected, however, the route has obviously been changed: the red and white route markers encourage you to follow the road as it loops up the hillside in a slightly longer and more gentle climb. Whichever route you take, the GR10 soon passes the entrance to the campsite. A short distance further on there is a road junction; go straight over, and after a couple of minutes leave the tarmac on a small path to the left. This path meets and crosses the road two or three times before coming to a farm access track. Turn left and follow the track for 300-400m, before taking a footpath which skirts around the farm buildings. Beyond the farm, the path runs through attractive woods for half a kilometre before abruptly doubling back on itself. As you walk southwards along a shady farm track, the **Plateau de Lhers** spreads out on the left.

After 1¹/₂km the track joins a small tarmac lane, near a farmhouse where milk, honey and cheese are for sale. The lane leads on, over a small bridge, to a road junction. Just south of the junction is a *gîte* and a grassy area suitable for *camping*. The gîte is looked after by Mme Nicole Rachau (☎ 05.59.34.77.27) but there is no guardian in residence so you'll need to make arrangements in advance if you wish to stay here.

From the road junction the GR10 goes north along the road past three or four houses, before leaving the tarmac and heading towards a rough-surfaced vehicle track which can be seen starting to climb the hillside. Before you reach the start of the track, however, the GR10 bends off to the right across the grass, and then begins to climb the hillside on a foot-path that runs through bracken. The path climbs steeply before joining a proper track and after a few minutes this joins a rough road used by log-ging vehicles. The road climbs in zigzags across the slopes and soon enters the woods, the trees providing welcome shade. Route-finding around here is easier than it used to be, but there is still scope for confu-sion because the foresters have daubed the trees with painted markers – some of them red and white! Thankfully, these marks are usually distinc-tive in some way (perhaps a red stripe with a white border around it or vice versa).

A considerable distance along the rough road, the GR10 cuts straight up the hill on footpaths to the **Col de Barrancq (1601m)** where there's a yellow sign: BORCE 2H; ETSAUT 2H 20. The col is a good spot for a lunch break, and if you head south-west along the ridge for a couple of minutes, the path leaves the trees, giving a decent view over the valley to the east.

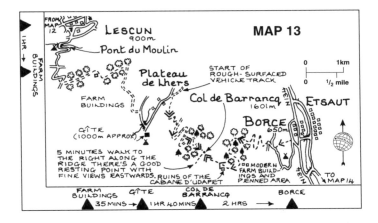

The footpath down from the col is steep initially but soon emerges at a grassy plateau. After five minutes you pass the ruins of the **Cabane d'Udapet**, and quarter of an hour later you come to two modern farm buildings. A sign, BORCE 1H 30, points the way into the woods along an old vehicle track. The GR10 soon cuts steeply downhill on a footpath; lower down the hill, at the edge of the wood, the gradient lessens and the path descends the open hillside in large, gentle loops. At the bottom of the slope, you come to a lane. Turn left along the tarmac following it down for a few minutes until the GR10 markers clearly indicate a turn off the road for a final shortcut down a footpath to the village.

BORCE AND ETSAUT
✉ code 64490
The two villages on either side of the River Aspe offer plenty of accommodation, plus a couple of basic shops. The SNCF bus service to and from Oloron-Ste-Marie is particularly useful and makes the villages a popular place either to start or finish a walking trip; the lodges can get very booked up.

Services
The bar near the gîte d'étape in Borce has a small **shop** attached to it where most essentials are available; there's a small general store in Etsaut. Etsaut also has a **post office**.There's a **Maison du Parc** (open 10.00-12.30, 13.00-18.00) which houses a rather boring display about brown bears; entry is €2/12F. The nearest bank and cash dispenser is in **Bédous**, to the north, which is accessible via the SNCF bus service which runs two or three times a day in each direction, the bus stop being in the main square in Etsaut. The nearest large town and railway station is **Oloron-Ste-Marie** which is also easy to get to on the bus.

Where to stay
● **Etsaut** The only hotel in either village is the **Hôtel des Pyrenees** ☆☆ (☎ 05.59.34.88.62, 🖹 05.59.34.86.96) which has rooms for €23-34/150-220F. It's pleasant enough and the restaurant is good. Apart from this, try the **Maison des Jeunes et de la Culture** (☎ 05.59 34.88.98, 🖹 05.59.34.86.91) which has

room for 66 people; it costs €9/60F per night or €12/75F for bed and breakfast. The interior of the building is pretty bleak, but the staff are very friendly and helpful. If all else fails, opposite the hotel is **La Maison d'Ours** (☎ 05.59.34.86.38), a rather crowded and scruffy **gîte**, which charges €12/75F for bed and breakfast, or €20/130F for demi-pension. There's an additional €1.50/10F fee to join the organization that runs the place.
● **Borce** The **gîte d'étape** (☎ 05.59.34.86.40) is the next best place to stay after the hotel. It's clean and modern, has 18 places, and the charge is a thoroughly reasonable €8/55F for the night (payable to the lady who runs the bar/shop nearby). The only problem is that it's right next to the church. Even the double glazing doesn't keep out the noise of the church bell which chimes throughout the night and, in true mountain tradition, repeats every set of chimes twice (eg at 2am it will strike twice, then pause and then strike twice again).

Camping de Borce (☎ 05.59 34.87.29) is above the village, not far from where the GR10 joins the road. Camping charges are €3/18F per tent and per person, and meals are available. There's also a small **refuge/gîte** here, which has 18 bunks and charges €8/49F per night. The refuge and the campsite are open from early June to mid September, and at other times by prior arrangement.

> **The Pau to Saragossa Railway**
> Running through the centre of Borce and Etsaut are the rusting remains
> of the old railway line which used to run from Pau to Saragossa, via the
> huge Tunnel du Somport-Canfranc. The international line, built in the 1920's
> was a major feat of engineering and saw its fair share of history. In February
> 1939, towards the end of the Spanish Civil War, train loads of fleeing
> Republicans were transported through the Pyrenees and placed in hastily con-
> structed refugee camps at Gurs, near Oloron-Sainte-Marie.
>   The railway itself stopped functioning after a derailment in the 1970's, and
> services have never been resumed.

BORCE/ETSAUT → GABAS   [MAP 14, p113]

Whichever side of the river you start on, the first part of the morning's walk
is along the road (the road leading out of Etsaut, or the lane out of Borce
and then the N134) to the Pont de Cebers. On the east side of the bridge near
a sign, CHEMIN DE LA MÂTURE 0H 30 & REFUGE D'AYOUS 5H 30, the GR10
turns off on a small side road. Follow the lane uphill a short way and
where it bends sharply back on itself continue southwards up a rocky trail.
As the path swings to the left, the Fort du Portalet comes into sight on the
opposite side of the gorge and the **Chemin de la Mâture** begins.

From the top of the Chemin, follow a level footpath through the
woods for 20 minutes, before another 5-10 minutes of steep ascent. At the
top of this, the path forks and the GR10 goes right (east). Ten minutes
later, you reach *Borde de Passette*, a shepherds' croft which was in the
process of being converted into a walkers' lodge over three years ago.
Now work seems to have stopped completely with no sign that it will ever
be finished.

Beyond the lodge continue climbing along the north-east side of the
valley, and after an hour you come to the **Cabane de la Baight de
Sencours (1560m)**. The cabane was completely renovated in spring 2000,
although whether it stays in good condition remains to be seen. There's

> **Chemin de la Mâture**
> Whatever you may hear about this part of the GR10, nothing quite pre-
> pares you for the first sight of the Chemin de la Mâture (the Way of the
> Masts). The project was initiated by the need for masts for the French navy.
> The forests of Béarn contained trees of a suitable size and quality, but getting
> them down from the mountains seemed impossible. This pathway, carved by
> convicts into the solid rock of an almost vertical cliff, was the solution. From
> its completion in 1772, huge tree trunks were brought down this slippery and
> precarious route, before being floated down river to the coast.

room to sleep 4-5 people quite easily on the sleeping platform. The cabane is just inside the boundary of the Parc National des Pyrénées (see p51).

Head south along the valley and, after crossing the stream, you arrive eventually in the bottom of a cirque, below the Pic d'Ayous. The path winds its way up the west slope of the bowl, arriving initially at a small col, which is also on the High Route, and soon afterwards at the **Col d'Ayous (2185m)**. Looking eastwards, the scene is dominated by the Pic du Midi d'Ossau (2884m), which stands isolated from the ridges and peaks around it. After 10-15 minutes' steep descent you come to the **Lacs d'Ayous** and the refuge. The *Refuge d'Ayous* (☎ 05.59.05.37.00) is a modern building with capacity for 50 people; accommodation costs €8/50F per night, or it's €24/155F for demi-pension.

The area around the Lacs d'Ayous, and indeed the whole area around the Pic du Midi d'Ossau, is popular with holiday makers and day trippers, so the walk down from here can be crowded, and the path is well worn. After descending across open hillside and then through woods, you come to a track junction next to the Gave de Bious. From here a rough road leads to the **Lac de Bious-Artigues**. If you're planning to spend a day doing the tour of the Pic du Midi d'Ossau (see p119) it's best to stay near the lake, as this is where the route starts and ends. Those continuing straight along the GR10 are better off heading down the road to Gabas.

BIOUS-ARTIGUES AND GABAS
✉ code 64440

Bious-Artigues
On the eastern shore of the lake near the dam is the *Refuge Pyrénéa Sports* (☎ 05.59.05.45.85), which charges €9/60F per night, or €22/145F for demi-pension. Self-catering facilities are practically non-existent and the dormitory is a bit cramped but otherwise it's fine. Next to the refuge are two *cafés*, and beyond these, about a kilometre down the hill, is *Camping de Bious-Oumette* (☎ 05.59.05.38.76). The campsite is open from mid June to mid September, and has a tiny but well-stocked shop. Overnight charges are reasonable at €2/14F per person and €1/7F per tent.

Opposite the gate of the campsite is the bus stop for the Pic Bus (see below). Only the morning service coming from Laruns, and the evening service heading back to Laruns make the detour up the hill to call at the campsite.

Gabas
Three and a half kilometres down the hill from Bious-Artigues is the village of Gabas. The *Chalet/Refuge de Gabas* (☎ 05.59.05.33.14) is right on the GR10. There are 34 places in four tiny dormitories and they charge €7/48F per night, or €21/139F for demi-pension. Despite being rather cramped, the refuge is recommended for the warm welcome and excellent food provided by the lady who runs it. About 500m down the road in the village itself there are two small hotels. The *Hôtel le Biscau* ☆ (☎ 05.59.05 31.37) has rooms for between €17/110F and €40/260F, and the *Hôtel Vignau* ☆ (☎ 05.59.05.34.06) has rooms for €23-34/150-220F; both hotels are reasonable.

Also in the village is a **National Park information centre** (open 10.00-12.30, 13.00-19.00). There's no shop but there are a couple of places selling cheese.

There are few **buses** passing through Gabas. In July and August the

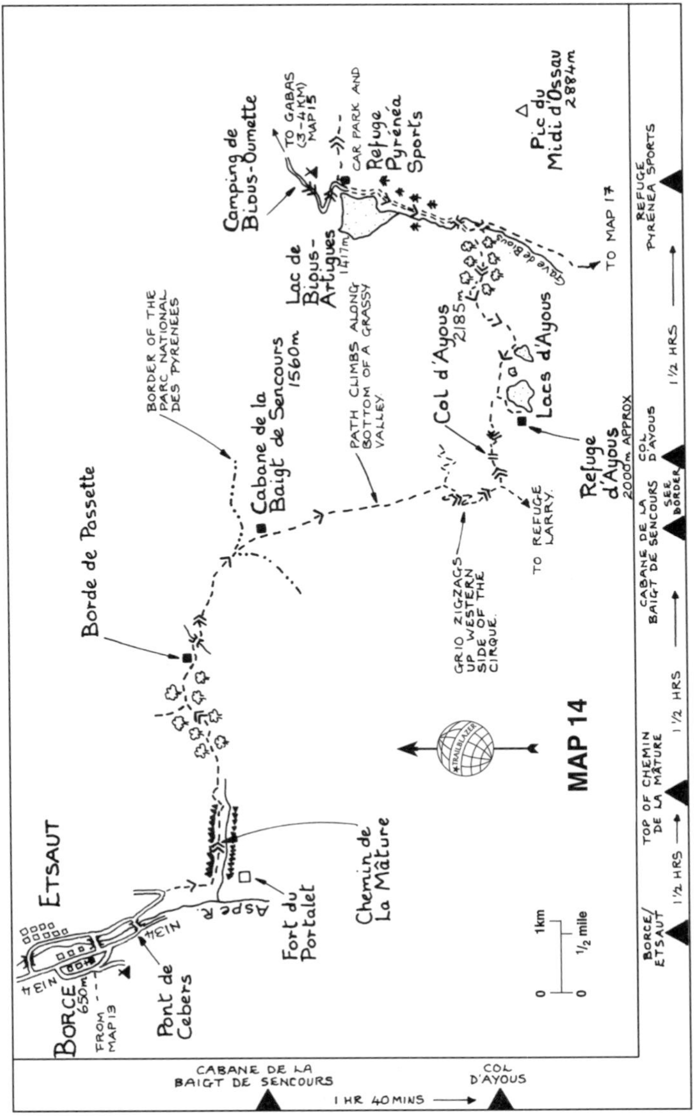

Map 14 – Borce/Etsaut to Gabas 113

MAP 14

BORCE 650m

Etsaut

FROM MAP 13

Pont de Cébers

Fort du Portalet

Chemin de La Mâture

Borde de Passette

BORDER OF THE PARC NATIONAL DES PYRÉNÉES

Cabane de la Baigt de Sencours 1560m

PATH CLIMBS ALONG BOTTOM OF A GRASSY VALLEY

Camping de Blous-Oumette

TO GABAS (3-4 KM) MAP 15

CAR PARK AND Refuge Pyrénéa Sports

Lac de Blous-Artigues 1417m

Pic du Midi d'Ossau 2884m

TO MAP 17

REFUGE PYRÉNÉA SPORTS

Col d'Ayous 2185m

Lacs d'Ayous

Refuge d'Ayous 2000m APPROX

TO REFUGE LARRY

GRID ZIGZAGS UP WESTERN SIDE OF THE CIRQUE.

0 1km
0 ½ mile

BORCE/ ETSAUT

TOP OF CHEMIN DE LA MÂTURE

½ HRS

CABANE DE LA BAIGT DE SENCOURS

SEE BORDER

COL D'AYOUS

½ HRS

REFUGE PYRÉNÉA SPORTS

½ HRS

CABANE DE LA BAIGT DE SENCOURS

COL D'AYOUS

1 HR 40 MINS

Pic Bus runs twice daily (excluding weekends and holidays) between Laruns, to the north, and the Col du Portalet, to the south. Currently, the morning service departs from Laruns at 08.55, calling at Gabas and the Camping de Bious-Oumette on its way south; on the return journey (departing from Portalet at 10.20) it stops only at Gabas. The afternoon service departs Laruns at 15.20 calling at Gabas (not Bious-Oumette) and returns via both Gabas and Bious-Oumette (departing from Portalet at 16.25). There's one additional daily (summer) service running from Pau via Laruns to Fabrèges (just south of Gabas) in the morning, and returning to Pau in mid afternoon. The company that runs the Pic Bus also operates **taxis** (☎ 05.59.05.30.31). A taxi from Laruns to the Lac de Bious-Artigues costs around €26/170F.

GABAS → GOURETTE   [MAP 15]

[**Includes high section – see warning on p20**] This section is a long one; try to get an early start so that you can take a decent break somewhere along the way.

The GR10 heads up a short stretch of old road behind the refuge, and joins the D934 going east. Ten minutes along the road, a yellow sign (PLATEAU DE CÉZY 3H, HORQUETTE D'ARRE 6H, GOURETTE 8H30), points left towards a footbridge. Cross the bridge and follow the path as it enters the tree line and climbs along the side of the valley. It soon passes over the top of the spur and starts to descend towards the north. Ahead, through the trees, the Pic de Cézy can be seen.

After ten minutes the footpath meets a forestry track, and the GR10 turns left along it. Don't allow yourself to be confused by the forestry markings painted on the trees, many of which have a single red line – this has nothing to do with the GR10.

After a further quarter of an hour you come to another yellow sign: PONT DU GOUA VARIANTE 0H 25 & CORNICHE ALHAS 0H 20 (PASSAGE VERTIGINEUX). Much is made of the dizzying walk along the **Corniche Alhas**, and for most people it will come as a bit of a disappointment. The drop beside the path is vertical in places but there's a handrail most of the way and the path is reasonably wide. The alternative to walking along the corniche is to take the other route via the Pont du Goua, a path which drops over 150m to the bridge and then has to gain height again to rejoin the main trail.

For those walking along the corniche, the path leads along the cliff face for 20 minutes before coming down to cross a footbridge below a waterfall. A few more minutes' along a level path through the trees brings you to a junction where both paths meet.

From here the serious climbing begins. The steep and rocky path eventually rises above the **Falaise de la Tume** and out of the trees. The views are excellent. To the south, on the opposite side of the valley, one can see the route of the Petit Train d'Artouste, and to the south-east the

Map 15 – Gabas to Gourette 115

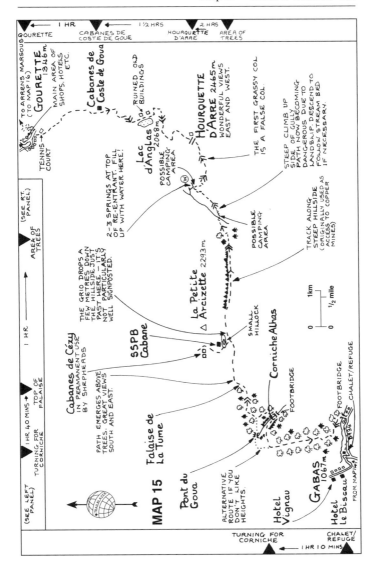

MAP 15

Gabas 1067m.

Pont du Gova

Falaise de La Tume

Cabanes de Cézy
IN PERMANENT USE
BY SHEPHERDS

PATH EMERGES ABOVE
TREES. GREAT VIEWS
SOUTH AND EAST.

ALTERNATIVE
ROUTE IF YOU
DON'T LIKE
HEIGHTS.

Hotel Vignau

Hotel Le Biscau

FROM MAP 14

SSPB Cabane

THE GR10 DROPS A
FEW METRES DOWN
THE HILLSIDE JUST
PAST HERE. IT'S
NOT PARTICULARLY
WELL SIGNPOSTED.

La Petite
Arcizette 2293m.

SMALL
HILLOCK

Corniche Alhas

FOOTBRIDGE

FOOTBRIDGE

CHALET/REFUGE

TRACK ALONG
STEEP HILLSIDE
(ORIGINALLY USED AS
ACCESS TO COPPER
MINES)

POSSIBLE
CAMPING
AREA

2-3 SPRINGS AT TOP
OF RE-ENTRANT. FILL
UP WITH WATER HERE!

Lac
d'Anglas
2068m.

POSSIBLE
CAMPING
AREA

RUINED OLD
BUILDINGS

Cabanes de
Coste de Goua

GOURETTE
1346m.

TO ARRENS MARSOUS
(TO MAP 16)

MAIN AREA OF
SHOPS, HOTELS
ETC.

TENNIS
COURT

Hourquette
D'Arre 2465m.

WONDERFUL VIEWS
EAST AND WEST.

THE FIRST GRASSY COL
IS A FALSE COL.

STEEP CLIMB UP
SIDE OF GULLY
PATH NOW BECOMING
DANGEROUS DUE TO
LANDSLIP. DESCEND TO
FOLLOW STREAM BED
IF NECESSARY.

0   1km
0   ½ mile

(SEE LEFT
PANEL)

TURNING FOR
CORNICHE

1 HR 40 MINS

TOP OF
FALAISE

1 HR.

AREA OF
TREES

(SEE RT.
PANEL)

GOURETTE

1 HR

CABANES DE
COSTE DE GOUE

1½ HRS

HOURQUETTE
D'ARRE

2 HRS

AREA OF
TREES

TURNING FOR
CORNICHE

CHALET/
REFUGE

1 HR 10 MINS

valley floor, the Plaine de Soussouéou, spreads out below. Heading east-wards on a level path, you are confronted by the fascinating sight of the twisted layers of rock which make up La Petite Arcizette (2293m). Soon the path is joined by an indistinct trail coming from the **Cabanes de Cézy**. Although the cabanes are in constant use by shepherds there is a possibility of some basic shelter near here: just to the north of the path junction, on the far side of the little hummock that blocks the Plateau de Cézy from view, is a tiny *cabane* with a roof so low that it looks as though it could actually be a covered sheepfold. On the metal door is a black badge with the letters SSPB. The cabane is left open and according to the shepherds may be used by walkers; it could sleep 3-4 people.

Continuing along the GR10 from the path junction, keep a careful look out for the route markers; the GR10 drops a few metres down the hillside to join a large track, but it's easy to miss. After three quarters of an hour on the new track, you reach a small area of trees and begin the second big climb of the day, towards the **Hourquette d'Arre**. Half an hour above the trees the path crosses to the east bank of the small stream it has been following and begins a steep ascent up a sharp-sided gully. In 2000 this section was precarious in places because a landslip had swept away the path. If in doubt, it would be safer to descend to the stream and follow the bank as far as possible. At the top of the gully, the gradient becomes more gradual and the track passes two or three springs. It's an excellent place to fill up with water: you can get it literally from the mountain side.

The path crosses a level area, goes past a tiny tarn and soon begins to climb again. The final approach to the Hourquette d'Arre is steep, but the views from the col in either direction are magnificent. There's a yellow sign at the col, GOURETTE 2H 30, and nearby a tiny *hut* that could be useful for shelter in an emergency. Heading north across the top of the hill, you soon begin to descend steeply to the **Lac d'Anglas**, which you can see below. Although camping is probably not allowed, it's a lovely spot, and people sometimes pitch their tents here.

Continue downhill from the lake for a further hour, towards the **Cabanes de Coste de Goua**. Gourette, an ugly and modern ski resort, soon comes into sight. The path drops down the final hillside to the out-skirts of the resort. From here, follow the road downhill to the main area of shops and hotels.

GOURETTE

✉ code 64440

Most of the facilities in Gourette are closed outside the ski season and particularly in the early summer (ie May/June) there is little choice of where to stay and where to eat. In July and August, how-ever, a few more places open up, and the bus service to/from Laruns and Pau also operates. The *Hôtel Au Péne Blanque* ☆☆ (☎ 05.59.05.11.29, 📠 05.59.05 10.85) is right next to the main road through the centre of town and is open in July and August; rooms are €41-53/270-

Map 16 – Gourette to Arrens-Marsous 117

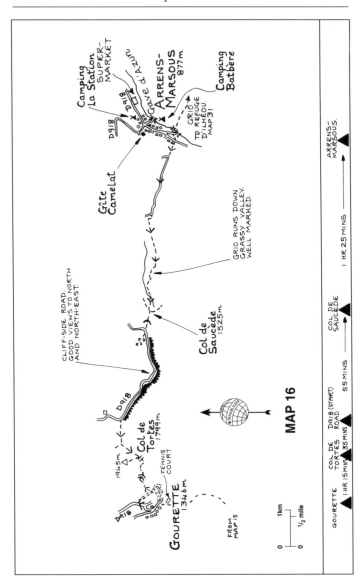

MAP 16

Camping La Station

SUPER-MARKET

D918

Gave d'Azun

ARRENS-MARSOUS 877m

Camping Batbère

D918

GR10 TO REFUGE D'ILHÉOU. MAP 31

Gîte Camelat

GR10 RUNS DOWN GRASSY VALLEY. WELL MARKED.

D918

CLIFF-SIDE ROAD. GOOD VIEWS TO NORTH AND NORTH-EAST.

Col de Saucède 1525m

1945m

Col de Tortes 1799m

TENNIS COURT

D918

GOURETTE 1346m

FROM MAP 15

0   1km
0   ½ mile

GOURETTE   COL DE TORTES   D918 (START) ROAD   COL DE SAUCÈDE   ARRENS-MARSOUS

1 HR 15 MINS   35 MINS   55 MINS   1 HR 25 MINS

350F. A short distance away, the **Hôtel la Boule de Neige** ☆☆ (☎ 05.59.05.10.05, 🖥 05.59.05.11.81) is open from mid July to mid September. The **CAF refuge** (☎ 05.59.05.10.56) is behind the Intersport shop. It costs €9/60F per night or €21/140F for demi-pension, and the refuge can take 40 people; it's open from early July until the end of August. By contrast the **Club Pyrénéa refuge** (☎ 05.59.05.12.42), near the Intersport shop, is open all summer. It's a large, modern place which charges €12/80F for the night or €23/150F for demi-pension.

Although the bank in the main building of the complex is closed, the **cash dispenser** (Crédit Agricole) remains in use. The **tourist office** (☎ 05.59.05.12.17), which opens full time only in July and August, is on the ground floor of the main building, and there's a post office next door to it. There are a couple of food **shops**, a sports shop and plenty of **cafés**. During July and August Citram Pyrénées (☎ 05.59 27.22.22) operates a bus service between Gourette and Pau (via Les Eaux Bonnes and Laruns); there are three buses a day each way.

GOURETTE → ARRENS-MARSOUS   [MAP 16, p117]

From the centre of Gourette, walk back up the road to the tennis courts/car park area where the GR10 entered the resort. The GR10 goes up a small tarmac lane in front of the large building with 'ASPTT' written on the front, and almost immediately passes a yellow sign: COL DE TORTES 1H 30. Follow the lane (which soon becomes a stony track) as it twists up the hillside to a point where another yellow sign clearly points the way up a footpath through the trees.

The path climbs steeply to the **Col de Tortes (1799m)**, before descending for half an hour to the main road (D918). At the road there's another yellow sign: ARRENS 3H 00; COL DE SAUCEDE 1H 15. Turn right, and follow the road south-eastwards for nearly 3km; halfway along the road a small waterfall marks the border between the Pyrénées Atlantiques and the Hautes Pyrénées.

Finally the GR10 leaves the road near a simple sign pointing uphill towards ARRENS. It's an easy walk up to the **Col de Saucède (1525m)**, beyond which the route heads straight down the valley, across rolling pasture land. After three-quarters of an hour the path drops down the side of a small ridge and joins a farm track which in turn leads to a tarmac road running into Arrens-Marsous.

ARRENS-MARSOUS
✉ code 65400

Although there is a hotel in Arrens-Marsous, the nicest place to stay is the **gîte Camelat** (☎ 05.62.97.40.94). The pretty and well-maintained building is immaculately clean and has seven rooms which can take 4-6 people each. There's access to a sauna (free access on Tuesday & Thursday, ask at other times) and, since the gîte is run by a chef, the food is fantastic. Staying here costs €11/70F for the night or €25/165F for demi-pension. On the way into Arrens the **Hôtel Le Tech** ☆☆ (☎ 05.62.97.01.60) is the first hotel you pass; it's a grey and impersonal place, where rooms cost €29-38/190-250F.

The **tourist office** (☎ 05.62.97.49.49) also has the details of three or four *houses* in the village offering chambres d'hôte.

There are several campsites around Arrens-Marsous. The two most central ones are the *Camping Batbère* (☎ 05.62.97.10.50) which is just across the river from the village centre and is next to the sports centre/swimming pool. It's €2/12F per person here, and €1/7F for emplacement. Just to the north-east of the village centre is the *Camping la Station* (☎ 05.62.97.00.56), open only during July and August, which is less crowded than Batbère; emplacement is €2/13F and it's €2/14F per person.

The village has a few shops including a small **supermarket** (half a kilometre from the centre of the village, past Camping La Station) and a **pharmacy**. Near the tourist office is a Crédit Agricole **cash dispenser** and you can normally also change money and travellers' cheques at the **post office**. There's a public **swimming pool** near the Camping Batbère.

Well worth looking into if you have a spare moment is the permanent **exhibition** about the Pyrenees which is in the gallery area of the tourist office.

There are two daily **buses** (not Sunday) to/from Lourdes and Tarbes.

Excursions around the GR10

PIC DU MIDI D'OSSAU   [MAP 17, p120]

The short, one-day tour around the base of the Pic du Midi d'Ossau is a popular hike through attractive but not spectacular scenery. As well as giving you a break from the routine of the GR10 it offers interesting alternatives: those with the necessary experience can climb the Pic itself (it's not difficult but you'll need a rope and some knowledge of climbing), while others can make an interesting diversion from the GR10 by continuing east from the Refuge de Pombie to the Refuge d'Arrémoulit, near Balaïtous. From Arrémoulit an excellent 1-2 day section of the HRP takes you direct to Refuge Wallon, near Cauterets.

From the Lac de Bious-Artigues, the route goes south up the rough road, towards the Col d'Ayous. At the top of the road, where the GR10 splits off to the right, is a sign, which includes an arrow: POMBIE PAR PEYREGET 2H 30. Follow the arrow left over a small bridge, and cross the plateau on the footpath which runs alongside the stream. After quarter of

> ❏ **The High Route**
> The Refuge de Pombie is on the High Route (HRP), and an interesting option here would be to join the HRP as it passes through some of the most spectacular scenery in the Pyrenees. See p121 for a recommended route via the Refuge d'Arrémoulit and Refugio de Respumoso to Refuge Wallon, near Gavarnie.

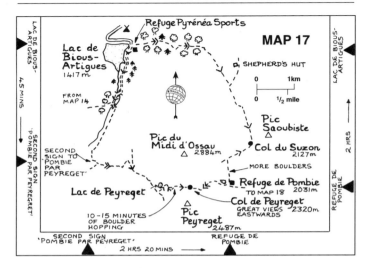

an hour you come to another sign; again follow the arrow (POMBIE PAR PEYREGET), as the path turns eastwards, climbs up the hillside, and then up a gully. At the top of the gully the path zigzags uphill across the grass to join a footpath running east. After a few minutes you come to the **Lac de Peyreget**.

From the lake the trail climbs eastwards over a low ridge, and descends to a little tarn. Beyond this is an area of boulders which must be negotiated before you reach the **Col de Peyreget (2320m)**. From the col there is a magnificent view eastwards towards Balaïtous. Descending from the col, you soon come to the refuge (2031m). The **Refuge de Pombie** (☎ 05.59.05.31.78) can take 50 people indoors, and a large tent outside allows for another 16 places in peak season. Accommodation costs €12/81F for the night and demi-pension is €29/192F. Food is available, and you're allowed to camp near the refuge.

From the refuge the track heads due north, wending its way through a mass of boulders for quarter of an hour before mounting a clear path to the **Col de Suzon (2127m)**. Beyond the col there's a long and gentle descent, mostly on grass, to the **Lac de Bious-Artigues**.

AROUND BALAÏTOUS

At 3144m, Balaïtous is one of the highest peaks in the Pyrenees, and the area around it is utterly unlike the landscape that one encounters on the GR10. Bare rock, perennial snow in some of the gullies and steep drops make the scenery appear savage and forbidding. It's an area which is unsuitable for the inexperienced walker but which offers plenty of excitement. It also provides some interesting variants to the GR10 which, at this stage, loops far to the north.

One of the best options is to leave the GR10 at the Pic du Midi d'Ossau and follow the HRP variant from the Refuge de Pombie, to the Refuge d'Arrémoulit. From Arrémoulit it's possible in a single, albeit long, day to cross the Col de Palas (2517m) into Spain and then cross back into France via the Col de la Fâche (2664m) arriving at the Refuge Wallon. The section from Arrémoulit to Wallon is a long one (9-10 hours' walking) which could easily be broken into two equal stages by stopping overnight at the Refugio de Respumoso. Whether you take two or three days to walk from Pombie to Wallon, it's still quicker than getting to Wallon via the GR10, and the scenery is superb. This route is described below. Note that both the Col de Palas and the Col de la Fâche may be impossible to cross in early summer because of snow. Even as late as early July it is advisable to check with the guardians of the refuges whether the cols are passable before setting out.

REFUGE DE POMBIE → REFUGE D'ARRÉMOULIT
[MAP 18, p122]

[Includes high section – see warning on p20] Next to the refuge, a sign points the way down towards the valley bottom where the path crosses the main road (D934): CAILLOU DE SOCQUES 1H 30. Head directly east from the refuge, following a clear path which descends across grassy slopes before skirting around to the right hand side of a large area of boulders. After half an hour you come to the **Cabane de Pucheaux** (approx 1730m) and, nearby, the **Cabane de la Glère**, both of which are in use by shepherds. Looking down to the left from the Cabane de Pucheaux, a clear path can be seen running along the far bank of the Ruisseau de Pombie. Descend from the cabane, cross the stream at a footbridge, and follow the path eastwards. After about 15 minutes the path crosses back to the south side of the stream via another footbridge, and enters a small wood. From here the path winds gently down the hillside until, after about 20 minutes, it leaves the trees and descends to cross the valley floor before climbing a short way to the road.

On the far side of the road a yellow sign points the way uphill: COL D'ARRIOUS 2H 30; ARREMOULIT 3H. The path makes a couple of sharp turns up the grassy slope before it enters the woods, climbing steeply for the next 20 minutes or so. As the gradient lessens, the path emerges from the trees, crosses a footbridge over the Ruisseau d'Arrious and begins the long climb up the Arrious valley. Half an hour after leaving the trees, you arrive at the **Cabane d'Arrious (1775m)**, which is in use by shepherds. Continue past

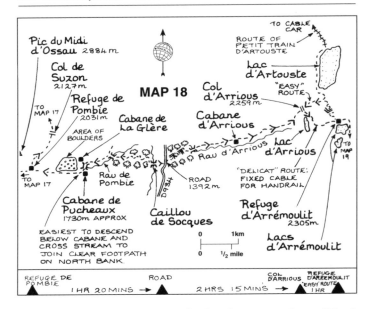

MAP 18

Pic du Midi d'Ossau 2884m

Col de Suzon 2127m

TO MAP 17

Refuge de Pombie 2031m

AREA OF BOULDERS

Cabane de La Glère

TO MAP 17

Rau de Pombie

Cabane de Pucheaux 1730m APPROX

EASIEST TO DESCEND BELOW CABANE AND CROSS STREAM TO JOIN CLEAR FOOTPATH ON NORTH BANK.

Caillou de Socques

ROAD 1392m

D934

TO CABLE CAR

ROUTE OF PETIT TRAIN D'ARTOUSTE

Lac d'Artouste

Col d'Arrious 2259m

"EASY" ROUTE

Cabane d'Arrious

Rau d'Arrious

Lac d'Arrious

TO MAP 19

"DELICAT" ROUTE: FIXED CABLE FOR HANDRAIL

Refuge d'Arrémoulit 2305m

Lacs d'Arrémoulit

0   1km
0   ½ mile

REFUGE DE POMBIE   ROAD   COL D'ARRIOUS   REFUGE D'ARRÉMOULIT
                                                    "EASY" ROUTE
▲ 1 HR 20 MINS → ▲   2 HRS 15 MINS → ▲   ▲ 1 HR

the cabane and some three quarters of an hour later you reach a small level area which is a good spot to take a break. Half an hour's further climbing beyond this point brings you to the **Col d'Arrious (2259m)**.

A yellow sign at the col indicates a choice of routes: ARREMOULIT (ATTENTION PASSAGE DELICAT) 0H 45; ARREMOULIT 1H 30. Although the 'passage délicat' to Arrémoulit is quicker (it's more direct and doesn't lose height – which the other path does, requiring a climb back up to the refuge) it's not a wise route to take if the weather is poor or if you haven't got a very good head for heights. The 'délicat' section consists of a narrow and uneven ledge above a steep drop (a cable has been fixed to the rock as a handrail). Many people do follow this path but if you're inclined to vertigo it's better to take the longer route which descends to the Lac d'Artouste and then climbs again. The 'easy' path takes around an hour, rather than the 1½ hours that the sign suggests.

Whichever route you choose you soon arrive at the refuge (2305m). The ***Refuge d'Arrémoulit*** (☎ 05.59.05.31.79) is a tiny place with space for 28 people indoors, and a further 10-12 people in the tent which is erected during peak season. A space in the refuge costs €12/80F, or a bunk in the tent costs €6/40F; supper is €13/85F and breakfast is €4.50/30F. Other drinks and snacks are available.

❏ **Getting to Refuge d'Arrémoulit – the easy option**

For the lazy or those who are short of time, there is a quick way up to this area. A **cable car** runs uphill from the northern end of the Lac de Fabrèges (near Gabas), to the starting point of the **Petit Train d'Artouste**. The narrow gauge train, normally crammed with tourists, takes 40 minutes to run around the hillside to the Lac d'Artouste, from which it's a 30-40 minute walk up to the Refuge d'Arrémoulit.

REFUGE D'ARRÉMOULIT → REFUGE WALLON [MAP 19, p125]

[Includes high section – see warning on p20] From the Refuge d'Arrémoulit, there are two ways across into Spain – via the Col d'Arrémoulit (2448m) which is visible from the refuge, or via the Col de Palas (2517m), which is hidden from view to the left, as you stand with your back to the refuge building. The route described here is via the Col de Palas. Note that although the route is not difficult it shouldn't be attempted in poor weather or bad visibility, as the way down from the col is indistinct: much of it is over boulders. Being able to see the lake below provides an important reference point which would be lost in poor visibility. Equally, unless you're properly equipped with crampons and an ice axe, the route is unsuitable in early summer when there is likely still to be snow on either side of the pass. If in doubt, ask the guardian of the refuge whether the col is passable.

From the refuge, go a short way around the north-east side of the lake before starting to climb steeply eastwards over rocks and boulders. There are no painted route markings but there are numerous small cairns which indicate the way up to the **Col de Palas (2517m)**, which you'll reach after about 50 minutes.

The route down from the col is steep and rocky and can be tricky to locate in some places although occasional cairns help to keep you on track. After a few minutes the northernmost of the **Lacs d'Ariel** becomes visible. Head down, across boulders, to the lakeside and then go around the eastern edge of the lake. The section around the lakeside is still mostly across boulders and consequently progress is fairly slow. Finally, just next to the small rocky hillock mid way down the eastern side of the lake (spot height 2259m on the IGN map), you'll come to a good path. Follow this path as it runs level past the first three lakes and then climbs slightly to reach the fourth lake. Just beyond the last lake the path passes the concrete foundations of an old building.

Continue along the same path as it climbs gradually around the hillside and soon you'll see the dam of the Embalse de Respumoso ahead of you. The path continues to climb at an easy gradient for some minutes before sinking down to arrive at the dam, where it meets the GR11 (the

Spanish trans-Pyrenean footpath) which has climbed up the valley below (for a description of this route see p150). From the dam the new refugio is visible ahead, and is reached after a further 10-15 minutes. The **Refugio de Respumoso** (2200m) (☎/🖳 (974) 49.02.23) is an extremely modern and comfortable place which is open all year and which charges €7/1200ptas for the night, €11/1800ptas for dinner, and €3.50/600ptas for breakfast. Drinks and snacks are available and the refuge sells some provisions such as puncture-type gas cylinders, chocolate, biscuits and peanuts.

From the refuge, walk around the side of the lake for short way and then follow the path as it continues in an east-south-easterly direction past the old refuge, a low building with a nissan hut type appearance, which is now firmly locked. As the path climbs and falls it passes two small tarns which have flat grassy areas beside them – perfect (and popular) for camping. Soon the small dam at the end of the Embalse de Campo Plano comes into view. The path descends to pass around the right hand side of the dam, and then skirts the south side of the grassy Campo Plano beyond, to arrive at the bottom of the climb up to the col.

The first part of the climb is at an easy gradient but gradually the path steepens and becomes rocky. After just over an hour of climbing you come to a 'lip', beyond which is a small lake. Even in mid July there is snow here, and the path around the south side of the lake crosses this. (You could avoid crossing the snow by taking an alternative path around the north side of the lake). From the far side of the tarn the path climbs in steep zigzags to a second lip, beyond which there is a short further climb up to the col itself. From the **Col de la Fâche (2664m)** there are wonderful views in both directions.

Hidden behind a rock just to the left as you reach the col is a yellow sign: WALLON 1H 45. The descent to Refuge Wallon is surprisingly gentle and along a well marked path, although even in mid/late July three or four patches of snow may have to be crossed. Since the path is hard to miss, there is little point in describing it in detail. The timing on the sign at the col is fairly accurate; after approximately an hour and three quarters you arrive at the **Refuge Wallon (1860m approx)**. (For details of Refuge Wallon and the possible routes beyond Wallon see p211 and p263).

❏ **Walking times on trail maps**
Note that on all the trail maps in this book the times shown alongside each map refer only to time spent actually walking. Add 30-40% to allow for rest stops.

Map 19 – Refuge d'Arriémoulit to Refuge Wallon 125

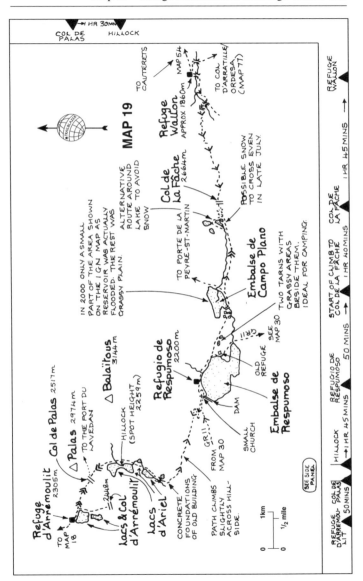

COL DE PALAS   HILLOCK

TO CAUTERETS

MAP 19

MAP 54

TO COL D'ARRAILLE/ ORDESA (MAP 77)

REFUGE WALLON

Refuge Wallon APPROX 1860m

IN 2000 ONLY A SMALL PART OF THE AREA SHOWN ON THE I.G.N MAP AS RESERVOIR WAS ACTUALLY FLOODED. THE REST WAS GRASSY PLAIN.

ALTERNATIVE ROUTE AROUND LAKE TO AVOID SNOW

Col de la Fâche 2664m

POSSIBLE SNOW TO CROSS EVEN IN LATE JULY

△ Balaïtous 3144m

TO PORTE DE LA PEYRE-ST-MARTIN

Embalse de Campo Plano

TWO TARNS WITH GRASSY AREAS BESIDE THEM. IDEAL FOR CAMPING.

△ Palas 2974m

TO THE PORT DU LAVEDAN

HILLOCK (SPOT HEIGHT 2259m)

Refugio de Respumoso 2200m

SEE MAP 30

GR11

OLD REFUGE

Col de Palas 2517m.

Refuge d'Arriémoulit 2305m.

Lacs & Col d'Arriémoulit

2048m

Lacs d'Ariel

CONCRETE FOUNDATIONS OF OLD BUILDING

PATH CLIMBS SLIGHTLY ACROSS HILL-SIDE.

FROM GR11 MAP 30

DAM

SMALL CHURCH

Embalse de Respumoso

TO MAP 18

0   1km
0   ½ mile

SEE SIDE PANEL

REFUGE D'ARREMOU- LIT	COL DE PALAS	HILLOCK	REFUGIO DE RESPUMOSO	START OF CLIMB TO COL DE LA FÂCHE	COL DE LA FÂCHE	REFUGE WALLON
50 MINS	1 HR 45 MINS	50 MINS	1 HR 40 MINS	1 HR 40 MINS	1 HR 45 MINS	

HR 30MN

Western Pyrenees – GR 11 (Spain)

The section of the GR11 (the Spanish trans-Pyrenean trail) described here passes through the province of Navarra and the western part of the province of Aragón. Although **Navarra** does not offer the best walking in the Spanish Pyrenees it does make a change from the GR10 and offers a chance to experience something rather different. Walking on the Chemin St Jacques is not the same as backpacking on the GR10, and the rolling hillsides to the east of Roncesvalles are almost deserted compared with the French hills. There are drawbacks: poor maps, lack of route marking and accommodation, but these are not insurmountable, and it's enjoyable to leave the carefully marked and often crowded French paths behind. **Aragón**, further to the east, contains some excellent walking routes, with the GR11 providing plenty of variety and some truly memorable days.

Route planning
This section describes the pilgrimage route (Chemin St Jacques) across the border from St-Jean-Pied-de-Port to the monastery at Roncesvalles. From Roncesvalles, the section describes a brief shortcut to join the GR11 which is then followed through the Western Pyrenees (this part of the book) and the Central Pyrenees (Part 4 of the book). There are numerous places to cross from the French to the Spanish Pyrenees (or vice versa), either to add some variety to your itinerary, or simply to make sense of your transport plans. The route across the border from St-Jean-Pied-de-Port is just one of these places. Others (eg via the Col de Palas (described above) or the Col d'Arratille (described in Part 4)) are mentioned in the text, where appropriate.

Chemin St Jacques – The Way of St James
Although pilgrims walking to Santiago de Compostela begin their journey from many places, St-Jean-Pied-de-Port is where the trails tend to converge, and where many walkers choose to make a start. The route to the shrine of St James (the French know him as St Jacques) is an ancient one, known locally as the Chemin St Jacques, and given the status of a footpath – the Grande Randonnée 65.

In mid summer, walking the Chemin is a truly international experience; some people have travelled across the world to make the pilgrimage. While many pilgrims are devoted Catholics, others complete the walk for a variety of reasons. For most there is an element of spirituality, even if only because walking every day for three weeks allows plenty of time to think. There's no need for it to be a religious experience, though; the GR65 offers some lovely walking across the north-west of Spain.

Map 20 – St-Jean-Pied-de-Port to France/Spain border 127

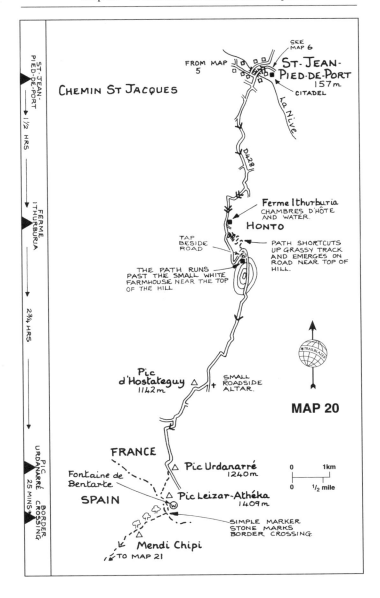

CHEMIN ST JACQUES

ST-JEAN-PIED-DE-PORT
157m

FROM MAP 5

SEE MAP 6

CITADEL

La Nive

D428

Ferme Ithurburia
CHAMBRES D'HÔTE
AND WATER.

HONTO

TAP BESIDE ROAD

PATH SHORTCUTS UP GRASSY TRACK AND EMERGES ON ROAD NEAR TOP OF HILL.

THE PATH RUNS PAST THE SMALL WHITE FARMHOUSE NEAR THE TOP OF THE HILL

Pic d'Hostateguy
1142m

SMALL ROADSIDE ALTAR.

TRAILBLAZER

MAP 20

FRANCE

△ Pic Urdanarré
1240m

Fontaine de Bentarte

SPAIN

△ Pic Leizar-Athéka
1409m

0   1km

0   ½ mile

SIMPLE MARKER STONE MARKS BORDER CROSSING.

Mendi Chipi

TO MAP 21

ST-JEAN-PIED-DE-PORT

1½ HRS

FERME ITHURBURIA

2¾ HRS

PIC URDANARRÉ

25 MINS

BORDER CROSSING

Chanson de Roland and Pyrenean folklore

Little is known about the Battle of Roncesvalles, fought in 778, in which the rearguard of Charlemagne's army was attacked and decimated by the Basques as it crossed the Ibañeta Pass. Nonetheless, the battle is one of the most famous of the early Middle Ages, owing to the work of the poet who immortalized it in the *Chanson de Roland*.

The poem's central character is Roland, commander of the rearguard, who too late sounds his horn to summon help from the main body of the army, a tragic delay that leads to the massacre of the élite of Charlemagne's knights. For his part in the tale Roland has passed into Pyrenean folklore. In the central Pyrenees, the Brèche de Roland (see p277) is said to have been formed when the hero, after a struggle with the Moors, found himself in a tight corner, and slashed a hole through the mountains with his sword, Durandal.

Nearly ten kilometres down the valley is a rock said to bear the hoof prints of his horse, as it leapt down from the newly-made hole in the ridge. At the battle of Roncesvalles, legend has it, Roland, overcome by the enemy, flung his sword in the air. The spot where it landed is still proudly marked by one of the villages on the plain below.

SAINT-JEAN-PIED-DE-PORT → RONCESVALLES
[MAP 20, p127 & MAP 21, p129]

Although the scenery is not particularly remarkable and most of the walk over the hills into Spain is along lanes or rough roads, interest is amply provided by the historical links of the area, and by the presence of the other pilgrims. The route is marked in a variety of ways. The most prominent and frequent markings are the red and white paint markings of the GR65 (the French have given the pilgrimage route the status of a long distance footpath and numbered it the GR65). The other key colour is yellow – yellow arrows painted on trees, wooden arrows with a carved cockleshell (*la coquille St Jacques*) and a yellow tip, or yellow stickers on the telegraph poles.

The initial part of the route is different from that shown on the IGN 1:50,000 map. The Chemin leaves St-Jean-Pied-de-Port along the Route de St Michel and goes south on the D428, a winding tarmac lane which climbs steadily to around 900m. A couple of kilometres before the top of the hill, at **Honto**, there are chambres d'hôte at *Ferme Ithurburia* (☎ 05.59.37.11.17). The farm is run by Mme Jeanne Ourtiague, double rooms cost €37/240F and an evening meal costs €13/85F. Above Honto, the path takes a shortcut, winding up a steep grassy track before rejoining the

---

(Opposite) The Aguas Tuertas valley (see p144) is undoubtedly one of the most memorable places in the Spanish Western Pyrenees. This ancient dolmen adds to the sense of timelessness. (Photo © Simon Mills).

Map 21 – France/Spain border to Roncesvalles 129

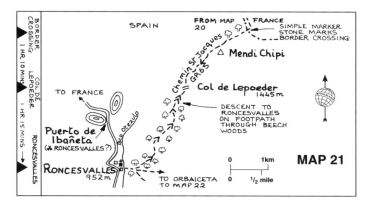

lane. Near where the path meets the tarmac there's a tap by the roadside, which provides a welcome chance to fill up with water (though it would be wise to treat the water before drinking it). From here continue along the road all the way to the **Pic Urdanarré (1240m)**, where you finally leave the lane for a footpath.

Beyond this point, the walk becomes more attractive, passing alongside and then through beech woods. Approximately 20 minutes after leaving the road by the Pic Urdanarré, the path passes the Fontaine de Bentarté, which provides another chance to fill up with water.Shortly after this the path crosses the border, which is marked by a stone, carved with the word 'Navarre'. From here, the path climbs slowly to the **Col de Lepoeder**. The route downhill to the monastery is through attractive beech woods.

RONCESVALLES
The **monastery** at Roncesvalles has been of considerable importance ever since the pilgrimage route to Santiago became firmly established in the twelfth century. The church of the monastery was originally built by the Navarrese monarch, Sancho el Fuerte at the beginning of the thirteenth century.

Next to the church, in the chapter house, is Sancho's mausoleum; the enormous statue of the king, which lies on top of the tomb, is said to be life-size. The stained glass window in the south wall of the chapter house shows Sancho at the battle of Las Navas de Tolosa (1212). The complex also houses a museum, a visitors' centre and a tourist office. Many pilgrims attend evening Mass in the cathedral church (timings are displayed), which is said to be very impressive.

(Opposite) Top: The beautiful Lac d'Arrémoulit, with the incredibly remote refuge perched beside it. **Bottom:** Although the younger generation has left many of the mountain villages, traditional life still goes on. This man, one of only 14 permanent residents in Estaon (see p250), is stripping bark for basket making.

RONCESVALLES (cont)
Services
If you need a taxi, try **Pedro Tellechea** (☎ 948-76 00 07, mobile 629 87 81 81). Unlike some other operators, he actually has set fares on a tariff card. He charges €36/6000ptas to Pamplona and €21/3500ptas to St-Jean-Pied-de-Port. He's a great character, who makes a fair bit of money transporting pilgrims who've decided to cheat.

Where to stay
Almost all pilgrims sleep in the accommodation provided within the monastery, but there are a couple of other places to stay if you don't fancy being crowded into the tiny dormitory. Just below the monastery is **La Posada** (☎ 948-76.02.25) a hotel/restaurant which has single rooms from €30/5040ptas and double rooms from €39/6500ptas. **Hostal Casa Sabina** next to the monastery has a few modern and very pleasant double rooms for €37/6200ptas.

In the northern courtyard of the monastery is the **Albergue Juvenil de Roncesvalles** (☎ 948-76.03.02) which has accommodation for 80 people in clean, modern dormitories. With a YHA card it's €9/1500ptas per night if you're under 26 years old, or €12/1900ptas if you're over 26. Even if you don't have a YHA card it's worth trying to see whether they'll allow you to stay. In 2000 they were underbooked and would allow anyone (YHA membership or not) to stay for one night at the standard membership rates. In comparison with the pilgrims' accommodation it's expensive but it's more civilized: there is plenty of space, washing facilities are good, and you don't have to wait till late afternoon to be admitted. The **pilgrims' accommodation** is controlled by the monastery, and the office opens from 10.00-13.00 and then after 16.00 in the afternoon. Visitors are allowed to stay for only one night and the system is rather regimented, but it's free (visitors are requested to make a contribution) so you really can't complain. The lights are turned out at 22.00 and all pilgrims must be out by 08.00 the next morning.

Where to eat
Food is available in the **Albergue Juvenil** if you're staying there, but for most people the choice is between the **Hostal Casa Sabina** and **La Posada**, both of which are next to the monastery. Normally both have cheap deals for pilgrims, although predictably the food is nothing special. If you can afford a little more, the 'tourist menu' at La Posada isn't cheap but is solid value at €11/1875ptas.

RONCESVALLES → EMBALSE (RESERVOIR) DE IRABIA [MAP 22, p131]

From the monastery retrace your steps 400m eastwards, along the previous day's route, to the point where the GR65 turns uphill on an earthen path, leaving the rough forestry road,. Don't follow the GR65, but instead take the rough road for 15-20 minutes, ignoring a left fork after 10-15 minutes, until the track meets another forestry road. Turn left along the new track, cross a small bridge, and follow the track for a kilometre as it climbs to the **Collado de Nabala** (1000m approx). There's a gate at the col, and just on the far side of it a concrete drainage duct has 'a Fabrica 9k' painted on it, with an arrow pointing north-east.

Follow the forestry track north-eastwards for about a kilometre, until it swings south-east and descends to a large trail junction at the base of a

Map 22 – Roncesvalles to Embalse (Reservoir) de Irabia 131

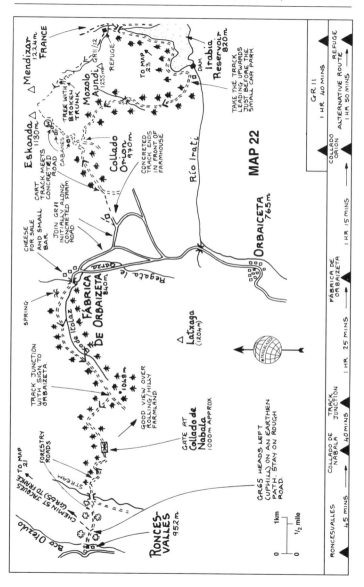

small hill (spot height 1048m on the map). A signpost here points left to: 'Fa ORBAIZETA'. This is the route to follow. Don't be tempted to take the path, shown on maps, which continues over the top of Latxaga (1204m) and appears to be a short cut to Orbaiceta; it starts off promisingly but peters out near the top of the hill. You then have to traipse back to this junction again.

From the junction, a stony vehicle track leads downhill through the trees for 5-6km. The latter half of the walk alongside the Bco de Itolaz is pretty and just before arriving at **Fábrica de Orbaizeta** there's a small spring on the left, a good opportunity to fill up with water. Fábrica de Orbaizeta is for the most part a fairly ramshackle collection of buildings, although three or four houses have recently been renovated. Cheese (and sometimes bread) is for sale at one of the houses (there's a notice on the door) and there's a small bar which sells drinks and sandwiches.

ORBAICETA

One option from Fábrica de Orbaizeta is to go south along the road to Orbaiceta, where there is accommodation.

Camping Irati (☎ 948-76.60.74) has a restaurant and shop. Casas Rurales include: *Casa Alzat* (☎ 948-76.05.55), *Casa Etzangio* 948-76.60.14), *Casa* *Mujurdin* (☎ 948-76.60.46), and *Casa Sastrarena* (☎ 948-76.60.93). Prices for a double room in all of the above range from €19/3200ptas to €24/4000ptas; all of them do breakfast but Casa Sastrarena is the only one where an evening meal is available.

The GR11 and GR12 pass through Fábrica de Orbaizeta and are marked clearly with red and white paint. They leave the hamlet on a concrete road which is followed for over a kilometre until it comes to an end in front of a farmhouse. Continue past the front of the house and beyond it join an old cart track. Follow this through the woods for 20-25 minutes, until it descends to meet a concrete road. Turn left along the road and follow it as it climbs slowly eastwards to the **Collado Orion (970m)**.

At the col there's a road/track junction and sign. From here you have a choice.

GR11

The GR11 leaves the concrete road at the Collado Orion and follows the rough road which zigzags up the hillside to the north of the signpost. After 5 minutes the track levels out and passes a shepherd's hut on the left. Beyond this it starts to climb again and after a further 5-10 minutes passes, on the left, a small hut with a corrugated iron roof. Here the GR11 leaves the rough road, descending on a grassy path to the right, and almost immediately passes another hut, beside which is a water source. The path, which is very poorly marked in this area, contours around a spur and, remaining just above the trees, crosses a tiny re-entrant before climbing towards the the grassy col between Mendizar (1224m) and

Pamplona

Pamplona, the ancient capital of Navarre, is a fascinating place. Easily accessible from both Roncesvalles and Ochagavia, it makes a memorable excursion from any walking itinerary in this area.

The city is famous for the annual fiesta of San Firmin, which takes place in the second week of July. The week-long festival is well known not only for the bull fights but also for the time-honoured tradition of **bull-running**. According to age-old custom, the bulls are herded through the heavily barricaded streets to the bull ring, and large numbers of brave (or crazy) participants dare to run through the streets with them. The ultimate adrenalin rush: the aim to get close but obviously not too close. Every year a few people get it wrong: if they're lucky it's simply a case of severe panic and some bruises but it's not unusual for runners to be badly injured or even killed.

Apart from the bulls, the fiesta is an excuse for a massive party. For a full week the town is packed to capacity and celebrations go on non-stop. If you plan to visit the festival, book somewhere to stay as far in advance as possible; turning up and expecting to find somewhere for the night is sure to end in disappointment. Above all pack some extra stamina. Ernest Hemingway summed up the atmosphere of the event in the novel *Fiesta*: 'The fiesta was really started. It kept up day and night for seven days. The dancing kept up, the drinking kept up, the noise went on. The things that happened could only have happened during a fiesta'.

Eskanda (1130m). Just below the col a couple of GR markings direct you onto a narrow and overgrown path which contours around the south slope of Mendizar. About 25 minutes after passing the col, the path, which has remained well above the trees up to this point, descends to meet the treeline. Look for a large tree with a broken trunk, on which there is a very faded GR marker. Go down into the woods near this tree to find the path. It's poorly marked and hard to distinguish at first but soon becomes clearer. After ten minutes' steep descent through the trees the path crosses a stream and becomes much easier to follow. A further 20-30 minutes' walking brings you to the *refuge* at the north end of the Embalse de Irabia. The hut is dirty and basic and could sleep five people at most, but the area is beautiful, and if you have a tent it's an ideal spot for (unofficial) camping.

Alternative route

A possible alternative route from Collado Orion, easier to find but longer, is to follow the road down to the reservoir and then walk around the shore. The road down to the barrage is rather long and tedious. Near the dam there's a small car park, and just before it a track leads uphill to the left. This route follows around the side of the reservoir and finally, 200m past the bridge (Puente de la Cuestión) at the northern end, comes to the *refuge* (see above).

EMBALSE (RESERVOIR) DE IRABIA → OCHAGAVIA [MAP 23]

From the refuge, the GR11 goes 200m south and crosses to the eastern side of the reservoir via the Puente de la Cuestión. On the far side of the bridge a sign points the way southwards: CASAS DE IRATI 1H 05; note that this timing is wildly optimistic: unless you're jogging it takes about 1¹/₂ hours. Follow the vehicle track all the way around the eastern side of the lake to the **Casas de Irati**, where there's a spring (this is a good opportunity to fill up with water) a car park and a tiny information booth but nothing else.

To get to Ochagavia from here the obvious option is to remain on the GR11. Because of problems locating the path I, however, ended up taking a shortcut uphill to join the GR11 near the Paso de las Alforjas. The following paragraph is a description of my alternative route – you may prefer to find your own.

Heading south from the Casas de Irati, I followed the road for 1500m past the first two major bends, before reaching, on the left of the road, a small area which had recently been cleared of trees. From this clearing two wide tracks had been bulldozed up the hillside, one of them widening an existing path (on the Editorial Alpina, 1:40,000 map it runs through the 's' of 'Bosque'). Take the right hand track and follow it as it climbs southwards, running straight up the hillside. After half an hour's steep climbing the track meets a loose surfaced forestry road (shown on the Editorial Alpina map) by a sharp bend.

On the other side of the forestry road, a clear footpath continues uphill, climbing gently at first, but becoming gradually steeper. Approximately 1500m beyond the forestry road, there's a fork in the path. I took the right fork. After three or four minutes, on the left of the path, there's a clear avenue running directly up the hillside between the plantations of beech trees. The partly-rocky, partly-grassy avenue leads steeply straight up the hillside until, after 5-10 minutes' climb you emerge above the trees on the north slope of Abodi Oeste, just below the summit. If you climb a little way up the grassy hillside you pass near to a large metal cow trough and find a few red and white GR markers on the rocks. The exact route of the GR11 around the north slope of Abodi Oeste is hard to locate, as the hillside is covered with numerous sheep tracks, but if you contour around the slope, remaining above the treeline, you soon arrive at the **Paso de las Alforjas (1430m)**, a grassy col with two large dips in the ground. If you have a little time to spare this is a great place to take a break. There are excellent views to the south and north and the route onwards to Ochagavia is all downhill from here.

A sign at the Paso points the way to Ochagavia. From the sign, go south-east past the large flat rock, and beyond it find a small building with a GR marking on the wall. Turn left (south-east) just before the building

Map 23 – Embalse (Reservoir) de Irabia to Ochagavia 135

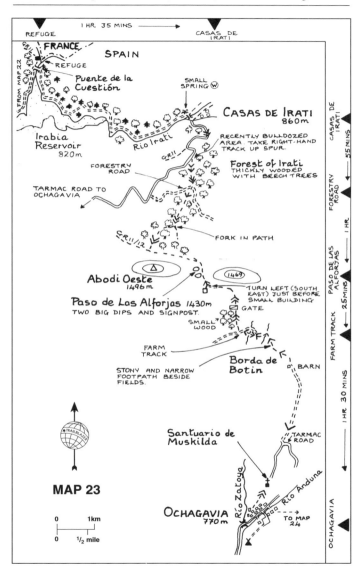

MAP 23

and follow the path as it gradually descends across the hillside. After a few minutes the path turns directly downhill and passes through a gate before descending a short way further to meet a farm track. The GR11 goes left on the track, which soon narrows to become a stony footpath, skirting the fields.

At the **Borda de Botin** you pass a barn and join a vehicle track, which runs south for 1500m to a tarmac road. Turn right along the road, and soon you come to the **Santuario de Muskilda**, a pretty little church with a conical roof on the tower. The path runs through the buildings and then down a steep and seemingly endless trail to Ochagavia.

OCHAGAVIA

Ochagavia is a sleepy, red-roofed village with several useful facilities.

Hostal Aunamendi (☎ 948-89 01.89) is right on the main square and has very pleasant single rooms from €30/5000ptas and doubles from €41/6800ptas. Also worth trying is the *Hostal Ori-Alde* (☎ 948-89.00.27) where doubles are €32/ 5300ptas. Both hotels have a restaurant.

There are a number of Casas Rurales, including *Casa Aisko* (☎ 948-89.03.30), *Casa Ballent* (☎ 948-89.03 73), *Casa Dukea* (☎ 948-89.00.62) and *Casa Eloico* (☎ 948-89.04.64). Double rooms in all of the above cost €21/ 3500ptas.

Camping Osate (☎ 948-89.01.84), five minutes walk from the main square, is a little run-down, but otherwise perfectly OK. Camping charges are €3/500ptas per person and €2.70/ 450ptas per tent. There's a reasonable restaurant/bar and a very poorly-stocked shop.

The **tourist office** ☎/🖳 948-89.06.41) is open 10.00-14.00 and 16.30-19.30 (except Sundays and holidays: 10.00-14.00). The **post office** is near the church (behind the tourist office). There are three **cash dispensers** and one small **bank** which is open Monday to Friday, mornings only.

There is a daily **bus** (not Sundays) to Pamplona, which leaves Ochagavia at 07.00.

OCHAGAVIA → ISABA [MAP 24]

The GR11 stage from Ochagavia to Isaba is rather dull, being mostly along a single rough road. By way of consolation, the Ermita Idoya is beautiful and Isaba is a very attractive little village in which to stop for the night. Moreover the following day's stage, over Ezkaurre (2049m), is excellent.

From the main square in Ochagavia, go up the east bank of the Río Anduña, past the building with 'Exposicion' written on the front of it. Pass to the left of another building which bears the words 'Estacion Patateria', and, on the wall of the building, a faded GR marking. The road swings right and becomes a rough track climbing north-eastwards. Although there are few route markers throughout the rest of the day, basically you follow this track almost all the way to Isaba.

The track makes a couple of large zigzags up the hillside and after 40 minutes passes a couple of old barns. At the barns the track swings left and continues to climb at an easy gradient, with occasional shade from

Map 24 – Ochagavia to Isaba   137

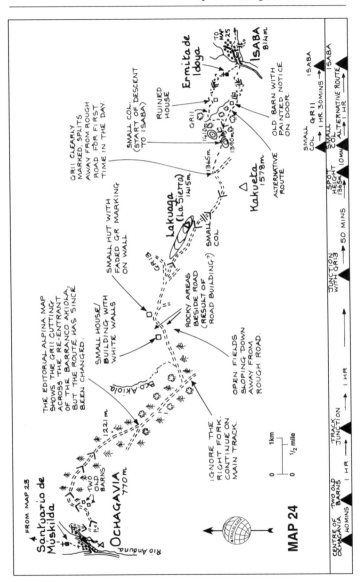

FROM MAP 23

Santuario de Muskilda

OCHAGAVIA 770m.

Rio Anduña

TWO OLD BARNS

1221m.

Bco. Akiola

IGNORE THE RIGHT FORK. CONTINUE ON MAIN TRACK.

THE EDITORIAL ALPINA MAP SHOWS THE GR11 CUTTING ACROSS THE RE-ENTRANT OF THE BARRANCO AKIOLA, BUT THE ROUTE HAS SINCE BEEN CHANGED.

OPEN FIELDS SLOPING DOWN AWAY FROM ROUGH ROAD.

ROCKY AREAS BESIDE ROAD (RESULT OF ROAD BUILDING?)

SMALL HOUSE/ BUILDING WITH WHITE WALLS

SMALL HUT WITH FADED G.R MARKING ON WALL.

GR11

Lakuaga (La Sierra) 1415m.

SMALL COL

Kakueta 1578m.

ALTERNATIVE ROUTE

GR11 CLEARLY MARKED. SPLITS AWAY FROM ROUGH ROAD FOR FIRST TIME IN THE DAY.

1365m.

1390m.

1410m.

SMALL COL. (START OF DESCENT TO ISABA)

GR11

RUINED HOUSE

Ermita de Idoya

OLD BARN WITH PAINTED NOTICE ON DOOR.

TO MAP 25

ISABA 814m.

MAP 24

1km
0
0   ½ mile

CENTRE OF OCHAGAVIA		TWO OLD BARNS		TRACK JUNCTION		JUNCTION WITH GR13		SPOT HEIGHT 1365m		SMALL COL		SMALL COL		ISABA
	40MINS		1 HR		1 HR		50 MINS		10MINS				GR11 1 HR 30MINS		
										ALTERNATIVE ROUTE 1 HR					

blocks of pine trees on either side. Gradually it swings round to the right to head south-eastwards and, about an hour beyond the barns, you come to a junction with another rough road. Continue south-eastwards passing, after about 15 minutes, a fork to the right, which you should ignore. Carry on along the main track as it swings around to head in a north-easterly direction. After a further 20 minutes the track leads past a small house on the left and ten minutes beyond this passes another tiny building with a very faded GR marker on the wall. A couple of minutes beyond this building there's another fork. Go left, and follow the track, which now climbs gently in a east-south-easterly direction to meet another rough road (the route of the GR13) at a very sharp bend.

A sign points the way from here straight up the rough road heading east-south-east. This soon passes around the south slope of Lakuaga (La Sierra) (1415m) and then, having descended a little to a small col, passes around the north side of Kakueta (1578m). At a point where the rough road bends sharply right to pass around the east slope of Kakueta, a handful of very clear painted markers direct the GR11 away from the rough road for the first time in the day. Follow the markers down an earthy track to the left before the footpath swings right to pass across a couple of grassy mounds to a small col. From here the GR11 heads down through young beech woods on a well established path. From the start of this descent there are two alternative routes down to Isaba.

GR11

Some 10-15 minutes after starting down through the trees, as the main path settles into an easy descent, the GR11 turns sharply left off the path without warning and with almost no marking. Keep a careful look out into the trees on the left of the path and you can just make out some red and white GR markings painted on the trunks of trees set well back from the path. Once you've spotted the turning itself, the GR11 is easy to follow as it doubles back sharply and heads northwards on a tiny earthen footpath. After 20 minutes the footpath crosses a stream and descends steeply through an area of overgrown bushes to pass a ruined building. The path doubles back sharply to the left and, after descending through more bushes, leads steeply downhill though woods. Half an hour after passing the ruined building you come to the beautiful **Ermita de Idoya**. Allow a little time here if possible. The immaculately tended garden, the small church and the whole setting make it a very special place. To continue down to Isaba, go through the arch, past the door of the church, and follow the stony footpath down to the village, which you'll reach 20 minutes after leaving the ermita.

Alternative route

If you miss the GR11 turning 10-15 minutes after starting down from the col, you needn't necessarily turn back to look for it; continuing on down the main path from the col, you soon pass a building on the left of the path, with the words 'Por Favor Cerrar la Puerta' painted on the door. Follow straight down the path which, although slightly overgrown in places, also leads straight down to Isaba, though it gets you there rather quicker than the GR11 route. Unfortunately by coming this way you'll miss the Ermita de Idoya.

ISABA

Isaba is an attractive village with a few useful shops, a tourist office and lots of places to stay and eat.

The smartest hotel in Isaba is the modern and rather soulless *Hotel Isaba* ☆☆☆ (☎ 948-89.30.00; 🖹 948-89.30 30) where a single room costs €40/ 6700ptas and a double goes for €58/ 9600ptas. A cheaper alternative is the *Hotel Ezkaurre* ☆ (☎ 948-89.33.03; 🖹 948-89.33.02).

There are several other hotels and hostals – contact the tourist office for details. Also worth considering for accommodation are the dozen or so Casas Rurales in the village. These include *Casa Francisco Mayo* (☎ 948-89.31.66) where French and English are spoken; *Casa Garatxandi* (☎ 948-89.32.61); *Casa Idoya* (☎ 948-89.32.49) and *Casa Inés* (☎ 948-89.31.55). All charge around €21/3500ptas for a double room (more if you want a room with an attached bathroom).

Isaba also has a **cash dispenser** and several useful shops. The **tourist office** (☎ 948-89.32.51, 🖳 www.surf.to/isaba) has plenty of information about facilities in the area.

ISABA → ZURIZA   [MAP 25, p141]

This is a really enjoyable day, the highpoint of which is undoubtedly the scramble to the top of Ezkaurre and the steep descent on the far side. If the weather is poor, however, or if any member of the party is likely to be uneasy with scrambling it might be wise to take an alternative route, possibly looping to the north, to avoid the crossing of Ezkaurre.

From the main road through Isaba, just above the area of the phone boxes, take a right fork down Calle Barrikata, a narrow cobbled street. Soon the road narrows to a footpath and this brings you to the tiny **Ermita de Belén**, where the path forks. Take the left fork and follow the narrow and occasionally overgrown path for 15 minutes until it descends to meet a rough road. Turn left and go eastwards along it for quarter of an hour, climbing steadily, to arrive at a junction with another rough road, just before a small gorge. A sign here indicates that the area is the **Ateas de Belabarze (920m)**. Cross the bridge and follow the road heading southeast until it comes to an end at a widened car park like area.

From the end of this rough road, the GR11 does **not**, as marked on the Editorial Alpina map, continue south-eastwards straight up the valley. Instead it makes a large loop, climbing up the spur to the south, before swinging north, back towards Ezkaurre. (See overleaf for the alternative route from here).

From the car park area, head down the short vehicle track and cross the stream. On the far side, follow the track as it climbs steeply in a north

❏ **An alternative route**

If you're feeling adventurous, the route as marked on the EA map should be quite possible but you'll need a compass as the path becomes difficult to follow. From the car park area a footpath climbs straight up the steep earth bank at the eastern end. The path remains fairly clear most of the way up the valley, at least until it has crossed the second stream marked on the EA map. After about 45 minutes it reaches a large open grassy area. From here the path is difficult to find and you'll need to set a compass bearing to follow through the relatively small area of trees and up to the col over the grassy hillside.

westerly direction. Ignore two left turns, but at the third left turning, follow the path as it doubles back and climbs in a south-easterly direction. A couple of faded GR markings near this turning help to reassure you that you're on track.

Follow this track as it climbs through trees until, after 10 minutes or so, the line of fencing on the right suddenly bends away from the track, at the corner of the enclosure. Leave the track here and follow a path alongside the fence for 100-200 metres, and as the fence bends around to the right continue with it for another 100 or so metres. The GR11 then splits left, away from the fence, climbing through bracken to join a steep track. This track climbs through trees for 10 minutes to a grassy area, in the middle of which is the ruin of an old building.

The GR11 goes south-west from the ruin and climbs through trees, following a few faded paint markers on the tree trunks. It crosses another grassy area and on the far side joins a very steep old earthen track which climbs in a southerly direction.There are only one or two faded paint markings as you go up this track, but after 10-15 minutes' hard climbing you arrive at another grassy area which also has a ruined building in the middle of it. Head straight across the grass, leaving the building just to your right, and follow the footpath as it runs through pine trees and along the top of a spur. Soon the path levels out and contours along the north slope of the hillside before emerging above the trees at a fine viewpoint from which you can pick out most of the remaining route to the base of Ezkaurre.

Don't allow yourself to be tempted by the two or three obvious paths leading away from this point across the hillside, as they all gradually lose height. The GR11 climbs a little further from this point, to follow a route which stays high, passing above the trees as you go round the side of the Berueta valley before arriving at the grassy col (1650m) at the end of it.

Go north from the col, heading directly over a small hillock, and then passing to the right of a second hillock and straight over a third beyond that, to reach a tiny tarn, the **Ibón de Ezkaurre (1680m)**. Some paint markings on the west side of the tarn point the way to the start of the

Map 25 – Isaba to Zuriza 141

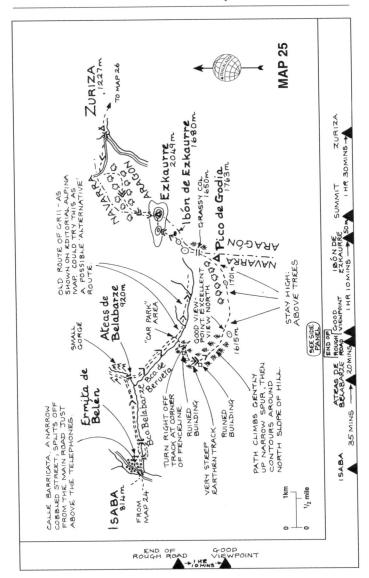

ZURIZA .1227m
TO MAP 26

MAP 25

OLD ROUTE OF GR11 - AS
SHOWN ON EDITORIAL ALPINA
MAP. COULD TRY THIS AS
A POSSIBLE ALTERNATIVE
ROUTE.

NAVARRA

ARAGÓN

Ezkaurre 2049m

Ibón de Ezkaurre 1680m

GRASSY COL 1650m

Pico de Godia 1763m

NAVARRA

ARAGÓN

1701m

STAY HIGH:
ABOVE TREES

SEE SIDE PANEL

Atxas de Belabarze 920m

SMALL GORGE

"CAR PARK" AREA

GOOD VIEW-POINT: EXCELLENT VIEW NORTH

1615m

Ermita de Belen

Bco Belabarze

Bco de Beruela

TURN RIGHT OFF
TRACK AT CORNER
OF FENCELINE.

RUINED BUILDING

VERY STEEP
EARTHEN TRACK

RUINED BUILDING

PATH CLIMBS GENTLY
UP NARROW SPUR, THEN
CONTOURS AROUND
NORTH SLOPE OF HILL.

CALLE BARRICATA, A NARROW
COBBLED STREET, SPLITS OFF
FROM THE MAIN ROAD JUST
ABOVE THE TELEPHONES.

ISABA 814m

FROM MAP 24

1km
0

½ mile
0

END OF
ROUGH ROAD
►1 HR
10 MINS

GOOD
VIEWPOINT

ISABA
35 MINS ►

ATXAS DE
BELABARZE
20 MINS ►

END OF
ROUGH
ROAD

GOOD
VIEWPOINT
1 HR 10 MINS ►

IBÓN DE
EZKAURRE
50 m ►

SUMMIT
1 HR 30 MINS ►

ZURIZA

scramble up the peak. The route up the side of Ezkaurre, mostly up a gully, is clearly marked with red and white GR markings. The ascent is not tricky and should be easily within most people's ability though possibly is not suitable in early summer if there's still snow, or if conditions are very wet. Once at the top of the scramble the path swings right to reach the concrete summit cairn of **Ezkaurre (2049m)**.

The descent from Ezkaurre starts in a roughly north-north-westerly direction with a large cairn helping to indicate the way. After ten minutes or so down a steep rocky path the gradient increases and there's an extremely steep section which leads down to a grassy shoulder at the top of a spur. Here the GR11 enters a dense beech wood through which it continues to descend very steeply on a narrow but well worn path. Approximately 40 minutes after entering the beech wood the trail levels off and emerges near the road and a large colourful sign which marks the border between Navarre and Aragón. Turn right down the road for a few metres, before heading off to the left on a footpath that parallels it for a short distance.

Eventually the path leads you back to the wood a short distance below the campsite. *Camping Zuriza* (☎ 974-37.01.96, 37.00.77) is a large place with good facilities including a reasonably well stocked shop (which keeps only puncture-type gas cylinders), bar and restaurant. There's also a guesthouse with 10 double rooms (€27/4500ptas, or €36/6000ptas with attached bathroom), and a hostel with 70 bunks in a clean but slightly crowded dormitory. A bed for the night in the hostel costs €6/1000ptas.

ZURIZA → SELBA D'OZA [MAP 26]

This day stage, ending at Selba d'Oza, is still included in the 'official' GR11 itinerary but may not actually be very relevant any more. The only reason for diverting to Selba d'Oza was the campsite and shop, but these are currently closed and show no signs of opening in the near future. Before starting from Zuriza ask around as to whether the facilities in Selba d'Oza are open again. If not it will be probably be better to continue beyond the Plano de la Mina for another couple of hours and find a place to camp around Aguas Tuertas.

From the campsite at Zuriza follow the rough road east-south-eastwards, as it climbs very gently, with the Barranco de Taxera on the right-hand side. After half an hour the road arrives at a car park area, beyond which it bends sharply to the right and crosses the stream via a concrete bridge. The GR11 splits off to the left here on a footpath which climbs past a small iron cross and, just above this, a ruined stone hut. Twenty minutes after leaving the car park area you come to the *Refugio de Taxera* **(1410m)**. The doors to both rooms have long since been removed and the floors are thick with animal dung; this is not a place to stay except in an emergency.

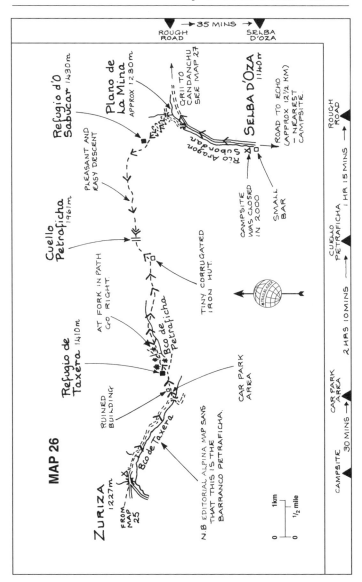

Map 26 – Zuriza to Selba d'Oza 143

MAP 26

Zuriza 1227m.
FROM MAP 25

Bco de Taxera

N.B EDITORIAL ALPINA MAP SAYS THAT THIS IS THE BARRANCO PETRAFICHA.

RUINED BUILDING

Refugio de Taxera 1410m.

AT FORK IN PATH GO RIGHT

Bco de Petraficha

CAR PARK AREA

TINY CORRUGATED IRON HUT.

Cuello Petraficha 1961m.

Refugio d'O Sabucar 1430m.

Plano de la Mina APPROX 1230m.

PLEASANT AND EASY DESCENT

Refugio d'O Sabucar 1430m.

GRILL TO CANDANCHU SEE MAP 27

Río Aragón Subordán

Selba d'Oza 1140m.

ROAD TO ECHO (APPROX 12½ KM) – NEAREST CAMPSITE.

CAMPSITE WAS CLOSED IN 2000

SMALL BAR

ROUGH ROAD → 35 MINS →
ROUGH ROAD   SELBA D'OZA

0 ——— 1km
0 ——— ½ mile

CAMPSITE — 30 MINS → CAR PARK AREA — 2 HRS 10 MINS → CUELLO PETRAFICHA — 1 HR 15 MINS → ROUGH ROAD

From the refuge climb north-eastwards on a footpath which has a few faded red and white GR markings. After 7-8 minutes the path enters an area of trees and levels out. After a further 2-3 minutes there's a fork; go right. The path soon leaves the trees and descends across the grassy hillside to pass alongside a stream bed (dry in late July). From here it climbs up the left side of a gully and contours around a rocky slope, before continuing upwards over grass. After passing a small corrugated iron shed on the right, the trail leads around a rocky outcrop and up to the **Cuello Petraficha (1961m)**.

With the exception of the first ten minutes of descent, during which the GR11 heads down a steep and rocky path, the way down from the col is mostly across grassy slopes covered with Merendera and Pyrenean Irises. In a couple of places the path becomes indistinct, but look out for some marks on low rocks. Approximately 50 minutes after leaving the col you come to a large grassy area near an old building, the ***Refugio d'O Sabucar* (1430m)** (which again is doorless and unsuitable for overnight shelter). Although the path is unmarked across this area, continue south-eastwards, towards the road and large barn seen below, and you soon pick up the path again, as it descends in long easy zigzags to meet the road at the area known as **Plano de la Mina (1230m approx)**. Turn right (south-west) and walk along the rough road, which soon crosses the river and joins the main road coming up from Selba d'Oza. If you are heading for Selba d'Oza, turn right and follow the tarmac road for half an hour. Apart from the campsite and shop (both currently closed) Selba d'Oza boasts a small bar which serves drinks and snacks (though it too may be closed outside peak season). If the campsite at Selba d'Oza is closed the nearest campsite is at Echo, some 13km down the road.

SELBA D'OZA → CANDANCHÚ   [MAP 27 p145, MAP 28 p147]

If you walked down the road to Selba d'Oza to make an overnight stop, the first half hour of the day is spent walking back up the tarmac to the point, just across the river from **Plano de la Mina (1230m approx),** where the rough road bends eastwards and starts to head up the Guarrinza valley. Follow this rough road for about $1^3/_4$ hours, as it climbs steadily east south eastwards. Near the end of the valley the road makes three or four long zigzags to climb the steep slope ahead, while the GR11 simply shortcuts up the hillside. At the top, just past an old refuge building (pretty filthy), you'll look down upon the beautiful plain of **Aguas Tuertas**. Although camping is probably not strictly allowed, there's ample opportunity to camp here as long as you're unobtrusive about it.

Follow the clearly marked path southwards, remaining on the west side of the Barranco de la Rueda. About halfway down the valley the markers disappear, but the route is fairly well trodden and is easy to discern. Near the south end of the plain the path finally crosses the stream

Map 27 – Selba d'Oza to Ibón d'Estanés 145

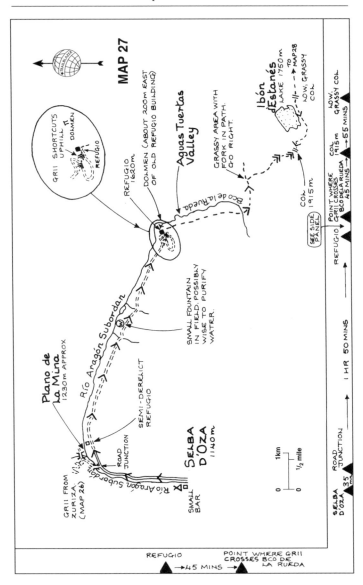

MAP 27

GRII SHORTCUTS UPHILL
DOLMEN
REFUGIO

REFUGIO 1620m
DOLMEN (ABOUT 200m EAST OF OLD REFUGIO BUILDING)

Aguas Tuertas Valley

Bco de la Rueda

GRASSY AREA WITH FORK IN PATH. GO RIGHT.

Ibón d'Estanés
LAKE 1750m
TO → MAP 28
LOW, GRASSY COL

SEE SIDE PANEL

COL 1915m

LOW, GRASSY COL

POINT WHERE GRII CROSSES BCO DE LA RUEDA
45 MINS →
← 55 MINS

REFUGIO
← 45 MINS →

Plano de la Mina
1230m APPROX

Río Aragón Subordan

SEMI-DERELICT REFUGIO

SMALL FOUNTAIN IN FIELD. POSSIBLY WISE TO PURIFY WATER.

ROAD JUNCTION

SELBA D'OZA 1140m

GRII FROM ZURIZA. (MAP 26)
Río Aragón Subordán

SMALL BAR

0   1km
0   ½ mile

SELBA D'OZA
35 MINS ►
ROAD JUNCTION
◄——— 1 HR 50 MINS ———►

REFUGIO
▲ →45 MINS →

POINT WHERE GRII CROSSES BCO DE LA RUEDA

and swings left (east). There are faded markers to indicate this. From here the path climbs gently for 5-10 minutes to a grassy area where there's a poorly-marked fork. Go right and follow a well-worn trail which begins to climb more steeply and soon arrives at a rocky-sided bowl with a grassy bottom. The GR11 climbs steeply up the east side of this bowl, below a crag that gives welcome shade even in mid morning. At the top of the climb the path swings left and crosses a rocky **col (1915m)**.

From the col you can see the **Ibón d'Estanés (1750m)**, a popular spot for day walkers and also for campers. The GR11 takes a time-consuming route all the way around the south side of the Ibon before arriving at a low grassy col on the south-east side of the lake. From here, you go eastwards down a wide path, much used by day walkers coming up from the car park below. After about quarter of an hour, at a very well marked junction ('GR11 → ' is painted on a rock), turn right off the large path and follow a footpath which contours south across the grassy hillside. After about 20 minutes the path enters beech woods and starts descending through the trees before coming to a crossing over the Gave d'Aspe where a waterfall and some large rocks make an excellent spot for sunbathing. Beyond the river the path narrows and crosses a steep scree slope (care is needed) before climbing to the **Cuello Causiat (1634m)**. Descend from the col to a rough road and follow this down through an area of deserted ski lifts and buildings to meet the main road through Candanchú.

CANDANCHÚ

Candanchú is a large and unattractive ski resort which, in common with most other Pyrenean ski resorts, feels like a ghost town during the summer. There are, however, enough facilities here to make it a good stopping point.

There's a reasonable choice of places to stay. The smartest place is **Hotel Tobazo** ☆☆☆ (☎974-37.31.25), although it's not strong on ambience. Prices include meals: €28/4620ptas per person for bed and breakfast or €38/6270ptas for a bed and supper. **Hotel Candanchú** (☎ 974-37.30.25; 974-37.30.50), almost directly opposite Hotel Tobazo, is slightly cheaper and generally nicer. Single rooms cost €24/4000ptas and doubles go for €34/5700ptas.

There's a choice of good budget accommodation. From the point where the GR11 meets the main road, walk down the tarmac for 150 metres and take the first road on the right; a short way down here are two excellent lodges. Both **Refugio-Albergue Valle de Aragón** (☎ 974-37.32.22) and **Refugio-Albergue El Aguila** (☎/ 974-37.32.91) are comfortable, friendly and modern and both charge the same prices: €9/1500ptas for the night, or €18/3000ptas for media-pensión.

There's a small **supermarket** just near the point where the GR11 meets the main road. Next to this is a small decrepit-looking bureau de change which has a **cash dispenser**.

Candanchú is a possible place to start or end a walk along the GR11 by virtue of the **bus service** which runs five times a day each way from Canfranc, via Candanchú to Jaca (where there's a railway station). You can get advance details of bus services from the company's website: 🖳 http://mavaragon.com. Buses currently depart daily from Candanchú, heading for Jaca, at 07.16, 10.36, 13.06, 16.06 and 20.36.

Map 28 – Ibón d'Estanés to Candanchú 147

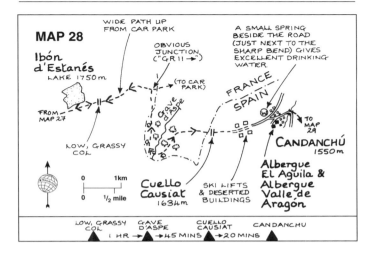

MAP 28

Ibón
d'Estanés
LAKE 1750 m

WIDE PATH UP
FROM CAR PARK

A SMALL SPRING
BESIDE THE ROAD
(JUST NEXT TO THE
SHARP BEND) GIVES
EXCELLENT DRINKING
WATER

OBVIOUS
JUNCTION
("GR11 →")

(TO CAR
PARK)

FRANCE
SPAIN

FROM
MAP 27

LOW, GRASSY
COL

TO
MAP
29

CANDANCHÚ
1550 m

0   1km
0   ½ mile

Cuello
Causiat
1634 m

SKI LIFTS
& DESERTED
BUILDINGS

Albergue
El Aguila &
Albergue
Valle de
Aragón

LOW, GRASSY   GRAVE   CUELLO   CANDANCHU
COL   D'ASPE   CAUSIAT
1 HR →   →45 MINS   →20 MINS

CANDANCHÚ → SALLENT DE GALLEGO   [MAP 29, p149]

From the area in front of Hotel Tobazo, walk down the main road to the
sharp right-hand bend, where the road crosses a bridge over the river. A
signpost on the far side of the bridge points the way for the GR11 (and the
GR65) up a footpath which climbs away from the road and soon meets
another road above. Cross this road and walk up a vehicle track (signposted: 'GR65.3 Santiago, Canfranc, Jaca') which climbs past a telecoms
mast. (Note, if you're using the Editorial Alpina map, that the road layout
appears to be wrongly depicted on the map).

At the end of the rough road go over a small rise and follow an obvious path downhill towards a road bridge over the river. Near the bridge the
path levels out and there's a fork – go right (on the lower path). The path
climbs, passes over a spur, and then swings left and descends to a large
white building, beyond which it joins a rough vehicle track coming up
from the road below. Follow this track past a signposted junction where
the GR65.3 and the southern variant of the GR11 turn off to the right. Just

❑ **Route options**
There are two possible GR11 routes between Candanchú and Sallent de
Gallego, a northern route via the Canal Roya which is considered the 'main'
route and a variant which runs to the south, via the Canal d'Izas. Both routes
take about the same time. The description below is of the main (northern) route.

beyond the junction you catch a glimpse through the trees of a campsite on the other side of the valley. There's no way directly across to the campsite from the path; to get there you need to retrace your steps and walk down the main road a short way.

Continue along the track, which soon passes two possible water points (although there's no indication that the water is fit for drinking). Some 20 minutes beyond the second of these, the track which has been climbing steadily comes to an end. From here follow the footpath which runs along the north bank of the stream to a footbridge. On the far side of the bridge the path climbs gently up to the **Refugio de Lacuars (1550m)**, one room of which is literally a foot deep in decomposing rubbish, making the refuge unsuitable for habitation.

Beyond the building the path climbs fairly steeply for 20-30 minutes before levelling out briefly and then beginning to climb again at a more gentle gradient. Slowly the trail starts to swing around to head south-eastwards and then southwards to arrive at the end of the valley in a grassy area called **Plano d'a Rinconada (1850m approx)**. To the left of the path, on the north side of the bowl is the wreckage of a light aircraft, and a small plaque attached to a rock. The GR11 continues southwards, however, somehow finding a path up the dauntingly steep rock face at the end of the valley. It's a well-made and well-marked trail but hard work. After nearly an hour of steep ascent you eventually reach the top of the climb and beyond this you come to the first of the **Ibones d'Anayet (2220m approx)**. Allow some time here if at all possible. The lakes themselves are pretty and the view northwards of the Pic du Midi d'Ossau is superb. The lakes are a popular day walk destination, so there are often quite a few people around here picknicking and even swimming. **(For walks/refuges around the Pic du Midi see p112 and p120)**

The path down from the Ibones d'Anayet is pleasant and easy to follow, much of it running alongside crystal clear mountain streams – no problem with getting water on this section. Approximately an hour after starting down, the GR11 arrives at the bottom of a ski lift with a couple of buildings and a huge car park area. Beyond the buildings, next to a small bridge, the GR11 heads off to the left, paralleling the road as it runs down to meet the main road (A136) by a small building, the **Corral deras Mulas**. From here it's a boring trudge 3km south-eastwards to a concrete bridge at the end of the Embalse de Gallego. The road is narrow and there's a considerable amount of traffic, so it may be more sensible to follow the track which runs just to the left of the road. This doesn't take you all the way to the bridge but it allows you to escape most of the walk along the road.

Just before the bridge the GR11 turns left off the road on to a footpath. From here it follows a well marked trail, mostly on old farm tracks, to Sallent de Gallego (1305m, see p150).

Map 29 – Candachú to Sallent de Gallego 149

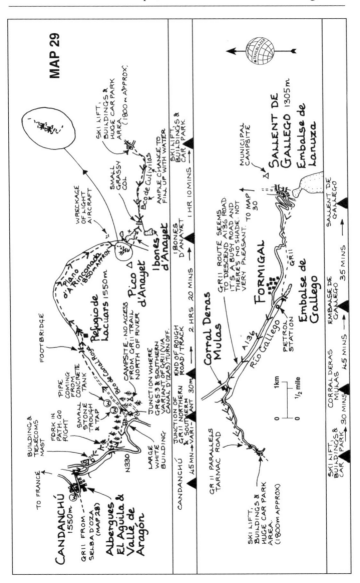

MAP 29

TO FRANCE

CANDANCHÚ 1550m.

GR11 FROM SELBA D'OZA (MAP 28)

Albergues EL Aguila & Valle de Aragón

SKI LIFT, BUILDINGS & HUGE CAR PARK AREA (1800m APPROX)

BUILDING & TELECOMS MAST

FORK IN PATH: GO RIGHT

SMALL STONE TROUGH & TAP

PIPE COMING FROM CONCRETE TANK

FOOTBRIDGE

N330

LARGE WHITE BUILDING

JUNCTION OF GR11 NORTHERN & SOUTHERN VARIANT

CANDANCHÚ — 45 MN → VARI- ANT 30m → 2 HRS 20 MINS

JUNCTION WHERE GR65.3 & SOUTHERN VARIANT OF GR11 (VIA CANAL D'IZAS) TURN OFF.

END OF ROUGH ROAD / TRACK

CAMPSITE: NO ACCESS FROM GR11 (VIA TRAIL NORTH OF RIVER

Refugio de Lacuars 1550m.

d'Añano Rinconada 1850m APPROX.

WRECKAGE OF LIGHT AIRCRAFT

Pico △ d'Anayet 1550m

Ibones d'Anayet

SKI LIFT, BUILDINGS & CAR PARK

SMALL GRASSY COL

IBONES D'ANAYET — 1 HR 10 MINS →

B° de Culivillas

AMPLE CHANCE TO FILL UP WITH WATER

Corral Deras Mulas

GR11 PARALLELS TARMAC ROAD

SKI LIFT, BUILDINGS & HUGE CAR PARK AREA (1800m APPROX)

0   1km
0   ½ mile

A136

Río Gallego

PETROL STATION

GR11 ROUTE SEEMS TO DESCEND A136 ROAD. IT'S A BUSY ROAD AND THERE'S NO SHADE. NOT VERY PLEASANT. TO MAP 30

FORMIGAL

Embalse de Gallego

MUNICIPAL CAMPSITE

SALLENT DE GALLEGO 1305m.

Embalse de Lanuza

GR11 SALLENT DE GALLEGO

SKI LIFT, BUILDINGS & CAR PARK — 30 MINS →

CORRAL DERAS MULAS — 45 MINS →

EMBALSE DE GALLEGO — 35 MINS →

SALLENT DE GALLEGO

Sallent de Gallego is a pretty little village with a few shops and plenty of places to stay and to eat. The most pleasant place to stay is the *Hotel Balaitus* ☆ (☎/▤ 974-48.80.59), a lovely old hotel in the centre of the village. Single rooms cost around €24/4000ptas and doubles around €36/6000ptas. The buffet breakfast is excellent. *Hostal Centro* (☎ 974-48.80.19) and *Hostal Faure* (☎ 974-48.80.07) are both also in the centre of the village and charge €36/6000ptas for a double room; both are comfortable.

The cheapest place in the village is the *Albergue Foratata* (☎/▤ 974-48.81.12), which specializes in taking groups but may accept individuals as well; media-pension here is €19/3200 ptas per person. The small municipal **campsite** is five minutes from the village centre to the north-east. There's no shop or bar here – just a basic campsite. The tariff is around €1.50/250ptas per person.

In the centre of the village there are a number of shops (including two small **supermarkets**) and a handful of good places to eat. There are two **cash dispensers**. The **tourist office** (☎ 974-48.80.12) is open only during July, August and the first half of September and is located in a wooden booth outside the town hall. You can get information on the local area (the Valle de Tena) before you travel from their website: ▢ www.valledetena.com

The tourist office has full details of possible activities in the area. Local operators worth trying include: *Aragon Aventura* (☎ 974-48.53.58; ▤ 974-48.53.48) and *Gorgol* (☎/▤ 974-48.76.26, ▢ www.gorgol.com). If you're starting or ending your walk in Sallent there's a local **bus service** that might be useful: it runs to Sabiñanigo and Jaca (both of which have railway stations). The service is currently run by *Automoviles La Oscense S.A.* (☎ (Sabiñanigo) 974-48.00.45; (Jaca) 974-35.50.60) and there are two daily buses each way, departing Sallent at 07.00 and 16.00 and departing Jaca at 10.15 and 18.15. The journey from Sallent to Sabiñanigo takes one hour, and Jaca (the final stop) is quarter of an hour further on. The same bus company runs buses from Sabiñanigo and Jaca to Pamplona. It's also possible to get a bus from Sabiñanigo to Huesca (approximately one hour) and get a connection there for Barcelona. Check all bus times locally. If you need a **taxi** try Taxis Domec (☎ 974-48.82.68; mobile 919-75.75.50)

SALLENT DE GALLEGO → BALNEARIO DE PANTICOSA [MAP 30, p153]

[**Includes high section – see warning on p20**] This section is a very long one so it's worth making an early start, in order to allow plenty of time for rest stops along the way. An alternative would be to break the section into two equal day stages, either by camping or by staying overnight at the Refugio de Respumoso.

Head through the main square of the village (with the modern sculpture and climbing wall) and walk up the back street (don't cross the bridge over the river – the GR11 remains on the west bank of the Río de Aguas Limpias). Where the road comes to an end the GR11 goes up a farm track which remains level for the first few minutes and then begins to gain height gradually. The GR markers, which have been absent on the way through the village, start again as soon as you reach the farm track. After a few minutes the GR11 splits left away from the farm track and climbs up a narrow path to meet the road. Walk north along the road to the **Embalse de la Sarra (1438m)** and, at the southern end of the reservoir, take a level footpath which leads around the west side of the lake. After 10 minutes the path descends slightly passing, on the right, a car park area near the **Puente de las Fajas**.

From here a clear path climbs along the west side of the valley, starting at a gentle gradient but becoming gradually steeper. Three quarters of an hour after passing the car park area the path crosses a small concrete bridge over the Barranco Garmo Negro and starts to swing round to head north-eastwards. Forty minutes beyond the bridge, at the **Paso de Pino (1700m approx)**, the path climbs around to the north side of a spectacular waterfall. Halfway up beside the waterfall there's a path splitting off to the left, signposted IBONES D'ARIEL 1H 30. (For information about the route over the Col de Palas via the Ariel lakes, see p123). Continue up the main path, which climbs steadily for a further hour until it reaches the huge dam at the end of the Embalse de Respumoso. From the dam the new refuge building (2200m) is visible ahead, and you'll reach it after a further 10-15 minutes. The ***Refugio de Respumoso*** (☎/▤ (974) 49.02.23) is an extremely modern and comfortable place which is open all year and which charges €7/1200ptas for the night, €11/1800ptas for dinner, and €3.50/600ptas for breakfast. The refuge sells some provisions such as puncture-type gas cylinders, chocolate, biscuits, peanuts etc.

From the refuge the GR11 passes around the side of the lake and then climbs past the old refuge building, which is locked, before descending steeply to cross the Barranco de Campo Plano and the torrent running down from the Ibón de Llena Cantal. Walk up the slope above the streams and you soon meet the well established trail around the southern side of the reservoir. Go left along this path ('GR11' is prominently painted on a rock) but almost immediately turn right off it onto a path heading south-east up the valley. The markings across the grass are vague at first but soon become more distinct. The path climbs at a fairly easy gradient for 20-30 minutes, then starts a steep ascent to the **Ibón de Llena Cantal (2450m approx)**. From here there's a further steep haul up a scree slope to the **Cuello Tebarrai (2782m)** which you reach approximately an hour after leaving the Ibón.

From the col the GR11 descends a short way and then contours across the slope above the Ibón de Tebarai to reach the **Cuello de L'Infierno (2721m)**. The path down from here is steep and rocky and even in early August you may find a few patches of snow to be crossed. After half an hour you come to the Ibón Azul Alto, where there's a grassy area suitable for camping. Beyond this, the path climbs over a rocky hummock and descends across an area of boulders to the Ibón Azul Baxo where the remains of an old metal refuge stand beside the water.

Descend from the Ibón Azul Baxo towards the **Ibón Alto de Bachimaña (2207m)**. Just above the lake the path climbs again, and remains high above the water as it runs around the west side of the lake. The trail leads you past the dam at the end of the higher lake and then past the lower lake before descending the steep hillside very rapidly in short zigzags. Despite the short distance that remains to Panticosa the rest of the walk down takes a surprisingly long time, as the GR11 climbs and falls, winding around obstacles, before making a final descent to Panticosa.

BALNEARIO (BAÑOS) DE PANTICOSA

Balneario de Panticosa is a strange place. Situated in a tiny bowl surrounded by steep mountainsides, this once fashionable spa resort with its handful of imposing buildings seems caught in a time warp. Two huge hotels stand opposite the grand building which once housed the casino; there's an ornamental garden, a boating lake and, of course, the thermal baths themselves. Apart from this, however, don't hold your breath.

The two hotels, the *Gran Hotel* and the *Hotel Mediodia*, are under the same management and share the same telephone number (☎ 974-48.71.61) and prices: €45/7500ptas for a single room, or €48-60/8000-10,000ptas for a double room. Both cater almost exclusively for visitors to the thermal baths, but will take walkers if they have space. In keeping with their history as part hotels, part sanatoriums both have an incredibly institutionalized feel, although the *Hotel Mediodia* has at least had a fresh coat of paint.

Most walkers stay at the *Refugio Casa de Piedra* (☎ 974-48.75.71) a large place, open all year, with dormitory accommodation for around 100 people. The refugio charges €7/1100ptas for the night, €7/1100ptas for dinner and €2.40/400ptas for breakfast.

Apart from this there's little else in Panticosa. Near the casino there's a small **swimming pool** which it might be possible to use, and in the central square there are a couple of **bars** and three small **shops** (one selling bread, the others selling souvenirs). The only bar with any life is *Casa Belio*, which is just above the central square. Definitely worth including in any plans for the evening, however, is a drink in the old **casino** building, where the long wooden bar and old card tables hint at what life must have been like when the resort was more fashionable. The casino building is also the unlikely location for a well-hidden **cash dispenser**. Perhaps they're planning to get rid of it in the near future, but the fully functioning machine is to be found just inside the main door of the casino building, on the left – half hidden by the coat racks.

The only other facility worth mentioning in Panticosa are the **baths** themselves. Either of the two large hotels can arrange visits. Prices include €12/2000ptas for a sauna, or €6/1000ptas for a treatment intriguingly known as a 'ducha nasal'.

For a description of the GR11 beyond Balneario de Panticosa see p222.

Map 30 – Sallent de Gallego to Balneario de Panticosa 153

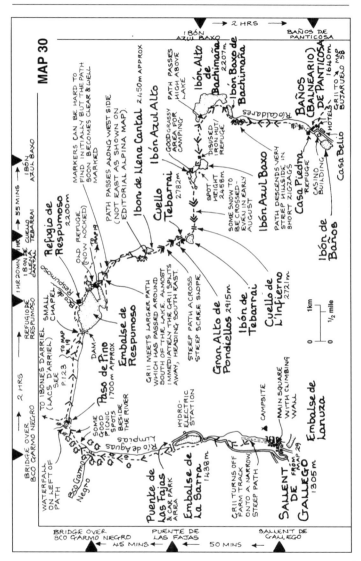

MAP 30

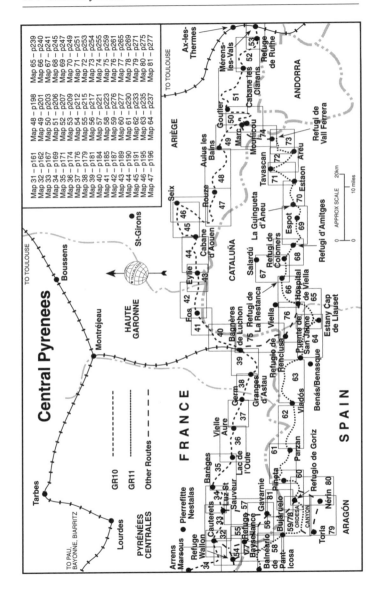

Central Pyrenees

GR10

GR11

Other Routes – – –

PYRÉNÉES
CENTRALES

TO PAU,
BAYONNE, BIARRITZ

Lourdes

Tarbes

Arrens
Marsous ● Pierrefitte
Refuge Nestalas
Wallon

FRANCE

HAUTE
GARONNE

Montréjeau

Boussens

TO TOULOUSE

St-Girons

ARIÈGE

TO TOULOUSE

Ax-les-
Thermes

Mérens-
les-Vals

Refuge
de Ruthe

ANDORRA

Cabane les
Clanans

Goutié

Marc

Mouhicou

Refugi de
Vall Ferrera

Aulus les
Bains

Areu

Estaon

Tavascan

Refugi d'Amitges

Espot

Refugi de
Colomers

La Guingueta
d'Aneu

Salardú

CATALUÑA

Rouze

Cabane
d'Aouen

Seix

Eylie

Fos

Bagnères
de Luchon

Refugi de
La Restanca

Viella

Hospital
de Viella

Estany Cap
de Llauset

St Joanne

Puente de
San Jaime

Refugio de
Benasque

Benás/Benasque

Viadós

Refugio de Goriz

Parzan

Bujaruelo

Torla

Nérin

ORDESA
CANYON

Balnéario
de Pantícosa

Refuge
Byssellance

Gavarnie

Lac de
l'Oule

Vielle
Aure

Granges
d'Astau

Germ

Barèges

Luz-St
Sauveur

Cauterets

SPAIN

ARAGÓN

APPROX SCALE

20km

10 miles

TO TOULOUSE

FRANCE

PART 4: CENTRAL PYRENEES

Facts about the region

GENERAL DESCRIPTION

The Central Pyrenees are defined here as the area of mountains contained within the French départements of Hautes Pyrénées, Haute Garonne and Ariège and in Spain within the eastern part of Aragón and the western part Catalonia.

The central region of the Pyrenees contains the highest mountains in the range and, to a greater extent than in the eastern or western Pyrenees, it is an area defined by its topography. Each valley holds its own community, and until the building of the first roads around a century ago, these settlements were often extremely isolated. During the nineteenth century, as explorers and academics began to take an interest in the mountains, it was discovered that there were still villages here where few inhabitants spoke French. Communication was channelled through passes in the mountains, leading to localized features such as ancient market areas (Marcadau), and hospices for pilgrims and traders who were travelling through the difficult terrain (Hospice de France, Hospital de Venasque, Hospital de Vielha).

Its geographical characteristics meant that, unlike either the Western or the Eastern Pyrenees, this central section of the mountains was never a thoroughfare for other people, and thus to a great extent it was left alone. Despite this, there are still remains of the Roman presence in the valleys, where they came to mine for iron and silver. The High Pyrenees largely escaped occupation by the Moors, and thus some of the earliest examples of Romanesque church architecture appear here in the mountains.

HAUTES PYRÉNÉES, HAUTE GARONNE AND ARIÈGE

Politics and history

For much of its early history, this area was a law unto itself. Although the lowlands at the base of the mountains may have experienced a succession

 Trekking in the Central Pyrenees – Highlights
The Ordesa National Park and the Aigües Tortes National Park both contain stunning scenery and are highly recommended, as is the Val d'Aran. The border area to the north of the Val d'Aran has many well-placed refuges amongst the high mountains, and there are any number of ways in which you can work your itinerary in this region.

of rulers, the mountain people largely went their own way. Nowhere is this clearer than in the case of the Cathar sect (see p281), centred in the eastern part of the area in the 12th century. Despite the best efforts of the Catholic church, which sanctioned a crusade against its followers, Catharism took over a century to eradicate.

Historical records start with the arrival of the Romans, who fought their way through the eastern Pyrenees around 200BC and, having overcome both Gaul and Spain, colonised the area. They were largely interested in mining, and much evidence of this still remains but there are also relics around spa sites such as Bagnères-de-Luchon and Ax-les-Thermes. The spas became renowned for their healing properties from the fifteenth century onwards but it wasn't until the early nineteenth century that they became popular as resorts. Cauterets, Gavarnie, Luchon, Bigorre and Ax all became fashionable places to be seen.

By the mid-nineteenth century the mountains themselves had become the focus of attention, and alpinism increasingly became popular. This century, with the arrival of skiing (the first skis appeared in the Pyrenees around 1902), and mountaineering, the region has become increasingly well-known.

Walking in the Hautes Pyrénées, Haute Garonne and Ariège

Above all, the central Pyrenees contain variety. From the deep, well-watered valleys, one can ascend to high barren landscapes of rock and snow. Marmots, izards, and even a few bears live in these mountains, and the flora, even in the highest areas, is magnificent. While the central Pyrenees attract huge numbers of walkers during the peak holiday season, most of them tend to stay on the main paths. A little exploration away from these main routes can reveal fantastic scenery with few other people to disturb the peace.

ARAGÓN AND CATALONIA

Politics and history

The Romans started mining activities in several places but the high valleys remained largely untouched by them or, later, by the Moors. Christianity appears to have reached the mountains in the seventh and eighth centuries, and at the end of the eighth century the region came under the control of the Franks when Charlemagne created the Spanish March.

With the slow disintegration of Charlemagne's empire, and the gradual retreat southwards of the Moors, the kingdoms of northern Spain began to sort themselves out. Aragón, initially an area of the March under a nominated governor, began to emerge as a separate entity from the eighth century onwards, and from the ninth century became linked by marriage to neighbouring Navarra. Catalonia, which had remained relatively free from Muslim rule, rose to fortune under the protection of the Franks and soon became one of the most powerful states in Spain.

Even after the union of Aragón and Castille in 1479, the kingdoms of Aragón, Catalonia and Navarra retained a large degree of self-rule, and it was not for some time that border questions were settled. The exact border between Aragón and Catalonia was constantly in a state of flux, the border with France not being finalized until the 1659 Treaty of the Pyrenees. Despite this agreement, the ownership of the Aran valley was still in dispute as late as the Peninsular War in the early 1800's.

In the twentieth century both Aragón and Catalonia were Republican strongholds in the Civil War, and the population of the villages was cut drastically when large numbers fled across the mountains.

Walking in eastern Aragón and western Catalonia

The central portion of the Spanish Pyrenees contains some of the best scenery in the whole of the range. The high mountainsides are different in character and appearance from the French Pyrenees; the colours are predominantly brown and grey, and the hills, which slope gently towards the south, are grass-covered. In Aragón, the Ordesa National Park makes a good week-long excursion, while in Catalonia, the Aigües Tortes National Park and the Aran Valley provide plenty of scope for a fortnight or more of walking.

FOOD AND DRINK

Spanish Pyrenean cooking, rather like its French counterpart, is heavy on substance and energy content. Large stews and thick soups frequently feature on the menu, as do sausages such as the Catalan speciality *butifarra traidora*. There are a selection of cheeses, including *serrat* and *brossat*, and the standard drink is red wine, or water. (You may even find that wine is served at breakfast, on the dubious theory that water will weigh you down as you head off into the mountains, whereas wine will lift you up!). There is also a selection of liqueurs – in Catalonia one of the best known is Ratafia – a syrupy sweet concoction.

GETTING THERE

Getting to the Central Pyrenees

Getting to the area of the central Pyrenees is covered in detail in Part 1 of the book. In outline, to get to the French Pyrenees there are airports in Pau and Lourdes for the western part of the region, or Toulouse for the eastern part. The nearest airport in Spain is Barcelona.

By rail, there are direct TGV services to Pau, Lourdes, Tarbes and Toulouse. By road there are coaches from London to Pau, Lourdes, Tarbes and Toulouse.

Getting to the walking

To get into the hills using public transport there are various options:

● **Arrens Marsous** (see p118 and p159) There are two buses a day between Tarbes and Arrens Marsous (every day except Sundays and holidays). The buses go via Lourdes (bus station) and Pierrefitte Nestalas (from where there are connections to Cauterets, Luz-St-Sauveur and, indirectly, Gavarnie). From Tarbes to Arrens the journey takes one and a half hours; from Lourdes to Arrens just over one hour. The buses are operated by Salt (☎ 05.62.34.76.69, 🖳 05.62.34.76.61).

● **Cauterets, Luz-St-Sauveur, Barèges, Gavarnie** From Pau and Tarbes there are trains to Lourdes, from where there are regular bus services (running from outside the railway station) to Cauterets. All services stop at Pierrefitte Nestalas, where you can change onto a bus headed for Luz-St-Sauveur and Barèges. From Luz, there are two daily buses to Gavarnie (see p168 for details of timings).

● **Bagnères-de-Luchon** From Toulouse, there are two daily trains, via Montréjeau, to Bagnères-de-Luchon. In addition there are a further three or four services daily to Montréjeau where you can change for a connecting bus service to Bagnères-de-Luchon.

● **Aulus les Bains** From Pau or Tarbes you can catch a train east (from Toulouse you'll need a west bound train) to Boussens, from where it's possible to catch an SNCF bus to St-Girons. During the summer there are three daily buses from St-Girons to Aulus (€4/28F). A taxi from St-Girons to Aulus costs €38/250F.

● **Ax-les-Thermes and Mérens-les-Vals** There are several direct trains daily from Toulouse to Ax-les-Thermes; some also stop at Mérens-les-Vals.

Spain

● **Torla** There are two daily buses between Torla and Sabiñánigo, where there's a railway station (see p266 for more details)

● **Sallent de Gallego** There are daily buses to Jaca and Sabiñánigo, where there are railway stations and other bus connections (see p150).

Car hire

This will obviously not be ideal for most people, as it's very expensive to hire a car and then go walking for several days. However if you want to have a very flexible itinerary, it may be suitable. There are car hire services in the following towns:

● **Lourdes** Avis (☎ 05.62.42.12.97) has an office at the railway station.

● **Tarbes** Avis (☎ 05.62.34.26.76), 40 route de Lourdes; Budget (☎ 05.62 93.91.60), 42 avenue de Maréchal Joffre; Europcar (☎ 05.62.51.20.21), 54 avenue Aristide Briand

● **Pau** Avis (☎ 05.59.13.31.33), ave Didier Daurat; Budget (☎ 05.59.62 72.54), 242 ave Jean Mermoz; Europcar (☎ 05.59.92.09.09), 115 ave Jean Mermoz

● **Toulouse** All major car hire companies have desks at the airport.

Central Pyrenees – GR10

ARRENS-MARSOUS → REFUGE D'ILHÉOU [MAP 31, p161]

Cross the Gave d'Azun via an old arched bridge just to the south of the village centre. On the far side of the river a small track leads uphill; stay on this track as it passes through woods and comes to a road. Join the road briefly before taking a footpath through the trees to meet the lane higher up the hillside. This time follow the lane to the **Col des Bordères (1156m)**. Just past the sign announcing the col, a footpath leads off to the left, only to rejoin the road after a few hundred metres. This used to be the route of the GR10, but in 2000 it was fenced off. Purists may choose to search out this tiny diversion, but in fact it's quicker and easier just to follow the road over the col. As the road starts to descend from the col, you pass the *Gîte le Relais du Pech* (☎ 05.62.97.44.93); it's not really a gîte d'étape for walkers, but you could try it if all else fails – the tariff is €15/100F per night.

Below the gîte, follow a footpath away from the road and down the hill. It soon re-emerges on a lane which it follows to the left past some buildings; skirt around a church and descend to meet the road (D103) run-

---

Route maps
● **Scale and walking times** All the following trail maps are drawn to a scale of 1:100,000 (10mm = 1km/0.625miles). Walking times are given along the side of each map, and the arrow shows the direction to which the time refers. Black triangles indicate the points between which the times have been taken. Note that the time given refers only to the time spent walking, so you will need to **add 30-40% to allow for rest stops**. Remember that these are **my timings** for the section; every walker has his or her own speed. With the first edition of this book, several readers commented that they found these timings on the fast side. The times are, however, consistent so you should err on the side of caution for a day or two until you see how your speed relates to my timings on the maps. When planning the day's trekking, count on between five and seven hours actual walking, and allow for an occasional rest day.
● **Up or down?** The trail is shown as a dotted line. An arrow across the trail indicates the slope; two arrows show that it is steep. Note that the arrow points towards the higher part of the trail. If, for example, you're walking from A (at 900m) to B (at 1100m) and the trail between the two is short and steep it would be shown thus: A—>>—B.
● **Refuges, gîtes and cabanes** Everywhere to stay that is within easy reach of the trail is marked. See the text for more details about each place.
● **Other information and symbols** Altitudes are given on the map in metres. Places where you can get water are shown by a 'W' within a circle.

ning south up the Vallée d'Estaing. Just to the right, a few metres up the road, is the very smart *Camping Pyrenees Natura* which charges €4/25F per person and per tent, although it's more geared up for cars and camper vans. The GR10 heads directly across the road and runs south alongside the stream for quarter of an hour to a point where it re-crosses the road and stream near a campsite. *Camping le Vieux Moulin* (☎ 05.62.97.43 23) boasts a swimming pool; it charges €2.50/15F for emplacement and €2.50/15F per person. The small shop and café, which used to be on the main road near the campsite, are now closed so if you're planning to stay here you'll need to have stocked up in Arrens.

After quarter of an hour along the west bank of the river, cross again and follow the road south past *Chez Place Bar and Restaurant* to the *gîte d'étape Les Viellettes* (☎ 05.62.97.14.37, 🗎 05.62.97.44.74). The gîte is open all year and charges €12/75F for the night or €25/165F for demi-pension. Ten minutes further south is the *Camping La Pose* (☎ 05.62.97 43.10) which has basic but adequate facilities; it's €1/7F for emplacement and €2/12F per person. Near the campsite the GR10 again crosses to the west side of the stream; it doesn't much matter if you miss this turning – it comes back onto the road again further up. At the top of the lane, just as the Lac d'Estaing comes into view is an attractive little hotel. The *Hôtel Restaurant du Lac d'Estaing* (☎ 05.62.97.06.25) is open from the beginning of May to mid October and has rooms ranging in price from €29-38/190-250F. The restaurant is far from cheap but the menu looks wonderful.

The Lac d'Estaing itself is not a place to linger as the area is generally packed with day trippers. Thankfully, few have the energy to walk more than a short way up into the hills, so the crowds are soon left behind. Five minutes' walk along the lake side and next to a sign, CABANES DU BARBAT 2H 30 & COL D'ILHÉOU 3H 45, the GR10 cuts uphill on a steep footpath through woods. After half an hour the path emerges from the trees near the **Arriousec Cabane**, which is normally locked; there's a water source near the cabane, although it might be wise to purify this water before drinking it. Ten minutes later, the GR10 crosses a rough vehicle track and heads south-east, climbing along the side of the valley. Fifty minutes' hard walking brings you to a path junction just east of the **Barbat Cabanes** and an hour beyond this, after a steep final ascent, you reach the **Col d'Ilhéou (2227m)**. There's a sign here, LAC D'ILHÉOU 1H, and a conveniently grassy slope where you can collapse. The descent to the refuge is gradual and undramatic.

The *Refuge d'Ilhéou* is one of the more expensive mountain huts in the Pyrenees, which is odd since the building is accessible to four-wheel

---

(Opposite) Tradition plays a large part in daily life in the Pyrenees, particularly in the Basque country. Local smuggling activities are re-enacted in this *contrabandiers* race, in which representatives from French and Spanish villages carry an 8kg sausage around a gruelling course over an old smuggling route. (Photo © Greg and Jane Knott).

Map 31 – Arrens-Marsous to Refuge d'Ilhéou 161

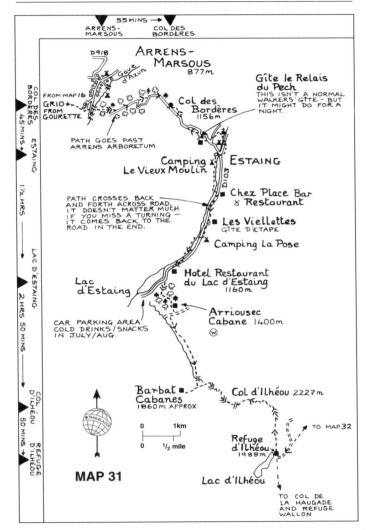

MAP 31

55 MINS →
ARRENS-MARSOUS
COL DES BORDERES

D918
ARRENS-MARSOUS
877m

Gave d'Azun

Gîte le Relais du Pech
THIS ISN'T A NORMAL WALKERS' GÎTE - BUT IT MIGHT DO FOR A NIGHT.

FROM MAP 16
GRIO
FROM GOURETTE

Col des Bordères
1156m

PATH GOES PAST ARRENS ARBORETUM.

ESTAING

Camping Le Vieux Moulin

PATH CROSSES BACK AND FORTH ACROSS ROAD. IT DOESN'T MATTER MUCH IF YOU MISS A TURNING — IT COMES BACK TO THE ROAD IN THE END.

Chez Place Bar & Restaurant

Les Viellettes
GÎTE D'ETAPE

Camping La Pose

Lac d'Estaing

Hotel Restaurant du Lac d'Estaing
1160m

Arriousec Cabane 1400m
Ⓦ

CAR PARKING AREA COLD DRINKS / SNACKS IN JULY/AUG.

Barbat Cabanes
1860m APPROX

Col d'Ilhéou 2227m

TO MAP 32

★ TRAILBLAZER

0   1km
0   ½ mile

Refuge d'Ilhéou
1988m

Lac d'Ilhéou

TO COL DE LA HAUGADE AND REFUGE WALLON

COL DES BORDERES
45 MINS →
ESTAING
← 45 MINS →
1½ HRS
LAC D'ESTAING
2 HRS 50 MINS
COL D'ILHÉOU
50 MINS
REFUGE D'ILHÉOU

(Opposite) Top: The Refuge d'Ilhéou (see p160) is just one of a number of well-placed refuges throughout the range, which offer food and shelter to trekkers.
Bottom: Many shepherds who spend their summers in cabanes in the high Pyrenees are only too happy to sell cheese to passing walkers. You may also be asked to help out with a few veterinary tasks, though! (Photo © Sarah Jane Riley).

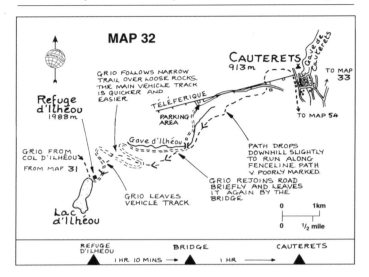

MAP 32

CAUTERETS
913m

TO MAP 33

GR10 FOLLOWS NARROW
TRAIL OVER LOOSE ROCKS.
THE MAIN VEHICLE TRACK
IS QUICKER AND
EASIER

TÉLÉFÉRIQUE

Refuge
d'Ilhéou
1988m

PARKING
AREA

TO MAP 54

Gave d'Ilhéou

PATH DROPS
DOWNHILL SLIGHTLY
TO RUN ALONG
FENCELINE. PATH
V. POORLY MARKED.

GR10 FROM
COL D'ILHÉOU
FROM MAP 31

GR10 REJOINS ROAD
BRIEFLY AND LEAVES
IT AGAIN BY THE
BRIDGE

GR10 LEAVES
VEHICLE TRACK.

Lac
d'Ilhéou

0   1km

0   1/2 mile

REFUGE
D'ILHÉOU

BRIDGE

CAUTERETS

1 HR 10 MINS →   1 HR →

drive vehicles which should make resupply easy. The refuge has space for 32 people and charges €12/80F per night and €37/240F for demi-pension. A beer here will set you back a whacking €2.50/16F – which must be four or five times the cost price in Cauterets! There's no telephone, only a radio link in the refuge itself, but reservations can be made on (☎ 05.62.92.52.38) or you can try their mobile phone (☎ 06.83.85.91.91). The refuge is named after a local lawyer and historian, Raymond Ritter, who devoted himself to writing about and promoting the Pyrenees.

REFUGE D'ILHÉOU → CAUTERETS   [MAP 32]

Follow the rough vehicle track downhill from the refuge for a few minutes, before turning off across the grass to the right (north). The footpath

---

❏ Refuge d'Ilhéou → Refuge Wallon

If you're heading for Gavarnie, or are just keen to explore the area, consider going south from the Refuge d'Ilhéou, instead of north-east towards Cauterets. By making directly for the Refuge Wallon, you can avoid Cauterets altogether and see some of the best of the scenery in this part of the Pyrenees. It takes about four hours via the Col de la Haugade (2311m) to the Refuge Wallon, and if you're feeling energetic you could carry on for a further 4½ hours to the Refuge Oulettes de Gaube. For details of the many alternative routes in the area see Excursions around the GR10 on p211.

crosses the hillside and descends to meet the rough vehicle track again. The GR10 crosses the track and continues on a narrow trail across the hillside over loose rocks. Depending on how you're feeling at the time, consider following the vehicle track: it's much faster and easier going. At the bottom of the slope the footpath rejoins this track a few hundred metres before a bridge over the Gave d'Ilhéou. Just before the bridge the GR10 turns right along a poorly defined grassy trail. After coming level with the large parking area on the far side of the valley, you go down the hillside to follow a fence line, and continue along a track between two fields. At the end of this, turn left along the road for a few metres before cutting downhill to the right, under the path of the cable car. A well-trodden trail leads down into Cauterets.

CAUTERETS
✉ code 65110

Cauterets came to the fore in the late 19th century as a spa town. It was a fashionable place to be seen, and it attracted a cross section of society figures: musicians, artists, writers and the nobility. These days, during high season, Cauterets is just as full of visitors as it ever was in the last century. After the calm and solitude of walking in the mountains, the crowded streets can be slightly bemusing but it's a good place to stock up on supplies, pick up mail and enjoy a night in a proper hotel. Because of its efficient bus connections it's also a convenient place to start or finish a walking trip.

Cauterets currently has no bureau de change. If you're travelling before 2002 and the introduction of the euro, note that you'll need to bring pesetas with you as the cash dispensers only give francs; the post office can provide pesetas but only if they are ordered in advance.

Services

Facilities in Cauterets include two **banks** (the Crédit Agricole has a cash dispenser), a **post office** where poste restante is kept efficiently, and two self-service **launderettes**. There are numerous **shops**: there's a photographic store with one-hour developing, a large Intersport which sells Coleman/Epigas

cylinders, and an indoor market which is laden with local specialities. The **tourist office** (☎ 05.62.92.50.27, 🖹 05.62.92.59 12, 💻 www.cauterets.com) is in the centre of town, and almost next door is the **Bureau des Guides** (☎ 05.62.92.62.02) where information is available on activities including mountain biking, climbing and canyoning.

The **Maison du Parc** is worth a visit if you want to find out more about the mountains. Entry is free and the well laid out exhibition covers flora, fauna and the traditional lifestyle of the montagnards. All captions are in French.

Just below the Maison du Parc is the wooden **gare**, from which buses depart. There are eight daily buses to and from Lourdes (€6/39F one way, one hour) and, during the summer, six daily buses to and from the Pont d'Espagne (25 minutes; €3/20F one way, €4.50/30F return). The Pont d'Espagne service leaves Cauterets at 08.00, 10.00, 12.00, 14.00, 16.00, 18.00 and Pont d'Espagne at 09.00, 11.00, 12.30, 15.00, 17.00, 19.00. If you're heading to Luz St Sauveur or Gavarnie, take the Lourdes bus north to Pierrefitte-Nestalas (€3/19F, half an hour) and change there for a bus to Luz (€3/19F, half an hour). For details of buses from Luz to Gavarnie see p168). There's an SNCF booking office inside the gare (open 09.00-12.30 and 15.00-19.00) where you can book train tickets for your onward journey from Lourdes. If you need a **taxi**, try Taxi Bordenave (☎ 05.62.92.53.68, mobile 06.71.01.46.86) or Taxi André Houssat (☎ 05.62.92.61.62, mobile 06.12.91.83.19).

Where to stay

The modern *Hôtel Club Aladin* ☆☆☆ (☎ 05.62.92.60.00, 🖹 05.62.92.63.30) which has double rooms starting at €82/540F, is probably the best place in Cauterets. A close competitor, however, is the *Hôtel Le Bordeaux* ☆☆☆ (☎ 05 62.92.52.50, 🖹 05.62.92.63.29) which has rooms from €49/320F.

Amongst the mid and lower range hotels in Cauterets, the friendly *Hôtel Le Pas De L'Ours* ☆ (☎ 05.62 92.58.07, 🖹 05.62.92.06.49) is good value with clean, pleasant double rooms from €40/ 260F, and, for a small amount extra, the best buffet breakfast you're likely to come across anywhere. Another place which has been recommended is the centrally located *Hôtel César* ☆☆ (☎ 05 62.92.52.57, 🖹 05.62.92.08.19) which has double rooms from €35/ 230F. Near to this, and right on the central square, is the *Hôtel de Paris* ☆☆ (☎ 05.62 92.53.85, 🖹 05.62.92.02.23) where double rooms start at €38/250F. There are lots of other hotels in the town, and the tourist office can usually assist in finding somewhere to stay.

At the cheaper end of the scale, the best *gîte* in the town is run by the Hôtel

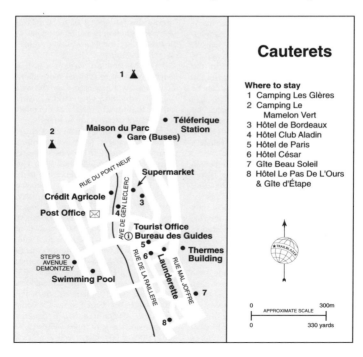

Cauterets

Where to stay
1 Camping Les Glères
2 Camping Le
   Mamelon Vert
3 Hôtel de Bordeaux
4 Hôtel Club Aladin
5 Hôtel de Paris
6 Hôtel César
7 Gîte Beau Soleil
8 Hôtel Le Pas De L'Ours
   & Gîte d'Étape

1 ▲

• Téléferique Station
Maison du Parc
• **Gare (Buses)**

2 ▲

RUE DU PONT NEUF

Supermarket

Crédit Agricole
Post Office ✉
4 AVE DE GÉN LECLERC
3

Tourist Office
ⓘ **Bureau des Guides**
5
6 • **Thermes Building**
RUE DE LA RAILLÈRE
Launderette
RUE MAL JOFFRE

STEPS TO AVENUE DEMONTZEY •
Swimming Pool

7 •

8 •

TRAILBLAZER

0   300m
APPROXIMATE SCALE
0   330 yards

Le Pas De L'Ours; a bed in the gîte costs €11/70F, or it's €26/170F for demi-pension. If this is full, try the *Gîte Beau Soleil* (☎ 05.62.92.53.52) which has a rather institutionalized atmosphere, and where they charge €14/90F per night and €28/180F for demi-pension.

There are two campsites close to the centre of town. *Camping Le Mamelon*

Vert ☆☆ (☎ 05.62.92 51.56) is fairly upmarket and charges €10/63F for two people and a tent. *Camping Les Glères* ☆☆ (☎ 05.62.92.55.34) is more crowded and further from the centre of town; the tariff is €5/32.50F for one person and a tent, and €2.50/16.50F for each extra person.

CAUTERETS → LUZ-ST-SAUVEUR   [MAP 33, p166]

The GR10 goes south from the Thermes (thermal baths) building, following the road uphill past the Gîte Beau Soleil, to a T-junction near a large crucifix. Turn left here, and follow the lane uphill past an old, deserted thermes building, where a collection of yellow signs adorn the area around some stone steps. Ignore the signs, and continue up the lane, which after 10 minutes becomes a loose-surfaced road. It climbs past a deserted forest lodge, and further up the hill past another empty building; nearby is a yellow sign: PLATEAU DU LISEY 1H 15; COL DE RIOU 2H 15.

A short way beyond the sign you come to a junction, where a barrier blocks vehicle access on the main track. Walk around the gate and continue for five minutes to a well-marked turn-off, where the GR10 cuts back steeply to the left. From this point a footpath zigzags upwards through pine woods. After 25 minutes the path emerges from the trees by a small farm building and, after a few minutes meandering, it climbs across open slopes to the **Col de Riou (1949m)**. You can see Luz-St-Sauveur from here, but the view is rather spoiled by the ski lifts just below the col itself.

The GR10 departs from the col on the vehicle track leading northeast, but soon heads down on a footpath to the ski station. From here, it goes almost straight down towards Luz, crossing the road each time it meets it. At first these short cuts are overgrown and hard to locate, but lower down the hill they become easier to find.

After nearly 1³/₄ hours of continuous descent, you arrive at the village of **Grust**. Drinking water is available from a tap next to the path, and there is also a *gîte d'étape* (☎ 05.62.92.34.79) which can accommodate 15 people. The tariff at the gîte is €11/70F for the night or €25/160F for demi-pension, and there is a small kitchen for self-catering. Opposite the gîte is the *Restaurant Auberge Les Bruyères* (☎ 05.62.92.83.03).

Half an hour downhill from Grust you come to **Sazos**, where there's a campsite: *Camping Caravaneige Pyrenevasion* ☆☆☆ (☎ 05.62.92.91 54) charges €10/65F for two people and a tent. Luz-St-Sauveur is a further 25 minutes' walk down the road.

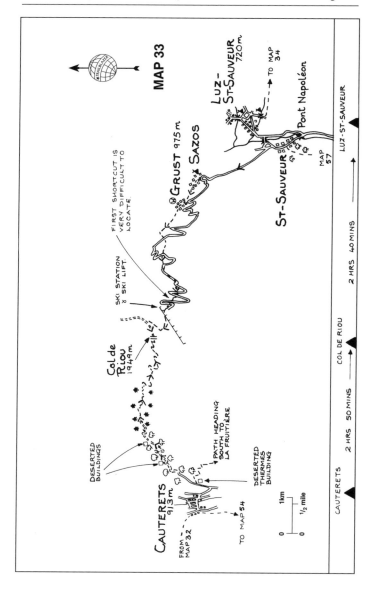

MAP 33

LUZ-ST-SAUVEUR 720m

TO MAP 34

Pont Napoléon

GRUST 975m

SAZOS

FIRST SHORTCUT IS VERY DIFFICULT TO LOCATE.

SKI STATION & SKI LIFT.

Col de Riou 1949m

ST-SAUVEUR

MAP 57

DESERTED BUILDINGS

PATH HEADING SOUTH TO LA FRUITTIÈRE

DESERTED THERMES BUILDING

CAUTERETS 913m.

FROM MAP 32

TO MAP 54

1km

½ mile

0

0

LUZ-ST-SAUVEUR

2 HRS 40 MINS

COL DE RIOU

2 HRS 50 MINS

CAUTERETS

LUZ-ST-SAUVEUR
✉ code 65120

Luz is another of the Pyrenean spa towns which capitalized on the thermal springs and the popularity of the mountains to thrive during the late nineteenth century. Today, as in Cauterets, summer finds the streets crowded with tourists, and the central area of the town is a mass of camping shops, pizza restaurants and bars. It's not a bad place to catch up on chores, but it's hardly the most peaceful or picturesque town in the Pyrenees.

Regular bus connections make it a good place to start or end a walk.

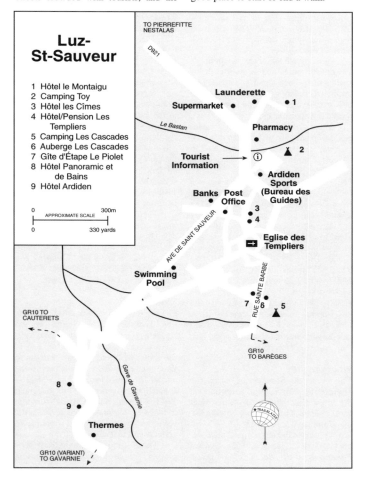

Luz-St-Sauveur

1 Hôtel le Montaigu
2 Camping Toy
3 Hôtel les Cîmes
4 Hôtel/Pension Les Templiers
5 Camping Les Cascades
6 Auberge Les Cascades
7 Gîte d'Étape Le Piolet
8 Hôtel Panoramic et de Bains
9 Hôtel Ardiden

0   300m
APPROXIMATE SCALE
0   330 yards

TO PIERREFITTE NESTALAS

D921

Launderette
Supermarket
Le Bastan
Pharmacy
Tourist Information
Ardiden Sports (Bureau des Guides)
Banks Post Office
3
4
Eglise des Templiers
AVE DE SAINT SAUVEUR
Swimming Pool
7 6 5
RUE SAINTE BARBE
GR10 TO BARÈGES
GR10 TO CAUTERETS
8
9
Gave de Gavarnie
Thermes
GR10 (VARIANT) TO GAVARNIE
TRAILBLAZER

Services
There are three **banks** (two of which have cash dispensers) near the centre of the town, opposite the **post office**. There is a **launderette** just to the north of the town centre. **Shops** near the centre include a pharmacy, a huge supermarket and five or six sports stores; Ardiden Sports, opposite the tourist office, sells Coleman/Epigas. The **tourist office** (☎ 05.62.92.81.60, 🖹 05.62.92.87.19) is on the central square, a few metres from the **Bureau des Guides**.

Entertainments include a **cinema**, a **swimming pool**, and a **nightclub**. If you're really lucky, and you reach Luz on a scheduled weekend, you could always have a go at **bungee jumping** off the Pont Napoléon.

There are four or five SNCF **buses** per day from Luz to Lourdes (€6/39F one way, one hour). To get from Luz to Cauterets, take the Lourdes bus as far as Pierrefitte Nestalas (€3/20F, half an hour) and change there for Cauterets (€3/20F, half an hour). Buses coming from Lourdes continue to Barèges (15 minutes) but go no further. During July and August there are also two daily services to and from Gavarnie. These services are currently run by Transports Claude Dubie (☎ 05.62.92.48.60, 05.62 92.48.51); buses depart from Luz at 09.00 and 17.30 and from Gavarnie at 11.40 and 18.30. The journey costs €5.50/35F and takes 40 minutes; the buses make one stop, at Gèdre, which is halfway between Luz and Gavarnie and is a possible starting place for a trip into the Cirque de Troumouse.

Where to stay
The area of St-Sauveur, near the Thermes building is more peaceful than the town centre but hardly convenient for the shops. There are two hotels here: the *Hôtel Ardiden* ☆☆ (☎ 05.62 92.81 80) is pleasant and has rooms from €29-55/190-360F. Nearby, the *Hôtel Panoramic et des Bains* ☆☆ (☎ 05.62

92.80.14) has a rather faded air, with rooms costing from €23-54/150-355F.

In the centre of town the top hotel is the *Hôtel Le Montaigu* ☆☆☆ (☎ 05.62 92.81.71) which is a modern, characterless building on a side street. Rooms cost between €43/280F and €69/450F. Much more lively is the *Hôtel Pension Les Templiers* ☆☆ (☎ 05.62.92.81.52, 🖹 05.62.92.93.05), a pleasant, friendly hotel where double rooms start at €32/210F. Next door, the *Hôtel Les Cîmes* (☎ 05.62.92.82.03) is more of a boarding house than a hotel but is very good value, with rooms from €18/120F for a single and €24/160F for a double.

There are two gîtes. The *Auberge Les Cascades* (☎ 05.62.92.94.14) is next to the campsite of the same name, and charges €8/55F per night or €20/130F for demi-pension; there's a kitchen for self-catering. Opposite the Auberge is the very pleasant *Gîte d'Étape Le Piolet* (☎ 05.62 92.92.67) where they charge €12/80F for bed and breakfast or €20 130F for demi-pension. There are no facilities for self-catering.

There are two campsites near the town centre. *Camping Les Cascades* ☆☆ (☎ 05.62.92.85.85) charges €4/25F per person, or a flat rate of €4.50/30F for one person and a tent. *Camping Toy* ☆☆ (☎ 05.62.92.86.85) charges €3/19F per person and €3/19F for a tent.

What to see
Spare a moment to look into the **Eglise des Templiers**, the church of the Knights Templar, a military and religious order. This lovely old building in the centre of the town bears witness to their strong influence in this part of the world. The ruined tower which stands on a small hill overlooking the Camping Toy is **Château Sainte Marie**; although it looks in reasonable shape from the town, an empty tower and a couple of walls are all that remain.

Those following the GR10 religiously will pass to the south of Luz and

Map 34 – Luz-St-Saveur to Barèges 169

cross the **Pont Napoléon** over the Gave de Gavarnie. The bridge usually features somewhere on local tourist literature, and it's an impressive piece of engineering but it's hardly worth making a special effort to see.

If you find yourself in the area in July you may be able to catch part of the **Jazz Altitude festival** which takes place in Luz. Even if you're not interested, try to book your place to stay in advance, as the town is packed during the festival.

LUZ-ST-SAUVEUR → BARÈGES [MAP 34]

Assuming that most walkers will have stayed a night in Luz, or at least walked through the town rather than following the path south to the Pont Napoléon, the easiest place to pick up the GR10 again is just south of the Camping Cascades. From the campsite entrance continue down the lane and cross a bridge, on the far side of which the GR10 markings head left (east). The path climbs gently at first before crossing a minor road (D146) and steepening through woods. Three quarters of an hour after leaving Luz the path emerges from the trees and continues climbing across the open hillside before levelling out and re-entering woods (the **Domaine du Gave de Pau**). From here the remainder of the walk is more or less level until the descent into Barèges.

Pass through the woods and on leaving them, turn south-east into the valley of the Rau de Bolou. In the valley below is the *Gîte d'étape Le Bolou* (☎ 05.62.92.80.83); there's no obvious way to get to it from the path so you'll need to phone for directions if you plan to stay here.

Walk south-east to the end of the valley, cross the stream and turn northwards along the level path. After about half an hour, the trail heads north-east and makes a gentle descent into Barèges.

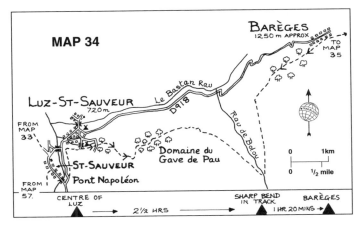

BARÈGES

✉ code 65120

Barèges is a tiny place spread out along the D918 road. There's little of interest here but the village is almost entirely devoted to tourism so there's plenty of accommodation and some useful shops.

Services

Barèges has most things you could need except a bank. There is a **post office**, **shops** (including a mini-supermarket and a sports store), a **cinema**, and a **swimming pool**. There's even a **paragliding school**.

The **tourist office** (☎ 05.62.92.16.00) is in the centre of the village.

Where to stay

The two best hotels in Barèges stand almost opposite each other. The *Hôtel Europe* ☆☆☆ (☎ 05.62.92.68.04, 🖹 05.62.92.65.29) has single rooms from €37/240F, while the *Hôtel Central* ☆☆ (☎ 05.62.92.68.05, 🖹 05.62.92.66.40) has singles starting at €32/210F.

For cheaper accommodation, try the *Hôtel Modern* ☆ (☎ 05.62.92.68.07) which has rooms from €14-37/90-240F.

There are two places with dormitory accommodation. The *Gîte d'étape L'Oasis* (☎ 05.62.92.69.47, 🖹 05.62 92.65.17) is very pleasant and can accommodate 40 people; it costs €12/80F for the night or €28/180F for demi-pension. Just above L'Oasis is *L'Hospitalet* (☎ 05.62.92.68.08, 🖹 05 62.92.66.13) a huge old place, which is the first building you reach as you enter Barèges on the GR10. Originally a military hospital, some people don't like it as the atmosphere is a bit gloomy, Conditions, however, are very civilized, and it's good value at €12/80F for the night and €4.50/30F for breakfast.

Seven hundred metres west of the village centre is the *Camping La Ribère* ☆☆ (☎ 05.62.92.69.01). Facilities at the campsite include a washing machine and tumble dryer; staying here costs €9/60F for two people and a tent.

🦌 Landslides in Barèges

Although the village's fate as a tourist stopover may seem a little sad, life is considerably better here today than in the past. Barèges was for years cursed by the steepness of the slopes above it and the instability of the soil. In the nineteenth century the threat became so great that the village was abandoned every winter. The inhabitants only returned once the snows had disappeared, often to start digging through the rubble of the houses that had been flattened. The woods that now cloak the hillside above the village have proved successful in stabilizing the slopes.

BARÈGES → LAC DE L'OULE   [MAP 35]

[Includes high section – see warning on p20] The GR10 goes straight past the front door of L'Hospitalet, dropping down briefly between the houses before climbing again on a footpath, to a tarmac lane. A sign points left along the road (PORTAZOUS GR10) and, after a hundred metres, you follow a farm track away from the road to the right. The track climbs for ten minutes and then descends to meet the D918. Turn right and follow the road, and after nearly a kilometre, take the slip road to the left, which leads past the *Auberge La Couquelle*, a restaurant/bar. Just beyond the

Map 35 – Barèges to Lac de L'Oule 171

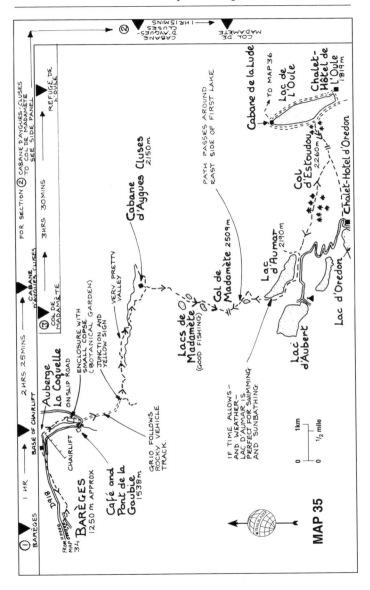

MAP 35

auberge is a large car park area at the base of some ski lifts. The path swings right near the corner of the car park and follows the stream south up the valley. After a few minutes' walk the footpath becomes clearer, and near the end of the valley it skirts a fenced enclosure (a botanical garden) and crosses the road just to the east of the **Pont de la Gaubie**.

On the far side of the road, the GR10 joins a stony vehicle track, which runs southwards to a track junction. To the right (south) the path leads to the Col d'Aubert (2h 30 according to the sign). The GR10, however, goes left (east) following the arrow towards the Cabane d'Aygues Cluses and the Col de Madamète. The rocky footpath climbs to a low col and makes its way up the valley beyond. The walk, alongside a tiny stream, is very pretty. After an hour you arrive at the *Cabane d'Aygues Cluses*, an empty and rather smelly stone hut with room for five or six people.

A sign outside indicates the way up to the Col de Madamète, and the path heads south. After half an hour you reach the beautiful and peaceful **Lacs de Madamète**. A further 35 minutes of easy climbing, negotiating a couple of areas of large boulders, brings you to the **Col de Madamète (2509m)**. The views in both directions are excellent: to the north you can see the observatory on the top of the Pic du Midi de Bigorre, while to the south are a range of peaks. The col marks the border of the Réserve de Néouvielle.

Follow the rocky path down the hillside and around to the east of the first lake. Beyond this the descent continues to the western end of **Lac d'Aumar** where the path levels out for the first time in the day. If the weather is fine this area may well be crowded – it's a popular spot for picnickers, and some brave souls even go for a swim.

At the far end of the lake the GR10 continues east, along the side of a wooded spur. There are views of the Lac d'Oredon and the Chalet-Hôtel d'Oredon below to the right. The *Chalet-Hôtel d'Oredon* (☎ 05.62.39.63 33) has 60 places: 44 in dormitories and 16 in private rooms. It is open (ie with a guardian) from mid-June to mid-September, and costs €12/75F per night and €28/180F for demi-pension.

Continuing on the main route, you soon reach the **Col d'Estoudou (2260m)** where there's a yellow sign: LAC DE L'OULE 1H. From here the path goes steeply downhill to the shore of the **Lac de l'Oule**. Turn right on reaching the vehicle track which runs around the lake side; ten minutes' walk brings you to the barrage, on the far side of which is the *Chalet-Hôtel de l'Oule* (☎ 05.62.98.48.62). There's space for 26 people: 16 in dormitories and 10 in rooms. It is staffed from the beginning of June to mid-September; charges are €10/65F per night and €25/160F for demi-pension.

LAC DE L'OULE → VIELLE AURE   [MAP 36, p174]

If you've stayed the night in the Chalet-Hôtel de L'Oule, it is easiest to follow the path up the east side of the lake. For those who have not, this description takes up again from the point where the GR10 comes down from the Col d'Estoudou to the west shore of the lake.

Go north around the lake shore and after about a quarter of an hour you reach the northern tip of the lake where the GR10 crosses a bridge. There's a yellow sign just above the *Cabane de la Lude*. This cabane appeared to be in permanent use when I visited, so don't rely on it as your overnight accommodation.

The GR10 heads straight uphill, swings right (south), and climbs gently through an area of pine trees. After about twenty minutes it veers sharply to the left and begins to climb northwards, leaving the trees. Finally it turns directly up the slope, passes close to the **Cabane de Bastan** (a private hut), and reaches a path junction. Although there is no sign to mark the junction, the rocks are literally covered with red and white markings, so it would be hard to miss. From here the GR10C goes north towards the Lacs de Bastan, and the GR10 turns south.

The next section is easy and relaxing. The GR10, now a grassy footpath, maintains an almost constant height and follows the hillside southwards and then eastwards. After passing beneath two ski lifts, the path sinks into a low dip and crosses two tiny streams. Beyond the streams there is a rough vehicle track which you follow (right) to the small parking area at the **Col de Portet (2215m)**.

The GR10 goes north from the car park but almost immediately swings eastwards. There are several trails across this bit of hillside; take the lowest one, which stays just above the tarmac road. The path descends gradually and then passes around the south flank of **Le Serre (2004m)**, on the far side of which it follows the line of the spur eastwards, descending to a grassy col.

Cross to the south of the col, and head down the hillside. There are literally dozens of sheep tracks which look as though they might be right, but which actually contour around the slopes; look out for the path which descends markedly – the lower part of it is along a fence line. On reaching a loose-surface road, near a sharp bend, follow it eastwards for about 200 metres. At the next sharp bend continue eastwards on a small footpath, which descends rapidly through young woods.

After about 25 minutes there is a fork: you can go either way – the tracks meet up again further down the hill. Five minutes beyond this the path crosses a road, and after a further quarter of an hour it enters Vielle Aure (see p175).

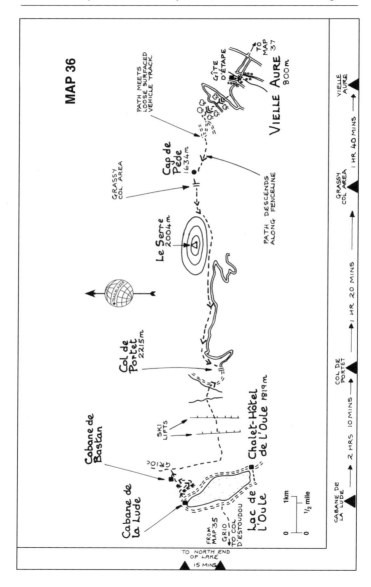

MAP 36

VIELLE AURE 800m

TO MAP 37

GÎTE D'ÉTAPE

PATH MEETS LOOSE SURFACED VEHICLE TRACK.

GRASSY COL AREA

Cap de Pede 1634m

Le Serre 2004m

PATH DESCENDS ALONG FENCELINE

Col de Portet 2215m

Cabane de Bastan

Cabane de la Lude

GR10

GR10

SKI LIFTS

Chalet-Hôtel de l'Oule 1819m

Lac de l'Oule

FROM MAP 35

TO COL D'ESTOUDOU

TO NORTH END OF LAKE
15 MINS

0   1km
0   ½ mile

CABANE DE LA LUDE ◄— 2 HRS 10 MINS —► COL DE PORTET ◄— 1 HR 20 MINS —► ◄— 1 HR 40 MINS —► GRASSY COL AREA ◄—— VIELLE AURE

VIELLE AURE AND ST-LARY-SOULAN

⌧ code 65170

Vielle Aure is a peaceful little village which, with St-Lary-Soulan nearby, has plenty of facilities. Unfortunately the excellent gîte which had opened in Vielle Aure when the first edition of this book was researched appears now to have closed.

Services

Within the village of Vielle Aure there is a **post office** and a **tourist office** (☎ 05.62.39.50.00). **Shops** include a small épicerie and a tabac.

Everything else you could need including **banks**, a **cash dispenser**, a **pharmacy** and a **launderette** can be found in St-Lary-Soulan.

There are three or four daily buses to and from Lannemezan, one of which continues to Tarbes; Lannemezan has a railway station. Buses stop in St Lary near the téléphérique, and in Vielle Aure near the tourist office.

Where to stay

St-Lary-Soulan is crammed with hotels including the plush *Hôtel Mercure* ☆☆☆ (☎ 05.62.99.50.00, 🖻 05.62.99 50.10) where double rooms start at €84/550F, and the equally nice *Hôtel La Pergola* ☆☆ (☎ 05.62.39.40.46, 🖻 05.62.40.06.55), which has rooms from €46/300F.

In Vielle Aure, *Hôtel Aurelia* ☆☆ (☎ 05.62.39.56.90, 🖻 05.62.39.43.75), with double rooms from €31-42/200-275F, is not quite in the same league, but is still good news; the owners are friendly, there's a pleasant terrace restaurant and a small swimming pool.

There are a few campsites near the two villages. The closest is *Camping Autun* which is near to Hôtel Aurelia. Alternatively you could try *Camping Municipal La Lanne* ☆☆☆☆ (☎ 05.62.39.41.58, 🖻 05.62.40.01.40)), which is in the centre of St-Lary-Soulan and charges €141/924F for emplacement and €4.50/29F per person.

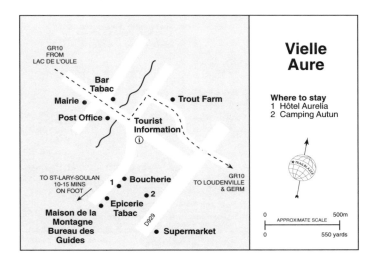

Vielle Aure

Where to stay
1 Hôtel Aurelia
2 Camping Autun

❏ **Walking times on trail maps**
Note that on all the trail maps in this book the times shown alongside each map refer only to time spent actually walking. Add 30-40% to allow for rest stops.

VIELLE AURE → GERM [MAP 37]

Cross the bridge over the Neste d'Aure and turn immediately left and then right, so that you follow the lane parallel to the D116 eastwards to the main road (D929). The GR10 goes straight across the road and enters the village of **Bourisp**, crossing a small bridge and swinging round to the left as it comes into the village itself. Almost immediately after the left hand bend, turn right up a concreted track between the houses. This soon bears right and then narrows to a footpath. The trail winds through the trees before climbing the hillside to **Estensan**, a tiny hamlet, where there's a water point next to the church.

Follow the lane through the village and turn left along the D225 before forking off immediately to the right along a small access lane. A few hundred metres up the lane the GR10 bears off to the left uphill along a stony farm track. Gradually the track narrows into a footpath which meets the road briefly, and then continues up the hillside to enter **Azet** (1172m).

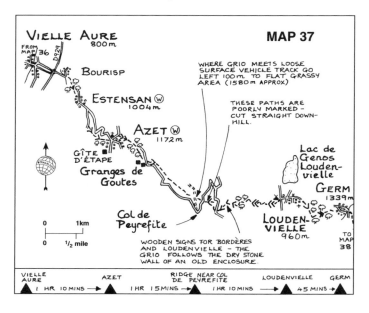

AZET

✉ code 65170

Azet is a peaceful and attractive village; there are no shops but there are three places to stay, all of which are on the lane running south from the church.

The best of the three is *La Bergerie* (☎ 05.62.40.08.98, 🖹 05.62.40.06.31), an attractive house which offers table d'hôte; it costs €18/120F for bed and breakfast, and €28/180F for demi-pension. Almost opposite, the *Auberge du Col* (☎ 05.62.39.48.97) is rather plain and unfriendly, and charges €11/70F for the night, and €28/180F for demi-pension. The *gîte d'étape* (☎ 05.62 39.41.44), about 50 metres down the lane from the other two, is simple but clean and has a small kitchen for self-catering.

The GR10 goes round the south side of the church, past a water fountain, and leaves the village on the lane running north-east. Just after the last house it turns up a steep vehicle track. The track bends south-eastwards, and narrows to a footpath which runs almost horizontally across the hillside through an avenue of trees.

Gradually the path climbs to pass above the **Granges de Goutes**; it soon meets and crosses the road. From here to the **Col de Peyrefite**, the GR10 is not well marked but is hard to miss. You follow a well-worn earthen path parallel to and only just above the road. As it rounds a small spur, the route ahead is visible all the way to the col.

Just north of the col you come to a loose-surface road. Turn left for about a hundred metres to a level grassy area, where there's a tiny concrete marker with the number '1' on it. Just below this the path starts to lead down towards Loudenvielle. The descent eastwards is not well marked. A short way below the crest of the hill the path meets the road for the first time; cross over and go straight down through the bracken – you'll rediscover the markers about half way down the slope. Where the track meets the road for the second time there is a steep bank. Head southwards above the road into the 'fold' of the valley where there are easier places to scramble down.

On the far side of the road a track runs down the centre of the valley, to the east at first but then bending around to the north-east and coming to a path junction. Wooden signs point to Bordères and Loudenvielle but the GR10 actually takes the middle option and heads eastwards along the dry-stone wall of an old enclosure. Slightly below this enclosure it meets a cart track; follow the track to the left for a short distance before taking a right fork, marked both with yellow paint and with red and white. A short way down this new track you pass a house and emerge from the trees on to a patch of open hillside with a good view over the valley. Almost immediately, the GR10 turns sharply right and down the steep hillside. Two thirds of the way down there is a path junction. To the right the path crosses a stream, to the left it goes down some steps. Go left and after a few minutes you reach the campsite on the edge of Loudenvielle.

LOUDENVIELLE

✉ code 65510

Loudenvielle is a pleasant enough little village with some useful facilities. The *Hostellerie des Templiers* (☎ 05.62.99 68.03, 🖹 05.62.99.60.94) is welcoming and has double rooms from €38/250F. The sunny terrace bar is good place to stop for a rest on your way through the village.

Camping de Pène Blanche ☆☆ (☎ 05.62.99.68.85) charges €2/14F for emplacement and €2.50/16F per person.

In the centre of the village, **shops** include a mini supermarket, sports store, newsagent and pharmacy. There's a Crédit Agricole **cash dispenser** and **tourist office** next to the shops. The **post office** is a short way to the east, near the church.

The GR10 goes straight through the village. Just by the post office, a wooden sign points the way left up a path which leads away from the buildings. Almost immediately, it turns right along a grassy track and climbs south-eastwards. The route is well-marked and there's some shade from trees but it's a tiring 45 minutes up to **Germ**. At the top of the hill, where the footpath meets the road, is a sign directing you left to the gîte. The *Gîte Montagne de Germ* (☎ 05.62.99 65.27) is well worth stopping at mainly because it has a swimming pool. Quite apart from this, however, it's very pleasant, and good value at €12/75F for the night or €20/130F for demi-pension. If there's room, campers can put up a tent in the garden for €4.50/30F. The *Auberge de Germ*, on the GR10 as you leave the village, is palatial by comparison with the gîte and charges proportionately higher prices. It costs €25/160F per person to stay here and, strangely, it appears to be closed on Mondays and Tuesdays.

GERM → GRANGES D'ASTAU   [MAP 38, p179]

Leave Germ on the lane leading south-east; just after crossing a stream turn left up a steep track. At the top of the rise the track swings southwards and passes the Granges de Béderèdes. Follow the rough vehicle track as it continues south, above and parallel to the tarmac lane. Just as the track begins to descend towards the road, and before a sharp switchback, the GR10 turns off left onto a small footpath.

The path heads south-eastwards, running almost horizontally around the hillside. After half an hour you reach a somewhat precarious section where a landslip has taken away the path, and you must be careful when crossing the steep slope. Quarter of an hour's walk beyond this there is a small artificially-made pool, and here the GR10 meets its variant, which has come up from Loudenvielle via the Pont des Chèvres. The two paths ascend the next part of the valley on opposite sides of the stream until, after a further 20 minutes, they arrive at the *Ourtiga Cabane* (approx 1620m). The hut is small and basic but is open for use by walkers.

From the plateau below the cabane, go south-east beside the stream to pick up the GR markings and the narrow footpath; beyond here the route

Map 38 – Germ to Granges d'Astau   179

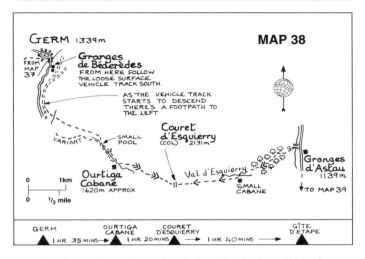

GERM 1339m   **MAP 38**

Granges
de Béderèdes
FROM HERE FOLLOW
THE LOOSE SURFACE
VEHICLE TRACK SOUTH.

FROM MAP 37

AS THE VEHICLE TRACK
STARTS TO DESCEND
THERE'S A FOOTPATH TO
THE LEFT.

VARIANT   SMALL POOL

Couret
d'Esquierry
(COL)   2131m

Granges
d'Astau
1139m

Ourtiga
Cabane
1620m APPROX

Val d'Esquierry

SMALL
CABANE

TO MAP 39

0   1km

0   ½ mile

GERM	OURTIGA CABANE	COURET D'ESQUIERRY	GÎTE D'ETAPE
1 HR 35 MINS →	1 HR 20 MINS →	1 HR 40 MINS →	

is well marked, and requires no description. There's about 500m of ascent to the **Couret d'Esquierry (2131m)**, a hard and tiring climb which is rewarded by the views from the top. The ridge which runs north-south on either side of the col marks the departmental border; as you cross the col you leave Hautes Pyrénées and enter Haute Garonne.

The walk down the Val d'Esquierry is easy and attractive. After three quarters of an hour you come to a small *cabane* which, judging by the amount of graffiti, has seen heavy service as a refuge. Below the hut the path crosses a stream and after five more minutes it enters a beech wood. The steep slope is negotiated in long zigzags until the path emerges at the valley bottom and crosses a stream to the **Granges d'Astau (1139m)**. The *Auberge d'Astau* (☎ 05.61.79.35.63, 🖹 05.61.94.34.59) has a restaurant/bar and, in a separate building, a well-maintained gîte. It costs €11/70F per night or €26/170F for demi-pension.

GRANGES D'ASTAU → BAGNÈRES-DE-LUCHON [MAP 39, p181]

Follow the rough road south from the parking area in front of the auberge. Gradually it gets more and more uneven and boulder-strewn until it is passable only on foot, winding up the wooded hillside in sharp turns. After about three quarters of an hour you come to a little building rigged with a cable and pulley system; a set of rails runs off around the hillside. Presumably this was used during the construction of the electricity installation which is tucked away below the lake. Twenty minutes further up the hill, you arrive at the **Lac d'Oô (1504m)**. The lake itself is quite pretty but the really eye-catching feature here is the 273 metre waterfall which tumbles down the cliffs on the south side of the lake. Just across the barrage is *Chez Tintin* (☎ 05.61.79.12.29) a refuge/café which has a terrace overlooking the water. It's open from the start of May to mid-October and has dormitory places for 20 people. A night in the dormitory costs €7/45F (or you can pay €15/100F for a double room) and the evening meal costs €10/65F. Camping is permitted nearby. A couple of walkers have noted that the reception they received in Chez Tintin was rather less than welcoming and that the facilities were pretty poor, but the good food is reputed to make up for this.

The path continues gaining height around the side of the lake, and thence makes its way up a gully to the east of the waterfall. The route is obvious and well-marked and attempts have clearly been made to stop people short-cutting. Just short of the **Col d'Espingo** there's a path junction which is marked by a painted sign on the rocks. From here the GR10 doubles back on itself and climbs north-eastwards. This last section towards the col is something of a slog; if you need encouragement, take a break halfway and admire the views to the south-west. Now that you're above the level of the lake, the glacier and snow-covered upper slopes around Pic Belloc can be seen to best advantage. Finally you reach the **Hourquette des Hounts-Secs (2275m)**. The views to the south-west are magnificent, and to the east the route of the GR10 is visible, until it disappears to the right just below the Sommet de la Coume de Bourg.

The next section is easy, as the path falls, climbs briefly over a ridge, descends again and finally makes a short, steep climb to the col (2272m) below the Sommet de la Coume de Bourg. The col and the **Pic de Cécire** above it are popular spots for day walkers, and the area can get fairly busy. There's a tiny spring just to the south-east of the col, in the middle of a pile of rocks, which provides a welcome chance to fill up with water.

From the col, descend north-eastwards to **Superbagnères (1800m)**. The ugly ski resort with its imposing central building is generally fairly crowded because the road running up here allows easy access to the hills. The area is popular in particular for mountain biking and paragliding. Although many of the facilities in the resort are closed during the summer, there are a couple of cafés which remain open.

If you're exhausted at this point one option is to take the **cable car**. The final stretch of the GR10 to Bagnères-de-Luchon is all downhill but is tiring nonetheless, as you lose over 1000m of height in a very short distance.

From the resort, follow the rough road heading north-west for ten minutes, to a small hexagonal building. The GR10 passes to the left of the building along an ill-defined path which, after a minute or two, bends right to join a clear forest track. The descent from here is well marked, and is almost entirely through woods.

Map 38 – Granges d'Astau to Bagnères de Luchon 181

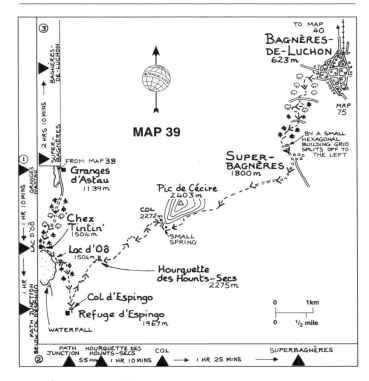

MAP 39

BAGNÈRES-DE-LUCHON
✉ code 31110

Luchon is the Pyrenean resort town to beat them all. A quick wander down the Allées d'Etigny, past the magnificent Thermes building and the casino, show that this was once a spa town of some importance. It still has a dignified atmosphere and the Thermes are still pulling in the customers. For the walker, Luchon suffers only from the lack of a gîte d'étape. Nonetheless, if you can stump up the cost of a hotel room for a night or two, it's an excellent place to take a break.

Luchon is on the junction of two good walking routes (see also p257), and has all the facilities you could want.

Services
The **tourist office** (☎ 05.61.79.21 21, 🖥 www.luchon.com) is on Allées d'Étigny, as is the **post office**. There are at least three **banks** (and cash dispensers) also on the Allées d'Étigny. Note that there's nowhere to change money once the banks and post office are closed (ie on Saturday afternoon and Sunday). There are two mini supermarkets in the town centre, and plenty of tabacs and

newsagents. There's a **launderette** near the Hôtel François 1er.

The **railway station** is to the north of the town centre; there's one direct train daily to Toulouse, and four SNCF buses daily from Bagnères to Montrejeau, where you can get connections to Toulouse, Tarbes and Lourdes. The journey from Bagnères to Toulouse via bus and train costs €16/103F. If you're in need of a **taxi**, try Jose Farrus (☎ 05.61.79.06.78) or Jean-François Gerdessus (☎ 06.09.32.37.44; ☎ 06.07 04.51.76; ☎ 05.61.79.06.57)

Where to stay

There are plenty of places to stay in Luchon unless you find yourself in town during the annual Flower Festival which takes place at the end of August – in which case, good luck.

The smartest spot in town is the *Hôtel Corneille* ☆☆☆ (☎ 05.61.79.36.22, ▤ 05.61.79.81.11) where during high season double rooms start at €85/560F. If you're after somewhere to relax and treat yourself this could be it. Among the more reasonably priced hotels are several good choices.

The *Hôtel Panoramic* ☆☆ (☎ 05.61.79.30.90, ▤ 05.61.79.32.84) is very friendly and is accustomed to walkers; clean, pleasant rooms are from €28/180F. The *Hôtel Bon Accueil* ☆☆ (☎ 05.61.79.02.20, ▤ 05.61.79.76.83) is almost opposite the Panoramic and has rooms from €36/235F. The *Hôtel Bellevue* ☆☆ (☎ 05.61.79.01.65, ▤ 05.61.79.74.27) has rooms from €38/ 250F.

Further out from the centre (and consequently quieter) the *Hôtel Dar-*

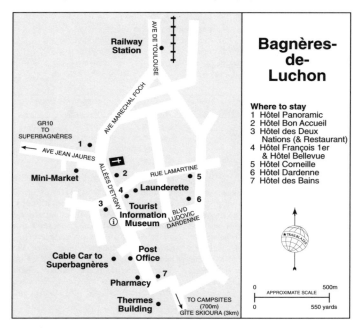

Bagnères-de-Luchon

Where to stay
1 Hôtel Panoramic
2 Hôtel Bon Accueil
3 Hôtel des Deux Nations (& Restaurant)
4 Hôtel François 1er & Hôtel Bellevue
5 Hôtel Corneille
6 Hôtel Dardenne
7 Hôtel des Bains

Railway Station

AVE DE TOULOUSE

AVE MARECHAL FOCH

GR10 TO SUPERBAGNÈRES

AVE JEAN JAURES

Mini-Market

ALLEES DETIGNY

RUE LAMARTINE

Launderette

Tourist Information Museum

BLVD LUDOVIC DARDENNE

Cable Car to Superbagnères

Post Office

Pharmacy

Thermes Building

TO CAMPSITES (700m)
GÎTE SKIOURA (3km)

★TRAILBLAZER

0   APPROXIMATE SCALE   500m
0   550 yards

denne ☆☆ (☎ 05.61.94.66.70, 📖 05 61.79.62.00), near the casino, has good rooms from €35/230F.

At the cheaper end of the scale, the **Hôtel François 1er** (☎ 05.61.79.03.94) has single rooms from €23/150F (although they're right above the town's noisiest bar).

The nearest gîte is 3km south along the D125. The **Gîte Skioura** (☎ 05.61 79.60.59) specializes in taking groups but will also take individuals for a night. It's €12/75F for a place in the dormitory and €24/155F for demi-pension.

There are three campsites, all of which are on the D125 leading south out of the town centre. Seven hundred metres from the centre is the **Camping des Thermes** (☎ 05.61.79.03.85) which is rather crowded and 'residential'; it's €10/67F for two people and a tent.

Four hundred metres further on is the **Camping Beauregard** ☆☆ (☎ 05.61

79.30.74) which has more space and even a few real tents; it's €3/20F for emplacement and €2.50/17F per person. Beyond this you come to **Camping Chanteclerc** (☎ 05.61.79.01.10).

What to see

At the southern end of the Allées d'Étigny is the imposing **Thermes building**, which was opened in 1848 on the site of the old Roman baths. Opposite the building is a statue of Baron d'Étigny himself. Unfortunately the appearance of this central square has been spoiled by the ugly new Thermes building which stands next to its older counterpart. A visit to the **museum** is recommended. It's open daily from 09.00-12.00 and 14.00-18.00, and houses a diverse and fascinating collection – everything from Roman masonry to old newspaper cuttings from the turn of the century. Entry is €1.50/10F.

BAGNÈRES-DE-LUCHON → FOS   [MAPS 40-41, pp184-5]

This stretch to Fos is a long one, and many people will prefer to break it up in some way, either by camping or spending a night in a cabane along the way.

Walk north past the railway station on the avenue de Toulouse and 300 metres past the station building, cross the line via a small underpass. Turn left on the D125 heading out of Bagnères and after half a kilometre, turn right at a roundabout towards **Juzet-de-Luchon**. Up to this point there have been few if any GR markers but they start again from here, marking the route through the middle of the village. Just on the north side of Juzet the climb begins as the path heads uphill, short-cutting between the stretches of road. After about half an hour of steep climbing through the woods, you come to the tiny and slightly ramshackle hamlet of **Sode**. Follow the markers, as the GR10 winds between the houses, and take a wide, level path leading north-west out of the village. Soon the climb begins again, and the path narrows considerably as it winds up through the woods. An hour and a quarter later you emerge at **Artigue (1224m)**, a village with a truly ancient feel to it. There's a restaurant/café here (closed on Mondays) towards the southern end of the hamlet, on the top 'level' of buildings. There's a spring with drinking water in the yard.

Although there is still a 500 metre climb above Artigue, it's fairly easy. Five minutes above the village there's a small spring which is a welcome chance to fill up with water. Beyond here the GR10 follows farm tracks that wind backwards and forwards across the open slopes. On a fine morning there's plenty to see; the hillside and village below are attractive, there are excellent views across the valley, and as a back drop there are the high peaks of the border. After an hour, the GR10 reaches a cabane just to the south-west of the **Serrat des Créspés**. The hut is private but the stone bench outside is a good place to take a break and enjoy the view.

Climb north-east from the hut, up the grassy hillside, and pass to the north of the Serrat des Créspés. After half an hour you reach a plateau and, some fifteen minutes later, come to a tiny pond next to a track junction. (Just to the south-east of the junction there's a basic cabane that could sleep six people). Turn left and climb the hillside to the Col des Taons de Bacanère where there are the remains of an old building. From here the path follows the line of the border, passing a series of numbered marker stones en route. After descending from the **Pic de Bacanère (2193m)** the path leads down into a col via two more border markers. It then cuts back

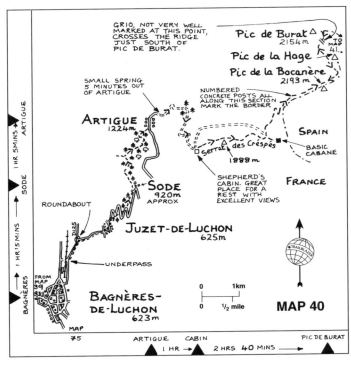

GRIO, NOT VERY WELL MARKED AT THIS POINT, CROSSES THE RIDGE JUST SOUTH OF PIC DE BURAT.

Pic de Burat △
2154m

TO MAP 41.

Pic de la Hage

Pic de la Bocanère
2193 m

SMALL SPRING
5 MINUTES OUT
OF ARTIGUE

NUMBERED
CONCRETE POSTS ALL
ALONG THIS SECTION
MARK THE BORDER

ARTIGUE
1224m

SPAIN

Serrat des Créspés

BASIC
CABANE

1888 m

SHEPHERD'S
CABIN. GREAT
PLACE FOR A
REST WITH
EXCELLENT VIEWS

FRANCE

SODE
920m
APPROX

ROUNDABOUT

D125

JUZET-DE-LUCHON
625m

UNDERPASS

1 HR 5MINS ► ARTIGUE

SODE

1 HR 15 MINS

BAGNÈRES

FROM
MAP
39

BAGNÈRES-
DE-LUCHON
623m

0   1km
0   ½ mile

MAP 40

MAP
#5

ARTIGUE   CABIN
▲ 1 HR → ▲ 2 HRS 40 MINS →

PIC DE BURAT
▲

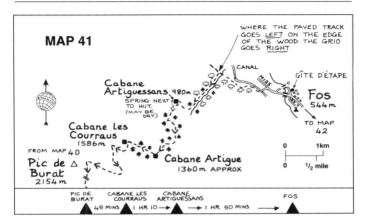

to the north-west before climbing again to cross the ridge running between the **Pic de la Hage** and the **Pic de Burat**, near an area of rusted fencing. This part is not well marked.

Cross the ridge and descend on a small footpath which, after 45 minutes, reaches the ***Cabanes des Courraus*** (**1586m**). The upper cabane can sleep eight people and has a fireplace, table and benches; the lower cabane is bare inside but would do for emergency shelter. Twenty-five minutes below the Cabanes des Courraus is the ***Cabane Artigue*** which though rather basic could sleep four or five people. The descent continues through pine woods and after 5-10 minutes the path joins a rough road, only to leave it almost immediately down an overgrown footpath which cuts steeply down the hillside. The GR10 rejoins the loose-surfaced road briefly before departing down a side track to the ***Cabane Artiguessans***, a hut which appears to be in permanent use by foresters. The spring beside the hut may be of use even if the cabane is not available as a shelter (although in a dry summer it may be barely more than a trickle).

Near the Cabane Artiguessans the route becomes a little difficult to locate; it runs from the south-east corner of the clearing below the hut. From here it descends through trees to meet an ancient paved pathway which runs steeply down the hillside next to a rushing stream. Be careful of your footing here as the stones are extremely slippery. At the bottom of the hill, and just inside the edge of the wood, the GR10 leaves the paved path and turns south-eastwards. A sign here (FOS: 45 MINUTES) points the way along the edge of the wood. Follow the woodline for some minutes before descending to the side of the canal. Soon you reach a bridge; cross it and follow the road into Fos.

FOS

✉ code 31440

There are several places to stay in Fos, although it's not a particularly exciting village. If you've got the energy you might consider continuing up the road to **Melles** (about 50 minutes further on), which is a much more attractive village with a very pleasant hotel.

In Fos, the *gîte d'étape* (☎ 05.61.79.44.51) is €8/55F per night. Meals are not available but there are reasonable self-catering facilities. The *Hôtel Gentilhommière* (☎ 05.61.79.29 00), on the main road through the village, has rooms from €18-31/120-200F. There's a bar/restaurant here, but check whether it's going to be open before you pin your hopes on it. It's closed on Sunday evenings and all day Monday. The *Camping Municipal de Fos* (☎ 05.61.79.29.28 or (Mairie) ☎ 05 61.79 41.61) is pleasant and good value – emplacement is €2/12F and it's €2/12F per person. In mid-summer you must book in advance.

There is an **épicerie/presse** and a **boulangerie/charcuterie** on the main road, at the south-eastern end of the village.

FOS → EYLIE   [MAP 42, p187; MAP 43, p189]

This is another long stretch which might be better completed over two days. Alternatively, you might be able to save a little time by hitching a lift up the road past Melles, and on to the point where the road ends.

Follow the main road (N125) south-eastwards, and just before the police and customs post, take the lane to the left, which climbs to the village of **Melles**. There are no shortcuts; the GR10 follows the lane all the way up the hill.

Melles is a pretty village, and the *Auberge du Crabère* (☎ 05.61 79.21.99, 🖹 05.61.79.74.71) has been recommended as a great place to stay. Double rooms (with demi-pension) start at €29/190F. The restaurant looks good too: the Menu Randonneur is a very reasonable €11/70F, and the Menu de Terroir for €22/145F should satisfy most appetites. Outside the mid summer high season the hotel is closed on Wednesdays.

Continue up the tarmac lane from Melles for another 4km, always climbing but on a gentle gradient. There are springs at regular intervals along the way. Near the end of the road is a perturbing sign which reads: 'Randonneurs Attention! Zone Frequentée par L'Ours...Evitez de vous deplacer seul. Ne quittez pas les sentiers balisés'. Your chances of seeing a bear (see p188) are practically nil but it concentrates the mind.

Just past the sign is a car park. Take the concreted access track to the left (there's a No Entry sign 'Sauf Riverains'); the lane leads only a few hundred metres further to a couple of houses, where the footpath begins.

The walk up to the Cabane d'Uls is very pretty but extremely hard work with around 1000m of ascent in the space of three and a half kilometres. The trail is well marked and needs little description. The initial part of the climb is through woods but after crossing a stream midway, the path mounts over open slopes. Finally after ascending the steep eastern end of the valley, the path begins to level out. After 10 minutes more across grassy

Map 42 – Fos to Étang d'Araing 187

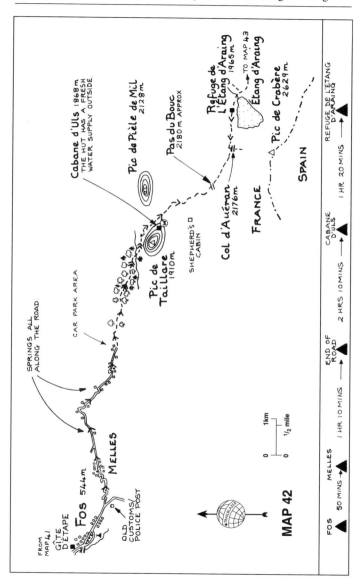

MAP 42

FOS	MELLES	END OF ROAD	CABANE D'ULS	REFUGE DE L'ÉTANG D'ARAING
50 MINS →	1 HR. 10 MINS →	2 HRS. 10 MINS →	1 HR. 20 MINS →	

Bears in the Pyrenees

Until the turn of the century bear hunting was a popular sport. Some of the hunters have even passed into Pyrenean folklore: it is said that one Bonnecaze of Laruns, who died in 1860, had killed 55 of the animals. Overhunting combined with deforestation saw to it that by the 1950's and 1960's numbers were so depleted as to make the recovery of the Pyrenean brown bear almost impossible.

In 1996, therefore, under a scheme to rescue the species, two female Slovenian brown bears were released into the wild above Melles. The experiment was fiercely opposed by many people whose criticisms appeared, at first, to have been justified when the bears ambled over the mountains and began slaughtering sheep in the Aran valley. Better times seemed to be ahead, when one of the bears, nicknamed Melba, produced three cubs. The project was dealt a crushing blow in September 1997 when Melba was shot by a hunter.

bog, you come to the *Cabane d'Uls* (**1868m**). The hut can sleep nine and has a table, benches, and a fireplace; there's a spring outside.

From the cabane, climb south-eastwards over a small grassy col and into a much larger bowl formed by the hill tops. There's a shepherd's hut to the right, but the GR10 passes well to the east of it. Follow the path around the edge of the depression and then around a hillside to a grassy col, the **Pas du Bouc (2170m)**. Contour around the side of the hill for quarter of an hour on a level path before arriving at the **Col d'Auéran (2176m)**. The col marks the border between Haute Garonne and Ariège Pyrénées; to the south, the impressive **Pic de Crabère** marks the border with Spain. Climb northwards briefly, and then head east down the spur to the refuge, which can be seen below. The *Refuge de l'Étang d'Araing* (☎ 05.61 96.73.73) is a modern building, which has a guardian in residence full time from mid June to mid October. The refuge is also manned at weekends in May, early June and October, and a small section with 12 places remains open for basic accommodation throughout the year. Accommodation is €12/80F for the night, and drinks and food are available.

Cross below the barrage and turn right (the path for the Tour de Biros goes left). As the path starts to climb, you pass an empty refuge; it's pretty spartan inside but quite adequate for a night if you don't want to stay in the staffed refuge. Continue past some old mines and after about 45 minutes of climbing south-eastwards, you reach a col (2221m) over the Serre d'Araing.

The path skirts a rocky outcrop and descends into the valley. After three quarters of an hour you reach the old mines at **Bentaillou**, and half an hour below these you come to another area of old workings. The final descent from here is through a wood on steep tracks, until the path brings you out at Eylie.

Map 43 – Étang d'Araing to Eylie 189

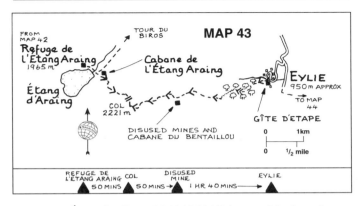

The **Gîte d'Étape d'Eylie** (☎ 05.61.96.14.00) is one of the best gîtes on the GR10. It's clean and well looked after with excellent kitchen facilities. Meals are available by prior arrangement. Accommodation here costs €11/70F for the night, or €26/170F for demi-pension.

EYLIE → CABANE D'AOUEN   [MAP 44, p190]

This section is one of the few on the GR10 where proper accommodation is not available in any form. The next gîte along the way is at Esbints, which is three days' walk, or two days if you're prepared to put in some extra hours. The route is described here as two long day stages. The only alternative to camping or staying in a cabane overnight is to leave the GR10 and follow a path down into the valley, possibly staying at Bornac.

Walk south from the gîte, following the path between buildings and past some old rusting machinery. Cross the rickety footbridge at the bottom of the valley and climb up the steep hillside. After about 20-25 minutes, the path reaches a small shoulder; it remains almost level around the next tiny valley, crossing a stream en route. Just before you reach a second stream, the Rau de Laspe, turn south-east along a fence line and begin to climb again. At first the gradient of the path is fairly gentle but after the track enters the woods it becomes progressively steeper. In the upper area of the woods the path passes under two steel cables, which run up the hillside, stretched between pylons.

Above the woods, the gradient of the climb lessens slightly. As the path approaches a dilapidated hut, a sign marked 'variante' points left towards an old mine working. Ignore this and turn right, following the path towards the Rau de Laspe. Climb beside the stream for a few metres, then cross it and make directly for the **Col de l'Arech (1802m)**. Once at

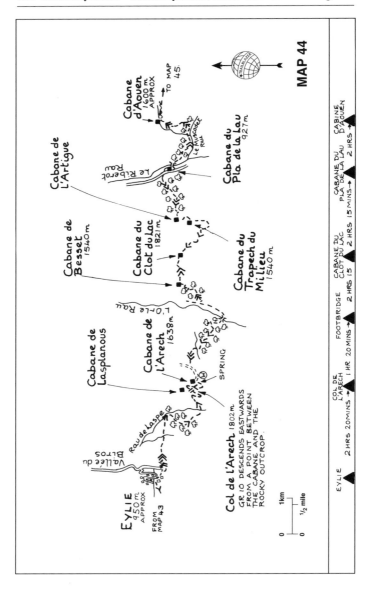

MAP 44

TO MAP 45

Cabane d'Aouen 1600 m APPROX

Cabane de L'Artigue

Cabane de Besset 1540 m

Cabane du Clot du Lac 1821 m

Cabane de Lasplanous

Cabane de L'Arech 1638 m

Rau de Laspe

Vallée du Biros

EYLIE 950 m APPROX

FROM MAP 43

Col de l'Arech 1802 m

GR 10 DESCENDS EASTWARDS FROM A POINT BETWEEN THE CABANE AND THE ROCKY OUTCROP.

SPRING

L'Orle Rau

Cabane du Trapech du Milieu 1540 m

Le Ribérot Rau

Le Muscadet Rau

Cabane du Pla de la Lau 927 m

0   1km
0   ½ mile

EYLIE	COL DE L'ARECH	FOOTBRIDGE	CABANE DU CLOT DU LAC	CABANE DU PLA DE LA LAU	CABANE D'AOUEN
2 HRS 20 MINS	1 HR 20 MINS	2 HRS 15	2 HRS 15 MINS	2 HRS

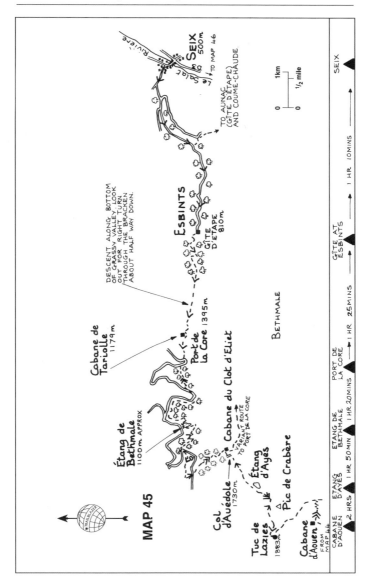

MAP 45

Cabane d'Aouen
FROM MAP 44

Tuc de Lazies
1883m.

Col d'Auédole
1730m.

△ Pic de Crabère

Étang d'Ayès

⌂ Cabane du Clot d'Eliet

VARIANT ROUTE
PORT DE LA CORE

Étang de Bethmale
1100m APPROX

Cabane de Tariolle
1179m.

Port de La Core 1395m.

DESCENT ALONG BOTTOM
OF GRASSY VALLEY. LOOK
OUT FOR RIGHT TURN
THROUGH THE BRACKEN
ABOUT HALF WAY DOWN.

BETHMALE

ESBINTS

GÎTE D'ÉTAPE 810m.

TO AUNAC
(GÎTE D'ÉTAPE)
AND COUME-CHAUDE

RIVIÈRE

Le Salat

SEIX 500m.

TO MAP 46

0   1km
0   ½ mile

CABANE D'AOUEN	ÉTANG D'AYÈS	ÉTANG DE BETHMALE	PORT DE LA CORE	GÎTE AT ESBINTS	SEIX
2 HRS	1 HR 50MIN	1 HR 20MINS	1 HR 25MINS	1 HR 10MINS	

the ridge, turn north along it towards the *Cabane de Lasplanous*. The GR10 descends from the ridge just south of the cabane, midway between the building and the rocky promontory which dominates the col. The descent to the Cabane L'Arech, accomplished in two long sweeps across the hillside, takes 20 minutes.

The *Cabane L'Arech* (1638m) is a small hut with a sign outside stating that walkers can stay here only if it's not in use by shepherds. There's a spring a few metres south of the cabane.

Follow the vehicle track which leads down from the cabane and, after about 10 minutes, turn right down a tiny footpath which descends through the heather. After some minutes the path swings to the right and heads into the gully. Cross the stream, the Rau de L'Arech, and descend south-east through mature beech woods. Eventually you reach the valley bottom and the footbridge over the stream.

Cross the footbridge and go north for about 15 minutes along a level path, to a wooden sign which points the way uphill. The footpath climbs across a meadow and enters the trees, making a steady ascent. Eventually it passes through the upper tree line and rises over grassy slopes to the *Cabane de Besset* (1540m). The tiny hut is in excellent condition: immaculately clean, it even has plates and cutlery, and a saw for cutting wood. The view from the front of the hut is superb and there's a spring a few metres from the door. At a real push it could sleep four or five.

Forty minutes' more climbing up steep grassy slopes brings you to the *Cabane du Clot du Lac* (1821m), which is very basic and could only sleep two people. There appears to be no water supply nearby. On the way down from the Cabane du Clot du Lac, the *Cabane Trapech du Milieu* (1540m) soon becomes visible below. Getting to it takes some time, however, as the GR10 makes a long detour to the south-east, almost to the banks of the stream, before it turns back northwards towards the cabane. The hut is dark and dirty; it could take four or five people. There's a spring just behind the building. Twenty five minutes further down the hill is the *Cabane de L'Artigue* which is smaller and in no better condition; two or three people at most could fit into this one.

From here, descend alongside the stream, Le Trapech Rau, through woods to the bottom of the valley. The area is a popular picnic spot so it may be packed with cars. Passing quickly through the mêlée, turn south-east along the river, Le Riberot Rau, to the *Cabane du Pla de la Lau* (927m). The location is excellent but the hut is not one of the best. The ugly concrete building has three rooms, two of which are suitable for sleeping in. One of these could take two people and the other could sleep four.

Cross the footbridge near the cabane and follow the river south-eastwards up the valley before turning eastwards along the bank of its tributary, Le Muscadet Rau. The path climbs through trees, alongside the waterfalls and white water of the Muscadet: it's a very attractive scene. The path finally leads away from the river and the trees and heads up the valley of the Rau d'Aouen. After some further steep climbing, you reach the *Cabane d'Aouen* (1600m approx). It's an ugly but functional hut, newly made out of concrete breeze blocks. The smaller room is left unlocked, and there's space here for only two people. There's a water supply via a hosepipe but a little investigation showed that the source was actually open to contamination in an area heavily grazed by sheep. You should purify the water before drinking it.

CABANE D'AOUEN → SEIX [MAP 45, p191]

From the Cabane d'Aouen, climb to a wooden signpost just below the top of the ridge. Follow the level path north-west across the hillside, which soon brings you to the **Tuc de Lazies** (near spot height 1883m on the map). The GR10 heads due east from the col, losing a little height and then rising again to pass just to the north-east of the **Pic de Crabère**.

The **Étang d'Ayes**, visible below, is reached after about 25 minutes. Go north-east from the lake along the hillside and climb slightly to the **Col d'Auédole (1730m)**, below which is the *Cabane du Clot d'Eliet*. The cabane is very basic and dirty, but could sleep about five people if necessary.

At this point there's a choice. The GR10 proper descends north-westwards and makes a loop via the **Étang de Bethmale**, an attractive lake which is popular with picnickers. The variant heads almost directly east, retaining its height and passing across rocky terrain before reaching the Port de la Core. A notice at the Port de la Core warns walkers not to use this route in stormy or wet weather.

The main GR10 goes steeply downhill through beech woods. It crosses a rough road, and then leaves the trees briefly to make a long zigzag across the open hillside. After re-entering the woods it meets the road again, and follows it to the right for a short distance before heading downhill to the left. The footpath leads down to the lake, emerging by the Refuge Forestier de Bethmale. The house is not for use by walkers but there's an *open-sided shelter* on the east edge of the lake which might be useful for cover from cloudbursts.

Take the footpath leading uphill beside the shelter; after four or five minutes it levels off and contours around the hillside, heading north at first and then swinging southwards. Finally it descends to join the road just below an area of heavy duty steel netting, erected to catch boulders tumbling down the hillside. Follow the road for several minutes and then take the clearly signposted footpath to the right and climb through the woods to the **Port de la Core (1395m)**.

A clear trail heads east from the Port de la Core to the *Cabane de Tariolle* (1179m). The hut is large and clean; the sleeping area in the rafters could probably take 8-10 people, but many more could fit in the main area. Continuing down the valley, look out for a turning to the right; some way below the cabane, without warning, the GR10 makes this turn through the bracken and then goes left along an old fence line. Soon after this you reach **Esbints**. The small *gîte d'étape* (☎ 05.61.66.86.83) situated in a renovated farm building, has only 10 places but occupies a beautiful position. Accommodation costs €9/55F per night or €22/140F for demi-pension; there's a well-equipped kitchen. Campers can pitch their tents nearby and pay €3/20F to use the facilities.

Although the GR10 skirts around the edge of Seix, the route described here goes into the town. Those who don't need to go into Seix can stay either at the gîte at Esbints or the gîte in Aunac. The turning where the GR10 heads south-east towards Coume-Chaude is twenty-five minutes' walk below Esbints; continuing down the lane you'll come to Seix some three quarters of an hour later.

SEIX

✉ code 09140

Seix is a pretty little town; a stopover here makes a pleasant change to life on the trail.

The *Auberge de Haut Salat* ☆ (☎ 05.61.66.88.03) on the central square is a friendly place; single rooms start at €22/140F and are comfortable and clean. The restaurant is good value. Just around the corner is the *Hôtel Restaurant Mont-Vallier* ☆ (☎ 05.61 66.83.68), which also has rooms from €22/140F and is of a similar standard. There are two campsites to the north of Seix, 1$^1/_2$ -2 km from the town centre.

Shops in Seix include a mini-supermarket, a tabac and a boulangerie. The

tourist office (☎ 05.61.96.52.90) is on the central square, and the **post office** is just to the north-east. There is a **bank** but this tiny branch of Crédit Agricole has inconvenient opening hours: only on Monday 14.00-16.00, and Thursday 09.30-12.00 and 14.00-16.00. There's no cash dispenser. If you find yourself in need of cash at other times, remember that post office branches can change money or travellers' cheques. Some walkers also reported that there was a cash dispenser at the post office, although whether this is suitable for use with foreign cards was not clear.

There are a couple of local **taxi** services (☎ 05.61.66.81.79 or 05.61.66 86.10).

SEIX → ROUZE   [MAP 46, p195; MAP 47, p196]

From the centre of Seix, walk south along the road (D3) to rejoin the GR10 near **Coume-Chaude**. Half a kilometre beyond the bridge to Coume-Chaude, where the road bears sharply left, the GR10 goes right over a small bridge, and along the lane past the hamlet of **Couflens de Betmajou**. Although the lane is level initially, it soon begins to climb, and after a while the tarmac surface gives way to loose stones. Eventually the track comes to an end by a footbridge and a building. A sign, CABANE D'AULA 3H, points the way up a footpath.

Map 46 – Seix to Refuge d'Aula 195

Follow the footpath up the pretty wooded valley. Twenty-five minutes beyond the sign there's a building which might do as a shelter in an emergency. An hour or so later the path leaves the trees, emerging into a huge open area near the **Cabane de l'Artigue (1053m)**, which is kept locked.

From the cabane the path begins to climb more steeply, heading south-west towards the end of the valley and then ascending through the trees to reach a cirque, in the middle of which is the *Refuge d'Aula* **(1550m)**. The hut is big but fairly spartan inside; the first room has a wooden sleeping platform large enough for two people, while the second room has nine bunks and lots of extra floor space.

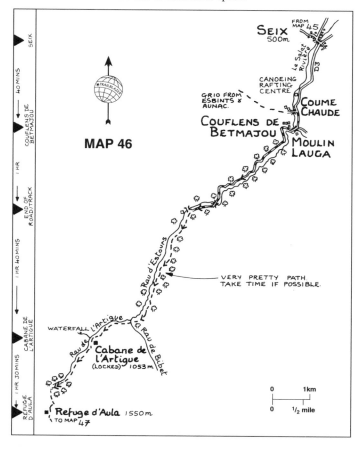

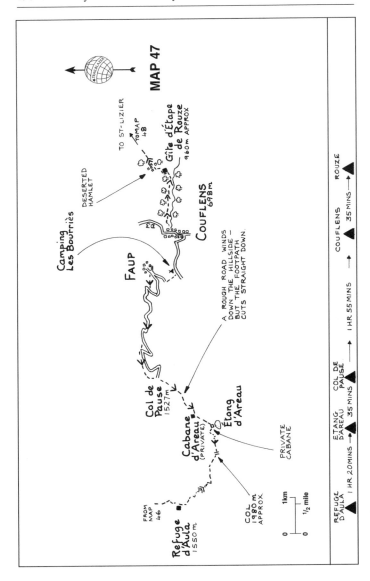

MAP 47

TO ST-LIZIER

TO MAP 48

Gîte d'Étape
de Rouze
960m APPROX

DESERTED
HAMLET

COUFLENS
698m

Camping
Les Bouriès

FAUP

920

A ROUGH ROAD WINDS
DOWN THE HILLSIDE –
BUT THE FOOTPATH
CUTS STRAIGHT DOWN.

Col de
Pause
1527m

Cabane
d'Areau
(PRIVATE)

Étang
d'Areau

PRIVATE
CABANE

FROM MAP
46

Refuge
d'Aula
1550m

COL
1980 m
APPROX

0 — 1km

0 — ½ mile

REFUGE
D'AULA — 1 HR 20 MINS — ÉTANG
D'AREAU — 35 MINS — COL DE
PAUSE — 1 HR 55 MINS — COUFLENS — 35 MINS — ROUZE

The GR10 zigzags up the hillside south-east of the refuge to a col (1980m approx), on the far side of which it descends to the **Étang d'Areau**. The cabane next to the lake is private, as is the **Cabane d'Areau** which you pass lower down. Below this second building, the path briefly cuts down the grassy slopes and then follows the rough road to the **Col de Pause (1527m)**. From the col, most of the descent to Couflens is along the road, although the GR10 takes a few short cuts. Just west of Couflens is the *Camping Les Bourriès*, a 'camping à la ferme' which has fairly basic facilities.

A kilometre further east along the lane is **Couflens**; there are no facilities here. Go north through the village and after about 400 metres there's a sign for the gîte d'étape. Thirty-five minutes' climb up the wooded valley brings you to the hamlet of **Rouze** (960m approx). The *gîte d'étape* (☎ 05.61.66.95.45) is in a lovely old building next to the farmhouse, with superb views westwards towards the Col de Pause. Among the attractions here are the excellent home-made cheese and a visit to the fromagerie. The gîte has a room for five or six people, and a larger dormitory for twelve people; there's a well-equipped kitchen area. It costs €9/60F per night to stay here, or €22/145F for demi-pension.

ROUZE → AULUS-LES-BAINS   [MAP 48, p198]

From the gîte, climb steeply on a sunken footpath through the woods, passing two deserted hamlets. It's a pretty and shady walk, and you emerge from the trees just below the **Col de la Serre du Cot (1546m)**, from which there is an excellent view westwards to the Col de Pause.

Two paths head away from the col in a north-easterly direction. Take the lower one, which soon enters the woods and winds down the hillside to meet a vehicle track running along the valley floor. Turn left along the track and follow it to **St Lizier (744m)**. There's a campsite here, *Camping Municipal d'Ustou* where they charge €2.50/16F per person and €3/18F for emplacement. Next to the campsite is a public swimming pool and small shop; there's also a café. The gîte d'étape which is marked on the IGN map has closed.

The GR10 heads south along the road and, just past the last building, turns left across an old footbridge. Almost immediately there's a track junction; turn right and start the climb towards the Pic de Fitté. The first 25 minutes are very steep but at least the path is shady.

Further up the hillside, the gradient lessens slightly but it's still hard work; after passing a few more deserted houses, you arrive at the **Pic de Fitté (1387m)**.

From the ridge, the modern ski resort of Guzet-Neige is clearly visible across the tiny valley. Turn south-east for a couple of hundred metres along a grass track to the point where the GR10 starts to climb again. It

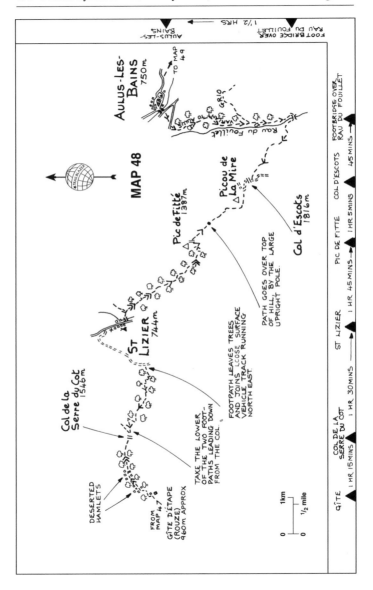

MAP 48

AULUS-LES-BAINS 750m.

TO MAP 49

AULUS-LES-BAINS

RAU DU FOUILLET   1/2 HRS

FOOT BRIDGE OVER

GR10

Rau du Fouillet

Picou de La Mire 1387m.

Pic de Fitté 1387m.

Col d'Escots 1816m.

PATH GOES OVER TOP OF HILL, BY THE LARGE UPRIGHT POLE

FOOTPATH LEAVES TREES AND JOINS LOOSE SURFACE VEHICLE TRACK RUNNING NORTH EAST.

ST LIZIER 744m.

Col de la Serre du Cot 1546m.

TAKE THE LOWER OF THE TWO FOOT-PATHS LEADING DOWN FROM THE COL.

DESERTED HAMLETS

FROM MAP 47

GÎTE D'ÉTAPE (ROUZE) 960m APPROX

0   1km

0   1/2 mile

GÎTE   COL DE LA SERRE DU COT   ST LIZIER   PIC DE FITTÉ   COL D'ESCOTS   FOOTBRIDGE OVER RAU DU FOUILLET

1 HR 15MINS   1 HR 30MINS   1 HR 45MINS   1 HR 5MINS   45 MINS

goes directly over the next hillock, passing by the base of a huge pole which stands on the top, and then skirts around to the south of the **Picou de la Mire** to arrive at the **Col d'Escots (1816m)**.

The descent into the next valley is rather long and drawn out, with the path running south-east across the hillside and even appearing at times to climb more than fall. Eventually, however, after crossing the footbridge over the Rau de Fouillet, it turns north, running parallel to the stream and passing numerous small waterfalls.

After 45 minutes you reach a fork; those wanting to break their journey at Aulus go left, while the GR10 proper goes right. The detour to Aulus is described here. The path continues descending through the woods, and meets the road twice before arriving in **Aulus-les-Bains (750m)**.

AULUS-LES-BAINS
✉ code 09140
Aulus is a small town with enough facilities to make it tempting as a stopover.

The smartest hotel is the *Hostellerie de la Terrasse* ☆☆☆ (☎ 05.61.96.00 98) where double rooms start at €34/220F. The restaurant on the riverside terrace looks very good and prices are quite reasonable; the menu du jour is €18/120F, and there are plenty of local specialities. Opposite the Hostellerie is the *Hôtel de Beauséjour* ☆☆ (☎ 05.61.96.00.06), which is a huge old place. Clean but rather plain rooms start at €28/180F; the terrace restaurant is good, and there's a swimming pool in the garden behind the hotel. More expensive but very pleasant is the *Hôtel Les Oussailles* ☆☆ (☎ 05 61.96.03.68, 🖹 05.61.96.03.70) where

single rooms start at €37/240F and doubles start at €46/300F. The *Gîte d'étape Le Presbytère* (☎ 05.61.96.02.21) in the centre of the village charges €12/75F for the night and €23/150F for demi-pension. Also near the centre of the village is the *Camping le Couledous* ☆☆☆ (☎ 05.61.96.02.26) which charges €3/19F per person and €3/19F for emplacement. Aulus also has a **tourist office** (☎ 05.61.96.01.79) and a food **shop**.

A bus service operates between St Girons (nearest point for SNCF buses) and Aulus. The service, running three times a day, is operated by Cars Antras (☎ 05.61.66.08.87) and costs €4/28F one way. A taxi to Girons (ask at the tourist office for taxi numbers, or try the taxis listed under Seix) costs around €38/250F.

AULUS-LES-BAINS → MOUNICOU   [MAP 49, p201]

Getting back on to the GR10 from Aulus is easy, as the path passes a few hundred metres to the east of the village. Rejoining it at this point means that you have missed out about three hours of the main route, but it's a lot quicker than trudging back up the hill to start again where you left off.

From the centre of Aulus, go north-east up the street past the Hôtel Les Oussailles, and follow the road as it leaves the village. Beyond the last houses you come to a small road junction; go down a cart track to the right and after a few minutes you arrive at a junction with the GR10. The path climbs back to the road, crosses it, and continues uphill; after a while it becomes less steep and follows along the hillside climbing gently through the trees. In the early morning it's a peaceful and pretty walk. After two or three kilometres the GR10 arrives at **Coumebière (1399m)**, where there's a parking area beside the road. Cross the road and follow the long easy climb to the **Port de Saleix (1794m)**.

The GR10 turns due south up the slopes of Mt Garias for a few minutes, but before reaching the top it heads off south-eastwards, passing the **Étang d'Alate**, and then crossing a flat rocky area. Soon, the **Étangs de Bassiès** and the refuge (1650m) can be seen below, and after a descent on a rocky footpath, you reach the building. The *Refuge de Bassiès* (☎ 05.61.64.89.98) is a large modern place; accommodation costs €9/60F for the night, €12/78F for the evening meal and €25/166F for demi-pension.

Go south-east from the refuge, and after an hour you reach the end of the easternmost lake, where the path starts to descend. The trail drops steeply for about an hour, passing two water sources, before arriving at a path junction. From here, Auzat is 45 minutes' walk to the north-east, while the GR10 heads south towards Mounicou.

Since it runs along the top of a concrete water duct, the route southwards along the side of the valley is perfectly flat. After three quarters of an hour, you emerge on the hillside above Marc. The GR10 goes around behind a two-storey brick tower and joins the road, which it follows for two or three minutes before cutting left, down a footpath, to the houses. The hamlet is tiny but there's some *accommodation* available if you phone in advance; the owners of one of the houses – the one advertising honey for sale (☎ 05.61.64.83.86) have two double rooms which they let to walkers. It costs €31/200F for the room and breakfast; evening meals are available by arrangement for €9-11/60-70F. If you're planning to stop in this area for the night, try these people before the gîte in Mounicou – you'd be much more comfortable here.

Follow the tarmac road down past the church and turn right past the families' holiday centre. The GR10 continues south along the river bank and soon comes to another road bridge. On the far side of the bridge is the gîte (1087m). The *gîte d'étape* (☎ 05.61.64.87.66) charges €11/70F per night, and is one of the dirtiest along the entire GR10. There are reasonable kitchen facilities but you will probably want to wash plates etc before you use them. There is a tiny bar in the same hamlet, but no food is served, so you'll need to carry supplies. The nearest shops are in Auzat, several kilometres away (see p202).

❏ **Walking times on trail maps**
Note that on all the trail maps in this book the times shown alongside each map refer only to time spent actually walking. Add 30-40% to allow for rest stops.

Map 49 – Aulus-les-Bains to Mounicou 201

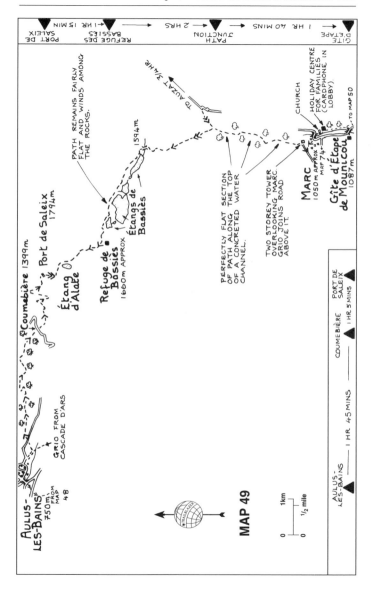

Port de Saleix 1794m

ºCoumebière 1399m.

Étang d'Alaze

Refuge de Bassiès 1660m APPROX

Étangs de Bassiès

1594m.

TO AUZAT 3½HR

PATH REMAINS FAIRLY FLAT AND WINDS AMONG THE ROCKS.

PERFECTLY FLAT SECTION OF PATH ALONG THE TOP OF A CONCRETED WATER CHANNEL.

TWO STOREY TOWER OVERLOOKING MARC. GRIO JOINS ROAD ABOVE IT.

CHURCH

HOLIDAY CENTRE FOR FAMILIES (CARDPHONE IN LOBBY)

TO MAP 50

MARC 1050m APPROX MAP 74

Gîte d'Étape de Mounicou 1087m

AULUS-LES-BAINS 750m. FROM MAP 48

GRIO FROM CASCADE D'ARS

PORT DE SALEIX ◄ 1 HR 15 MIN

REFUGE DES BASSIES ◄ 1 HR 15 MIN

2 HRS → JUNCTION PATH

1 HR 40 MINS → GITE D'ÉTAPE

MAP 49

0   1km
0   ½ mile

AULUS-LES-BAINS —— 1 HR. 45 MINS —— COUMEBIÈRE —— 1 HR. 5 MINS —— PORT DE SALEIX

Auzat and Vicdessos

For those not continuing along the GR10, **Auzat**, a small town dominated by a huge factory, is seven kilometres down the road. Three kilometres beyond it is **Vicdessos**, which is much prettier, and which boasts a **tourist office** (☎ 05.61.64.87.53), **bank**, **cash dispenser**, **pharmacy**, and a handful of **shops** and cafés.

The nearest railway station is in Tarascon sur Ariège. According to the guardian of the Refuge du Pinet there is a daily bus from Marc to Tarascon which leaves Marc at 06.30, but it would be wise to confirm this with another source before dragging yourself out of bed at such an hour. Alternatively you could try to hitch a ride down to Auzat/Vicdessos, or you could phone a taxi (there's a pay phone in the holiday centre). For taxis, try **Transports Bernard Pujol** in Vicdessos (☎ 05.61.64.88.02, 🖹 05.61.03.80.26).

Once you get to Vicdessos there's a daily **bus** service to Tarascon, which again leaves at a horribly early hour. A taxi from Vicdessos to Tarascon costs about €17/110F.

MOUNICOU → GOULIER [MAP 50]

Cross the river via the road bridge and walk a short way south along the lane. The GR10, signposted to the left, climbs steeply from the tarmac for about 35 minutes before levelling out and heading northwards. After a further 25 minutes you pass the hut at **Prunadière** (1600m approx), a reasonably large *shelter* with room for at least five or six people. There's a small (and possibly unreliable) water source next to the cabane.

The GR10 continues almost level along the wooded hillside for another 1500m before reaching the end of the spur and beginning to descend. At the bottom of the hill, the path passes straight through the hamlet of **Arties (985m)** to the road, where there is a tap with drinking water. Turn left (south) along the lane, and follow it as it climbs gently up the valley bottom. After half an hour, next to some buildings you pass a sign, GOULIER 3H 30, pointing uphill to the east. Although the timing on this is questionable, this shortcut, shown on the IGN map, appears worth considering if you're in a hurry. The climb is, however, particularly steep and exhausting, so if you're not in any great rush, the longer route is more enjoyable.

Ten minutes south of the sign, you come to the electricity installation at **Pradières**. Take the left fork, past the power station itself, and after about five minutes the lane doubles back to the left to a small parking area. From here the GR10, well signposted, continues as a footpath. It's about an hour's climb to the **Étang d'Izourt (1647m)** where there are a number of abandoned buildings at the northern end of the lake. The first building you come to has a large and very dirty room open as a shelter.

Map 50 – Mounicou to Goulier 203

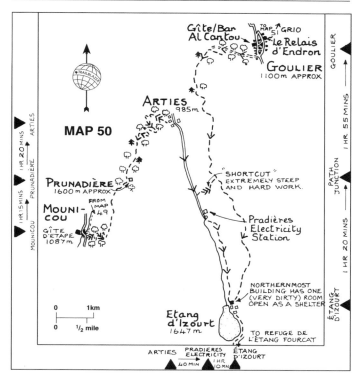

The GR10 climbs very briefly and then settles into a long, gradual descent northwards. After an hour and twenty minutes, you reach a path junction, at the top of the shortcut mentioned earlier. Continue along the hillside, eventually rounding the spur to another junction where you take the left hand path. The footpath soon turns into a broad track which descends through the woods to the village of **Goulier (1100m)**.

GOULIER

Thoroughly recommended is the excellent *Gîte Al Cantou* (☎ 05.61.64.81.84). The gîte, which is in the centre of the village, is well laid out, with individual beds, good washing facilities, and a well-equipped little kitchen. The warmth of the welcome is what really makes this place great, though. Demi-pension is €27/175F, but you can pay for just the night, too. There is a small bar downstairs.

Just above the village is the other gîte, the modern *Relais d'Endron* (☎ 05.61.03.87.72, 📄 05.61.03.80.66). It seems to be planned more as an activity centre, with lots of information about what's on in the area. Accommodation is either in the gîte which has nine beds, or in individual rooms. Demi-pension is €25/160F in the dormitory, or €27/175F in a private room. The night only in the dormitory is €11/70F. There are no shops in Goulier.

GOULIER → CABANE LES CLARANS   [MAP 51]

This section is a very long one and many people will prefer to split it up in some way. If you have tent, of course, accommodation will not be a problem; if you don't, the only real option is to try to get a space in the room which has been set aside for walkers in Siguer. Note that there are no shops or cafés in any of the villages on this section.

The GR10 climbs north-eastwards from Goulier and after quarter of an hour passes a spring. Just beyond this, the route-marking becomes very poor; follow the path upwards picking up the waymarks again near the top of the climb. At the **col (1330m)** just south of **Pic de Risoul**, turn south-eastwards and follow a level footpath which runs just above a loose surface road. After 25 minutes you reach a path junction; the GR10B runs off to the south-west while the GR10 goes north-east.

The track climbs slightly over the Col de l'Esquérus and then turns south-east along the hillside above a forest road. It soon descends and joins the road, which it follows to the **Col de Grail (1485m)**. There's a *foresters' hut* here which is reasonably well kept and could sleep three people. Go along the track behind the hut for a minute or two, before turning right on a level footpath which heads north-east. After about 35 minutes the path joins a large track which leads to a tarmac lane. Follow the lane down to **Lercoul** (1140m approx); the GR10 goes through the centre of the village and continues on a footpath which descends steeply to **Siguer (743m)**.

There are no facilities in Siguer (ie no shop, café or gîte), but the village has set aside a *room* which is for use by passing walkers. There are six bunks, a table, chairs and a fridge but no cooking facilities. There are also toilets, a basin and a shower. It's free.

From Siguer, climb directly uphill to **Gesties (958m)** – a bit of a slog which takes about half an hour. There's a water fountain in Gesties but little else. Pass through the village and continue uphill to the **Col de Gamel (1390m)** on a tiny, steep path which is not very well marked.

From the Col de Gamel, the route to the Col du Sasc is also very poorly marked and the tiny footpath soon peters out among the long grass and bracken. The easiest option is to keep close to the edge of the woods on your left, as the GR10 runs along much the same line. You soon see the triangulation point on the top of the **Pla de Montcamp (1904m)**; the GR10 passes over the top of this hill and descends south-southeastwards. The markers come back into evidence here, and every second rock is plas-

Map 51 – Goulier to Cabane les Clarans 205

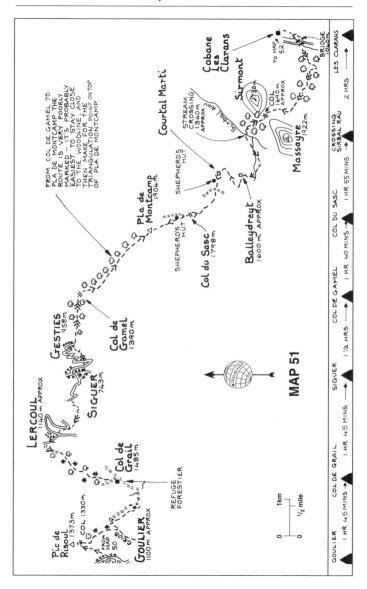

Pic de Risoul △1373m

⌂ COL 1330m

LERCOUL 1140 m APPROX

GESTIES 958m

Col de Gamel 1390m

SIGUER 743m

Col de Grail 1485m

REFUGE FORESTIER

GOULIER 1100m APPROX

FROM MAP 50

Pla de Montcamp 1904m

SHEPHERD'S HUT

Col du Sasc 1798m

SHEPHERD'S HUT

Balleydreyt 1600 m APPROX

FROM COL DE GAMEL TO PLA DE MONTCAMP THE ROUTE IS VERY POORLY MARKED – IT'S PROBABLY EASIEST TO STAY CLOSE TO THE WOODLINE AND THEN MAKE FOR THE TRIANGULATION POINT ON TOP OF PLA DE MONTCAMP

Courtal Marti

STREAM CROSSING 1340m APPROX

Massayre 1922m

Sirmont 1730m

COL 1640m APPROX

Cabane Les Clarans

TO MAP 52

BRIDGE 1040m

LES CLARANS

MAP 51

0 1km
0 ½ mile

GOULIER	COL DE GRAIL	SIGUER	COL DE GAMEL	COL DU SASC	CROSSING SIRBAL RAU	LES CLARANS
1 HR 45 MINS	1 HR 45 MINS	1½ HRS	1 HR 40 MINS	1 HR 55 MINS	2 HRS	

tered with red and white paint as you head down to the shepherd's hut at the **Col du Sasc (1798m)**.

Go south-east around the top of a small valley, and then follow the route markings eastwards. The GR10 crosses a dirt road and descends past a smart new shepherd's hut to the refuge of *Courtal Marti*. This tiny shelter could sleep two people at most and is not a place to spend the night if you can help it. From Courtal Marti the path continues down through undergrowth into the small valley to the south, at the bottom of which is the *Cabane de Balleydreyt* (1600m approx). The building is semi-dilapidated, with two huge holes in the roof; it might just do for shelter from a cloudburst, but is good for little else.

Cross the stream just below the cabane, and follow it north-eastwards down into the wooded valley of the **Sirbal Rau**. From the stepping stones across the Rau (1340m approx), climb steeply through beech woods to the grassy col (1690m approx) south of Sirmont.

The path swings southwards, enters the woods and then makes a long and steep descent to reach the **road bridge** (1040m) over the **Aston Rau**. Cross the bridge and immediately turn left up a footpath which leads, after 5-10 minutes, to a large clearing, on the north-west side of which is the *Cabane Les Clarans*. The cabane has room for four; the attached barn-type room could also sleep several people if they were prepared to put up with a dirty floor and a few bats.

CABANE LES CLARANS → REFUGE DE RULHE   [MAP 52]

From the clearing by Les Clarans, follow an overgrown but clearly marked path up the valley to the south-east. The gradient is initially fairly gentle but after about half an hour the path turns directly uphill and becomes much steeper. About 45 minutes later the path begins to level out and it passes through an extremely overgrown area of head-high bushes. If it's been raining or there's a heavy dew, prepare to get soaked, as the needle-like leaves retain lots of water. Some people seem to have skin allergy to these plants which are known as *Cystisus scoparius*; struggling through them and getting wet could leave you scratching for the rest of the day. Just beyond the bushes you come to the *Cabane d'Artaran* (**1695m**). It's in good condition and has two rooms; the smaller one could sleep five, while the larger room has a picnic table and could sleep three or four more if necessary. No water source is apparent.

Walk north-north-east along a grassy vehicle track and after half an hour reach the *Centre d'Accueil*. The modern building is really for use during the ski season but the bar/restaurant stays open all year. There's no accommodation but it's a good place to stop for a coffee or a snack; business hours are 09.30-18.00. The GR10 goes past the building and follows the large vehicle track southwards – markers are a bit scarce at this point but you just have to stick to the track. After half an hour you pass the

Map 52 – Cabane les Clarans to Refuge de Rulhe 207

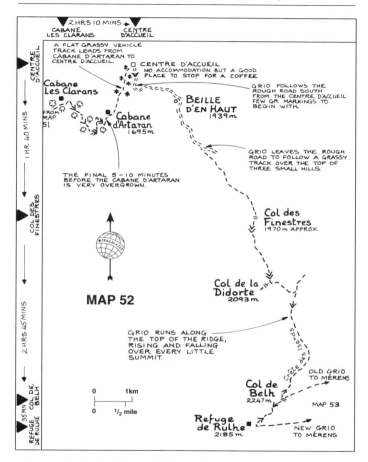

MAP 52

FROM MAP 51

MAP 53

2 HRS 10 MINS

CABANE LES CLARANS   CENTRE D'ACCUEIL

CENTRE D'ACCUEIL

A FLAT GRASSY VEHICLE TRACK LEADS FROM CABANE D'ARTARAN TO CENTRE D'ACCUEIL.

CENTRE D'ACCUEIL. NO ACCOMMODATION BUT A GOOD PLACE TO STOP FOR A COFFEE.

Cabane Les Clarans

GR10 FOLLOWS THE ROUGH ROAD SOUTH FROM THE CENTRE D'ACCUEIL. FEW GR MARKINGS TO BEGIN WITH.

BEILLE D'EN HAUT 1939m

Cabane d'Artaran 1695m

GR10 LEAVES THE ROUGH ROAD TO FOLLOW A GRASSY TRACK OVER THE TOP OF THREE SMALL HILLS.

THE FINAL 5–10 MINUTES BEFORE THE CABANE D'ARTARAN IS VERY OVERGROWN.

TRAILBLAZER

Col des Finestres 1970m APPROX.

Col de la Didorte 2093m

GR10 RUNS ALONG THE TOP OF THE RIDGE, RISING AND FALLING OVER EVERY LITTLE SUMMIT.

Crête des Isards

OLD GR10 TO MÉRENS

Col de Belh 2247m

Refuge de Rulhe 2185m

NEW GR10 TO MÉRENS

0   1km
0   ½ mile

1 HR 40 MINS

COL DES FINESTRES

2 HRS 45 MINS

35 MN   COL DE BELH

REFUGE DE RULHE

cabane at **Beille d'en Haut (1939m)**, which is not currently available for use by walkers. After a further 25 minutes, where the vehicle track bears left, the GR10 continues south along a grassy track. Again, markers are extremely well spaced along here, but the track takes you all the way to the **Col des Finestres** (1970m approx).

Climb up the ridge to the south of the col, and then descend slightly before climbing again past the **Col de la Didorte (2093m)**. From here, head south-east briefly and then south along the top of the ridge which leads to the **Crête des Isards**. This section is quite tiring, as the path climbs and falls over every hummock. Eventually you reach the **Col de Belh (2247m)**. There's little to mark it except a sign pointing south-west towards the refuge (2185m), which you reach in half an hour. The *Refuge de Rulhe* (☎ 05.61.64.40.20, 06.72.20.20.60) is a modern place with room for 50 people. It costs €10/65F to stay the night here and €27/175F for demi-pension.

REFUGE DE RULHE → MÉRENS-LES-VALS   [MAP 53]

A yellow sign near the refuge building points the way onwards towards Mérens-Les-Vals: MÉRENS 5H 30. Follow the GR10 markings eastwards towards the col just south of the **Pic des Calmettes**. Keep on the left slope, as the path passes over the left side of the col. Beyond the col the going becomes very slow, as the GR10 runs around the northern shore of the **Étang Bleu**, across an area of rocks and large boulders. Finally the path climbs very steeply up a grass track to the **Crête de la Lasse** (2400m approx).

❏ **GR10 to Mérens**
The route down to Mérens-les-Vals is now different from that shown on the IGN 1:50,000 map, and the path heading north-east from the Col de Belh has been superseded: the new GR10 runs eastwards from the Refuge de Rulhe. The old route of the GR10, which descends north-eastwards from the col is still marked with red and white way marks, as is the newer path towards the refuge.

Go east a short distance before doubling back and descending into the valley to the south-east. Follow a clear path downhill, passing above the **Étang de Comte** and into the valley bottom to the north-east of the lake. Here there is a tiny *cabane*; it has no door and the inside of the building is bare and dirty but it would serve as temporary shelter. The level grassy area beside the Rau de Mourgouillou is popular with day-trippers, and consequently the path down the valley to the north-east is well trodden. About half an hour beyond the cabane, join an unsurfaced road leading down from a car park, and a few minutes later take a footpath away from the road again. After a further 40 minutes you reach **Mérens-les-Vals (1052m)**.

MÉRENS-LES-VALS
✉ code 09580
Mérens makes an obvious starting or finishing point for a walk along part of the GR10, because of its easy access by rail; direct trains from Toulouse pass through en route to La-Tour-de-Carol. There are few facilities – there's a small **shop** on the main road and a **post office** (which doesn't change money).

The *gîte d'étape* (☎ 05.61.64.32.50, 🖹 05.61.64.02.75) is slightly above the village. Walkers rate it as one of the best along the GR10, partly for the clean and smart accommodation, but mostly for the excellent food. It costs €10/65F per night, and €27/175F for demi-pension. If the gîte is full, you could try the *Hôtel/Bar Rouaix* (☎ 05.61.64.24.13) which is on the main road through the

Map 53 – Refuge de Rulhe to Mérens-les-Vals 209

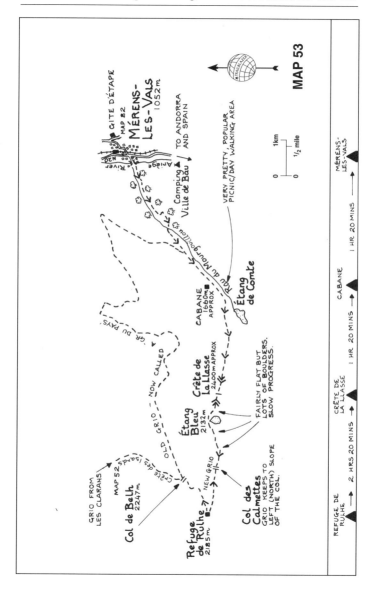

MAP 53

GITE D'ÉTAPE

MAP 52

MÉRENS-LES-VALS
1052m

TO ANDORRA
AND SPAIN

Camping
Ville de Bau

Ariège

River

VERY PRETTY, POPULAR
PICNIC/DAY WALKING AREA

0 1km
0 ½ mile

RU du Mourgouillou

CABANE
1660m
APPROX

Étang
de Comte

GR10 – NOW CALLED

GR DU PAYS

CRÊTE DE
LA LLASSE

Crête de
La Llasse
2400m APPROX

Étang
Bleu
2132m

FAIRLY FLAT BUT
LOTS OF BOULDERS.
SLOW PROGRESS.

GR10 FROM
LES CLARANS

CRÊTE DES ISARDS

MAP 52

Col de Belh
2247m

OLD

Refuge
de Rulhe
2185m

NEW GR10

Col des
Calmettes
GR10 KEEPS TO
LEFT (NORTH) SLOPE
OF THE COL.

REFUGE DE
RULHE ← 2 HRS 20 MINS → CRÊTE DE
LA LLASSE ← 1 HR 20 MINS → CABANE ← 1 HR 20 MINS → MÉRENS-LES-VALS

village. Rooms here are €17/110F but there's no food available apart from breakfast, and the place is rather run down and smelly. The Auberge de Jeunesse, which is signposted from the road, is no longer open.

One kilometre south of the village is the *Camping Ville de Bau* (☎ 05.61 02.85.40, ≣ 05.61.64.03.83), which has a small shop on site; the tariff is €2.40/15F per person and €2.50/16F for emplacement.

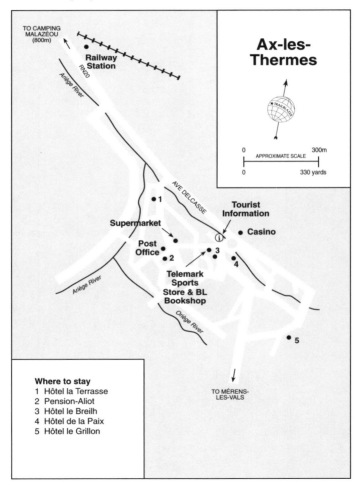

Ax-les-Thermes

TO CAMPING MALAZÉOU (800m)

Railway Station

RN20

Ariège River

AVE DELCASSE

TRAIL BLAZER

0   300m
APPROXIMATE SCALE

0   330 yards

● 1

Tourist Information

● Casino

Supermarket

ⓘ

Post Office

● 2

● 3

● 4

Telemark Sports Store & BL Bookshop

Ariège River

Orlège River

● 5

Where to stay
1 Hôtel la Terrasse
2 Pension-Aliot
3 Hôtel le Breilh
4 Hôtel de la Paix
5 Hôtel le Grillon

TO MÉRENS-LES-VALS

AX-LES-THERMES

✉ code 09110

Ax-Les-Thermes is eight kilometres north of Mérens. Whereas Mérens has few facilities, Ax has plenty.

Services

Ax has three **banks** with cash dispensers, at least one of which gives pesetas as well as francs. Shops include a couple of **food stores**, a good **book shop**, a **pharmacy**, a **photo shop** and two **newsagents**.

Telemark Sports (💻 www.tele mark-pyrenees.com), which is run by an English/Italian couple, has Coleman Epigas for sale, as well as a good range of outdoor kit.

There are three or four trains a day between Mérens and Ax. The journey takes about 15 minutes and costs €4.50/30F one way. There are also a couple of buses which depart from the bus stop opposite the shop. If all else fails, hitching the few kilometres down the road is easy.

There are regular trains to **Toulouse**, via Tarascon and Foix, as well as a useful night service between Paris and La Tour-de-Carol, which conveniently stops in Ax as well.

Where to stay

Ax has plenty of reasonably priced hotels. The best of these is the *Hôtel le Grillon* ☆☆ (☎ 05.61.64.31.64) which is slightly away from the bustle of the town centre; double rooms start at €34/225F.

At the cheaper end of the scale, the friendly *Hôtel la Terrasse* (☎ 05.61 64.20.33, 🖹 05.61.64.66.89) has double rooms from €22/140F – make sure that there's access to a shower, though. *Pension-Aliot* (☎ 05.61.64.22.01) is also good value with rooms from €22/140F.

Approximately one kilometre north-west of the railway station is the *Camping Malazéou* (☎ 05.61.64.69.14) where they charge €3/18F per person and €3/18F for emplacement.

Excursions around the GR10

CAUTERETS → REFUGE WALLON [MAP 54, p212]

There are several options for the southern route out of Cauterets although the most direct route, along the avenue Demontzey, has been closed for some time (ie a couple of years) because of the danger of rockfalls. An alternative route (marked on the 1:50,000 map) runs along the eastern side of the valley towards La Fruitière, while another option is simply to walk up the road to La Raillère. A fourth is to take the bus to Pont d'Espagne, and start walking from there: for bus details see the Cauterets section.

The route via avenue Demontzey is both the most pleasant and the quickest route and is therefore recommended, but you'll need to check with the tourist office or Bureau des Guides whether it has been reopened. Assuming that it has, to get to the start of the avenue from the centre of town, walk up the steps just to the north-west of the swimming pool. There's a large modern sculpture of a bird halfway up, which is hard to miss, and a yellow sign, LA RAILLÈRE 0H 40 & PONT D'ESPAGNE 2H 15, at

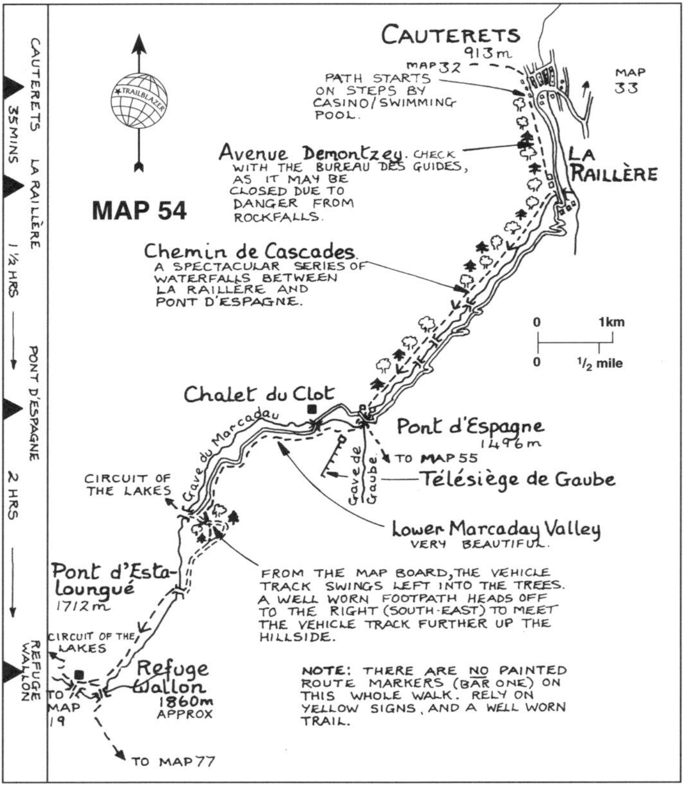

MAP 54

CAUTERETS
913m

MAP 32

PATH STARTS
ON STEPS BY
CASINO/SWIMMING
POOL.

MAP 33

Avenue Demontzey. CHECK
WITH THE BUREAU DES GUIDES,
AS IT MAY BE
CLOSED DUE TO
DANGER FROM
ROCKFALLS.

LA RAILLÈRE

Chemin de Cascades.
A SPECTACULAR SERIES OF
WATERFALLS BETWEEN
LA RAILLÈRE AND
PONT D'ESPAGNE.

0   1km
0   1/2 mile

Chalet du Clot

Gave du Marcadau

Pont d'Espagne
1496m

TO MAP 55

Télésiège de Gaube

CIRCUIT OF
THE LAKES

Gave de Gaube

Lower Marcaday Valley
VERY BEAUTIFUL.

Pont d'Esta-
loungué
1712m

FROM THE MAP BOARD, THE VEHICLE
TRACK SWINGS LEFT INTO THE TREES.
A WELL WORN FOOTPATH HEADS OFF
TO THE RIGHT (SOUTH-EAST) TO MEET
THE VEHICLE TRACK FURTHER UP THE
HILLSIDE.

CIRCUIT OF THE
LAKES

TO
MAP
19

Refuge
Wallon
1860m
APPROX

NOTE: THERE ARE NO PAINTED
ROUTE MARKERS (BAR ONE) ON
THIS WHOLE WALK. RELY ON
YELLOW SIGNS, AND A WELL WORN
TRAIL.

REFUGE WALLON

TO MAP 77

CAUTERETS   35 MINS   LA RAILLÈRE   1 1/2 HRS   PONT D'ESPAGNE   2 HRS

the bottom. Above the steps, the path climbs the hillside in a few long gentle zigzags before heading off southwards. This shady 2km stretch of path, known as avenue Demontzey, is named after the Inspector General of Waters and Forests, Prosper Demontzey (1831-1898), who was responsible for a drive to replant huge areas of woodland in the Pyrenees.

At the end of the avenue go past a building which until recently housed the Thermes, and on to the tiny village of **La Raillère**. Just before the bridge over the river is a yellow sign pointing to the right: CHEMIN DES CASCADES; PONT D'ESPAGNE 1H 30. From here the path climbs steadily for an hour and a half beside a series of impressive waterfalls to the **Pont d'Espagne (1496m)**. The area around the bridge is generally packed with people, and the most prominent building is the *Hôtellerie du Pont* *d'Espagne* (☎ 05.62.92.54.10) where food and drink are served, and rooms are available from €28/180F. Follow the well-beaten trail a little beyond the waterfall and you'll arrive at the bottom of the telesiège (chair lift) de Gaube. For information on the route up to the Lac de Gaube, and the Refuge de Bayssellance beyond it, see p214.

From here, two paths head up the Marcadau valley, on either bank of the Gave du Marcadau, – it doesn't much matter which one you take. After only a few hundred metres you pass a building on the right. The *Chalet du Clot* (☎ 05.62.92.61.27, ▤ 05.62.92.07.93) is a bar/restaurant/refuge, with room for 40 people. Bed and breakfast costs €14/90F or it's €23/150F for demi-pension.

Beyond the Chalet, the Vallée du Marcadau is very pretty. After half an hour you reach a mapboard, and next to it a sign: CIRCUIT DES LACS 6H 30. Follow the vehicle track as it bends left into the trees, and just past a tiny parking area take a footpath to the right. This climbs a short way, before rejoining a large track to head south-west.

After 25 minutes you come to a footbridge, the **Pont d'Estaloungué (1712m)**, to the south of which is a large open area: the remains of a lake which has become silted up. The footpath onwards is unmistakable and after 50 minutes or so you reach the Refuge Wallon (1860m approx).

Refuge Wallon/Marcadau (☎ 05.62.92.64.28) is one of the largest refuges in the French Pyrenees. This area of the Pyrenees is very popular and Wallon, which is also known as Refuge Marcadau, can easily get booked out. In summer, with a guardian and several helpers it can take

---

Circuit des Lacs

According to the signs, the tour is supposed to take six and a half hours. If you leave your rucksack at Wallon and carry only a light day pack, the walk can be accomplished in more like five hours. There are few route markers along the way, but the path is well trodden and would be hard to miss; at the two points where the path divides there are clear signs.

From the refuge go north-west, leaving the small **chapel** on your left. After climbing the rocky slope above Wallon for 20-25 minutes you come to the first track junction and sign. The climb continues for a further half hour or so until you reach **Lac Nère**. It's a desolate scene: clear blue water, bare rock and a chaos of boulders. Quarter of an hour beyond Lac Nère is the **Lac du Pourtet**, which is of a similar appearance. Throughout this part of the climb there are good views south and south-east towards Vignemale.

When almost at the northern end of the Lac du Pourtet, the path bears east, away from the lakeside and starts to descend steeply. From here the route is all downhill; halfway down, near the **Lacs de l'Embarrat**, you pass the junction with the path heading towards the **Lac d'Ilhéou**, and eventually after a steep and rocky descent you arrive at the **Gave du Marcadau**.

The return journey to the Refuge Wallon takes about an hour and is as described above, in the main body of the text.

115 people, and some die-hard mountain walkers complain that it's more of a hotel than a refuge. Summer accommodation is in a mixture of dormitories and private rooms. It costs €12/80F to stay the night in a dormitory, or there's a €2.50/15F per person supplement if you want a private room. The evening meal costs €14/88F. Washing facilities consist of a few handbasins.

Next to the refuge is a tiny **chapel**, built in the 1960's. Every year on 5th August the chapel is the destination of a pilgrimage in memory of those who have been lost in the mountains.

CAUTERETS → REFUGE BAYSSELLANCE   [MAP 55]

[Includes high section – see warning on p20] From Cauterets to the Pont d'Espagne is as described in the section above. Once at the bridge, follow signs for the Lac de Gaube, and climb the well-trodden track up the eastern side of the Gave de Gaube. The rocky path climbs through an area of mature pine trees, and after three quarters of an hour, reaches the northern edge of the **Lac de Gaube (1725m)**. There's a *café/bar* here (open from the beginning of June to the end of October) but no accommodation.

Follow the path around the west side of the lake, and past a flat grassy area which is popular with picnickers. From here the trail starts to climb and soon passes the ***Cabane du Pinet***, a bare hut which could sleep five or six people. Half an hour further up the hill is the **Cascade Esplumouse (1949m)**. Above the waterfall, the path continues to climb gradually for another fifty minutes or so to the refuge (2151m). The ***Refuge des Oulettes de Gaube*** (☎ 05.62.92.62.97) is situated at the base of Vignemale and has an excellent view of the mountain. Camping is possible on a large flat area below the building. Accommodation in the refuge costs €12/80F for the night, or €30/195F for demi-pension.

Near the refuge, a sign points the way onwards towards the Refuge Bayssellance: HOURQETTE D'OSSOUE 2H. Approximately three quarter of an hour's climb up the steep and rocky trail above the refuge, there's a path junction, and approximately fifty minutes beyond this you reach the

---

> ### The English Couple
> The Lac de Gaube became assured of a place in Pyrenean folklore when, in 1832, it was the scene of a much-publicized accident. The newly-wed Pattisons, out from England on their honeymoon, hired a rowing boat. Their brief excursion was to end in their deaths, drowned in the lake. This tragic event so caught the imagination of other visitors that a plethora of stories soon grew up. In one the couple had formed a suicide pact, in another the husband slipped overboard and his wife, failing to see him surface, chose to follow him. For several years the lake itself was an attraction because of the accident, rather than anything else.

Map 55 – Pont d'Espagne to Refuge Bayssellance 215

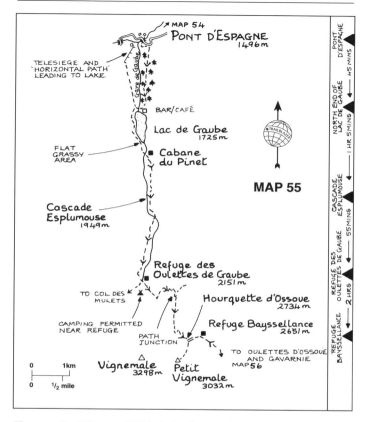

Hourquette d'Ossoue (2734m). In the mornings and early afternoons you may well find it crowded, as it's a popular excursion to climb from here to the top of Petit Vignemale (3032m). The path up Petit Vignemale is not difficult and takes about half an hour.

The *Refuge Bayssellance* (2651m) (☎ 05.62.92.40.25), a space-age looking building, is visible just below the col and is only ten minutes' walk down the track; it has places for 58 people but gets booked out in mid-season. Note that there were plans to close the refuge for part of the 2001 season so that it could be renovated. It's worth checking with a tourist office (or with another refuge) whether Baysellance is open if you're planning to use it.

Count Henry Russell (1834-1909)
Henry Killough Russell, born to an Irish father and French mother, is one of the great characters in Pyrenean history. After completing his studies, he embarked on a series of travels which even today seem impressive. He toured North America and lived with the Sioux Indians; he journeyed across Siberia from Moscow to Peking before the railway was built, he crossed the Gobi desert and visited, among other countries, Japan and Australia.

He eventually returned and settled in the Pyrenees, where he developed something of an obsession with Vignemale, the highest peak in the French Pyrenees. In 1888 he succeeded in renting the Glacier d'Ossoue on a 99 year lease, and he subsequently had three caves carved in it, so that he could stay up on the mountain during the summer. His book *Souvenir d'un Montagnard* is one of the classic Pyrenean texts but is hard to come by nowadays.

REFUGE BAYSSELLANCE → GAVARNIE   [MAP 56]

[Includes high section – see warning on p20] The path descends rapidly from the refuge, with magnificent views. After twenty minutes you pass the **Grottes Bellevue**: three caves, hewn out of the rock, which have been extended with some brickwork.

After a further hour of descent you arrive at the western end of the plateau, the **Oulettes d'Ossoue**. Cross the stream by a small footbridge, and walk across the plateau for 30-35 minutes to arrive at the barrage, and the locked **Cabane d'Ossoue** (1840m approx). According to the yellow sign next to the cabane it's two hours' walk to Gavarnie if you follow the rough road.

The GR10 crosses a small footbridge just below the barrage and comes to another sign: CABANE DE LOURDES 0H 30 & GAVARNIE 2H 45. Most of the walk from the barrage is very pleasant on an almost horizontal path along the hillside. The *Cabane de Lourdes* had one room open (space for four people) when I passed; the Cabane de Saus Dessus, thirty five minutes further along the way, was locked. Half an hour beyond this, the path begins a gradual descent and soon reaches the road.

The GR10 goes straight across the road and cuts down the hillside towards the *Refuge de la Grange de Holle* (☎ 05.62.92.48.77, 🖹 05.62 92.41.58). Accommodation in the refuge is €8/50F for the night, and €22/142F for demi-pension. The refuge (1450m) is an ideal place to stop if you're following the GR10 and aren't too bothered about not staying in Gavarnie itself, since the GR10 turns northwards from here avoiding the village altogether.

Twenty minutes' more walking down the road brings you into **Gavarnie** (1365m, see p218).

Map 56 – Refuge Bayssellance to Gavarnie 217

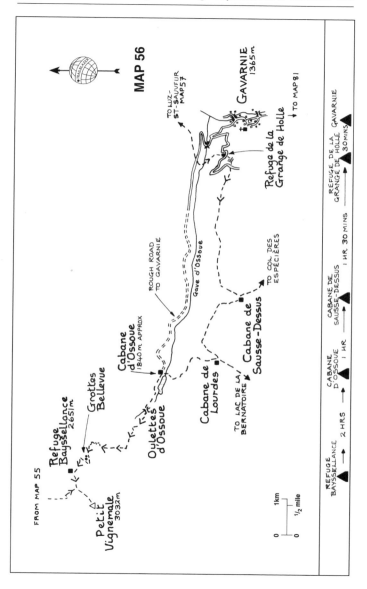

MAP 56

FROM MAP 55

Petit Vignemale 3032m

Refuge Bayssellance 2651m

Grottos Bellevue

Oulettes d'Ossoue

Cabane d'Ossoue 1840m APPROX

ROUGH ROAD TO GAVARNIE

Gave d'Ossoue

Cabane de Lourdes

Cabane de Sausse-Dessus

TO LAC DE LA BERNATOIRE

TO COL DES ESPÉCIÈRES

TO LUZ-ST-SAUVEUR MAP 57

GAVARNIE 1365m

Refuge de la Grange de Holle

TO MAP 81

1km
0

½ mile
0

REFUGE BAYSSELLANCE ← 2 HRS →

CABANE D'OSSOUE ← 1 HR. →

CABANE DE SAUSSE-DESSUS ← 1 HR. 30 MINS →

REFUGE DE LA GRANGE DE HOLLE ← 30 MINS →

GAVARNIE

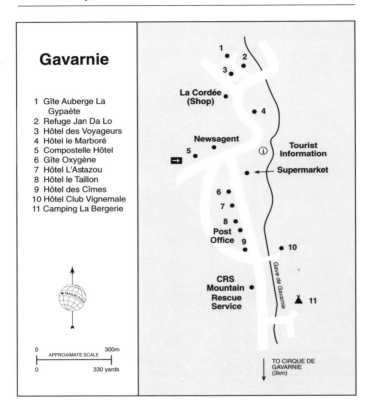

Gavarnie

1 Gîte Auberge La
   Gypaète
2 Refuge Jan Da Lo
3 Hôtel des Voyageurs
4 Hôtel le Marboré
5 Compostelle Hôtel
6 Gîte Oxygène
7 Hôtel L'Astazou
8 Hôtel le Taillon
9 Hôtel des Cîmes
10 Hôtel Club Vignemale
11 Camping La Bergerie

La Cordée
(Shop)

Newsagent

Tourist
Information

Supermarket

Post
Office

CRS
Mountain
Rescue
Service

Gave de Gavarnie

★ TRAILBLAZER

0   300m
APPROXIMATE SCALE
0   330 yards

TO CIRQUE DE
GAVARNIE
(3km)

GAVARNIE

✉ code 65120

Gavarnie must be the best known village in the Pyrenees. The breathtaking cirque, with its soaring cliffs and the 423m waterfall has attracted visitors from around the world since the village first became accessible.

Today, Gavarnie is as popular as ever and hosts a drama festival in early summer with the cirque as the backdrop. It's a good place to start or finish a trip and has enough shops to make it worth a stop to stock up on supplies. Many people, however, will find the crowds, donkey rides and souvenir shops a little too much and will move on quickly.

Services

There's no bank but the **post office** can change cash or travellers' cheques, and there's a Crédit Agricole cash dispenser next to the **tourist office** (☎ 05.62.92 49.10, 🖥 www.gavarnie.com).

Shops in the village include a mini supermarket, boulangerie and newsagent. Two shops, La Cordée and the sports shop opposite the supermarket, sell Coleman/Epigas. The sports shop also sells Editorial Alpina maps of the Spanish Pyrenees. Near the campsite, at the southern end of the village is the **CRS mountain rescue service** (☎ 05.62.92.48.24).

Buses run from the bus stop near the Hôtel le Taillon. There are currently two buses a day from Gavarnie to Luz-St-Sauveur, via Gèdre (depart Gavarnie at 11.40 and 18.30); the trip takes about 40 minutes and costs €5/35F one way. From Luz there are regular buses to Lourdes, via Pierre-fitte-Nestalas where you can change for Cauterets.

Where to stay
The best hotel in Gavarnie is the *Hôtel Club Vignemale* ☆☆☆ (☎ 05.62.92 40.00, ▤ 05.62.92.40.08) where prices start at €56/368F for a single room.

Next down the line is the *Hôtel le Marboré* ☆☆ (☎ 05.62.92.40.40, ▤ 05.62.92.40.30) which has rooms from €38/250F, and its own bar/pub, Le Swan, to make Brits feel at home. There are several other hotels with prices in this range, all of which are fine: *Hôtel Le Taillon* ☆☆ (☎ 05.62.92.48.20), *Hôtel L'Astazou* ☆☆ (☎ 05.62.92 48.07), *Hôtel des Cimes* ☆☆ (☎ 05.62

92.48.13), and *Hôtel des Voyageurs* ☆☆ (☎ 05.62.92.48.01). Worth a special mention is the *Compostelle Hôtel* ☆☆ (☎ 05.62.92.49.43), a friendly place run by Mme Laporte, where clean, pleasant double rooms start at €32/210F.

There are three gîtes. *Gîte Oxygène* (☎ 05.62.92.48.23) is a modern, rather soulless place which seems to specialize in taking large groups, although individuals can stay here too; accommodation costs €12/80F per night and demi-pension costs €25/165F. *Refuge Jan Da Lo* (☎ 05.62 92.40 66) is the place to try if you fancy getting away from the crowd, as it seems to have lost all its business to La Gypaète, next door. There are no self catering facilities, but otherwise the place is fine; it's €12/79F for bed and breakfast. *Gîte Auberge La Gypaète* (☎ 05.62.92.40.61) is in a pretty, old building, and is by far the most popular of the three. Demi-pension costs €22/145F, but there are no self-catering facilities.

Camping La Bergerie (☎ 05.62 92.48.41) is run by the friendly Mme Sacaze and has a pleasant position next to the river. It costs €1.50/10F per person, and €1.50/8F for emplacement. Meals are available in the little café/bar and a hot shower costs an extra €1.50/8F.

GAVARNIE → LUZ-ST-SAUVEUR [MAP 57, p221]

To get back onto the GR10, follow the road north-west out of Gavarnie to the first sharp switchback. Take the small lane (signposted 8 BARRAGE D'OSSOUE) which runs westwards and soon crosses the **Gave d'Ossoue**. Twenty minutes' walking brings you to a yellow sign pointing the way to LE SAUGÉ 1H.

The path climbs gradually across the hillside before rounding the spur and heading north, past several farm buildings; eventually you join a rough road which leads to the gîte. The *Gîte d'étape Le Saugué* (1627m) (☎ 05.62.92.48.73) is an attractive thatched building; there are two dormitories, a small kitchen for self-catering, and a large dining area. Accommodation here costs €9/60F for the night or €23/150F for demi-pension. Camping (€3/20F) is permitted on the lawn next to the gîte, but only for those on foot and only for one night.

From the gîte, continue north, to a point where the track swings left into the side valley. Just past the corner, the GR10 takes a poorly marked turning and cuts up the embankment on the left along a small footpath. Follow the path to a **footbridge**, on the far side of which it turns northeast and climbs again. This part is poorly marked, and the multitude of small tracks made by people and animals can be confusing. Keep a careful eye out for markers.

The path slowly climbs to the ridge, becoming steeper as it nears the top. Soon, the power station at Pragnères comes into view, and after a further 20 minutes' climbing you reach a level area where the path turns west, heading into the valley of the Gave de Cestrede. The descent across the side of the valley is almost entirely through the trees of the **Sapinière de Bué**.

Near the bottom of the valley, the GR10 turns back on itself and veers east, soon passing above a small parking area which is at the end of a rough road leading down the valley. Although the GR markers indicate that the route continues down the footpath, there have been landslips on this section and the path may still be impassable. It is wiser, therefore, to cut down to the car park and follow the rough road downhill for approximately 900 metres to a point where the GR10 crosses it. Rejoin the GR10 at this point as it heads down to the left of the road, into the valley. After a 10-15 minutes you cross a small footbridge and continue down the valley to a group of houses on a tarmac lane. Turn left, and follow the lane to the main road (D921) opposite the **Pragnères power station**. Turn left along the D921 and follow it for 1½ kilometres to the *Camping St Bazerque* ☆☆ (☎ 05.62.92.49.93). The campsite is uninspiring but adequate; it costs €2.50/16.50F per person and €2.50/16.50F for emplacement, and there's a small bar.

Beyond the campsite, the GR10 parallels the main road via a narrow and overgrown footpath, soon reaching a **tiny hamlet**. From here, the path climbs on wooded tracks until you reach a summit with a rough wooden cross, the **Croix de Sia**. From here you go down to St-Sauveur; the final descent is on a steep footpath which enters St-Sauveur near the Thermes building. It's a fifteen-minute walk to the centre of **Luz-St-Sauveur** (see p166 for more information).

For a description of the GR10 beyond Luz, see p169.

Map 57 – Gavarnie to Luz-St-Saveur 221

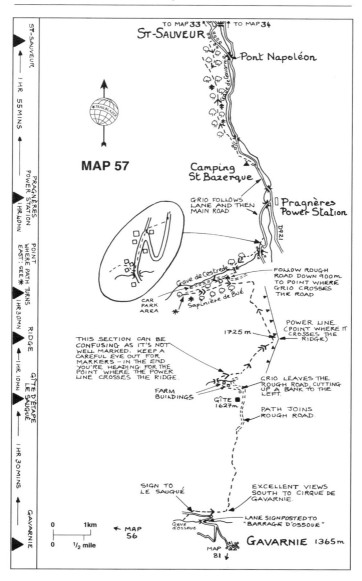

MAP 57

TO MAP 33   TO MAP 34

St-Sauveur

Pont Napoléon

Gave de Gavarnie

Camping
St Bazerque

GRIO FOLLOWS
LANE AND THEN
MAIN ROAD

Pragnères
Power Station

D921

Gave de Cestrede

FOLLOW ROUGH
ROAD DOWN 900m
TO POINT WHERE
GRIO CROSSES
THE ROAD

CAR
PARK
AREA

Sapinière de Bué

POWER LINE.
(POINT WHERE IT
CROSSES THE
RIDGE)

1725 m

THIS SECTION CAN BE
CONFUSING AS IT'S NOT
WELL MARKED. KEEP A
CAREFUL EYE OUT FOR
MARKERS – IN THE END
YOU'RE HEADING FOR THE
POINT WHERE THE POWER
LINE CROSSES THE RIDGE.

FARM
BUILDINGS

GRIO LEAVES THE
ROUGH ROAD, CUTTING
UP A BANK TO THE
LEFT.

GÎTE
1627m

PATH JOINS
ROUGH ROAD.

SIGN TO
LE SAUGUÉ

EXCELLENT VIEWS
SOUTH TO CIRQUE DE
GAVARNIE.

LANE SIGNPOSTED TO
"BARRAGE D'OSSOUE"

Gave
d'ossoue

0   1km

0   ½ mile

← MAP
56

MAP
81 ↓

GAVARNIE 1365m

ST-SAUVEUR ← 1 HR 55 MINS ←

PRAGNÈRES
POWER STATION ← 1 HR 40 MIN ←

POINT
WHERE PATH TURNS
EAST: SEE ✳ ← 1 HR 30 MIN ←

RIDGE ← 1 HR 10 MIN ←

GÎTE D'ÉTAPE
LE SAUGUÉ ← 1 HR 30 MINS ←

GAVARNIE

Central Pyrenees – GR11

The GR11 route through the Central Pyrenees contains some of the best walking in the entire range. Quite apart from the fantastic scenery of the Ordesa National Park, the GR11 also passes through the beautiful Maladetta region, and continues through the Aigües Tortes National Park. While travel to and from the region from the Spanish side of the mountains may not be ideal, it's easy to pick a route that starts and ends in France, crossing over a high mountain pass at each end to join and leave the GR11. Possible itineraries include:

● Tour of the Ordesa National Park, starting at Cauterets and ending at Gavarnie (4-7 days) (see p263)

● GR11 though the Aigües Tortes National Park, starting at Bagnères de Luchon and ending at Mounicou (14-17 days)

For the GR11 route through the Western Pyrenees (as far as Panticosa) see p126.

BALNEARIO/BAÑOS DE PANTICOSA→ BUJARUELO [MAP 58]

[Includes high section – see warning on p20] Walk up the steps beside Casa Belio and follow the clear GR markings which lead left to a stony path. The path, well marked and easy to follow, climbs the steep hillside gradually via long, gentle zigzags. After walking for an hour or so you'll leave behind the grass and the few pine trees while the path continues to climb through a moonscape of bare rock.

Two hours after starting from Panticosa you'll reach the dam of the **Ibón de Brazato (2360m)**.The path remains level around the north shore of the lake for five minutes and then climbs steeply across a scree slope to reach the top of a spur. On the far side of the spur the GR11 contours around the side of a bowl, high above another lake. The slope is covered with boulders, so there's no path as such but the paint markings on the rocks are enough to keep you on track and lead you up to the **Cuello de Brazato (2550m)**. Looking east from the col you have an excellent view of the imposing shape of Vignemale (3298m).

Head straight down from the col on an indistinct path which is hard to pick out at times, although the route markings are generally adequate. The path passes to the left (north) of the three **Ibóns de Batans**, crossing several areas of boulders. Below the third lake the path crosses the stream and descends a small gully, again mostly across boulders. Below the gully you pass a flat grassy area (possible for camping in late summer) and continue to

Map 58 – Panticosa to Bujaruelo 223

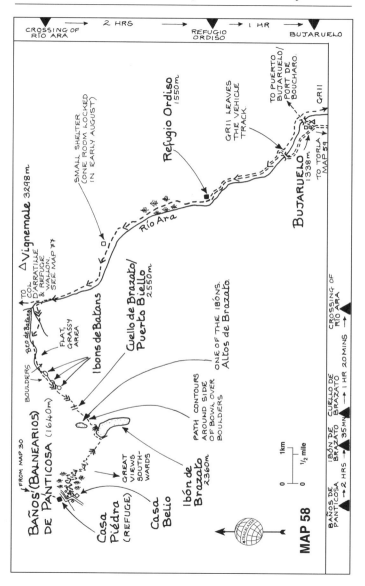

CROSSING OF RIO ARA → 2 HRS → REFUGIO ORDISO → 1 HR → BUJARUELO

△Vignemale 3298m.

SMALL SHELTER (ONE ROOM LOCKED IN EARLY AUGUST)

Refugio Ordiso 1550m.

GRII LEAVES THE VEHICLE TRACK

TO PUERTO BUJARUELO/ PORT DE BOUCHARO

GRII

BUJARUELO 1338m.

TO TORLA MAP 59

Río Ara

(TO COL D'ARRATILLE & REFUGE WALLON, SEE MAP 7)

Bco de Batans

FLAT, GRASSY AREA

Ibons de Batans

Cuello de Brazato/ Puerto Biello 2550m.

BOULDERS

ONE OF THE IBÓNS. Altos de Brazato

FROM MAP 30

BAÑOS (BALNEARIOS) DE PANTICOSA (1640m)

Casa Piédra (REFUGE)

Casa Belio

Ibón de Brazato 2360m.

GREAT VIEWS SOUTH-WARDS

PATH CONTOURS AROUND SIDE OF BOWL OVER BOULDERS

1km
0

½ mile
0

MAP 58

CROSSING OF RIO ARA →

CUELLO DE BRAZATO → 1 HR 20 MINS →

IBÓN DE BRAZATO → 35 MN →

BAÑOS DE PANTICOSA → 2 HRS →

descend eastwards, crossing the Barranco de Batans two or three more times before descending finally into the Ara valley. Follow the Río Ara downstream for a few minutes before crossing to join the path on the far bank.

Follow the footpath down the valley. After about 45 minutes you come to a small, empty **shelter** with two rooms (one of which was locked when we tried it). The hut is far from clean but would do for an overnight stop. An hour further down the valley, at the end of a rough road, is the **Refugio Ordiso (1550m)**, a tiny building which looks (and smells) as though it has been used as a sheep shelter. Follow the rough road down from the refuge, and then take the marked trail along the east side of the river to the old bridge of **Bujaruelo**.

BUJARUELO

Bujaruelo (1338m) consists of only three buildings but fortunately for backpackers they're the right sort: a modern building with facilities for the campsite, some public loos, and a bar/restaurant/lodge. Both the bar and the campsite (*Camping San Nicholas de Bujaruelo* (☎ 974-48.64.28)) have been closed for renovation, so check in Panticosa that they're open again before you rely on them. (If the facilities are closed, the next nearest campsite is half an hour's walk down the rough road).

BUJARUELO → REFUGIO DE GORIZ   [MAP 59/78, p226]

❏ Owing to various factors the first part of the route description for this stage is not the 'official' GR11 route. From Bujaruelo the proper GR11 route continues along a footpath on the east bank of the Río Ara and then crosses the **Puente de Santa Elena** and heads up a footpath over the cliffs on the west side of the river, eventually descending near to the Puente de los Navarros. The route described here is the quick but boring option of walking down the rough road for two hours to the Puente de los Navarros and rejoining the GR11 there.

Head down the rough road leading south from Bujaruelo. After half an hour you come to the **Camping Valle de Bujaruelo** ☆☆ (☎ 974-48.63.48) which has a shop, bar and restaurant, and even a few rooms: a double room costs €16/2700ptas, a triple €23/3800ptas, and a quadruple €29/4800 ptas. Camping costs €3/475ptas per person and per tent. Three and a half kilometres below the campsite is the main road and the **Puente de los Navarros (1050m approx)**, which is just below the entry to the National Park. The roof tops of Torla can be seen to the right, down the valley.

(For information on Torla and a one-week itinerary around the Torla area, see p263)

(Opposite) The Ordesa Canyon. The Parque Nacional de Ordesa y Monte Perdido, just across the border from Gavarnie, has some of the most spectacular scenery in the entire Pyrenees.

At the Puente de los Navarros a red and white GR marker on the stonework indicates the way under an arch of the bridge and down a footpath. A sign here points the same way: CAMINO VIEJO A ORDESA. A short way down here the path crosses a bridge and beyond it comes to a junction. The GR11 heads eastwards, climbing up into the Ordesa valley. (If you're going to Torla follow the path south until it emerges near the Camping Río Ara, just below the town).

Following the GR11 route eastwards, the path climbs at a steady but easy gradient through trees with occasional excellent views to the left. After about an hour you come to the Cascada Tomborrotera and ten minutes beyond this the Cascada Abelos. Just beyond the second waterfall you pass a turning to the left, leading to the Puente Luciano Briet (there's a monument and plaque to Briet, who was the first person to champion the cause of the Ordesa area). You can either cross this bridge and walk up the road to the car park area or, better, continue along the same bank of the river for a further 20 minutes until another sign points you left across a bridge to 'aparcamiento'. Cross the river via this bridge and arrive at the car park area. There's a bar/restaurant here, with a water point and toilets nearby.

The GR11 leaves the car park heading eastwards on the path towards the Refugio de Goriz. After about an hour you pass the **Cascada de Arripas**, and there's a water point at the side of the path. Ten minutes beyond this there's a fork; go left, following signs: GRADAS DE SOASO. The section above here, running past a series of low waterfalls and clear blue pools, is perfect for picnicking and sunbathing. Nearly two hours beyond the fork in the track, you reach the eastern end of the canyon, the **Circo de Soaso (1760m approx)**, where a tiny bridge crosses the stream just below an impressive waterfall, **Cascada de Cola de Caballo**.

For those who have a good head for heights, just to the right of the waterfall (north-east of the bridge) a chain has been fixed to the rocks to facilitate the climb up this direct but very steep route to the Refugio de Goriz. Most people, however, opt for the easier option and take the main path which winds up the scree slope to the east, before heading north to join the other path just above the cliff. A further three quarters of an hour's climbing brings you to the refugio (2200m). The ***Refugio de Goriz*** (☎ 974-34.12.01) is very popular, and you should book in advance if you're visiting during peak season (mid-July to mid-August), or make an effort to turn up as early in the afternoon as possible. In the evening the area around the refuge is often crammed with tents, too. The refuge has a guardian in residence all year, and has 90 places; charges are €7/1100ptas

---

(Opposite) Top: After a long haul over the Brèche de Roland (see p276-8) the Refuge des Sarradets is a welcome sight. **Bottom:** The alternative route down to Gavarnie from the Refuge des Sarradets is easier than the HRP route but meltwaters from the Glacier du Taillon can add plenty of excitement. (Photos © Sarah Jane Riley).

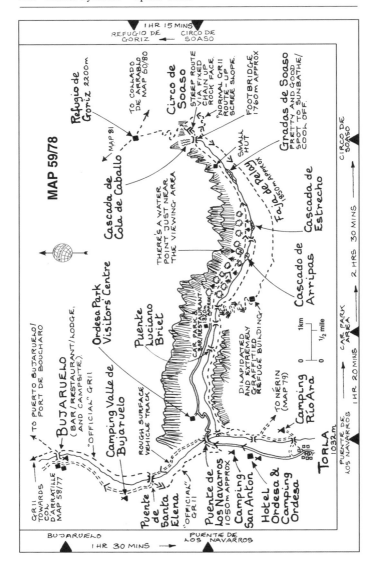

MAP 59/78

1 HR 15 MINS
REFUGIO DE   CIRCO DE
GORIZ ←   SOASO

Refugio de Goriz 2200m

TO COLLADO DE ARRABIO MAP 60/80

MAP 81

Circo de Soaso

STEEP ROUTE VIA FIXED CHAIN UP ROCK FACE.

"NORMAL GR11 ROUTE - UP SCREE SLOPE.

FOOTBRIDGE 1760m APPROX

Cascada de Cola de Caballo

SMALL HUT

Gradas de Soaso
PRETTY AND GOOD SPOT TO SUNBATHE/COOK OFF.

THERE'S A WATER POINT JUST NEAR THE VIEWING AREA

Faja de Pelay (850m APPROX)

Cascada de Estrecho

Cascado de Arripas

CIRCO DE SOASO

2 HRS 30 MINS

Ordesa Park Visitors' Centre

Puente Luciano Briet

CAR PARK AND CAR/REST AURANT 1320m APPROX

CAR PARK AREA

Camping Valle de Bujaruelo

ROUGH SURFACE VEHICLE TRACK

BUJARUELO
(BAR/RESTAURANT/LODGE AND CAMPSITE).

TO PUERTO BUJARUELO/ PORT DE BOUCHARO

"OFFICIAL" GR11

DILAPIDATED AND EXTREMELY GRAFFITIED REFUGE BUILDING

0   1km
0   ½ mile

TO NÉRIN (MAP 79)

Camping Río Ara

1 HR 20 MINS

GR11 TOWARDS COL DE ARRATILLE MAP 58/77

Puente de Santa Elena

"OFFICIAL" GR11

Puente de Los Navarros 1050m APPROX

Camping San Anton

Hotel Ordesa & Camping Ordesa

TORLA 1032m

PUENTE DE LOS NAVARROS

BUJARUELO   PUENTE DE LOS NAVARROS
1 HR 30 MINS →

Map 59 – Ordesa Canyon; Map 60 – Goriz to Circo de Pineta 227

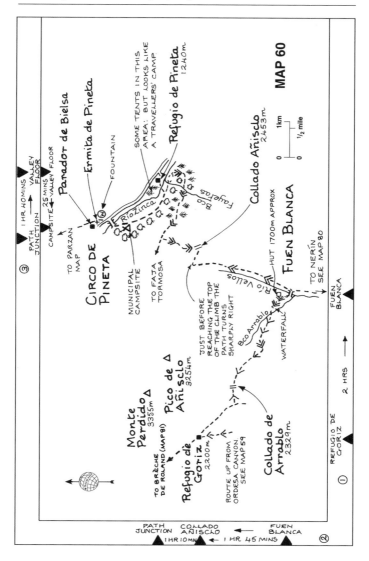

per night, €12/1900ptas for the evening meal and €3.60/600ptas for breakfast . Some provisions are sold at the refuge, including pasta, chocolate and puncture-type camping gaz cylinders.

REFUGIO DE GORIZ → CIRCO DE PINETA   [MAP 60, p227]

[Includes high section – see warning on p20] The section from Goriz to the Circo de Pineta is a long one, albeit through spectacular scenery.

From the refuge, head south-east along a level and clearly marked path for twenty minutes or so, before climbing to the **Collado de Arrablo (2329m)**. From the col continue south-eastwards across a grassy plateau before reaching a very steep descent. The path crosses a couple of grassy ledges with steep sections between them before crossing the Barranco Arrablo and heading down a very steep slope to arrive at **Fuen Blanca**. There's a tiny *stone shelter* here (for use only as a last resort; it's fairly dirty and could take no more than two or three people). The Fuen Blanca area, with a string of small waterfalls along the Río Vellos and with steep canyon walls on either side is extremely beautiful and a popular camping spot.

Just below the level of the small stone shelter the GR11 crosses the stream via a footbridge and the heads north-eastwards climbing up the valley at a fairly steep gradient. The path remains on the east side of the stream throughout the climb and just before reaching the top it turns sharply right, and heads south-east for 10 minutes contouring round to reach the **Collado Añisclo (2453m)**.

The descent from the col is very steep and hard work (there's a drop of approximately 1200m to the valley floor) so allow plenty of time and energy. From the col, the Parador, refuge and campsite can be seen far below but the markers must be followed carefully as the path, precipitous as it is, winds around the mountainside to avoid cliffs. Initially (for the first hour or so) the path goes almost straight down, zigzagging in short sharp turns. After about an hour you come to a junction where there's a sign pointing left to the Faja Tormosa. Don't take this turning, but continue on the main path as it slowly bends to the right and contours around the mountainside before going down into pine trees. Several fallen trees and three or four steep sections which need to be scrambled down, make the descent time-consuming. Approximately $1^1/_2$ hours below the path junction and sign, the path crosses the Barranco Fayetas. Continue the descent for a further half hour before arriving at the valley floor.

Just before the path finally flattens out at the bottom of the valley, the GR11, not very well signed, goes left on a path along the base of a cliff. It doesn't matter much if you miss this turn; the alternative path continues across an open grassy meadow and meets the GR11 in the trees on the far side. From here the GR11 winds through a small wood before emerging on a stony riverbank. A sign here points the way (right) to the Refugio de Pineta, which is some five minutes' walk to the east, across the stream. The GR11, however, continues towards the north-west, without crossing the stream, and after a further quarter of an hour arrives at the campsite.

Pineta

The Pineta area has little in the way of facilities.

The large hotel which can be seen from the Collado Añisclo is the *Parador de Bielsa* (☎ 974-50.10.11; 🖹 974-50 11.88). It's a very smart place which is generally fully booked and is probably beyond most walkers' budgets anyway. In mid summer (July and August) a single room here costs €80/13,200ptas and doubles go for €99/16,500ptas. While the hotel itself is probably too costly to be of interest, if you have some extra cash to spare, you could consider splashing out on a meal in the restaurant. The menu for €21/3500ptas seems very expensive but the food is wonderful and a beer or two beforehand on the terrace, with its superb view of Monte Perdido,

is the perfect way to relax after the day's walking. Non residents should try to get to the restaurant relatively early (ie 8pm) to ensure that there's a table.

The *Refugio de Pineta* (☎ 974-50.12.03) is a smart new refuge that is open all year. A place in the dormitory costs €7/1100ptas, dinner is €7.20/ 1200ptas and breakfast is €2.70/ 450ptas.

The municipal **campsite** is extremely popular and generally very crowded, possibly because, although there's meant to be a charge for staying there, very often the collector doesn't seem to turn up. The down side of this is that the facilities are very basic (two cold showers, and some smelly toilets). There's a small **bar** where sandwiches and snacks are for sale.

CIRCO DE PINETA → PARZÁN   [MAP 61, p230]

From the campsite entrance, walk up the road towards the hotel and follow the route markers around the back of the Ermita de Pineta, passing between the ermita and the water fountain. The clearly marked path climbs steeply for half an hour through trees, before meeting a vehicle track. The path shortcuts directly uphill between the loops of the track, finally meeting it again at a grassy plateau and following it (left) to **Refugio La Larri (1560m)**. The refuge building is now in use as a cowshed and is unsuitable for walkers.

The GR11 swings right here and begins to climb steeply. After a halfhour's ascent across an almost bare hillside with only a few trees, the trail enters an area of pine trees and the climb becomes even steeper for about 10 minutes. At the top of this the path emerges at a flatter area and then follows a small gully up to a grassy plateau. Head roughly south-east across the grass until after quarter of an hour you come to a vehicle track. Go right along the track for a few metres, then turn off left up a gully to reach a small **col (approx 2100m)**.

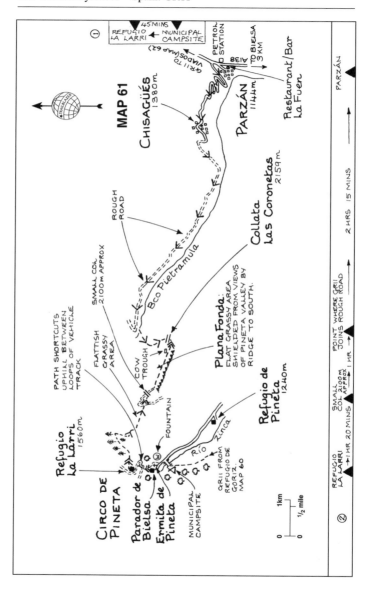

MAP 61

REFUGIO LA LARRI ← MUNICIPAL CAMPSITE 45 MINS

CHISAGÜÉS 1380m.

GR11 TO VIADÓS (MAP 62)

PETROL STATION

A138 TO BIELSA 3 KM

PARZÁN 1144m.

Restaurant/Bar La Fuen

ROUGH ROAD

Collata Las Coronetas 2159m.

Bco Pietramula

SMALL COL 2100m APPROX

PATH SHORTCUTS UPHILL BETWEEN LOOPS OF VEHICLE TRACK

FLATTISH GRASSY AREA

COW TROUGH

Plana Fonda: FLAT GRASSY AREA SHIELDED FROM VIEWS OF PINETA VALLEY BY RIDGE TO SOUTH.

Refugio La Larri 1560m.

CIRCO DE PINETA

Parador de Bielsa

Ermita de Pineta

FOUNTAIN

RÍO ZINCA

Refugio de Pineta 1240m.

GR11 FROM REFUGIO DE GORIZ MAP 60

MUNICIPAL CAMPSITE

0   1km
0   ½ mile

REFUGIO LA LARRI → 1 HR 20 MINS → SMALL COL 2100m APPROX → 1 HR → POINT WHERE GR11 JOINS ROUGH ROAD → 2 HRS 15 MINS → PARZÁN

The GR11 descends gently from the small col and continues south-east-wards across the **Plana Fonda**, a flat grassy area screened from views of the Pineta valley by a rocky ridge along the right-hand side. After 10 minutes you pass a cow trough, and then follow a distinct path climbing the slope north-eastwards to the **Collata las Coronetas (2159m)**. The route down from the col, mainly over grass, swings from north-west through to north-east before crossing the Barranco Pietramula and coming to a rough mountain road. Follow this all the way to Parzán. After about $1^1/_2$-2 hours the road passes through the tiny hamlet of Chisagüés, and the loose surface gives way to tarmac. Beyond the hamlet the lane descends the hillside in long zigzags for $3^1/_2$ km, to meet the main road next to the village of Parzán (1144m).

Parzán

There's not much to Parzán but it does offer the chance to stock up on supplies and the possibility of somewhere to stay for the night. On the main road, the *Restaurant/bar La Fuen* (☎ 974-51.10.47) seems to be more of a holiday home than hotel, but could be worth trying for somewhere to stay – particularly if you can phone in advance. Otherwise there are a couple of houses in the village which advertise 'habitaciones' (rooms) to rent (look for the signboards). Alternatively you could head 3km down the road to Bielsa. The petrol station on the main road has a small snack bar and a tiny but very well-stocked supermarket.

PARZÁN → REFUGIO DE VIADÓS [MAP 62, p233]

From the petrol station, walk north up the main road for just over a kilometre to a turning off to the right, signposted 'Lago de Urdiceto 11'. Take this turning down across the bridge, and follow the mountain road as it climbs south-south-eastwards. From here the GR11 follows the rough road almost as far as the Collata Chistau with only a couple of short deviations.

After about an hour the track passes a flattish grassy area with two huts (the first possible spot to camp since leaving Parzán); about ten minutes beyond this there's a spring on the left-hand side of the path. An hour or so above the huts the GR11 leaves the rough road briefly to climb past the buildings of a small hydroelectric station (Central Electrica de Urdiceto). Just above these buildings there's a tiny refuge which could sleep two or three people, as well as a grassy area which is suitable for camping.

From the refuge, continue uphill along the vehicle track for a further half hour until the road makes a sharp switchback to the left. Here the GR11 splits away on a footpath which continues straight up the valley, level at first and then climbing directly towards the col. The footpath rejoins the rough road a few metres before reaching the **Collata Chistau (2314m)**.

From the col, follow the obvious path leading eastwards, which descends for quarter of an hour across a bare hillside before climbing briefly again to reach the top of a spur. The path descends along the top of the spur for 10 minutes before swinging left (north) and leading down to a grassy area where there's stone hut, the roof of which has collapsed. Go down past the hut, and you'll soon cross the Barranco Montarruego and pass through an area of pine trees. Just beyond the trees, on the right, a small hut with a corrugated roof offers possible shelter for three people. The path continues to descend through pine trees before crossing a stream and climbing for five minutes to reach a small col just to the north of Las Collas.

Despite the maps showing this part of the GR11 as a footpath there is actually a new vehicle track here which zigzags down the hillside. The remains of the GR11 footpath can still be seen but they are now blocked with fallen trees, so it's easiest to follow the vehicle track. Approximately quarter of an hour after leaving the col you pass, on the right, another tiny hut with space for 3-4 people. Just below this you arrive at a junction with a more permanent rough road which runs east-west past the **Bordas de Lisier (1730m)**. Follow this rough road eastwards as it descends into the valley where it meets an earthen road running along the valley floor. There's an information board here and a GR11 sign pointing north-east up the road towards Viadós.

Follow the road and after five minutes you pass a fairly basic camping area. There's a building here with some washing facilities but it's in poor condition: dirty sinks, smelly toilets and very doubtful showers. Five minutes further up the road you pass a youth camp, the **Campamiento Virgen Blanca**. Just beyond this the road crosses a bridge and swings around to the right to pass **Camping Forcalla** a small campsite with adequate facilities and a bar/café. Beyond the campsite the rough road winds up the hillside, but the GR11 shortcuts between the loops on a well worn path. Above a parking area the GR11 climbs again, crosses a ridge and descends to the refuge (1760m). The **Refugio de Viadós** (☎ 974-50.61.63) is a lovely place to stay. It's immaculately clean and from the benches outside the door there's a fantastic view across the valley to the impressive peaks around Pico Posets (3375m). The tariff is very reasonable: €4.20/700ptas for the night, €9/1400ptas for supper and €3/500ptas for breakfast. The refuge is open from 25 June to 25 September and on some weekends outside this period.

Map 62 – Parzán to Refugio de Viadós 233

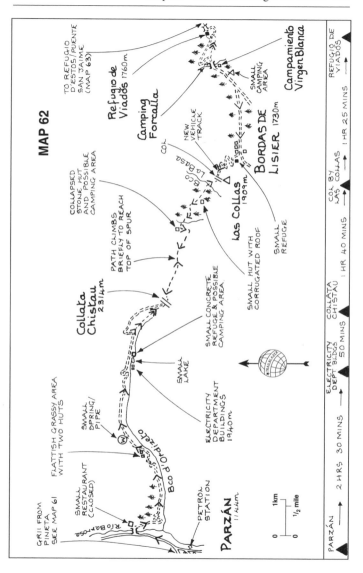

MAP 62

GRILL FROM PINETA SEE MAP 61

FLATTISH GRASSY AREA WITH TWO HUTS

SMALL RESTAURANT (CLOSED)

RÍO BARROSA

PETROL STATION

PARZÁN 1144m

SMALL SPRING/PIPE

Bco d'ORDIZETO

ELECTRICITY DEPARTMENT BUILDINGS 1940m

SMALL LAKE

Collata Chistau 2314m

PATH CLIMBS BRIEFLY TO REACH TOP OF SPUR

COLLAPSED STONE HUT AND POSSIBLE CAMPING AREA

SMALL CONCRETE REFUGE & POSSIBLE CAMPING AREA

SMALL HUT WITH CORRUGATED ROOF

SMALL REFUGE

las Collas 1909m

Bco de la Basa

COL

La Basa

NEW VEHICLE TRACK

BORDAS DE LISIER 1730m

Camping Forcalla

Refugio de Viadós 1760m

TO REFUGIO D'ESTOS/PUENTE SAN JAIME (MAP 63)

SMALL CAMPING AREA

Campamento Virgen Blanca

REFUGIO DE VIADÓS

0 1km
0 ½ mile

PARZÁN ◄ 2 HRS 30 MINS ◄ ELECTRICITY DEPT BLDGS ◄ 50 MINS ◄ COLLATA CHISTAU ◄ 1 HR 40 MINS ◄ COL BY LAS COLLAS ◄ 1 HR 25 MINS ◄ REFUGIO DE VIADÓS

REFUGIO DE VIADÓS → PUENTE DE SAN JAIME   [MAP 63]

[Includes high section – see warning on p20] Head down a narrow foot-path from the refuge and, on reaching the vehicle track below, follow it left across the bridge. The track almost immediately narrows to a footpath, and runs eastwards through the middle of a cluster of old stone barns. After a few minutes it meets another path and a sign next to the junction points the way: REFUGIO D'ESTOS 4H 30. Continue along the footpath which heads north-east across the side of the valley, climbing at a gentle gradient. After approximately three quarters of an hour the path turns directly uphill and the climb is very steep for five minutes before you turn north-eastwards again, continuing on a gradual ascent.

Quarter of an hour beyond this, the Río Zinqueta d'Añes Cruzes curves north-eastwards through a tiny gorge and the GR11 follows it closely, climbing steeply alongside the gorge. Having reached the top of the ravine the path leads down into the **Pleta d'Añes Cruzes (2080m)**, a small bowl in which there is a stream junction and, next to it, a sign: COL-LADO DE ESTOS 1H 30. The GR11 crosses two streams before starting to climb eastwards up the south slope of the valley of the Barranco El Puerto. After a tiring ascent the path levels off slightly near the top and finally reaches the **Puerto de Chistau/d'Estós (2592m)**.

Descend from the col on a steep, narrow path running across the valley side. On reaching the valley bottom the path crosses the course of the Barranco d'Estós (which is dry by mid/late summer) a couple of times before finally crossing to the north bank of the Río Estós, where it remains, parallelling the river down the valley. Approximately an hour after leaving the col, the path climbs slightly away from the river and soon arrives at the refuge (1875m). The ***Refugio d'Estós*** (☎ 974-55.14.83) is a large place (space for 185 people) which is open all year. It costs €7/1200ptas for the night, €11/1800ptas for an evening meal and €3.60/600ptas for breakfast.

Beyond the refuge, the GR11 descends briefly before following a shady and level path through pine trees. After 20 minutes it descends again to cross a footbridge over the river. Just beyond the bridge the path joins a vehicle track which is, with one small exception, followed all the way to Puente de San Jaime. Five minutes' walk down the track there's a brief diversion to the left, where the GR11 takes a shortcut across a loop of the vehicle track. Actually the shortcut probably takes longer than remaining on the vehicle track, so it's hardly worth it.

Approximately three quarters of an hour after starting down the vehicle track you pass, on the right, the ***Cabana Santa Ana***, which appears to be open for use by walkers. Ten minutes beyond this the track crosses a bridge over the river and 20-30 minutes later you'll arrive at the parking area just above **Puente de San Jaime (1254m)**.

Map 63 – Refugio de Viadós to Puente de San Jaime 235

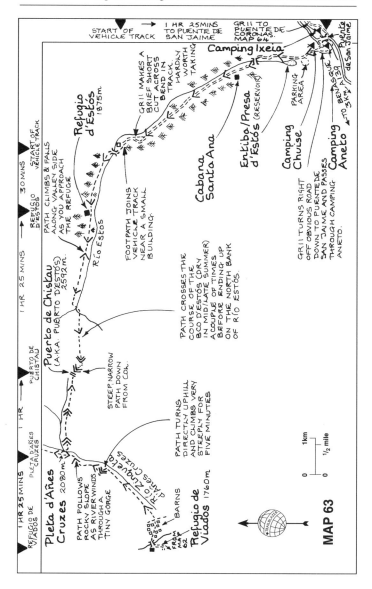

START OF VEHICLE TRACK → 1 HR 25MINS TO PUENTE DE SAN JAIME

GRILL TO PUENTE DE CORONAS. MAP 64

Camping Ixeia

GRILL MAKES A BRIEF SHORT CUT ACROSS BEND IN TRACK. HARDLY WORTH TAKING.

Refugio d'Estós 1875m.

PATH CLIMBS ALONG VALLEY SIDE AS YOU APPROACH THE REFUGE

Entibo/Presa d'Estós (RESERVOIR)

PARKING AREA

TO BENASQUE A139 Puente de San Jaime

TO 3KM A139

FOOTPATH JOINS VEHICLE TRACK NEAR A SMALL BUILDING.

Cabaña Santa Ana

Camping Chuise

Camping Aneto

GRILL TURNS RIGHT OFF OBVIOUS ROAD DOWN TO PUENTE DE SAN JAIME AND PASSES THROUGH CAMPING ANETO.

Río Estós

PATH CROSSES THE COURSE OF THE BCO D'ESTÓS (DRY IN MID/LATE SUMMER) A COUPLE OF TIMES BEFORE ENDING UP ON THE NORTH BANK OF RÍO ESTÓS.

Puerto de Chistau (A.K.A. PUERTO D'ESTÓS) 2592m.

STEEP NARROW PATH DOWN FROM COL.

1 HR 25 MINS

30 MINS

REFUGIO D'ESTÓS →

START OF VEHICLE TRACK

1 HR

PUERTO DE CHISTAU →

1 HR 25 MINS

PLETA D'AÑES CRUZES →

Pleta d'Añes Cruzes 2080m.

PATH FOLLOWS ROCKY SLOPE AS RIVER WINDS THROUGH A TINY GORGE

PATH TURNS DIRECTLY UPHILL AND CLIMBS VERY STEEPLY FOR FIVE MINUTES

R. Añes Cruzes

BARNS

Refugio de Viadós 1760m.

FROM MAP 62

REFUGIO DE VIADÓS →

0 1km
0 ½ mile

MAP 63

TRAILBLAZER

Puente de San Jaime

The area around the Puente de San Jaime is a popular holiday spot and consequently there's a choice of campsites. Other facilities, including hotels and shops are available in the village of Bénasque, 3 km down the road.

Just below the parking area, the *Camping Chuise* has a slightly jaded appearance but it's perfectly adequate and it's considerably quieter than its enormous neighbour. Beyond Camping Chuise the GR11 leaves the road and passes, via a rough road and then a footpath, down to the enormous *Camping Aneto* (☎/🖳 974-55.11.41). The campsite has excellent facilities including a large bar/restaurant, a well-stocked

supermarket (puncture-type gas cylinders only) and washing machines. Camping here costs €3/475ptas per person and per tent, and there's also an albergue which charges €9/1500ptas for a bed for the night. The reception sells maps of the area and has lots of information on local activities and transport. Just beyond the Puente de San Jaime is the *Camping Ixeia*.

There's currently a daily **bus service** running three or four times a day from Bénasque to the area of La Besurta, just below the Port de Bénasque/ Vénasque and the Refugio de Renclusa (see p258). The bus service stops at, among other places, Puente de San Jaime and the Hospital de Benasque.

PUENTE DE SAN JAIME → ESTANY CAP DE LLAUSET [MAP 64]

[Includes high section – see warning on p20] This section is far from ideal because it doesn't have any accommodation at the end of it. Alternatives include stopping overnight in or near the small refugio at Puente de Coronas, or continuing beyond Estany Cap de Llauset to stop overnight in or near the Refugio d'Angliós. If you don't have a tent, the problem with either of these options is that the refuges could well be already occupied when you get there (as was the case when I passed through this area).

Cross the stone footbridge, the Puente de Cubera, in the middle of Camping Aneto, and turn left along the river bank, passing under the road bridge. Beyond the bridge the GR11 joins a rough road running north-north-east, past the Camping Ixeia. Just below the dam of the Embalse de Paso Nuevo the rough road doubles back sharply to the right and the GR11 leaves the track, shortcutting uphill for ten minutes. Where it meets the track again, turn left and follow the road past the reservoir, over the Puente de Ballibierna and to a track junction where there's a sign: VALLEBIERNA GR11.

Go up the rough road which soon leads past a concrete water container on the right. Just past the container the GR11 splits away from the track, climbing very steeply for quarter of an hour through an area of large pine trees. Where the path rejoins the vehicle track, turn right and follow the track, which climbs at a constant and fairly easy gradient. After almost an hour you pass the *Refugio d'El Quillón*, almost hidden up a steep bank on the left; it could sleep six or seven people. After a further 45 minutes you come to the **Puente de Coronas (1920m approx)** and, just beyond it,

Map 64 – Puente de San Jaime to Estany Cap de Llauset 237

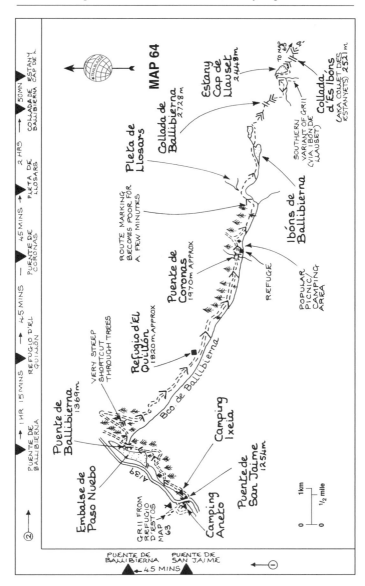

MAP 64

Estany Cap de Llauset 2448m

Collada de Ballibierna 2728m

Pleta de Llosars

Collada d'Es Ibons (AKA COLLET DES ESTANYETS) 2521 m.

SOUTHERN VARIANT OF GR11 (VIA IBON DE LLAUSET)

TO MAP 65

Ibóns de Ballibierna

REFUGE

POPULAR PICNIC/ CAMPING AREA

ROUTE MARKING BECOMES POOR FOR A FEW MINUTES

Puente de Corónas 1970m APPROX

Bco de Ballibierna

VERY STEEP SHORTCUT THROUGH TREES

Refugio d'EL Quillón 1820m APPROX

Puente de Ballibierna 1369m

Embalse de Paso Nuebo

A139

GR11 FROM REFUGIO D'ESTOS MAP 63

Camping Ixeia

Camping Aneto

Puente de San Jaime 1254m

0   1km
0   ½ mile

PUENTE DE BALLIBIERNA ← 1 HR 15 MINS → REFUGIO D'EL QUILLÓN ← 45 MINS → PUENTE DE CORÓNAS ← 45 MINS → PLETA DE LLOSARS ← 2 HRS → COLLADA DE BALLIBIERNA ← 50MN → ESTANY CAP DEL.

PUENTE DE BALLIBIERNA   PUENTE DE SAN JAIME
← 45 MINS →

the *refuge*. The building is in good condition, contains an emergency SOS radio, and can sleep 12 people on two tiers. The area around the refuge is popular as a picnic area, and for camping.

Follow a wide, stony track eastwards from behind the refuge building. After about seven minutes, at a fork, clear GR markings direct you to the right. Beyond this the path becomes narrower, rockier and steeper. Approximately half an hour after leaving the refuge the route temporarily becomes less well marked; keep an eye out for a few cairns which assist. Soon you arrive at a flat grassy area, the **Pleta de Llosars**. This is shown on the map as marshy ground, but in late summer it's possible to camp here. Cross the Barranco de Llosars and climb up the steep rocky slope to reach the lower of the Ibóns de Ballibierna. The GR11 goes around the north side of the lower lake, then crosses the rocky area between the two lakes, and passes around the southern side of the upper lake. A stream feeding the upper lake provides a possible water source.

From the edge of the second lake the climb to the col takes a fairly direct route (the paint markers are faded and can be hard to spot), first up a grassy path and then across boulders in the last part of the climb. Finally you arrive at the **Collada de Ballibierna (2728m)** from which there are magnificent views to the east and west.

The descent from the col starts directly down towards the Estany Cap de Llauset, which can be seen below. A short way down from the col, however, the path swings right, heading south to a flattish area before descending eastwards alongside a stream which soon meets the outflow coming from the Estany Cap de Llauset. At this point the path divides – one route of the GR11 going north and the other south. Both routes are clearly marked on the rocks. This description follows the north route.

The north route runs across an area of boulders, then crosses the stream coming from the lake above and climbs to the side of the **Estany Cap de Llauset (2448m)**. Although camping is probably not strictly allowed here, the grassy western shore of the lake provides a suitable overnight spot.

ESTANY CAP DE LLAUSET → HOSPITAL DE VIELLA [MAP 65]

[Includes high section – see warning on p20] The GR11 heads around the western side of the Estany Cap de Llauset and then climbs across boulders to the **Collada d'es Ibóns (2521m)**. The descent from the col is via a steep rocky path, and then across boulders to the edge of the first of the Estanys Cap d'Angliós. From here the GR11 runs around the south side of the first two lakes and then crosses an area of boulders to pass around the north side of the third lake before finding a grassy path which leads down to the refuge. The *Refuge d'Angliós* **(2220m)**, a tiny wooden shelter with only four bunks, is open for use by anyone (including shepherds – so you may find it already full).

Map 65 – Estany Cap de Llauset to Hospital de Viella 239

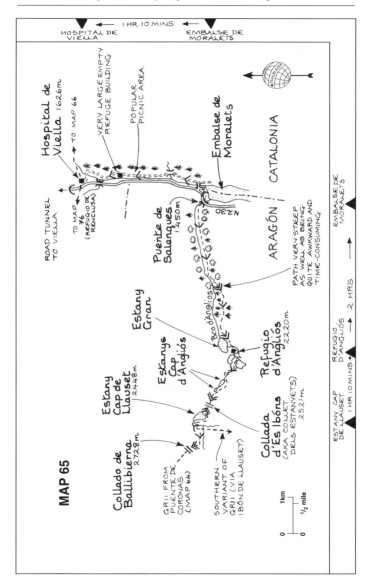

MAP 65

Collado de Ballibierna 2728m.

GRII FROM PUENTE DE CORONAS (MAP 64)

SOUTHERN VARIANT OF GRII (VIA IBÓN DE LLAUSET)

Collada d'Es Ibóns (AKA COLLET DELS ESTANVETS) 2521m.

Estany Cap de Llauset 2448m.

Estanys Cap d'Angliós

Estany Gran

Refugio d'Angliós 2220m.

Bco d'Angliós

PATH VERY STEEP AS WELL AS BEING QUITE AWKWARD AND TIME-CONSUMING

Puente de Salenques 1450m.

N230

ARAGÓN   CATALONIA

Embalse de Moralets

ROAD TUNNEL TO VIELLA

TO MAP 76 (REFUGIO DE RENCLUSA)

Hospital de Viella 1626m.

TO MAP 66

VERY LARGE EMPTY REFUGE BUILDING

POPULAR PICNIC AREA

← 1 HR 10 MINS ←
HOSPITAL DE VIELLA   EMBALSE DE MORALETS

TRAILBLAZER

1km
0
1/2 mile
0

ESTANY CAP DE LLAUSET
1 HR 10 MINS →

REFUGIO D'ANGLIÓS →
2 HRS →

EMBALSE DE MORALETS

Below the refuge the GR11 circles around the edge of the Estany Gran and descends quite steeply along the side of the small gully below it. It levels out slightly through an area of pine trees before descending very steeply through mixed coniferous and deciduous woods. This section is very awkward and time-consuming. After 1½-1¾ hours of descent from the refuge the gradient lessens and the path descends gently through deciduous woods to the north end of the **Embalse de Moralets**. The route markers invite the walker to ford the stream above the road bridge, the **Puente de Salenques (1450m)**, but it's easier to cross via the bridge and walk up the tarmac for 200-300m to a parking area. At the north end of the parking area, a small concrete bridge crosses a stream. Cross the bridge, passing as you do so from the province of Aragón into the province of Catalonia, and turn left, heading north along the rough vehicle track. The track initially runs close alongside the stream, at first as a stony cart track and then across grass. About 10 minutes later the path climbs a little to cross a concrete footbridge and then descends again to run alongside the river. A short way beyond this it passes a large and popular picnic area and then a huge empty refuge building, before reaching the Hospital de Viella and the *Refugi Sant Nicolau* (**1626m, see p262**).

HOSPITAL DE VIELLA → REFUGI DE LA RESTANCA   [MAP 66]

(**For the linking stage from Bagnères-de-Luchon, see p257**) If you're short of time this section could be combined with the next stage to Colomers. The walk takes about 4½-5 hours and after a long but fairly gentle climb to the Port de Rius it's pretty much all downhill to Restanca.

From the Hospital de Viella the route is well defined with the familiar red and white paint-markings. A sign points the way along the path running eastwards from the refuge (REFUGI DE LA RESTANCA 4H 40) and after a few minutes you start to pick up the route markers. These become

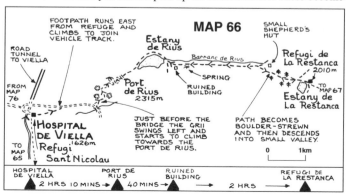

increasingly clear as the GR11 joins a vehicle track which you follow eastwards into the Vall de Conangles.

Just before a small **bridge** across the Barranc de L'Hospital, the path heads left, and the climbing begins. The path zigzags back and forth, and about two hours after leaving the refuge, you reach the **Port de Rius (2315m)**, from which there is an excellent view westwards towards the Tuc de Mulleres.

Follow the path to and around the northern edge of the **Estany de Rius**. The shores of the lake are boulder-strewn, and the scene is some-

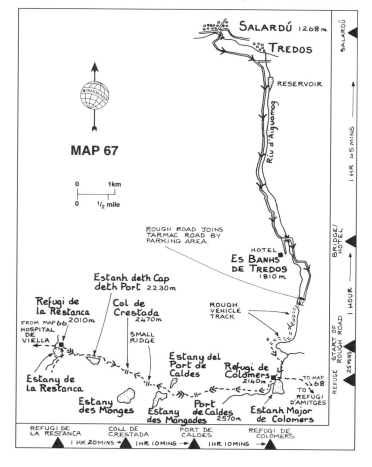

how both attractive and extremely desolate. From the eastern end of the lake the path starts to descend gently into the valley below, passing a ruined building and soon afterwards a tiny spring. Finally, just before passing above a **shepherd's hut**, the GR11 turns south-east and climbs gently across the hillside. As it rounds the spur it passes through an area of rocks and then descends into a valley.

The climb up the far slope of the valley is short but steep and follows roughly along a line of telegraph poles. At the top of the climb the path crosses the ridge and soon the **Estany de la Restanca** and the refuge (2010m) come into sight below. Walk down the hill and across the barrage to get to the refuge. The *Refugi de la Restanca* (☎ 908-03.65.59) is a large and rather ugly building, with 86 places. The guardians are friendly and the place is generally very well run. It costs €10/1600ptas for the night and €11/1850ptas for the evening meal; you can get a hot shower for €1.20/200ptas. Visa cards are accepted.

REFUGI DE LA RESTANCA → REFUGI DE COLOMERS [MAP 67, p241]

[Includes high section – see warning on p20] Take the path which climbs rapidly up the hillside to the south-east. After 25 minutes you come to a small plateau, and the **Estanh deth Cap deth Port**, a pretty little lake with a good area for camping on its north shore, although, reportedly, there are lots of mosquitoes. Follow the markers around the north-eastern edge of the lake and climb through an area of boulders to the **Col de Crestada (2470m),** from which there's a good view south over Estany des Monges.

The GR11 continues south-eastwards, crossing a grassy bowl and climbing a small ridge from which you can see, in the valley below, the Estany des Mangades and the Estany del Port de Caldes.

After a steepish descent into the valley, the painted markings lead you between the two lakes and up the rocky slope on the far side to the **Port de Caldes (2570m)**. Head straight over the pass and down the other side; the footpath is steep in places but after about half an hour it levels out into an attractive route alongside the stream. Following the path and stream as they turn north you soon reach the *Refugi de Colomers* (2140m) (☎ 973-25.30.08). The refuge is small (40 places) but attractive and is a popular destination for day trippers. It costs €10/1600ptas for the night and €11/1800ptas for an evening meal. Camping is permitted nearby.

❏ **Refuges in Val'd'Aran**
For further information on the refuges in the Val d'Aran and on the area generally, try the website, 🖳 www.refugis.com, which has some useful information on access to the region and on opening dates for the refuges.

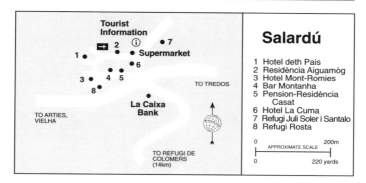

Salardú

1 Hotel deth Pais
2 Residència Aiguamòg
3 Hotel Mont-Romies
4 Bar Montanha
5 Pension-Residència Casat
6 Hotel La Cuma
7 Refugi Juli Soler i Santalo
8 Refugi Rosta

Tourist Information
2
7
1
Supermarket
6
3 4 5
8
La Caixa Bank
TO TREDOS
TO ARTIES, VIELHA
TO REFUGI DE COLOMERS (14km)

0   200m
APPROXIMATE SCALE
0   220 yards

SALARDÚ

There are several places in the Aran valley where you can pick up supplies. Viella is the largest town in the valley, and Espot also has a few shops; there's a store in the campsite in La Guingueta d'Àneu, and there are several shops in the nearby village of Esterri d'Àneu. Alternatively you could choose to head down from Colomers to Salardú. The village is not big but it has two banks, a shop and several places to stay. The only problem is that Salardú is about 14 weary kilometres down the road from Colomers. There's nowhere from which to phone for a taxi, so the only other option (apart from walking) is to try hitching a lift from near the main parking area, one hour below the refuge.

From the refuge, descend below the barrage and follow the clear footpath northwards. After 25 minutes you arrive at the rough road which leads down towards Salardú. Turn right and follow the track; after half an hour it passes through a large parking area, beyond which the road is metalled. Half an hour later it crosses a small bridge, near the hotel/bar/restaurant at *Es Banhs de Tredos* (☎ 973-25.30.03). The newly-constructed hotel, built on the site of some hot springs, is far from cheap. Double rooms go for between €90-102/ 15,000-17,000ptas (including breakfast)

– a lot of money to stay in the comfortable but rather characterless building. The evening meal (€18/3000ptas) is, however, reported to be very good. After a further 1¾ hours' walk down the lane you come to Salardú.

Services

There are two **banks**. During the period June-September, La Caixa is open 08.15-14.00 Monday to Friday (presumably the hours are shorter outside this period), and there's a cash dispenser outside the building. The only **shop** in Salardú is the small supermarket, although some walkers have reported that there's a pharmacy which is open from 14.00-16.00 only. The **tourist office** (☎ 973-64.57.26) is in a tiny wooden hut near the supermarket; they can give details of accommodation throughout the Aran valley. If you need to see a doctor, try the place opposite the *Residència Aiguamòg*, which is open for consultations from 12.30-13.30 daily. The nearest hospital (☎ 973-64 00.04) is in Viella.

The **taxi service**, though far from cheap, is useful to avoid having to trudge back up to Colomers. The taxi driver (☎ 973-64.50.33) lives next to the La Caixa bank. If he's busy, the next nearest taxis are in Viella; try Ignacio Gallardo Rufaste (☎ 973-64.18.20;

mobile 629-31.43.34) or Javier Martinez Solé (☎ 973-64.20.87) who has an Espace-type van (up to eight passengers). He charges about €48/8000ptas to make the trip up to just below Colomers. From Viella to Bagnères de Luchon costs €54/9000ptas. There are three or four daily **buses** from Salardú to Viella, and the journey takes about half an hour.

Where to stay

There's a good range of reasonably priced accommodation in Salardú. The smartest place is the **Hotel Mont-Romies** ☆☆ (☎ 973-64.58.16, 🖹 973-64.45.39) which is on the Plaça Major. Double rooms start at €63/10,500ptas (including breakfast). **Hotel deth Pais** ☆☆ (☎ 973-64.58.36) is very comfortable but perhaps a little lacking in character; doubles start at €43/7200ptas (including breakfast) in July, although they rise to €49/8200ptas in August. **Hotel la Cuma** ☆ (☎ 973-64.50.17, 🖹 973-64.58.48) is also modern,and charges similar prices to Hotel deth Pais: €44/7300ptas in early/mid July, rising to €49/8200ptas in late July/August. The rooms are reportedly very clean and the management are friendly and helpful;

the owner swears that her restaurant is *the* place to try local specialities. Just around the corner from La Cuma is the **Residència Aiguamòg** (☎ 973-64.54 96), a pretty old house, the inside of which has been completely modernized; double rooms start at €30/5000ptas, triples are €39/6500ptas or there's a quadruple room for €48/ 8000ptas.

Coming down in price, in the lane running east from the Plaça Major are two little places. The **Bar Montanha** (☎ 973-64.41.08) has doubles with attached bathroom from €27/4400ptas, or it's €21/3400ptas for a double with a common bathroom. Almost next door, the **Pension-Residència Casat** (☎ 973-64.50 56) has doubles from €27/4500 ptas.

Finally, there are two cheapies in Salardú. **Refugi Rosta** (☎ 973-64.53.08, 🖹 64.58.14), has private rooms (€24/3975ptas for media-pensión) and dormitory accommodation (€12/1980ptas for the night). **Refugi Juli Soler i Santalo** (☎/🖹: 973-64.50.16) is open between June and October and offers very basic accommodation. A bed in a four-bedded room costs €15/2400ptas per night, or a bed in the dormitory costs €9/1500ptas.

REFUGI DE COLOMERS → REFUGI D'AMITGES   [MAP 68]

[Includes high section – see warning on p20] Cross the barrage, and follow the path as it dips down into the bowl just north-east of the dam; it then climbs eastwards up a short, steep slope, to pass over a col. From here the path heads south-east, remaining level and passing a succession of idyllic lakes. Some fifty minutes after leaving the barrage you pass the southern end of Estanh Obago and start to climb to the **Port de Ratera** (2530m approx). The steep ascent is made considerably easier by the fact that the path is well-trodden and weaves back and forth maintaining a manageable gradient. In the middle of the col a sign points towards the *Refugi de Saboredo*, 45 minutes away.

Descend south-eastwards from the col to a grassy shoulder where there's another sign. The direct path to the Refugi d'Amitges is signposted to the left, while the arrow to the right points to the Estany de Sant Maurici (via the GR11). It is possible to follow the GR11 and then double back to the refuge, but it's not a great idea as the path loses a lot of height,

Map 68 – Refugi de Colomers to Refugi d'Amitges 245

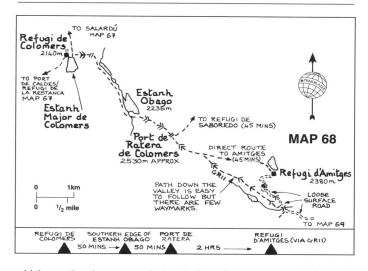

REFUGI DE COLOMERS — SOUTHERN EDGE OF ESTANH OBAGO — PORT DE RATERA — REFUGI D'AMITGES (VIA GR11)

50 MINS → 50 MINS → 2 HRS →

which you then have to regain by climbing the very steep vehicle track. (If you do follow the main GR11, towards Estany de St Maurici, don't be surprised to find that it is poorly marked until you get about halfway down the valley. The path isn't hard to follow, but for some reason, almost all the markings disappear for a while). If you're taking the direct path to Amitges, follow the yellow marker posts away from the grassy shoulder. As you come around the corner, stay high above the area of moraine, which is both difficult and time-consuming to cross.

The **Refugi d'Amitges (2380m)** (☎ 973-25.01.09) is a large modern building with all comforts; media-pensión costs €23/3775ptas.

REFUGI D'AMITGES → LA GUINGUETA D'ÀNEU [MAP 69, p247]

This is not the most interesting of the sections in this circuit. The countryside is attractive but undramatic, and much of the day's walk is on roads and vehicle tracks. Despite this, Espot is a good place to stop for a break, and beyond here, as you pass out of the National Park, you suddenly have the countryside almost entirely to yourself.

From the Refugi d'Amitges, follow the vehicle track downhill to join the GR11. Despite what is shown on the IGN 1:50,000 map, the GR11 follows the track all the way to the eastern end of the **Estany de Sant Maurici**, passing en route the ruins of a large old building which used to be a military barracks. An hour's walking brings you to the edge of the lake where there's a small **information booth** with a few displays and some leaflets about the National Park. For those in a hurry to get to Espot, there's a regular service up and down the hill in Land Rovers during the summer months; it's €3.60/600ptas per person and stops running around 20.00. On the south side of the lake, under the huge shape of Gran Encantat, is the *Refugi Ernets Mallafré* (1950m) (☎ 973-25.01.18), a tiny place opened in October 1975. The building is so small that there's only room for sleeping (28 people) and for eating, the rucksacks stay outside. The refuge is open from 1 June to 30 September: it costs €10/1600ptas for the night and €11/1850ptas for the evening meal.

The path running towards Espot on the southern bank of the Riu Escrita has suffered from avalanche damage and is hard to follow, so the only option is to take the vehicle track eastwards. Ten minutes after leaving the refuge, you pass the **Chapel of Sant Maurici** and five minutes beyond this the track joins the tarmac road. Follow the road for ten minutes until, by a small cabane, the GR11 heads off on a grassy footpath. After quarter of an hour there's a junction. The path to the right descends to a footbridge across the river, while the GR11 climbs slightly from the junction and continues along the northern slopes of the valley on a wide track.

After about forty minutes, the GR11 crosses the river at the **Pont de Suar** and continues down to Espot on the road. En route you pass the *Camping Vora Park* (☎ 973-62.41.08, 🖹 62.41.43), a pleasant and peaceful campsite with its own shop, bar and restaurant. Charges are €3.75/625ptas per person and €3.75/625ptas per tent, and the campsite is open from June to the end of September. Quarter of an hour further down the road is the *Camping Solau* (☎ 973-62.40.68), where the tariff is €3.45/575ptas per person and per tent. There's a poorly stocked shop and a bar.

ESPOT

The village of Espot is enjoying a rebirth as a tourist centre, and is consequently well-stocked with restaurants, cafés, bars and shops. The tiny La Caixa **bank** is open from Monday to Friday 11.00-14.00, but there's also a cash dispenser. The **National Park Information Centre** is open 09.00-13.00 and 15.30-19.00 daily.

The best place to stay in Espot is the *Hôtel Saurat* (☎ 973-62.41.62, 🖹 62 40.37), which is the large whitewashed building in the centre of the village – during peak season (August) it costs up to €46/7600ptas per person for room and breakfast, but the prices are considerably lower in late June/early July. The *Hotel Roya* (☎ 973-62.40.40, 🖹 62.41 44) comes a poor second to *Saurat*; the

management are less than helpful, and in summer they only offer media-pensión (€34/5600ptas per person).

There are four Cases de Pagès in the village. *Casa Colom* (☎ 973-62.40.10) is self-catering and charges €15/2500ptas per person per night. It's run by two friendly ladies, has a well-equipped kitchen and is open all year round. *Casa Felip* (☎ 973-62.40.93) charges €12/2000ptas per person, is equally friendly, and all rooms have a shower. *Casa Palmira* (☎ 973-62.40.72) is a much larger, and slightly impersonal place where they charge 3800ptas for media-pensión, or €30/5000ptas for full board. Finally, *Casa Peret de Peretó* (☎ 973-62 40.68) is attached to Camping Solau and has apartments for four or six people; they charge €15/2500ptas per person.

Map 69 – Refugi d'Amitges to La Guingueta d'Àneu 247

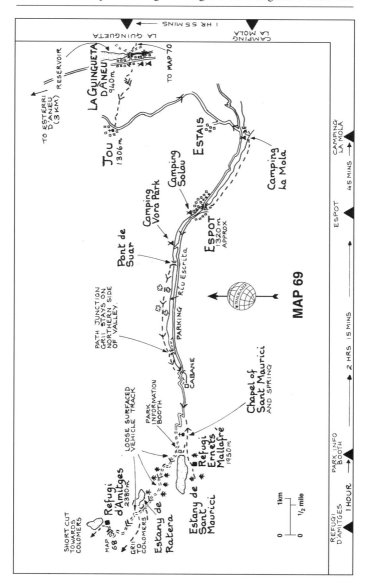

MAP 69

From the centre of Espot, the GR11 goes east down an alley and then follows a grassy vehicle track away from the village. After half an hour you come to a path junction, where a signpost points left to: ESCALÓ. Follow the path downhill, cross the river and climb to the road on the other side, near the entrance to the *Camping La Mola* (☎ 973-62.40.24). The campsite has a shop, café and bar, and they also have a few apartments for rent, generally for periods of two or more days. The campsite is open from mid-June to the end of September and charges €3.75/625ptas per person and €3.75/625ptas per tent.

From the campsite, the GR11 follows the minor road north-eastwards all the way to **Jou**. The village is pretty but has no shops or other facilities. A clearly marked footpath leads downhill from Jou to **La Guingueta d'Àneu**.

LA GUINGUETA D'ÀNEU

Despite being so small, La Guingueta has several places to stay. The best of these is the very friendly *Hotel Poldo* ☆☆ (☎ 973-62.60.80, 📠 62.63.85), which boasts a swimming pool and a good restaurant (the gazpacho, and 'creme Cataluno' are highly recommended). A double room here costs €51/8400ptas. Opposite is the *Hostal Orteu* (☎ 973-62.60.86), a bar restaurant which has double rooms available for €24/4000ptas. At the *Hostal Cases* (☎ 973-62.60.83), a double room (with a real bath as well as a shower) costs €25/4200ptas. Nearby, the *Pensio Abril* (☎ 973-62.60.89, 📠 62-62-93) charges €24/4000ptas for a double.

There are two large campsites in the hamlet, both of which have swimming pools. *Nou Camping* (☎ 973-62.60.85) charges €3.75/625ptas per person and €3.75/625ptas per tent; it's very smart and has a well-stocked shop, restaurant/bar, mountain bike hire and laundry service; it's open in the summer only. *Camping Val d'Aneu* ☆☆☆ (☎ 973-62.63.90) charges €3.50/575ptas per person and €3.50/575ptas per tent, and also has a restaurant and bar; it's open from Easter to the end of November.

The nearest shops (apart from campsite shops) are 3km north (along the road) from La Guingueta, in Esterri d'Àneu. There are two **supermarkets**, a well-stocked **chemist**, a **post office** and an outdoor adventure centre.

If you need a **taxi**, try Pere Cortina (☎ 619-55.56.31) who charges €48/8000ptas for the trip from La Guingueta to Estaon. There is a daily **bus** service to Llavorsi (the local transport hub) from which you should be able to catch buses onwards.

LA GUINGUETA D'ÀNEU → ESTAON   [MAP 70]

This fairly short section will only be possible if you have a tent, as the accommodation which used to be available in Estaon has now closed. It is quite possible to continue beyond Estaon to Lleret or even Tavascan, but you'll need to make a very early start, as it's a long section.

From La Guingueta, the GR11 crosses the **concrete bridge** to the east side of the reservoir and turns right (southwards) down the vehicle track. Despite the route shown on the IGN map (which has it that the path follows a road/track to Dorve) the GR11 actually leaves the rough road with-

Map 70 – La Guingueta d'Àneu to Estaon 249

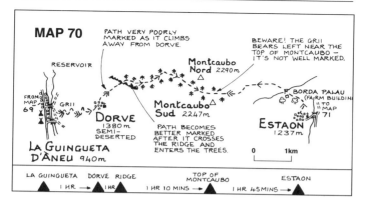

MAP 70

in a couple of minutes. The footpath up to the left is marked only by a cairn but after some 200 metres the first red and white waymarks appear. The steep climb to **Dorve**, best undertaken in the early morning when the hillside is in shade, takes about an hour. With the exception of one house which has part-time residents, the attractive little hamlet is deserted. It's a lovely shady spot to stop for a rest; the houses are in remarkably good condition, and there's picturesque **chapel**, dedicated to San Bartolomé. There's a **water fountain** next to the path as you enter the village.

The route marking, which up to this point has been excellent, becomes much less clear above the village. It's not easy to spot the faded paint splashes as the rocky hillside is covered with low vegetation and criss-crossed by animal tracks. If in doubt, climb north-eastwards, making your own loops across the hillside; the markers will be picked up again eventually. Once at the ridge, the GR11 enters a shady pine forest and the path becomes well marked again adopting a gentler gradient. The climb to the top of **Montcaubo** is still quite steep in places but at least there's shade, and the views, when they come, are excellent.

At the top of the climb, and just to the south of Montcaubo Nord, the GR11 suddenly bends left and begins its descent. It's easy to miss the turning, not least because another path continues across the hilltop in a straight line. The *other* path is indicated with yellow and white paint markings. Take note! These are not some strange local alternative to the proper GR waymarks.

The descent to **Estaon** is long and in some places steep (1000m of height is lost in a little over 3km). It's well marked, however, and after about 1³/₄ hours you come to the village. Sadly the only accommodation in Estaon closed in 1999 and the next nearest place to stay is in Lleret some 3¹/₂ hours further along the GR11.

Catalonia's vanishing mountain communities

Estaon is a lovely little place – an example of an old mountain village being given new life. Many of the houses have been restored and the narrow alleys between them are lined with flower baskets and banks of flowering shrubs. It is one of the lucky villages – although it has a permanent resident community of only 14 people, it's undergoing a rejuvenation at the hands of city dwellers. People from Barcelona, in particular, are buying up the houses and undertaking massive refurbishment – a process you see in villages throughout the Spanish Pyrenees.

The village emptied in the 1960's when factory work in the cities offered well-paid employment and an easier alternative to the harsh mountain life. In a way, though, the ruin had started before this. In the 1930's many of the local Romanesque churches were stripped of their artefacts by collectors, and the villages were further ravaged by the effects of the Civil War.

The **Church of St James**, below the village, is definitely worth a visit; the key is kept by a neighbour near the large house named Casa Pau, which used to be the only guesthouse in the village. Although the church has a venerable and time-worn appearance (it dates from the 18th century), in the centre of the village are the remains of a much older structure. The chapel, which was dedicated to Saint Eulalia, dates from the 12th century. The early frescos that used to adorn the walls of the chapel are now kept in various museums.

ESTAON → TAVASCAN   [MAP 71]

Follow the road eastwards away from the village. At the bridge over the Ribera d'Estaon, ignore the GR markings alongside the stream (this was the old route), and continue on the road a little further to find the vehicle track which runs north up the valley. Eventually it narrows to a footpath, which continues along the peaceful and shady valley bottom. About an hour after leaving Estaon, you pass **Bordes de Nibrós**, a collection of farm buildings.

A couple of minutes beyond the hamlet, the path makes a sudden right turn, doubling back on itself and starting up the hillside. After 10-15 minutes on a good footpath, you come to the **ruins** of a large old barn. The route marking becomes a little vague above here but it's no great problem, and after a further half hour of climbing you'll reach the top of the **ridge** (1820m approx).

From here, the GR11 actually follows a route quite different from that marked on the IGN map. Cross straight over the ridge, and head directly down the hillside on a steep earthen path. Near a sign, LLERET, AINETO, TAVASCAN, the GR11 joins an old cart track which winds down the hillside to **Lleret**. Only a handful of houses in the village are occupied, one of

Map 71 – Estaon to Tavascan 251

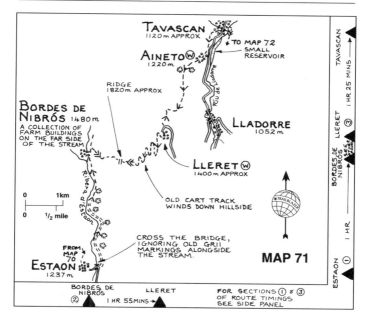

which is a casa de pagè called ***Casa Rabassó*** (☎ 973-62.32.12). It would make a good place to stay: the house is beautiful, the owner is very friendly and Lleret has a wonderful sleepy atmosphere to it. The tariff is €25/4100ptas per person for media-pensión. There are two water points in the village.

Leave the village on the rough access road, and at the first sharp bend, literally 200-300 metres from the houses, continue northwards on a footpath. The junction is not well marked, so keep an eye out for the path and for the paint-markers. The footpath climbs initially and then levels out heading northwards along the valley side. It's an easy route although in a couple of places you need to watch your footing.

After about an hour you come to **Aineto**, where there is a water point. Quarter of an hour beyond Aineto you reach **Tavascan**.

TAVASCAN

There are four places to stay in Tavascan. The ***Hotel Llacs de Cardós*** ☆ (☎ 973-62.31.78, 🖹 62.31.26) is a newish and comfortable place where media-pensión costs €31/5200ptas (although if business is slow they may be prepared to give you a much better price). Separate but under the same management is the plush new ***Hotel Estany Blaus*** ☆☆☆ where media-pensión is €39/6500ptas.

The *Hotel Marxant* (☎ 973-62.31.51, 🖹 62.30.39) is cheaper than either of these, and good value: media-pensión costs from €24/4000ptas, and a double room costs €36/6000ptas.

Finally, the *Bar Restaurant Feliu* (☎ 973-62.31.63) has recently added a vast new extension; the rooms are fairly small and basic but the price isn't bad: media-pensión costs €24/4000ptas per person if you have a room with with common bathroom, or €27/4500ptas with private bathroom. The owner claims that she serves the best local food in the village.

The nearest campsite, *Camping Serra* (☎ 973-62.30.17), is in Lladore.

Tavascan has a well-stocked **shop**, and there's a public **swimming pool** just north of the church. There's a small **tourist office**.

The **church** itself is well worth looking into; the key is kept behind the bar in the Hotel Llacs de Cardos. Also interesting is the ancient **bridge**, west of the church.

TAVASCAN → ÀREU   [MAP 72]

Cross the Riu de Lladore via the bridge near the church and begin a steep climb. Soon the footpath settles into a pattern of regular turns up the hillside, through a young wood of beech, birch, hazel and oak. After 35 minutes there's a painted sign on a rock beside the path indicating a fountain to the right of the trail; it's possible that there's a spring slightly further away from the path, but there's no sign of any water source. The area directly above this point is poorly marked; go straight uphill across the grass to find the markers again. After just over an hour's ascent, the path levels out and contours around the hillside, passing above **Boldis Jussa** and entering **Boldis Sobira**, a sleepy little village with several fountains.

From Boldis Sobira, the route to the **Coll de Tudela** is simple but bears no relation to that shown on the IGN 1:50,000 map. The GR11 leaves the village heading eastwards along a rough vehicle track, which you follow for the next 1-1½ hours. The track itself takes a different route from that shown on the map, and the GR markings are, in some places, hundreds of metres apart. No matter, stay on the track. Towards the top of the climb with the coll almost in sight, the track follows a long leg eastwards. After a tight left bend and then entering a right bend to head northwards, you'll find the markers suddenly reappearing to the right, indicating the way up a rocky path which runs straight up the hillside. This area is fairly overgrown, and following the trail up to the coll is tricky. Once you reach the coll, however, the view is superb. To the west are the high rocky peaks of the Aigües Tortes; to the east are the peaks of Andorra. The rolling grassy hill tops of the Pallars Sobira region contrast with the land on either side.

Despite the fact that you have to lose around 1000m in height to get down to Àreu, it's a surprisingly easy descent – much of it through shady pine woods and on gently sloping footpaths. After about an hour, you reach the two barns of **Borda de Costuix**, and join a vehicle track which leads down to **Àreu**.

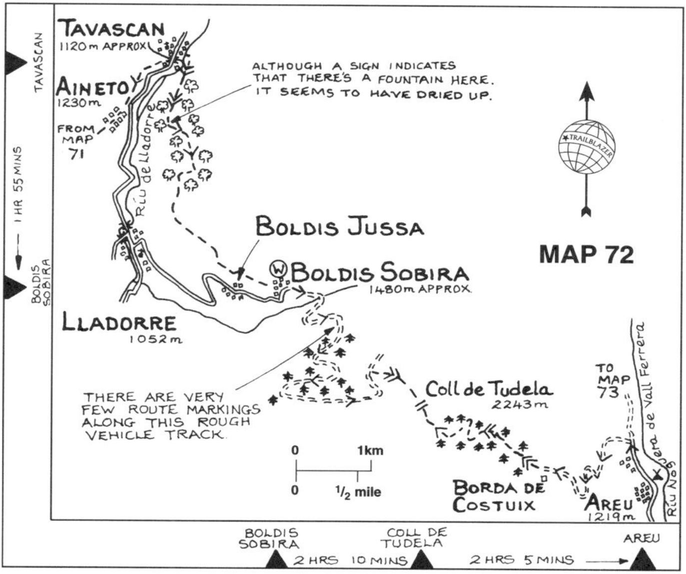

Map 72 – Tavascan to Àreu 253

TAVASCAN
1120 m APPROX

AINETO
1230 m

FROM
MAP
71

ALTHOUGH A SIGN INDICATES
THAT THERE'S A FOUNTAIN HERE.
IT SEEMS TO HAVE DRIED UP.

RÍU de Lladorre

TAVASCAN

1 HR 55 MINS

BOLDIS SOBIRA

BOLDIS JUSSA

BOLDIS SOBIRA
1480m APPROX

LLADORRE
1052 m

THERE ARE VERY
FEW ROUTE MARKINGS
ALONG THIS ROUGH
VEHICLE TRACK

MAP 72

TRAILBLAZER

Coll de Tudela
2243 m

TO
MAP
73

Ríbera de Vall Ferrera

0   1km
0   ½ mile

BORDA DE
COSTUIX

ÀREU
1219 m

RÍU Noguera de Vall Ferrera

BOLDIS   COLL DE
SOBIRA   TUDELA   ÀREU
      2 HRS 10 MINS   2 HRS 5 MINS

ÀREU

Hostal Val Ferrera (☎ 973-62.43.43) is the only hotel in Àreu; the rooms are comfortable and prices for media-pensión start at €36/5915ptas per person. There are several casas de pagès, including *Casa Besoli* (☎ 973-62.44.15) where a double room costs €24/4000ptas, and media-pensión is €26/4350ptas per person. *Camping Pica d'Estats* (☎ 973-

62.43 47), on the northern edge of the village, is pleasant and shady, and the swimming pool and bar make it all the more enticing. The tariff is €3.75/ 625ptas per person and €3.75/625ptas per tent; non residents can use the pool for a small fee. The campsite is open from Easter-October.

Àreu has a small **shop**, and there's a **museum** open only at weekends.

ÀREU → REFUGI DE VALL FERRERA   [MAP 73, p254]

Walk north from the village to rejoin the GR11 and continue along the road as it parallels the Ríu Noguera de Vall Ferrera. The tarmac lane soon turns into an unsurfaced track, and the GR markings become increasingly rare. Just over 3km from the village, the track crosses the river. A short way north of the bridge, a sign (ROUTE VIA PLA DE BOET TO PORT DE BOET) marks the spot where GR11 turns right up a footpath through the birch and pine trees. The footpath climbs through the trees and then passes along the grassy hillside, near the two barns of the **Borda Gavatxo**.

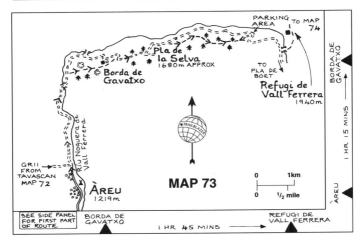

Beyond the barns, the GR11 rejoins the vehicle track near a sharp right-hand bend. Follow the track around the bend and on up the hill, past the **Pla de la Selva**. Three quarters of a kilometre beyond the Pla, the GR11 heads off to the right along a well-marked footpath. The path climbs, quite steeply at times, through pine woods. After some minutes it widens into a new logging track which soon starts to descend, passing an open area with a track junction. Half a kilometre beyond this, the GR11 again heads off to the right on a footpath, which soon leads downhill to join the main vehicle track (marked on the map) near a small parking area.

As the vehicle track swings south-eastwards towards the Pla de la Boet, there's a tiny area set aside for camping and a sign, pointing left: REFUGI DE VALL FERRERA. After another ten minutes you come to the refuge (1940m). The **_Refugi de Vall Ferrera_** (☎ 973-62.43.78) was built in 1935, and has recently been renovated. At a squeeze, 30 people can fit into the tiny dormitory. The refuge has a guardian from June to October; the tariff is €10/1600ptas per night, €11/1850ptas for supper, and €4.20/700ptas for breakfast.

REFUGI DE VALL FERRERA → MARC   [MAP 74]

[Includes high section – see warning on p20] The route to Marc via the Refuge du Pinet is excellent. It's mountainous, pretty and it provides the option of climbing up one, two or even three peaks of over 3000m en route. It's also a fairly long and tiring (though very satisfying) day, so an early start is recommended.

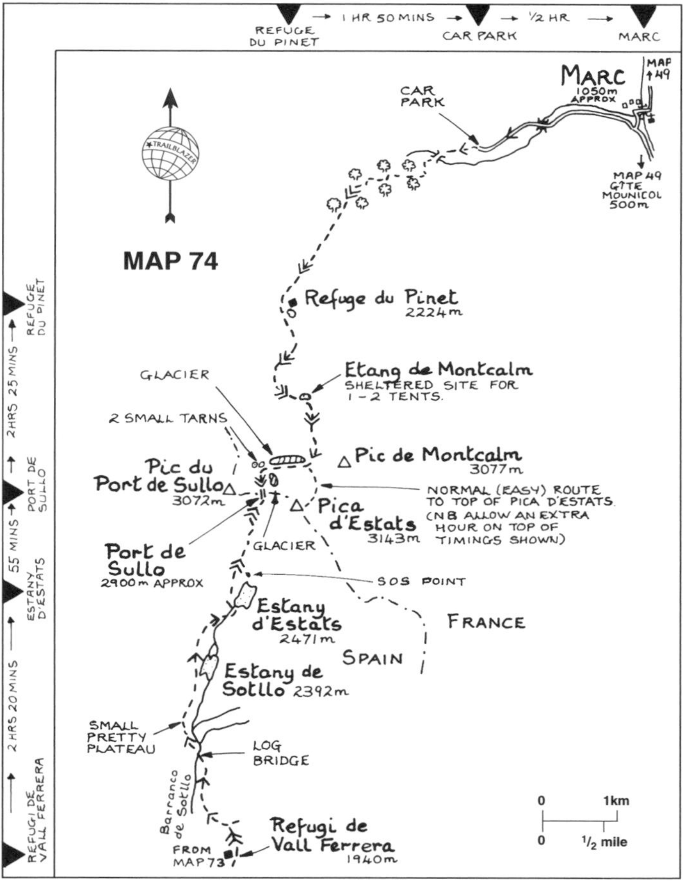

Map 74 – Refugi de Vall Ferrera to Marc 255

MAP 74

Next to the Refugi de Vall Ferrera is a sign: PICA D'ESTATS 5H. Follow the path almost straight up the hill for 15 minutes to a junction where another sign points left. The trail is well trodden and easy to follow; it heads west and then swings northwards, contouring around the hillside and soon following the valley above the Barranc de Sottlo. After a short scramble down a rocky outcrop, the trail leads to a **log bridge** over the Barranc, beyond which is a **small plateau** where several streams meet. At the north end of the plateau, as the path starts to climb again, there is a metal plaque fixed to one of the rocks: three ice axes and a rope make up the simple design. Follow the path above the plaque and soon you reach the **Estany de Sottlo**, which has a flat grassy area at its northern end, ideal for camping (it's also possible to camp at the southern end, which has far less space but is much more sheltered). Continue up to the **Estany d'Estats**, from which, with the Pica d'Estats towering above, you have a clear view of the climb to the **Port de Sullo**. Passing around the west side of the Estany, the path passes an SOS point on a rocky mound, and then begins its climb, heading straight up the very steep shale slope towards the Port. From the northern end of the lake up to the Port is approximately an hour's climb.

Your effort is rewarded by excellent views when you get to the top. Immediately west of the Port is the **Pic du Port de Sullo (3072m)**, while to the east is the **Pica d'Estats (3143m)**. The direct route from the Port to the top of the Pica requires considerable scrambling/climbing and is best not attempted by those who are inexperienced. Most walkers follow the easier route to the top, going past the **Pic de Montcalm (3077m)**, and approaching the Pica d'Estats from the north-east.

From the Port, head down towards the **small tarn** which you can see below. Although a path leads eastwards only a short way below the Port, it's better to ignore this, and continue down until you are just above the tarns (as you get lower down, a second one comes into view). Finding a suitable spot, scramble east over the ridge, and cross the rocks below the steep glacier beyond. The path can now be seen heading directly east, climbing beside a long glacier which stretches down the valley. Follow this route up to a small cirque below the Pic de Montcalm, and the Pica d'Estats, from which ascent to either is easy. To the north, the way to the Refuge du Pinet is prominently marked with circles of yellow paint on the rocks.

The descent to Pinet is steep and rocky. Halfway down you pass the **Étang de Montcalm**, which has a suitably sheltered area at its western end where you could pitch a tent. Forty minutes later you come to the refuge (2224m). *Refuge du Pinet* (☎ 05.61.64.80.81) is a modern and rather ugly building which can take 57 people. The tariff is €12/80F for the night, €12.50/82F for the evening meal and €4.50/30F for breakfast; payment in pesetas is accepted. There are facilities for self-catering and it's possible to camp beside the refuge. It's open from 1 June to 30 September.

The descent from Pinet is on a clear path waymarked with yellow paint. It takes a little over 1½ hours to get down to the car park, and a further half hour along the road to Marc. For information on accommodation in **Marc** and **Mounicou**, and facilities in **Auzat** and **Vicdessos**, see p200 and p202.

(Opposite) Top: The superb views from the Collada de Ballibierna (see p238) are just one of many memorable aspects of the GR11 route through the Central Pyrenees. **Bottom:** If you have time to spare, the walk up from Torla into the Ordesa Canyon is highly recommended. The area around Puente Luciano Briet (see p268) is beautiful and wonderfully peaceful.

GR10-GR11 route link
Bagnères-de-Luchon to Hospital de Viella

This two-day section from Bagnères-de-Luchon to Hospital de Viella will not be possible in early summer (due to snow), or in bad weather (due to problems with route finding). The second day in particular is extremely arduous – requiring a very early start, some hard walking and a reasonable head for heights. Having said all this, the section is worth considering as it passes through a wonderful area (the Maladetta Region) and links up with a great stretch of the GR11 through the Aigües Tortes National Park. If you can get past the tough first couple of days, the route provides a challenging but excellent two week itinerary.

BAGNÈRES-DE-LUCHON → REFUGIO DE RENCLUSA
[MAP 75, p259]

[Includes high section – see warning on p20] Many would advise cutting out the first part of this section by taking a taxi (approximately €21/140F, 20 minutes) or hitching a lift to the Hospice de France, as the walk up to the Hospice is mainly along roads and tracks. For diehard pedestrians, however, the route is easy to follow. From the centre of Luchon, follow the road (D125) south out of the town past the campsites. After half an hour, as the road begins to climb, you pass the *Gîte Skioura* (☎ 05.61 79.60.59), a friendly place which specializes in taking groups, although they'll take individual walkers, too. There's a kitchen area for self-catering, and meals are also available by prior arrangement; it costs €11/75F for the night and €24/155F for demi-pension. One hundred metres further up the road is the *Auberge de Castel Vielh* (☎ 05 61.79.36.79), a tiny place set in a delightful garden. There are only three (double) rooms here, ranging in price from €38/250F-€46/300F, but one gets the impression that people don't really come here for the accommodation – the food's the thing. The Menu Castel-Vielh at €29/190F looks mouth-watering, and local dishes are a speciality.

Another half hour's walking up the road brings you to a **bridge** over the river. Immediately on the far side of the bridge, a footpath goes off to the left. Follow this uphill for a couple of hundred metres and then follow the yellow pointer, No 20. The path climbs across the hillside in a south-

---

(Opposite) **Top:** Above the clouds on the Tuc de Mulleres (3010m, see p260). **Bottom:** Banyuls-sur-Mer, on the Mediterranean coast, is the finishing point for the GR10 and HRP High Level Route. Relax, sunbathe and celebrate your achievement!

easterly direction, eventually swinging eastwards. After an hour and twenty minutes it levels out and comes to the *Cabane de Barguères*. The hut is in regular use by foresters and is consequently in good condition; there is space for four people.

From the hut, follow a large forestry track east to the end of the valley, and then south-west around the hillside. After about a kilometre it is joined by another, larger track; turn right and follow this steeply downhill. On reaching a junction with the tarmac road, turn left and walk up to the **Hospice de France**, which you come to about an hour after leaving the cabane. There's little to see at the Hospice. Three ruined houses stand just above the car park and there's a monument to those who escaped across the mountains during the war. The area is popular with day walkers and picnickers.

The climb to the Refuge de Vénasque (2248m) is long and steep but at least the stream running down the centre of the valley means that water is available throughout the walk. The *Refuge de Vénasque* (☎ 05.61.79.26.46) is a small place that, with the addition of the tent next to the building, can sleep 25 people. They charge €12/80F for the night, and €14/90F for an evening meal; camping is permitted (although there's not much space) next to one of the nearby lakes. It's open from the beginning of June to the end of September annually – even if to open it they have to dig it out of the snow first.

From the refuge, it's a 25-minute walk up to the gap in the ridge which constitutes the **Port de Vénasque (2444m)**. Passing through the narrow gap is rather like entering another world; suddenly the views on the French side of the mountains seem tame in comparison with the dramatic scenery of the Maladetta massif. You can see below you the car park at the end of the road from the Hospital de Benasque; beyond it, and slightly to the right, the Refugio de Renclusa is visible, midway up the opposite mountain side.

The path heads south initially before veering south-east along the top of a steep slope. It eventually descends in a series of zigzags to the road below. Turn left to the car park, where there is a snack stall during the summer months and from which there's a regular bus service running down to Bénasque.

A large path, waymarked with yellow and white paint, runs south-eastwards. It soon veers south-west, and climbs the hillside to the *Refugio de Renclusa* (**2140m**) (☎ 974-55.14.90), where food and accommodation are available. The refuge was opened in 1913, and consequently has loads of character but rather primitive facilities. A new extension has recently been completed, but there's still no shower.

Map 75 – Bagnères de Luchon to Refugio de Renclusa 259

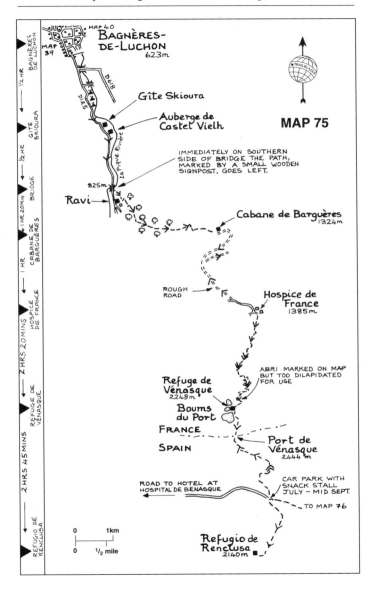

MAP 75

BAGNÈRES-DE-LUCHON 623m

Gîte Skioura

Auberge de Castel Vielh

La Pique Rivière

IMMEDIATELY ON SOUTHERN SIDE OF BRIDGE THE PATH, MARKED BY A SMALL WOODEN SIGNPOST, GOES LEFT.

825m

Ravi

Cabane de Barguères 1324m

ROUGH ROAD

Hospice de France 1385m

ABRI MARKED ON MAP BUT TOO DILAPIDATED FOR USE

Refuge de Vénasque 2248m

Boums du Port

FRANCE

SPAIN

Port de Vénasque 2444 m

ROAD TO HOTEL AT HOSPITAL DE BENASQUE

CAR PARK WITH SNACK STALL JULY – MID SEPT.

TO MAP 76

0   1km
0   ½ mile

Refugio de Renclusa 2140m

MAP 40

MAP 39

D618

D125

BAGNÈRES DE LUCHON

½ HR

GÎTE SKIOURA

½ HR

BRIDGE

1 HR 20MIN

CABANE DE BARGUÈRES

1 HR

HOSPICE DE FRANCE

2 HRS 20MINS

REFUGE DE VÉNASQUE

2 HRS 45 MINS

REFUGIO DE RENCLUSA

REFUGIO DE RENCLUSA → HOSPITAL DE VIELLA [MAP 76]

[Includes high section – see warning on p20] From the refuge, walk back down almost to the car park and follow the sign pointing to FORAU D'AIGUALLUT. After 35 minutes you arrive at the **Forau d'Aiguallut**, a spectacular chasm where a rushing stream tumbles down a waterfall and disappears underground. From here the water passes through a maze of limestone tunnels to emerge in the next valley, where it joins the River Joeu and becomes a tributary to the Garonne. There's a small *refuge* hidden just behind the trees to the west.

> ❏ **Weather alert**
> This section should be tried only in good weather and with plenty of time (locals recommend a 7am start or earlier); not only is it a fair distance, but the path can be hard to locate in some places, necessitating extra time for route-finding. The descent from the Col de Mulleres involves a steep scramble/climb down from a ridge, unsuitable for those who dislike heights. It could be dangerous in poor conditions. Having said all this, if weather permits, the walk has lots to recommend it: spectacular views, peaceful valleys and a variety of scenery.

The path follows the eastern side of the grassy **Plan d'Aiguallut** to the southern edge of the plateau, where it approaches the steep-sided entrance to the Valleta de la Escaleta. Cross to the southern bank of the torrent (easier said than done if the water is high) and then scramble up the side of the gully to find a path a short way above the stream. Follow the track south-eastwards into the valley, and you soon pass the Cova de la Escaleta and Grutas de Toro. To your left at this point is the **Col de Toro**. The area has a dense population of marmots and they are in evidence all along the route.

Climbing still to the south-east, the path, marked by tiny cairns, leads into a steep-sided little valley where it comes to an apparent dead end. Scramble a few metres up the rocks to find a path slightly higher up, and continue south-eastwards. Low cairns assist with route-finding as the track is at times clearly visible and at other times practically non-existent. Follow the route past two small tarns, before climbing south-south-east across a rocky scarp, next to a rushing stream with waterfalls. The water issues from an upper tarn, to which the path climbs, passing across the stream just at the point where it comes from the tarn.

At this point, the path changes direction, and climbs up a gully heading south-west before crossing an area of large boulders. On the far side of the boulders is a weird but beautiful landscape, as the route, marked only by a few tiny cairns, crosses enormous sloping plates of granite. The path passes within a few hundred metres of another tarn and then heads south, parallel to a stream.

Soon the vague line of cairns brings you up just to the west of the **Tuc de Mulleres (3010m)**, a rounded boulder-covered summit with an iron

Map 76 – Refugio de Renclusa to Hospital de Viella 261

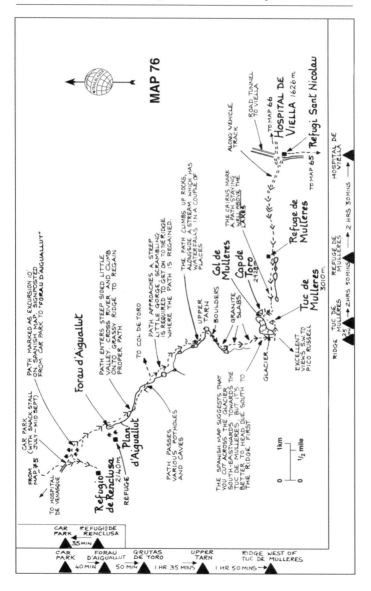

MAP 76

TRAILBLAZER

Forau d'Aiguallut

PATH MARKED AS EXCURSION 10' ON SPANISH MAP. SIGNPOSTED FROM CAR PARK TO "FORAU D'AIGUALLUT"

CAR PARK (WITH SNACK STALL JULY – MID SEPT)

FROM MAP 75

TO HOSPITAL DE VENASQUE

Refugio de Renclusa 2140m

REFUGE

Plan d'Aiguallut

PATH PASSES VARIOUS POTHOLES AND CAVES

PATH ENTERS STEEP SIDED LITTLE VALLEY, CROSS RIVER AND CLIMB ONTO GRASSY RIDGE TO REGAIN PROPER PATH

TO COL DE TORO

PATH APPROACHES A STEEP LITTLE GORGE, SCRAMBLING IS REQUIRED TO GET ON TO THE RIDGE WHERE THE PATH IS REGAINED.

THE PATH CLIMBS UP ROCKS, ALONGSIDE A STREAM WHICH HAS WATERFALLS IN A COUPLE OF PLACES

UPPER TARN

BOULDERS

GRANITE SLABS

Col de Mulleres

Cap de Toro 2908m

GLACIER

EXCELLENT VIEWS S.W TO PICO RUSSELL

THE SPANISH MAP SUGGESTS THAT YOU CUT ACROSS THE GLACIER SOUTH-EASTWARDS TOWARDS THE TUC DE MULLERES, BUT IT'S BETTER TO HEAD DUE SOUTH TO THE RIDGE FIRST

Tuc de Mulleres 3010m

THE CAIRNS MARK A PATH STAYING WELL ABOVE THE LAKES

Refuge de Mulleres

ALONG VEHICLE TRACK

ROAD TUNNEL TO VIELLA

TO MAP 66

HOSPITAL DE VIELLA 1626m.

Refugi Sant Nicolau

TO MAP 65

HOSPITAL DE VIELLA

0   1km
0   ½ mile

CAR PARK	REFUGIO DE RENCLUSA
	◄── 35 MIN ──

CAR PARK	FORAU D'AIGUALLUT	GRUTAS DE TORO	UPPER TARN	RIDGE WEST OF TUC DE MULLERES
	40 MIN	50 MIN	1 HR 35 MINS	1 HR 50 MINS ──►

RIDGE	TUC DE MULLERES	REFUGE DE MULLERES	HOSPITAL DE VIELLA
	25 MINS	2 HRS 50 MINS	2 HRS 30 MINS ──►

cross on top of it. Before climbing the Tuc, take time on the ridge; there is a magnificent view south-west across the Valle de Salenques to the Pico Russell (3205m). Despite the fact that a path is shown on the map, there's no real route up to the top of the Tuc de Mulleres; clamber across the boulders as best you can. The iron cross has a box below it with a notebook where walkers can record their visit. Again, the views are stunning.

The eastern side of the ridge leading to the Col de Mulleres is near vertical, so stick to the western side above the glacier, as you move towards the col – there are a few cairns here which take a suitable line. You need to go almost to the northern end of the col to find the point to cross – looking down, you can see a route which has been much used. Great care needs to be taken when descending this part; there are good foot and hand holds, but it's very steep. Even in July there may be snow at the bottom of the scramble down; again great care is required as the slope is steep and there are rocks at the bottom.

From the area just below the col, follow the cairns, which lead east, staying high above the lakes below. Eventually the cairns lead down to the valley bottom near the easternmost lake. On a spur above the tarn is the *Refuge de Mulleres*, a bright orange metal shelter that can sleep twelve people. Note that the position of the refuge is incorrectly shown on the Editorial Alpina map.

The path continues its steep descent down the valley, becoming increasingly clear and easy to follow. Finally, in the lower valley, join a vehicle track which leads directly to the refuge/auberge. The *Refugi Sant Nicolau* (☎ 973-69.70.52) can sleep 49 people in the huge dormitory in the basement. It's a comfortable place with a good restaurant/bar on the ground floor. Bed and breakfast costs €11/1800ptas, and media-pensión is €20/3300ptas. The refuge is open every day from 30 June to 15 September; outside these times, apart from the odd day on which it is closed, it basically remains open on every day except Monday. (For details of taxi services in the area, see p243.)

For the continuation of the two week itinerary through the Aigües Tortes region, see p240.

Ordesa National Park (Spain)

Spain's Ordesa region, just across the border from Gavarnie, contains some of the most spectacular scenery in the Pyrenees. The Ordesa Canyon, carved by glacial action up to a million years ago, is justifiably the most famous feature, but the narrow Añisclo Canyon is just as impressive and is considered by many to be much prettier. Monte Perdido, at 3355m the third highest peak in the Pyrenees, dominates the area, while the Brèche de Roland (see p128), a jagged hole in the frontier ridge between France and Spain, is a landmark of legendary status. A combination of the wonderful scenery, and the fact that the weather is generally more stable on the Spanish side of the mountains means that a visit to the Ordesa region, whether by itself or as part of a longer itinerary, is highly recommended.

There are, of course, many ways to do this. The GR11 passes through the region anyway, but for those not intending to follow the GR11, the route suggested below is a four- to seven- day circuit which starts from Refuge Wallon and arrives back in France, via the Brèche de Roland, at Gavarnie. If you have the time, and particularly if you're carrying a tent (and thus have some flexibility over accommodation) it's worth allowing at least six days. Each of the four stages of the circuit outlined here involves a very long day's walking. (Note, too, that both the Col d'Arratille, at the start of the circuit, and the Brèche de Roland, at the end of the circuit, are high passes that may not be passable without proper equipment in the early summer.)

REFUGE WALLON → TORLA (VIA ARA VALLEY) [MAP 77, p265]

[Includes high section – see warning on p20] Just to the east of the Refuge Wallon a sign points the way towards the Col d'Arratille (LAC D'ARRATILLE 1H 30; COL D'ARRATILLE 2H 30). From here the path heads across a footbridge and starts to climb south-eastwards. The trail, which also links with the Col des Mulets and the Refuge des Oulettes de Gaube beyond, is popular in high season, so try to make an early start; it's a beautiful walk and best enjoyed without crowds.

Beyond the Lac d'Arratille the gradient steepens, and the final part of the climb to the col involves picking your way through an area of boulders and then crossing the steep slope above a small lake. (This section will be hazardous for walkers without proper equipment if there is still snow, so in early summer it's worth asking the guardian at Wallon whether the col is passable before starting out).

Approximately $2^1/_2$ hours after leaving the refuge you reach the **Col d'Arratille (2528m)**. The Ara valley, with Vignemale on the far side, lies before you. In sharp contrast with the landscape to the north of the col, the valley slopes gently down towards the south; it seems strangely deserted after the busy trails around Wallon. The route down from the col, clearly indicated with red and white paint marks, makes a wide loop towards the Col des Mulets. You can save a little time by cutting down the slope when the opportunity arises and crossing the stream to join the footpath on the eastern bank of the Río Ara.

Follow the footpath down the valley. After $1^1/_2$-2 hours you come to a small, empty *shelter* with two rooms (one of which may be locked). The hut is far from clean but would do for an overnight stop. An hour further down the valley, at the end of a rough road, is the *Refugio Ordiso* **(1550m)**, a tiny building which looks (and smells) as though it has been used as a sheep shelter. Follow the rough road down from the refuge, and then take the marked trail along the east side of the river to the old bridge of **Bujaruelo**.

BUJARUELO

Bujaruelo (1338m) consists of only three buildings but fortunately for back-packers they're the right sort: a modern building with facilities for the campsite, some public loos, and a bar/restaurant/ lodge. Both the bar and the campsite (*Camping San Nicholas de Bujaruelo* (☎ 974-48.64.28)) have been closed for renovation, so phone ahead to check that they're open again before you rely on them. (If the facilities are closed, the next nearest campsite is half an hour's walk down the rough road).

On the next section, from Bujaruelo to the **Puente de Los Navarros**, there are two options. The more interesting is to follow the GR11 which runs down the east side of the Río Ara, then crosses the river via the **Puente de Santa Elena** and climbs the cliffs on the west side of the river. The quicker but more boring option is to head straight down the rough road. For various reasons (mainly that I was making for the closest campsite) the route described here is along the rough road.

After half an hour you come to the *Camping Valle de Bujaruelo* ☆☆ (☎ 974-48.63.48) which has a shop, bar and restaurant, and even a few rooms: a double room costs €16/2700ptas, a triple €23/3800ptas, and a quadruple €29/4800ptas. Camping costs €2.85/475ptas per person and per tent. Three and a half kilometres below the campsite is the main road and the **Puente de los Navarros (1050m approx)**, which is just below the entry to the National Park. The roof tops of Torla can be seen to the right, down the valley.

There are two ways to get to Torla. You can either walk straight down the road (approximately 40 minutes), or follow the attractive footpath which heads down the valley along the side of the river ($3/_4$ hour to 1 hour). If you're taking the old path, a red and white marker on the arch of

Map 77 – Refuge Wallon to Torla 265

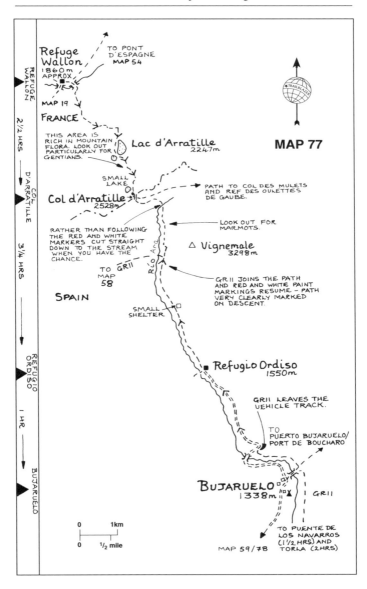

MAP 77

Refuge
Wallon
1860m
APPROX

TO PONT
D'ESPAGNE
MAP 54

MAP 19

FRANCE

THIS AREA IS
RICH IN MOUNTAIN
FLORA. LOOK OUT
PARTICULARLY FOR
GENTIANS.

Lac d'Arratille
2247m

SMALL
LAKE

Col d'Arratille
2528m

PATH TO COL DES MULETS
AND REF DES OULETTES
DE GAUBE

RATHER THAN FOLLOWING
THE RED AND WHITE
MARKERS CUT STRAIGHT
DOWN TO THE STREAM
WHEN YOU HAVE THE
CHANCE.

LOOK OUT FOR
MARMOTS.

△ Vignemale
3298m

TO GR11
MAP
58

RÍO ARA

SPAIN

GR11 JOINS THE PATH
AND RED AND WHITE PAINT
MARKINGS RESUME – PATH
VERY CLEARLY MARKED
ON DESCENT.

SMALL
SHELTER

Refugio Ordiso
1550m

GR11 LEAVES THE
VEHICLE TRACK.

TO
PUERTO BUJARUELO/
PORT DE BOUCHARO

BUJARUELO
1338m

GR11

TO PUENTE DE
LOS NAVARROS
(1½ HRS) AND
TORLA (2 HRS)

MAP 59/78

REFUGE WALLON   2½ HRS   COL D'ARRATILLE   3¼ HRS   REFUGIO ORDISO   1 HR   BUJARUELO

0   1km
0   ½ mile

the bridge indicates the way, and there also a sign: CAMINO VIEJO A ORDE-SA. A short way down the path you come to a junction; continue south-wards until the path brings you out just below the town, next to the Camping Río Ara.

If you're heading down the road, after quarter of an hour you come to the *Camping San Anton* ☆☆ (☎ 974-48.60.63) where there's a shop and bar/restaurant; the tariff is €2.85/475ptas per person and per tent. Ten minutes further south, you come to *Hotel Ordesa* (☎ 974-48.61.25, 📧 48.63.81), a large complex which includes *Camping Ordesa* (☎ 974-48.61.46, 📧 48.63.81). During high season, the hotel has double rooms from €44/7530ptas, and a space in the campsite costs €3.50/600ptas per person and per tent. Campers can use the hotel swimming pool. Just beyond the hotel you come to **Torla**.

TORLA

A pretty little village with a relaxed atmosphere and plenty of good facilities, Torla is a great place to take a break. In mid season it can get very crowded, so don't rely on getting a space in either of the refugios unless you have booked in advance.

Services

Shops in Torla include a couple of mini supermarkets, two camping stores (one of which sells Coleman/Epigas) and a pharmacy. There are two small **banks**, both of which have cash dispensers. The **post office**, through an unmarked door near the main square, is open from 10.00-11.30 on weekdays; if you want to send a parcel note that it and it will accept only small ones. The **tourist office** is on the main square and is open daily (hours vary). Rather confusingly the office seems to be abandoned in all but high season in favour of a small wooden booth on the road into Torla, from which the tourist office representative dispenses leaflets and information.

There are currently two daily buses between Torla and Sabiñánigo (where there's a railway station). Buses leave Torla at 15.30 and 20.00 for Sabiñánigo, and depart Sabiñánigo for Torla at 11.00 and 18.30; the journey takes an hour. There is also one daily bus between Torla and L'Ainsa, leaving Torla at 12.00 and leaving L'Ainsa at 14.30; again the journey takes an hour.

From the start of July to mid October (and at Easter) an excellent bus service runs between Torla and the car park area in the Ordesa Canyon (stopping en route to drop off and pick up at the Visitors' Centre). The service runs roughly every 15 minutes between 07.00 and 19.00 and costs €2.25/375ptas for a return ticket.

Taxi Bellavista (☎ 974-48.61.53) operates from the Hostal Bellavista. They use Espace-type vans, so if there are several of you it becomes a viable option. A taxi to Nerín costs €30/5000ptas. Other taxi operators include **Taxi J Lardiés** (☎ 616-72.25.31) and **Taxi J Soler** (☎ 974-48.62.43).

Where to stay

Probably the best hotel is the *Hotel Villa de Torla* ☆☆ (☎ 974-48.61.56, 📧 48.63.65), which is right on the central square and has single rooms for €28/4600ptas and doubles for €40/6750ptas. (Try to avoid Room 110: the double glazing is no match for the noise at turning out time from Discoteca As Proas). There are several other hotels of similar standard and with the same sort of prices. *Hostal Bellavista* ☆☆ (☎ 974-48.61.53) has single rooms for €23/

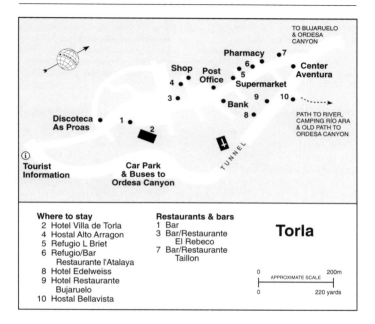

Where to stay
2 Hotel Villa de Torla
4 Hostal Alto Arragon
5 Refugio L Briet
6 Refugio/Bar
   Restaurante l'Atalaya
8 Hotel Edelweiss
9 Hotel Restaurante
   Bujaruelo
10 Hostal Bellavista

Restaurants & bars
1 Bar
3 Bar/Restaurante
   El Rebeco
7 Bar/Restaurante
   Taillon

Torla

```
0                          200m
    APPROXIMATE SCALE
0                       220 yards
```

3750ptas and doubles for €33/5500ptas; *Hotel Restaurant Bujaruelo* ☆ (☎ 974-48.61.74, 🖹 48.63.30) has double rooms for €39/6500ptas; *Hotel Edelweiss* ☆☆ (☎ 974-48.61.73, 🖹 48.62.73) has singles from €20/3300ptas and doubles from €36/5900ptas. There are others. For budget accommodation, a good place is the *Refugio L Briet* (☎ 974-48.62.21 🖹 48.64.80) which takes its name from the French explorer who studied and photographed this part of the Pyrenees. It's very clean and modern, and excellent value at €6/1000ptas for a dormitory bed. They also have three private rooms (a double, a triple and a four-bedded room) available. There are no self-catering facilities. Similarly priced accommodation is also available at *Refugio/Bar/Restaurante l'Atalaya* (☎ 974-48.60.22).

Several campsites have already been mentioned above, but the nearest to Torla is the *Camping Río Ara* ☆☆ (☎ 974-48.62.48) which is situated in a peaceful shady area near the river. There's a shop and bar/restaurant; the tariff is €2.85/475ptas per person and per tent.

What to see

The national park **Visitors' Centre** is worth a look if you're going up towards the canyon. It's open daily from 09.00-13.30 and 16.00-19.00, and entry is free. The displays cover the geology, flora and fauna, and the local history and culture of the area.

Activities in the area include climbing, horse riding, mountain biking, rafting and caving. For information try the tourist office in Torla, or contact a local company direct. **Compañia de Ordesa** (☎/🖷 974-48.64.17) has a website at 🖥 www.pirineo.com/guiasordesa.

Entertainment in Torla is limited, but the **Bar/Restaurant l'Atalaya** is worth a mention: at €9/1400ptas, the menu del día (which includes wine) is excellent value, and the bar (next door) plays great blues music. The restaurant in **Bar/Restaurante El Rebeco** is more expensive but also looks worth a try. If you're feeling energetic, you could pay a visit to **Discoteca As Proas**, which opens at midnight.

THE ORDESA CANYON   [MAP 78/59]

Many walkers visit the Ordesa Canyon en route to or from the Refugio de Goriz. Another option, however, if you're staying in Torla, is to do a one-day circuit. It's a fairly long day, but if you leave your gear in Torla and carry only a light day sack, it's a very enjoyable walk. Alternatively, if you want to spend more time in the canyon itself and less time getting there, you could use the excellent bus service which runs from Torla to the car park in the canyon, either to get up there, or to get back, or both.

The walk up to the canyon from Torla is highly recommended. From near the Hostal Bellavista, take the path leading down towards the Camping Río Ara. On the far side of the river bridge, and just below the entrance to the campsite, take the large path which runs north along the side of the river. Various signs in Torla and along the path, point the way: CAMINO DE TURIETO ORDESA. After 15-20 minutes the path forks, the right fork being marked as the CAMINO TURIETO and the left fork PUENTE DE LOS NAVARROS, VALLE DE BUJARUELO. Go right, following the red and white markers of the GR11, which has come down from Bujaruelo.

The path climbs at a steady but fairly easy gradient through the trees, which provide welcome shade. As the path swings eastwards into the entrance of the canyon, there are excellent views northwards towards the Visitors' Centre (see p265). Approximately half an hour after leaving the fork in the path, you pass the impressive **Cascada Tomborrotera** which is visible from a small viewing platform, and ten minutes beyond this you come to the **Cascada Abelos**. Just beyond this second waterfall there's a fork in the trail. The left-hand path leads down to the **Puente Luciano Briet**, beside which there's a monument to the French naturalist. It's probably better not to cross the river here, but if you have time to spare, wander down to the bridge and admire the view up the canyon.

Continuing along the south side of the river, the path is now wide and level and runs through mature woods which provide plenty of shade. Twenty minutes beyond the Puente Luciano Briet, you come to a sign pointing left across the river towards the car park ('aparcamiento'), where there are a few useful facilities including a *restaurant/bar*, *toilets*, a *drinking fountain*, and *buses* back to Torla.

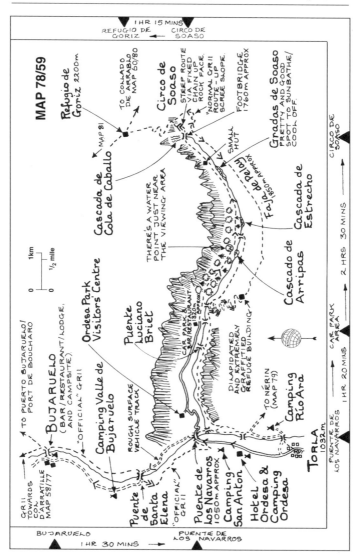

MAP 78/59

1 HR 15 MINS
REFUGIO DE GORIZ ← CIRCO DE SOASO

Refugio de Goriz 2200m

TO COLLADO DE ARRABLO MAP 60/80

MAP 81

Circo de Soaso

STEEP ROUTE VIA FIXED CHAIN UP ROCK FACE

"NORMAL" GR11 ROUTE - UP SCREE SLOPE

FOOTBRIDGE 1760m APPROX

Cascada de Cola de Caballo

SMALL HUT

CIRCO DE SOASO

Gradas de Soaso PRETTY AND GOOD SPOT TO SUNBATHE/ COOL OFF.

Faja de Pelay 1850m APPROX

Cascada de Estrecho

THERE'S A WATER POINT JUST NEAR THE VIEWING AREA

Cascada de Arripas

Ordesa Park Visitors Centre

Puente Luciano Briet

CAR PARK & BAR/RESTAURANT

1320m

1300m

DILAPIDATED AND EXTREMELY GRAFFITIED REFUGE BUILDING

2 HRS 30 MINS

CAR PARK AREA

BUJARUELO (BAR/RESTAURANT/LODGE AND CAMPSITE).

"OFFICIAL" GRILL

Camping Valle de Bujaruelo

ROUGH SURFACE VEHICLE TRACK

TO PUERTO BUJARUELO/ PORT DE BOUCHARO

GR11 TOWARDS CON D'ARRATILLE MAP 58/77

Puente de Santa Elena

"OFFICIAL" GRILL

Puente de los Navarros 1050m APPROX

Camping San Anton

Hotel Ordesa & Camping Ordesa

TO NÉRIN (MAP 79)

Camping Rio Ara

TORLA 1032m

1 HR 20 MINS

CAR PARK AREA

PUENTE DE LOS NAVARROS

1km
½ mile
0

The route from the eastern end of the car park is well signposted and the circular tour of the canyon begins and ends here. There is, however, a choice – which direction to complete the circuit? On either side of the Río Araza two main paths follow the valley floor as far as the Puente de Arripas, where the path on the north side of the river becomes the only option. Running high around the south side of the canyon, however, is the Faja de Pelay, a promontory some two thirds of the way up the canyon wall, from which there are spectacular views. If you walk up the valley floor and then back along the Faja de Pelay you find yourself climbing slowly but constantly for two thirds of the route, then completing a level section along the Faja, before descending very steeply to the car park. If you do it the other way around there's a long and incredibly steep climb to begin with, after which it's all either level or downhill. The description here is of the first option.

It doesn't much matter whether you take the path on the south or north side of the river for the first part of the walk – both are shady and very pleasant. If you take the southern path, after about forty minutes you come to the **Puente de Arripas** at which point you are forced to cross the river and join the northern route. The (northern) path climbs steadily from here, gaining height above a series of waterfalls until, about an hour's walking beyond the Puente de Arripas you come to the **Gradas de Soaso** a series of low waterfalls and clear blue pools which provide a perfect place to stop for a break. Approximately an hour beyond the Gradas, you reach the eastern end of the canyon, the **Circo de Soaso (1760m)**, where a tiny bridge crosses the stream just below an impressive waterfall, **Cascada de Cola de Caballo**.

North-east of the bridge, a chain has been fixed to the rocks to facilitate the steep climb towards the *Refugio de Goriz* (there's also an easier path to the refugio, which runs up the scree slope to the right). The path to the Faja de Pelay, however, is much less strenuous, and runs south-west, climbing gradually up the hillside. The path soon levels off, continuing around the side of the valley horizontally while the bottom of the canyon sinks away below. There are superb views westwards towards the mouth of the canyon, and across to the towering walls on the far side.

At the western end of the Faja de Pelay, the descent into the canyon begins near a large and decrepit refuge building, marked on the map as 'Ref y Mirador'. It takes an hour to get down the unrelentingly steep path, to the car park. From the Circo de Soaso back to the car park via the Faja takes about three and a quarter hours. In all, the circuit starting from and returning to the car park has taken about 6-6½ hours.

TORLA → NERÍN   [MAP 79]

This section from Torla to Nerín is not going to be a highlight of anyone's trip; it's a thirsty, tiring walk, almost entirely along a single rough road,

Map 79 – Torla to Nerín 271

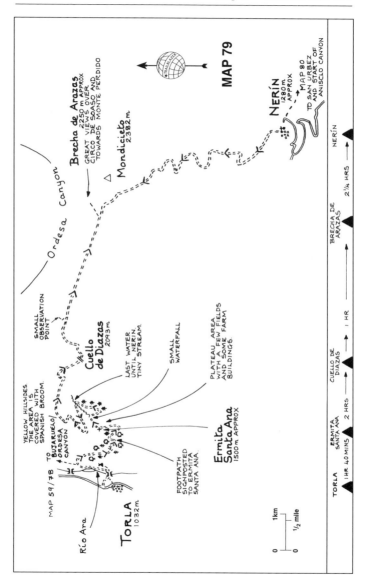

MAP 79

Brecha de Arazas
2250 m APPROX
GREAT VIEWS OVER
CIRCO DE SOASO AND
TOWARDS MONTE PERDIDO

Mondicieto
2382 m.

NERÍN
1280 m
APPROX

MAP 80
TO SAN URBEZ
AND START OF
ANISCLO CANYON

Ordesa Canyon

SMALL
OBSERVATION
POINT

Cuello
de Diazas
2093 m.

LAST WATER
UNTIL NERÍN.
TINY STREAM.

SMALL
WATERFALL

PLATEAU AREA
WITH A FEW FIELDS
AND SOME FARM
BUILDINGS.

YELLOW HILLSIDES.
THE AREA IS
COVERED WITH
SPANISH BROOM.

TO BUTARUELO/
ORDESA
CANYON

MAP 59/78

Ermita
Santa Ana
1500 m APPROX

FOOTPATH
SIGNPOSTED
TO ERMITA
SANTA ANA

TORLA
1032 m.

Río Ara.

0 —— 1km
0 —— ½ mile

TORLA ◄ 1HR. 40 MINS ► ERMITA SANTA ANA ◄ 2 HRS ► CUELLO DE DIAZAS ◄ 1 HR ► BRECHA DE ARAZAS ◄ 2¼ HRS ► NERÍN

and there's a large uphill section to begin with. It does get you to Nerín, however, which is the ideal starting point for a hike up the Añisclo Canyon, and walking over the tops of hills is a lot better than walking down the road, which is the only alternative. If you're keen to avoid all or part of this section, you could consider taking a taxi. In 2000, Taxi Bellavista in Torla was charging €30/5000ptas for the trip to Nerín; the journey takes one hour.

From Torla, follow the footpath over the old river bridge and go left along the track which passes below the Camping Río Ara. After about twenty minutes, the vehicle track bends sharply right and the footpath continues towards Ordesa. Follow the vehicle track, which starts to climb the hillside. After forty minutes you pass a rough sign: STA ANA. The little path is rather overgrown and presumably forms an alternative route to the Ermita, for some twenty minutes further up the vehicle track you reach the **Ermita Sta Ana** (1500m approx) anyway.

Up to this point, if you've started at a reasonable hour, the trees and the steep slopes above the path will have provided welcome shade. From here, however, there is little in the way of shelter from the sun. Five minutes beyond the Ermita there's a small waterfall and twenty minutes later you cross the same stream further up the hillside. This is literally the last water until Nerín. Ensure that you are carrying at least two litres, as the entire walk from here is exposed to the sun and is arid and dusty.

Another hour and a half of climbing brings you to the **Cuello de Diazas (2093m)**, from which there are good views west to Mondiciero (2296m) and south into the Valle de Vío. Ten minutes further east along the track you get a glimpse of the Ordesa Canyon, where a break in the rocks allows a footpath to a **small observation point**.

Fifty minutes later, there's a better view; a grassy vehicle track leads across the hillside to the **Brecha de Arazas**. The view from anywhere around here is unbelievable: way below you, you can see people on the Faja de Pelay, and as far below again, walkers on the path alongside the Río Araza. The view of the Circo de Soaso with Monte Perdido towering above it is memorable. From the Brecha de Arazas, it's about $2^1/_4$ hours down the rough road to **Nerín**. (For details of the bus service from here to Nerín, see below).

NERÍN

Nerín, a tiny, pretty hamlet of 10-15 houses, has somehow avoided the fate that has befallen some of its neighbours (such as Sercué) which have simply been abandoned. In summer a substantial part of Nerín's income must come from tourism, both from the walkers who stay in the two small lodges and from the day trippers who use the coach service up to the Brecha de Arazas. In winter it's a different matter: only one family remains in the hamlet year round.

There are two places to stay. The *Albergue Añisclo* (☎ 974-48.90.10) is run by a friendly family, has a good selection of walking books, and a big

terrace facing east towards the mountains around Ainsa. A bed in the clean and modern dormitory costs €6/1000 ptas, or it's €15/2500ptas for media-pensión.
    Pension al Turista (☎ 974-48.90.16) is slightly less welcoming, but has the attraction that the proprietress speaks French (which makes reservation easier, if your Spanish isn't too hot). They charge €6/1000ptas for a bed in the dormitory (€15/2500ptas for media-pensión), or €30/5000ptas for a double room (€45/7500ptas for media-pensión).

For those who are feeling terminally lazy, a bus service runs three times a day from Nerín, up the rough road to the Brecha de Arazas (near **Mondicieto (2382m)**). The idea is that this takes day walkers up to the same level as the Refugio de Goriz, so that they can walk to the refuge around the top of the canyon without having to climb any hills. The bus currently leaves Nerín at 07.00, 10.00 and 15.00; the 10.00 and 15.00 services will also bring walkers back to the village from the Brecha; there is a late service at 20.00 to bring walkers down to Nerín.

NÉRIN → REFUGIO DE GORIZ [MAP 80, p275]

On the lane leading east out of the village there's a signpost and a map board showing all the local paths. The GR15 is the one you want; the actual signpost points down into the stony valley and simply reads :SERCUÉ, AÑISCLO. The path is easy to follow, and after three quarters of an hour you come to the deserted village of **Sercué (1160m)**. One house is in use, but the other buildings are all in various states of ruin. Just above the houses is a flat grassy area which would be good for camping, but the village might be a little too spooky for most people.

Twenty minutes' walk beyond Sercué you come to the lip of the canyon, from which a steep but well-made path descends to the main trail along the valley floor. Heading north along the canyon, the scenery gets progressively more attractive, with waterfalls, clear pools and a tiny spring en route. About half an hour past the spring, the path starts to climb steeply, zigzagging up the hillside, eventually levelling out when it has gained enough height to pass over the top of the cliffs. After a further three quarters of an hour you come to **La Ripareta (1405m)**, a perfect spot for a break. The river edge is lined by an area of flat rock and grass: just right for a spot of sunbathing.

From La Ripareta, continue up the valley along a narrow and sometimes indistinct footpath, which runs through the trees. After about 50 minutes you come to the **footbridge** marked as *pasarela* on the map. Although a path is shown (on the Editorial Alpina map) as continuing on the west bank of the stream, it is not recommended. Having passed over a short stretch of *clavijas* (a cable and some iron pins to enable walkers to traverse a vertical bit of rock) the path becomes hard to follow and then peters out completely. Whichever route you take, therefore, it's best to cross here to the eastern bank of the stream, where a clear path winds northwards towards **Fuen Blanca**.

Ramond de Carbonnières

The first ascent of Monte Perdido was masterminded by Frenchman Ramond de Carbonnières, one of the great figures in Pyrenean history. Following a stay in Barèges in 1787, Ramond became fascinated with the mountains. In 1789 he published *Observations faites dans les Pyrenées*, and over the following years he travelled widely, recording details of all aspects of Pyrenean life. After several attempts to scale Monte Perdido, he finally succeeded on 10 August 1802; in the same year he published his account of the feat in *Voyage au Mont Perdu*. Ramond's contribution to scientific knowledge of the mountains was commemorated in 1865 by the formation of the Société Ramond – an organization dedicated to intellectual enquiry about the Pyrenees. There is also a flower named after him – Ramondia Pyrenaica.

On the far side of the bridge, the narrow path climbs steeply at first, before levelling out and running across the side of the canyon to arrive at Fuen Blanca. Opposite the tiny footbridge at Fuen Blanca is a *stone shelter*. The area is beautiful with little waterfalls and pools, and impressive mountains on all sides. It's a popular camping spot, and many walkers use it as a stopover. The shelter is picturesque but only for use as a last resort; it's extremely dirty and could take no more than two or three people.

From this hut, the route to the Refugio de Goriz is clearly indicated with the red and white waymarks of the GR11. After $3/4$ of an hour of steep climbing, the path crosses the stream above the waterfall. Fill up here, as there's more climbing to come. The trail now rises in three or four stages, mounting to a grassy ledge, crossing it and then climbing again. Finally you reach a grassy plateau, and you'll see the **Collado de Arrablo (2329m)** ahead; the river runs almost next to the path, and there's another chance to get water. Having reached the col, the path starts to head south-west; within a short distance, you take an obvious turning to the north-west and follow the path to Goriz.

The *Refugio de Goriz* (☎ 974-34.12.01) is very popular: you should book in advance if you're visiting during peak season (mid-July to mid-August), or make an effort to turn up as early in the afternoon as possible. In the evening the area around the refuge is often crammed with tents, too. The refuge has a guardian in residence all year, and has 90 places; charges are €7/1100ptas per night, and €11/1900ptas for the evening meal. Some provisions are sold at the refuge, including pasta, chocolate and blue camping gaz cylinders.

❏ Walking times on trail maps
Note that on all the trail maps in this book the times shown alongside each map refer only to time spent actually walking. Add 30-40% to allow for rest stops.

Map 80 – Nerín to Refugio de Goriz 275

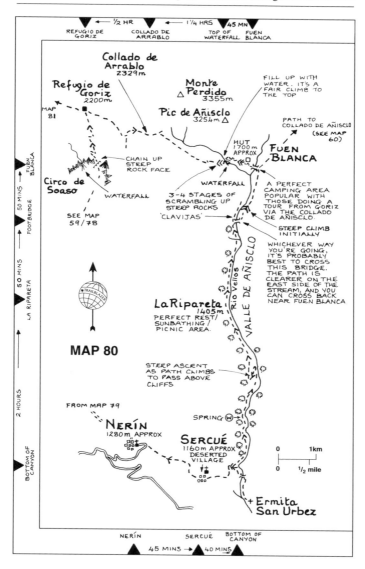

REFUGIO DE GORIZ ← ½ HR ← COLLADO DE ARRABLO ← 1¼ HRS TOP OF WATERFALL ◄45 MN► FUEN BLANCA

Collado de
Arrablo
2329m

Monte
△ Perdido
3355m

Refugio de
Goriz
2200m

MAP
81

Pic de Añisclo
3254m △

FILL UP WITH
WATER. IT'S A
FAIR CLIMB TO
THE TOP

PATH TO
COLLADO DE AÑISCLO
(SEE MAP
60)

CHAIN UP
STEEP
ROCK FACE

HUT
1700m
APPROX

FUEN
BLANCA

Circo de
Soaso

WATERFALL

WATERFALL

3-4 STAGES OF
SCRAMBLING UP
STEEP ROCKS

'CLAVIJAS'

A PERFECT
CAMPING AREA
POPULAR WITH
THOSE DOING A
TOUR FROM GORIZ
VIA THE COLLADO
DE AÑISCLO

SEE MAP
59/78

FUEN BLANCA

50 MINS

FOOTBRIDGE

50 MINS

LA RIPARETA

STEEP CLIMB
INITIALLY

WHICHEVER WAY
YOU'RE GOING,
IT'S PROBABLY
BEST TO CROSS
THIS BRIDGE.
THE PATH IS
CLEARER ON THE
EAST SIDE OF THE
STREAM, AND YOU
CAN CROSS BACK
NEAR FUEN BLANCA

Río Vellos

VALLE DE AÑISCLO

La Ripar[e]ta
1405m
PERFECT REST/
SUNBATHING/
PICNIC AREA.

TRAILBLAZER

MAP 80

STEEP ASCENT
AS PATH CLIMBS
TO PASS ABOVE
CLIFFS

2 HOURS

FROM MAP 79

SPRING Ⓦ

Nerín
1280m APPROX

Sercué
1160m APPROX
DESERTED
VILLAGE

BOTTOM OF
CANYON

0   1km

0   ½ mile

Ermita
San Urbez

REFUGIO DE GORIZ → GAVARNIE [MAP 81]

[Includes high section – see warning on p20] This section over the Brèche de Roland and down to Gavarnie is not especially difficult but it is quite arduous and should definitely not be attempted in bad weather. The route is unmarked apart from a few low cairns and there are areas where, even in reasonable visibility, it is easy to lose the way amongst the rocks. Equally, in early summer there may still be a fair amount of snow around the south side of the Brèche, and it's worth asking for advice from the guardian at the Refugio de Goriz about whether the Brèche is passable for walkers.

From Goriz, follow the well-worn track along the hillside to the west of the refuge, as it climbs to a small ridge. Scramble up the rocks and continue in a westerly direction along a mostly level and grassy track to the **Cuello de Millaris** (2480m approx). From the bare and desolate hummock of the col, you'll see in front a large flat area, the **Plana de San Ferlús**. Most of it is completely bare, covered with small rocks, while the southern part is grassy and has a weather-monitoring stand.

A path marked by tiny cairns leads off to the right, and contours around the northern side of the bowl. Gradually it climbs the hillside and, as it starts to bend northwards, it steepens, leading towards the **Gruta Casteret** (see below). The actual route is very indistinct; keep an eye out for the cairns which lead you up a steep scramble to a rocky promontory just to the south of the cave (although the mouth of the cave remains out

---

Gruta Casteret

In July 1926, Norbert Casteret, one of France's leading speleologists, set out on an expedition looking for caves with his wife, mother and brother. Catching a brief glimpse of what appeared to be the opening of a cavern, they struggled up a snow slope towards it, half expecting that they would find only another overhang. The cave, however, complete with a 'a river of ice...from the bowels of the mountain' was beyond their wildest dreams.

Casteret's account of their initial exploration makes modern caving techniques look positively wet. 'Pushed by Martial, wielding my pick, and holding the candle in my teeth, I finally managed to scramble to the top. I started to crawl up a flattened tube in the thick ice, white as porcelain; but at each attempt an air-current trumpeting through the tunnel blew out the candle...'

Turning back only because the candle was about to run out, Casteret had to wait a month until he and his wife could return to have another look – again by candlelight. 'Our first step was to explore the huge hall which we had glimpsed a month before. Its vast roof was all in one piece, spanning an ice-field with an estimated area of three thousand three hundred and fifty square yards...Huge blocks off the ceiling were set in ice which was so clear that we could see tiny pebbles frozen six or seven feet deep. Cracks in the vault furnished a considerable influx of ice to feed the lake. The largest of these streams filled a vertical cleft and formed a translucent cascade sixty or eighty feet high. Its top was lost to sight'.

Map 81 – Refugio de Goriz to Gavarnie: Brèche de Roland 277

of sight until you're very close to it). As you reach the promontory, the frontier ridge suddenly comes into view, and you can see to the north two prominent gaps in the ridge. The left of these has a pillar of rock standing in the middle of it, while the right one is simply a huge rectangular breach in the chain. This latter is the **Brèche de Roland (2804m)**.

From here it's possible to continue up and around the promontory to get to the cave; the entrance is accessible to all walkers but in order to go into the cave you'll need to be properly equipped. The best route towards the Brèche, however, involves descending again, down the rocky ridge which runs westwards. There's no defined path, but from the vantage point near to the cave you should be able to pick out a route down the

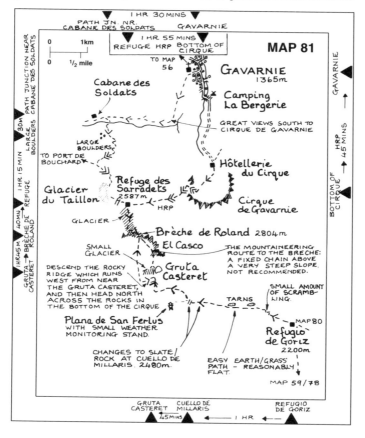

ridge. Having descended, you then need to head north across the bottom of the cirque, finally ascending the relatively straightforward slope directly below the Brèche. (For those with a strong head for heights, a **high path** runs under the vertical walls of El Casco, with the aid, in places, of a steel cable. Considerable care, and proper equipment is required: the scree and snow slopes are extremely steep and slippery).

The descent from the Brèche to the Refuge des Sarradets (also called the Refuge de la Brèche Rolande) takes 30-40 minutes, and is across the Brèche glacier. In mid summer, although many people carry an ice axe, there's little need for one; a stick is useful, however, to give a little extra stability. The *Refuge des Sarradets* **(2587m)** (☎ 05.62.93.37.20) has 60 places and charges €12/80F for the night and €12/75F for an evening meal. The refuge accepts both francs and pesetas and, like other huts around Gavarnie, gets heavily booked in the summer.

There are two ways down to Gavarnie from the refuge:

The HRP route The HRP route, which runs eastwards into the Cirque de Gavarnie, has the twin advantages of being both less busy and of having spectacular views. Although it's shown in dots on the IGN map it's not difficult; the path can, however, be slippery after rain. Some easy scrambling is required in three or four places. Following this route, it takes about 1³/₄ hours to get to the bottom of the cirque; ten minutes' walk further down is the Hôtellerie du Cirque. There is no accommodation here, and the whole area is generally packed during the summer. Follow the rough road which runs to the left of the hôtellerie for three kilometres to arrive in Gavarnie. For details of where to stay and information on facilities in Gavarnie see p218.

The alternative route Most walkers doing the trek between Gavarnie and the Refuge des Sarradets follow this route, rather the HRP path. From the refuge follow the clear path running north-westwards for a few minutes to the adjacent col. On the far side of the col the path descends steeply to pass below the Glacier du Taillon. About twenty minutes after leaving the refuge, there's a fork, with the path to the Port de Boucharo heading west and the path towards Gavarnie starting a steep descent beside the meltwater streams coming from the glacier. The path is difficult to pick up in places but soon becomes clearer.

About 1¹/₄ hours below the refuge the path comes to a small level area with three or four huge boulders, where some flat grass provides an ideal camping spot. From here the path descends for half an hour to meet the main trail coming down from the Cabane des Soldats which can be seen to the left. At the path junction there's a yellow sign pointing back up the hillside: REFUGE DE LA BRÈCHE 2H 15. Follow the main trail eastwards until, after about 40 minutes, the path swings north-eastwards to begin the descent to Gavarnie. A further half hour's walking brings you to Gavarnie.

PART 5: EASTERN PYRENEES

Facts about the region

GENERAL DESCRIPTION

The area dealt with here is entirely on the French side of the border, in the département of Pyrénées Orientales.

This area, which starts just to the east of Mérens-les-Vals is distinctive in several ways. There is a noticeable climatic change as you move towards the Mediterranean. The short, violent thunderstorms of the high mountains give way to more consistent, calmer weather. Good news as this may sound, it also means that trekking in this part of the Pyrenees can be a hot and dusty experience – carry plenty of water!

The landscape alters as you move east, too. Andorra, the Aran Valley and the high mountains to the west of Mérens soon become memories. As you cross the border from Ariège to Roussillon and approach the Étang de Lanoux, the differences start to become obvious. The huge shallow valleys of the Lacs de Lanoux and Bouillouses are in contrast to anything so far experienced along the GR10, and the meandering course of the Têt River is a surprise. The Pic du Carlit (2921m) and the Pic Canigou (2784m) are the last mountains of any size on the way east. Within five or six hours of descending from Canigou you find yourself in Arles-sur-Tech, which sits at only 282m.

With the change of altitude and climate, there is a marked change in lifestyle. The remote world of the montagnard is left behind, and everywhere the plains start to close in. Villages are no longer slate-roofed mountain hamlets perched on hillsides but groups of red-tiled, white-washed houses huddled in the valleys. The Eastern Pyrenees, like their western counterparts, have been a traditional access route to the peninsula, and so there is a variety of influences at play.

 Trekking in the Eastern Pyrenees – Highlights
While there are plenty of places to see away from the walking trail, your choices are rather limited if you are on foot.

Mont Louis is extremely impressive and makes a great stopover for the night. Likewise, the abbey in **Arles-sur-Tech**, with its miraculous Holy Tomb is well worth seeing. A visit to the old Cathar stronghold at **Montségur** is also most interesting but you'd need to hire a car.

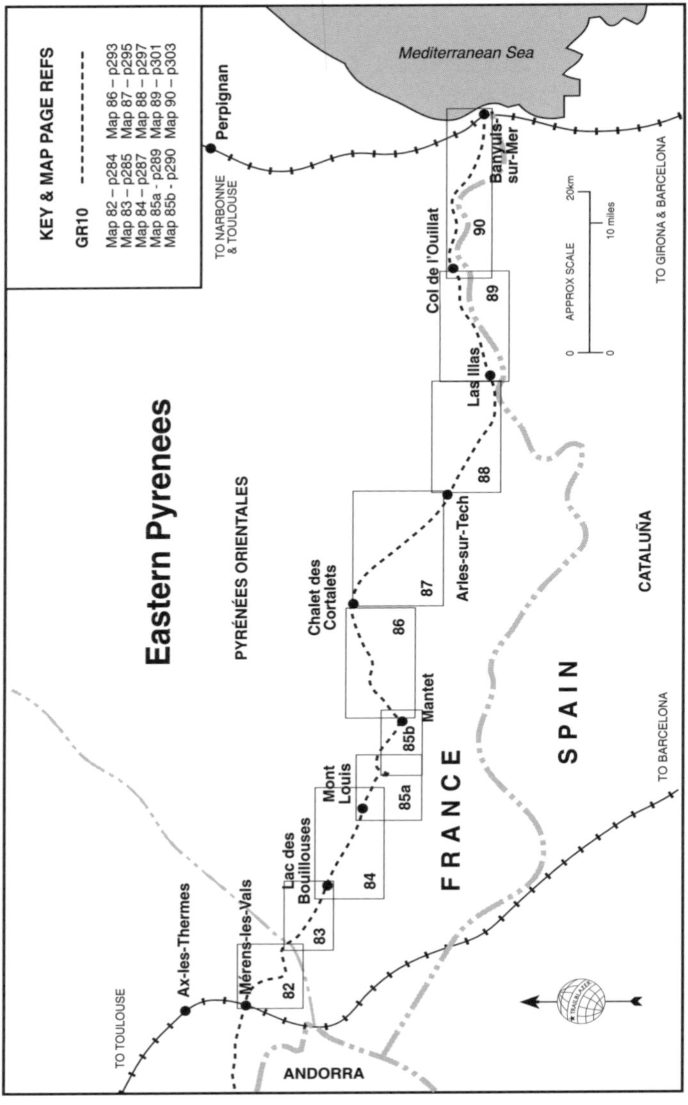

Eastern Pyrenees

PYRÉNÉES ORIENTALES

KEY & MAP PAGE REFS

GR10

Map 82 – p284
Map 83 – p285
Map 84 – p287
Map 85a – p289
Map 85b – p290
Map 86 – p293
Map 87 – p295
Map 88 – p297
Map 89 – p301
Map 90 – p303

Mediterranean Sea

Perpignan

TO NARBONNE & TOULOUSE

Banyuls-sur-Mer

Col de l'Ouillat

90

89

Las Illas

88

Arles-sur-Tech

Chalet des Cortalets

87

86

Mantet

85b

Mont Louis

85a

Lac des Bouillouses

84

83

Ax-les-Thermes

Mérens-les-Vals

82

TO TOULOUSE

ANDORRA

FRANCE

SPAIN

CATALUÑA

TO GIRONA & BARCELONA

TO BARCELONA

APPROX SCALE

20km

10 miles

0

0

Politics and history

The Roussillon region, which encompasses the Pyrénées Orientales, has one of the richest cultural histories of any part of the Pyrenees. In 218BC Hannibal passed through here, and the Romans later used this access route to get into the peninsula for themselves. The slopes of Canigou still have the traces of Roman iron mines, and the remains of the Via Domitia which connected the Iberian peninsula to Rome show the importance of the area as a natural corridor. After the Roman departure, when the nation states of Europe were beginning to take shape, the foothills of the Eastern Pyrenees were home to the Cathars. This ill-fated Christian sect pursued a teaching of non-violence but was brutally suppressed in a persecution sponsored by the Catholic Church. The most famous reminder of them is the castle at Montségur, north of Ax-les-Thermes.

This area has not always belonged to the French. In 1213 Peter II, King of Aragon and Count of Barcelona, intervened on behalf of the Cathars, and for many years Roussillon was a Catalan province. Having been exchanged during a series of treaties in the latter half of the fifteenth century, the area was finally given to France in 1659, under the Treaty of the Pyrenees.

Walking in the Eastern Pyrenees

The Eastern Pyrenees are not the most interesting part of the range for walking but they have their attractions. Settled weather is one obvious

---

 The Cathars

The Cathar sect is believed to have originated around the tenth century, probably in the Balkans. Over the ensuing years it spread through Europe and by the twelfth century had arrived in south-west France.

Cathar doctrine held that the material world was corrupt and worthless, and that salvation depended on escaping a cycle of reincarnation which tied the soul to an earthly existence. A pure life, and the blessing or consolation given by a priest just before death were the keys to freeing the soul and its return to God.

The Cathars had fundamental doctrinal differences with the Catholic Church and these combined with an alarming spread of Catharism prompted swift action. In 1209, the Pope sanctioned a crusade in which many notable Crusaders like Raymond of Toulouse refused to take part. Nevertheless a period of random violence was unleashed as a band of northern nobles, led by Simon de Montfort the Elder, ravaged the country. For a brief period from 1216 to 1224 the Languedoc dignitaries managed to regain their property. In 1226, however, a further crusade took place, accompanied by the work of the Inquisition which hunted down individual members of the Cathar priesthood. By this stage, many of the remaining Cathar priests had withdrawn to the protection of the the fortress at Montségur.

On 16 March 1244, the fortress eventually fell, and 225 Cathars who refused to renounce their faith were burnt alive below the walls of the castle.

bonus, and there's also the pleasant prospect of finishing a walking trip at the Mediterranean, where you can relax and sunbathe to recuperate. The Pic du Canigou (2784m) is fun to climb and the sections from Mérens to the Lac des Bouillouses, from Mont Louis to Mantet and from Marialles to Cortalets are particularly attractive.

GETTING THERE

Getting to the Eastern Pyrenees
Getting to the area of the Eastern Pyrenees is covered in detail in Part 1 of this book. In outline there are airports in Toulouse and Perpignan, and to the south of the border there is also an airport in Barcelona.

By rail, there are direct TGV services to Toulouse, and by coach, there's a summer service from London to Perpignan.

Getting to the walking
Getting into the mountains is particularly easy in the Eastern Pyrenees because of the direct access to both Mérens-les-Vals and Banyuls-sur-Mer. Mérens is on the line from Toulouse to La Tour-de-Carol, and there's even a direct train from Paris. It's also possible to get a direct train from Paris to Banyuls. The *Train Jaune* also provides a scenic route up into the mountains, from Villefranche-de-Conflent via Prades and Font Romeu, to La Tour-de-Carol. In addition to these services, both Mont-Louis and Arles-sur-Tech are served by buses which connect to Perpignan.

Route maps

● **Scale and walking times** All the following trail maps are drawn to a scale of 1:100,000 (10mm = 1km/0.625miles). Walking times are given along the side of each map, and the arrow shows the direction to which the time refers. Black triangles indicate the points between which the times have been taken. Note that the time given refers only to the time spent walking, so you will need to **add 30-40% to allow for rest stops**. Remember that these are **my timings** for the section; every walker has his or her own speed. With the first edition of this book, several readers commented that they found these timings on the fast side. The times are, however, consistent so you should err on the side of caution for a day or two until you see how your speed relates to my timings on the maps. When planning the day's trekking, count on between five and seven hours actual walking, and allow for an occasional rest day.

● **Up or down?** The trail is shown as a dotted line. An arrow across the trail indicates the slope; two arrows show that it is steep. Note that the arrow points towards the higher part of the trail. If, for example, you're walking from A (at 900m) to B (at 1100m) and the trail between the two is short and steep it would be shown thus: A—>>—B.

● **Refuges, gîtes and cabanes** Everywhere to stay that is within easy reach of the trail is marked. See the text for more details about each place.

● **Other information and symbols** Altitudes are given on the map in metres. Places where you can get water are shown by a 'W' within a circle.

Eastern Pyrenees – GR 10

MÉRENS-LES-VALS → LAC DES BOUILLOUSES [MAPS 82-83]

[Includes high section – see warning on p20] You can cover this long section in one day although many walkers prefer to break the journey at the Refuge des Bésines or at the Cabane du Solà.

From the main road (N20) in Mérens, pass under the railway line and follow the clearly marked route uphill, past the remains of the ancient church. The church, along with much else in the village, was burnt to the ground by Spanish bandits in 1811; it is believed that the tower which still stands was built in the tenth or eleventh century. A short way above the church, the route goes right, passes between some houses, then immediately turns left and begins to climb on a well-trodden footpath. A sign here gives the following rather pessimistic timings: PORTEILLE DE BÉSINES 4H 45; REFUGE DE BÉSINES 5H 30.

The climb along the valley is not too steep but is, nevertheless, hard work. After an hour and a half, the waymarks lead across a small **footbridge**, and the ascent continues on the other side of the stream. Twenty five minutes' walk beyond this, the path turns sharply to the south-southwest and begins a steep climb towards the Porteille de Bésines, which you'll see ahead. After a further 35-40 minutes, the route levels out a little near a small lake; the gradient stiffens again beyond the tarn and a short, hard climb brings you to the **Porteille de Bésines (2333m)**. You reach the refuge (2104m), which is visible from the col, after a further forty minutes. The *Refuge des Bésines* (☎ 05.61.05.22.44) is brand new and has room for 60 people. A night here costs €12/80F and it's €11/70F for an evening meal. The small *cabane* at the north end of the lake is an alternative if the refuge is full.

The GR10 heads north-eastwards from the refuge along a reasonably level path. As it swings eastwards, however, towards the **Coll de Coma d'Anyell (2470m)**, the gradient steepens and you have to cross a couple of areas of large granite boulders. Approximately one and a half hours after leaving the refuge, you arrive at the col, where the path crosses from Ariège into the département of Pyrénées Orientales. The view from the col comes as something of a surprise. After the high and bare mountains to the west of Mérens, the Étang de Lanoux sits in a huge, shallow bowl. With its rounded, boulder strewn slopes and the apparent emptiness of the scene, the lake and its surroundings seem almost enchanted.

The path descends and passes around the northern tip of the lake. A ten-minute detour southwards at this point brings you to the *Cabane du Solà*, a

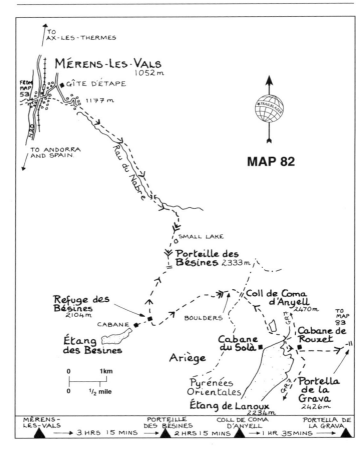

tiny shelter available for use by walkers. Continuing on the GR10 you come to a junction with the GR7, at the north-east corner of the lake. Turn southwards and follow the path, which at first parallels the lake side, and then climbs eastwards, away from the water. Soon you'll arrive at the *Cabane de Rouzet*, a tiny shelter with a single bed frame and a fireplace. 'Cabane du Berger' is painted prominently above the window, so it's not the best place to rely on for overnight shelter. From the cabane, the **Portella de la Grava (2426m)** is clearly seen and soon reached. Keep an eye out for *mouflons*, wild mountain sheep which roam the area in large herds.

The GR10 heads down from the col into the wide, flat-bottomed valley below. Although the landscape is not dramatic in the same way as the mountains that have been left behind, it's extremely pretty, and the walk down to the Lac des Bouillouses is one to be savoured. As the GR10 approaches the north-west corner of the lake, a yellow sign points the walker southwards. About three quarters of an hour later you come to the **barrage**.

LAC DES BOUILLOUSES

There's plenty of accommodation near the lake. On the western side of the barrage is the huge *Refuge des Bones Hores* (☎ 04.68.04.24.22. 🖳 04.68 04.13.63). Despite its massive size, a large part of the building seems to be closed – they have only two dormitories and four rooms open. A night in the dormitory costs €12/80F, or it's €29/190F for demi-pension (money well spent, as the food is excellent). On the eastern side of the dam, the *Auberge du Carlit*

(☎ 04.68.04.22.23) has a friendly owner and a choice of accommodation in private rooms or in the gîte. Demi-pension, if you're staying in the gîte, is €24/ 160F, and a bed for the night costs €11/ 70F.

Slightly further down the hill is the CAF's *Refuge des Bouillouses* (2005m) (☎ 04.68.04.20.76) which has a pleasant terrace. It can take 42 people and charges €12/75F for the night or €27/ 175F for demi-pension.

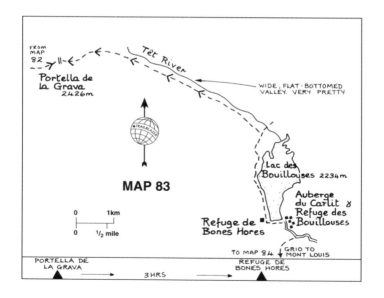

LAC DES BOUILLOUSES → MONT LOUIS [MAP 84]

Walk down the road from the eastern side of the barrage, and four hundred metres beyond the CAF refuge, turn off to the right and cross a small bridge. The twenty-minute walk to the **Estany de la Pradella** is almost level. At the western end of the lake is a well-maintained *cabane*, with room for at least four people.

Cross the stream near the cabane, and follow the wide path on the south side of the lake. The path soon enters the pine wood and you begin a rocky descent; after about 40 minutes you'll pass over a piste and under a **chairlift**, and twenty minutes later come to a large clearing. Beyond the clearing, continue through the woods, mostly on substantial forestry tracks, as far as the D618. Cross the road and continue, mostly on tarmac now, to **Bolquère**.

BOLQUÈRE

Bolquère wins no prizes for being attractive but there's accommodation and a small shop here which might come in handy.

The *Hôtel/Restaurant l'Ancienne Auberge* ☆ (☎ 04.68.30.09.51) is reasonable: it has double rooms from €31/200F. The *Lassus Hôtel/Café/Restaurant* ☆ (☎ 04.68.30.09.75) is a little more lively. Doubles here cost €34/220F. The cheapest place in the village is the grubby *Chez Guillamo* (☎ 04.68.30.15.82) which has single rooms from €14/90F and doubles from €23/150F.

From Bolquère, continue down the road to the **Col de la Perche (1579m)**, and the busy N116. If you should want to stay near the main road the *Relais Les Melezes* (☎ 04.68.04.22.85) is a good spot. A night in the gîte accommodation is €12/80F, and there's a bar/restaurant in the main building.

Go south from the crossroads and almost immediately turn left along the edge of the small pine wood, and then go down an overgrown track between the fields, which leads to **La Cabanasse**. There are three or four shops in the village (including a good épicerie), and a water point near the church but there's nowhere to stay. To get to **Mont Louis**, take the left fork out of La Cabanasse, and walk up the road.

MONT-LOUIS

✉ code 66210

There are two hotels within the fort. The *Hôtel La Taverne* (☎ 04.68.04.23.67, 🖹 04.68.04.13.35) is extremely comfortable, with double rooms from €41/265F; the hotel has its own upmarket pizza restaurant next door. *Hôtel Restaurant Lou Baillou* (☎ 04.68 04.23.26), with double rooms from €41/270F, also looks good, and the restaurant has been recommended by just about every good food guide you've ever heard of. Set menus range in price from €19-30/125-195F. Outside the fort, the *Hôtel le Clos Cerdan* (☎ 04.68.04.23.29, 🖹 04.68.04.23.79) has zero atmosphere, but is very comfortable; double rooms cost from €43/280F.

Shops inside the fort include a pharmacy, a tabac and a small food store. There is a **bank** of sorts, a tiny branch of Crédit Agricole which is open only on Tuesday and Thursday 13.30-15.30. There's a cash dispenser on the corner of the Hôtel le Clos Cerdan.

Map 84 – Lac des Bouillouses to Mont Louis 287

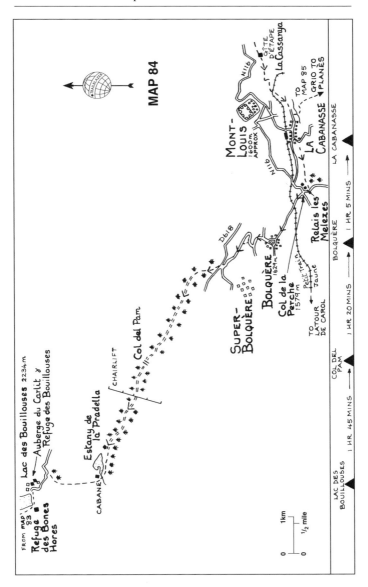

MAP 84

FROM MAP 83

Refuge des Bones Hores

Lac des Bouillouses 2234m

Auberge du Carlit & Refuge des Bouillouses

Estany de la Pradella

CABANE

CHAIRLIFT

Col del Pam

D618

SUPER-BOLQUÈRE

Col de la Perche 1579m

Bolquère 1624m

Petit Train Jaune

TO LATOUR DE CAROL

Relais les Melèzes

Mont-Louis 1600m APPROX

N116

N116

La Cassanya

GÎTE D'ÉTAPE

TO MAP 85

GR10 TO PLANÈS

LA CABANASSE

0   1km
0   ½ mile

LAC DES BOUILLOUSES	COL DEL PAM	BOLQUÈRE	LA CABANASSE
← 1 HR 45 MINS →	← 1 HR 20 MINS →	← 1 HR 5 MINS →	

The Fortress of Mont Louis

The Pyrenees are rich in reminders of the past, from the Roman Via Domitia to the Cathar fortress at Montségur. No monuments have survived so well, however, as the fortresses which the French constructed during the seventeenth century to bolster the border with Spain.

Louis XIV's famous military architect was Sébastien le Prestre de Vauban (1633-1707) and examples of his Pyrenean work can be found as far apart as Bayonne in the Basque Country, and Le Perthus, near the Mediterranean coast. Vauban built for war; subtlety didn't come into it. His citadels were constructed to last, with unbelievably thick walls made of huge blocks of stone. Mont Louis has outer and inner walls, a moat, and a triple main gate. All that, of course, is before you get to the citadel, which contained all the essentials to survive a long siege.

It isn't hard to see why the French chose this site for one of their eastern fortresses – the hill top commands a view across the Col de la Perche, one of the most accessible corridors through the Pyrenees. What is surprising is how short a time it took to build: work started in 1679 and the fort was completed in 1681. The testimony to the workmanship lies in the fact that after more than 300 years, the place looks pristine, and it's easy to imagine that it will look just as good after another three centuries.

Although the walled town is open to the public, the citadel remains the preserve of the military, housing a French commando training centre. There's a marked route which you are allowed to take around the walls, provided you stay on the path, and don't touch any of the training gizmos that are lying around. Part of the fun of following the path is trying to figure out how all the apparatus is used. There are ropes, pulleys, bungees, steps, ladders and jumps – let your imagination run wild as you try to figure out how the unfortunate trainees tackle this nightmare assault course. The citadel is interesting, too.

The walking tour takes about forty minutes, and you can pick up the trail by the gendarmerie, within the walled town.

MONT LOUIS → MANTET   [MAP 85a, p289; Map 85b, p290]

This is another long section, which might be better split into two parts, with a stopover at the Refuge del Ras de la Carançà.

From the fort, walk back down to **La Cabanasse**, and rejoin the GR10 as it leads south out of the village. After crossing a little stream, the path runs across the fields to **Planès**. A *gîte d'étape* should be opening soon in the village. The route through the village is clearly marked, and above the houses you come to a lane junction. A yellow sign here points the way to a forestry track heading south-east. After a long climb through pine woods, the track narrows to a footpath which soon comes to the **Pla de Cédeilles (1911m)**.

The path heading down from the Pla is narrow and, at times, quite steep. It emerges eventually in the valley bottom, beside a stream, which you cross via a small footbridge near a tiny stone shelter. Three hundred metres north of the bridge, on the east bank of the stream is the *Refuge de l'Orry* (**1810m**). The hut can sleep 6-8 people but it is often occupied by shepherds or hunters, so don't rely on its being available.

Walk north from the refuge, along a large track which slopes downhill through pine trees. After about 1500 metres it meets another rough road at a sharp bend. Turn right, and after five minutes you pass a tiny stone *shelter* and a penned area. Near here the GR10 breaks off to the right and climbs steeply to the **Els Collets d'Aval (1996m)**. It doesn't matter hugely if you miss the turning; the rough vehicle track which you're on takes about an hour to climb to the same point.

The ascent from Els Collets d'Aval to the **Coll Mitja** is steep and takes around 50 minutes, passing a small **spring** en route. A stony footpath leads down from the col to the refuge (1830m) which you reach in about 50 minutes. The *Refuge du Ras de la Carança* (☎ 04.68.30.33.52) takes 30 people and has a guardian during peak season. It's a convenient stopping place though facilities are pretty basic (ie if you want to wash, it'll have to be in the river). During the guarded period, it costs €7/45F to stay the night here, or €20/130F for demi-pension.

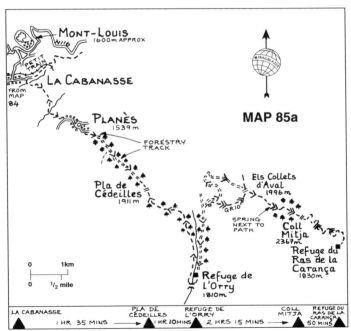

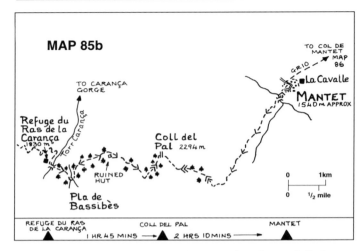

Cross the Carançà Torr by the footbridge near the refuge and climb eastwards. The waymarks, excellent up to this point, suddenly become very scarce, and in many places the paint is so faded that small cairns become the best way of route finding. Having reached a flat open area, the **Pla de Bassibès**, where you have to hop across several small streams, the path re-enters the pine trees heading north and then east. Finally, near a ruined hut you begin the steep climb to the **Coll del Pal (2294m)**.

From the col, the path initially heads south-east, contouring around the hillside, but it soon begins its descent eastwards down a small footpath. Gradually the path swings north-eastwards towards **Mantet**, and after coming down along the side of the valley, you arrive at the village.

MANTET
⊠ code 66360

There are three places to stay in Mantet. The *gîte municipal* is in the centre of the village; it's instantly recognizable, as the word 'gîte' is scrawled in spray paint on the door. According to walkers who've stayed there it's quite basic and dirty, and there's no food available, – but at €8/50F for the night you can't really complain. Above the village is *La Cavalle* (☎ 04.68.05.57.59, 🖹 04.68 05.29.50), an equestrian centre where

there is a small gîte and a few chambres d'hôte. The rooms cost from €34/220F, and a night in the dormitory is €8.50/ 55F. According to recent reports, the food is excellent. The third option is the *auberge/café/restaurant* (☎ 04.68.05 51.76) on the road below La Cavalle. Demi-pension costs €27/175F and you'll need to phone in advance to ensure a room, as there isn't much space. If you're staying in the municipal gîte and want to eat here (the food is good) try to warn them in advance.

Crossing the Mountains – 1937
In December 1937, **Laurie Lee** crossed the Eastern Pyrenees on foot, to join the International Brigade, fighting with the Republicans in the Spanish Civil War. *In A Moment of War*, he recalls his arrival at a Spanish farmhouse: ' "He's come to join us", said one of the youths; and that set them off again, and even the girl lifted her gaunt head and simpered. But I was pleased too, pleased that I had managed to get here so easily after two days' wandering among peaks and blizzards. I was here now with friends. Behind me was peace-engorged France. The people in the kitchen were a people stripped for war – the men smoking beech leaves, the soup reduced to near water; around us hand-grenades hanging on the walls like strings of onions, muskets and cartridge-belts piled in the corner, and open orange-boxes packed with silver bullets like fish. War was still so local then, it was like stepping into another room.'

MANTET → CHALET DES CORTALETS   [MAP 86, p293]

Stage 1: Mantet to Refuge de Marialles

The GR10 leaves Mantet along the road, but just beyond the auberge it turns up the track towards La Cavalle, and then up the hillside to the left, on a footpath. After an easy twenty-five minute climb you come to the **Col de Mantet (1761m)**. On the far side of the col, go downhill on a steep, rough footpath; there are no GR markings initially but they restart after a few minutes. The descent to Py is almost entirely on footpaths, although you cross the road several times and in a couple of places follow it for a short while.

Py is a sleepy, red-roofed village, with a small *gîte d'étape* (☎ 04.68.05.58.38) which charges €7/45F for the night, and which shuts in mid September. There's a *café/restaurant* with a little épicerie. Check the prices in the shop before you buy anything, as some items are surprisingly expensive.

The GR10 continues out of the village on the road, and after a few minutes a yellow sign marks its turn off to the right. Cross the bridge over the river, and follow a lane northwards for 500m before turning off on a footpath to the right. This climbs the hillside to a promontory with a good view down over the town of Sahore, and across to the Tour de Goa on the opposite hill top. The path turns sharply south-east from here and descends to cross the valley, before climbing to the **Col de Jou (1125m)**.

From the col follow a steep vehicle track uphill through pine woods. Gradually it narrows to a footpath, and after three quarters of an hour it joins a level earthen road. Follow the road for four or five minutes, before the GR10 descends to the left on a tiny path which winds through the trees, climbing gradually to the refuge (1700m). The *Refuge de Marialles*

(☎ 04.68.05.57.99) is clean and pleasant, with space for around 40 people. The food is excellent. It costs €11/70F to stay the night here, and €25/165F for demi-pension.

Stage 2: Refuge de Marialles to Chalet des Cortalets

From the refuge, climb the short distance to the car park area, then follow the footpath descending past a **forester's hut** into the pine trees. Almost immediately the path starts to climb again; after about 35 minutes you reach the **Col Vert (1861m)**, beyond which the ascent continues towards the **stream crossing** (near spot height 1964m on the map). Quarter of an hour beyond the stream you reach the junction of the GR10 and the HRP. Those wanting to go over the top of the Pic du Canigou must take the HRP from this point.

The GR10 follows a pleasant, shady and level route around the mountainside to the **Col de Segalès (2040m)** where there's a yellow sign giving timings for the main path, and also a wooden sign pointing down the hill: ST MARTIN DU CANIGOU 5.5KM, 1H. Five minutes past the col there is a good spring.

The path continues level for another half an hour to a shoulder next to the **Roc des Bassoues (2061m)**; from here, it turns sharply east and starts to descend. Quarter of an hour later it levels out briefly, then continues the descent, still on a clear path, across several areas of boulders. At the bottom of this descent, the path joins a vehicle track; a yellow sign points along the GR10, and a separate wooden sign points downhill: VERNET 2H 15.

The **vehicle track** is grassy in places and obviously rarely used; follow it north around the hillside for 15 minutes to another yellow sign, this time pointing uphill. The climb eastwards to just below the Pic Joffre takes about an hour and a quarter. From the hillside where the path levels out, the Chalet des Cortalets (2200m) is visible below, and you reach it after a further 15 minutes.

The *Chalet/Refuge des Cortalets* (☎ 04.68.05.63.57) has two lots of accommodation. In the large hotel building there are private rooms, while in the refuge building, a night in the dormitory costs €8/55F. There is a bar and restaurant – an evening meal is €13/87F and breakfast is €4.50/30F. Try to book in advance, particularly if you're planning to stay during a weekend, as the Pic du Canigou is a popular destination for weekend walkers.

❑ **Walking times on trail maps**
Note that on all the trail maps in this book the times shown alongside each map refer only to time spent actually walking. Add 30-40% to allow for rest stops.

Map 86 – Mantet to Chalet des Cortalets 293

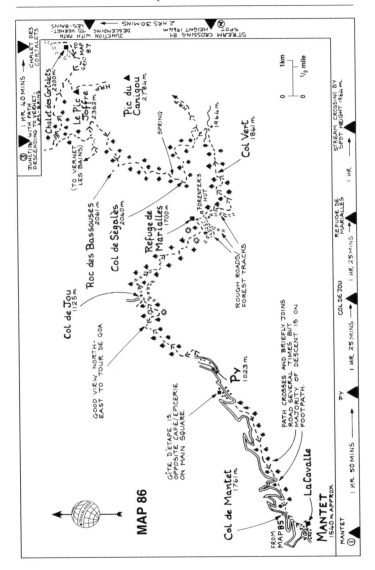

MAP 86

FROM MAP 85

Col de Mantet 1761 m.

La Cavalle

MANTET 1540 m APPROX

GÎTE D'ÉTAPE, IS OPPOSITE CAFÉ/ÉPICERIE ON MAIN SQUARE

Py 1023 m.

PATH CROSSES AND BRIEFLY JOINS ROAD SEVERAL TIMES BUT MAJORITY OF DESCENT IS ON FOOTPATH.

GOOD VIEW NORTH-EAST TO TOUR DE GOA

Col de Jou 1125 m

Roc des Bassouses 2061 m

Col de Ségalès 2040 m

Refuge de Marialles 1700 m

ROUGH ROADS/ FOREST TRACKS

FORESTER'S HUT

SPRING

Col Vert 1861 m.

1964 m.

(TO VERNET LES BAINS)

Le Pic Joffre 2362 m.

Pic du Canigou 2784 m.

Chalet des Cortalets 2200m.

1 HR. 40 MINS Chalet des Cortalets

JUNCTION WITH PATH DESCENDING TO VERNET-LES-BAINS

TO GO TO MAP 87

STREAM CROSSING BY SPOT HEIGHT 1964m

JUNCTION WITH PATH DESCENDING TO VERNET-LES-BANS

2 HRS 30 MINS

0 1km
0 ½ mile

MANTET	PY	COL DE JOU	REFUGE DE MARIALLES	COL VERT	STREAM CROSSING BY SPOT HEIGHT 1964 m.
1 HR. 50 MINS	1 HR. 25 MINS	1 HR. 25 MINS	1 HR.		

CHALET DES CORTALETS → ARLES-SUR-TECH   [MAP 87]

Walk down the path from the Chalet to the vehicle track down the hillside. It's a tedious walk along the rough road to the **Ras del Prat Cabrera (1739m)**, where the GR10 once again joins a footpath. The path goes south-west, remaining almost level around the hillside. At the end of the valley (**La Carnisserie** on the map), the GR10 turns eastwards, remaining level but now running through trees, to the *Abri du Pinateil* **(1680m)**, a very basic wooden shack with room for 6-8 people. The path begins to go downhill from here and after a further 35 minutes it passes a *foresters' hut*. The hut, which has recently been renovated, has room for at least eight people.

Just beyond the hut, the path begins to climb steeply. It levels out briefly after quarter of an hour, and then climbs again to the **Col de la Cirère (1731m)**. A wide loose-pebble path leads down from the col initially, but within minutes the surface is grass. The GR10 heads down past a ruined hut to join the rough road which can be seen below. Follow the road for nearly a kilometre to the gîte/auberge. The *Auberge du Batère* (☎ 04.68.39.12.01) is a large place with a bar/restaurant, chambres d'hôte and gîte d'étape. Accommodation costs €11/70F per night in the clean and pleasant dormitory, €15/95F in a single room and €25/165F in a double. The food is very good.

From the auberge, follow the road downhill for about ten minutes to the **Col de la Descarga**. The GR10 drops down into the gully just to the left of the low hilltop, and follows a line of faded markers which can be difficult to see. The path gradually becomes better defined and runs down a steep hillside past rusting cables – the remains of iron-mining operations. After half an hour's steep descent, the GR10 joins an earthen vehicle track, which continues downhill to a ruined building (**Stn Intermed des Vigourais** on the map). From here most of the rest of the descent is on footpaths, much of it along the line of an old cable lift. The GR10 briefly joins vehicle tracks in three or four places but soon leaves them again for the footpath which leads to Arles.

ARLES-SUR-TECH
✉ code 66150

Arles's most famous sight is La Tombe Sainte (see p296), the Holy Tomb which rests in the courtyard of the eleventh century Benedictine abbey in the centre of the town. There's no gîte in Arles but there are two hotels and enough facilities to make a stop here worthwhile.

Facilities in Arles include a **tourist office** (☎ 04.68.39.11.99), **post office**, **cash dispenser** (Crédit Agricole) and several **shops**.

There are regular **buses** to Perpignan.

Hôtel les Glycines ☆☆ (☎ 04.68.39 10.09, ▤ 04.68.39.83.02) is quite upmarket and the rooms are very comfortable; singles/ doubles start at €31/200F, although if the cheapest rooms are booked, you may be forced to pay more like €43/280F for a double. The *Bar/ Hôtel le Commerce* (☎ 04.68.39 11.75) has double rooms for €18/120F. *Camping du Riuferrer* ☆☆ (☎ 04.68 39.11.06, ▤ 04.68.39.12.09) is near the sports centre.

Map 87 – Chalet des Cortalets to Arles-sur-Tech 295

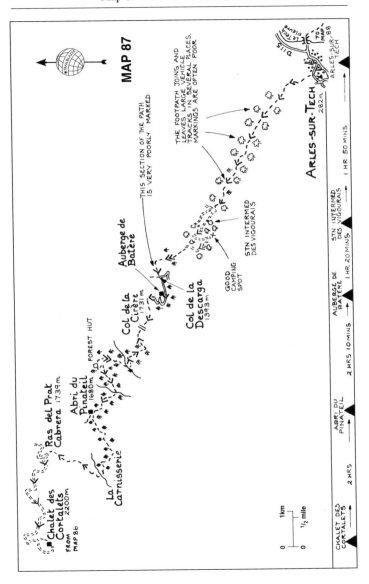

MAP 87

Chalet des Cortalets 2200m
FROM MAP 86

Ras del Prat Cabrera 1739m

La Carnisserie

Abri du Pinateil 1680m

FOREST HUT

Col de la Cirère 1731m

Col de la Descarga 1343m

Auberge de Batère

GOOD CAMPING SPOT

STN INTERMED DES VIGOURAIS

THIS SECTION OF THE PATH IS VERY POORLY MARKED

THE FOOTPATH JOINS AND LEAVES LARGE VEHICLE TRACKS IN SEVERAL PLACES. MARKINGS ARE OFTEN POOR.

TO MAP 88

LE TECH FLEUVE

D 115

ARLES-SUR-TECH 282m

0 1km
0 ½ mile

CHALET DES CORTALETS	ABRI DU PINATEIL	AUBERGE DE BATÈRE	STN INTERMED DES VIGOURAIS	ARLES-SUR-TECH
2 HRS	2 HRS 10 MINS	1 HR 20 MINS	1 HR 50 MINS	

La Tombe Sainte

This marble coffin, believed to date from the fourth century, is held by many to be miraculous: despite the fact that it is covered with a lid the sarcophagus is constantly filled with water, which many claim has healing properties.

Popular belief links this mysterious quality to the fact that, during the tenth century, the coffin was used to store the holy relics of two Christian martyrs, St Abdon and St Sennen. The bones, which had been brought to Arles from the catacombs in Rome, were subsequently removed and placed in silver reliquaries but the coffin soon gained a reputation for producing the inexplicable flow of water. Over the centuries there have been several official enquiries none of which could explain the phenomenon. More recently, attempts to account scientifically for the production of the water, estimated at 500-600 litres per year, have also been unsuccessful.

Water is regularly drawn off for distribution to those who request it, and during the Saints' feast day, on 30 July, large quantities are taken from the coffin to be given to supplicants. Anthony Fitzherbert's book, *A Coffin of Clear Water*, which is on sale in the town book shop, goes into greater detail about the mystery.

ARLES-SUR-TECH → LAS ILLAS [MAP 88]

The section from Arles to Las Illas is quite a long one, with a fair amount of climbing; there are few places to get water en route, so ensure that you have enough from the outset.

The GR10 leaves Arles from the eastern side of the town, near the large car park, and crosses a modern footbridge over the river Tech. On the far side of the bridge the path begins to climb; for the most part it is narrow, steep and rather overgrown, and it comes as a relief to reach the **Col de Paracolls (902m)**. The descent from the col is gentle at first, through chestnut woods but the gradient steepens after about a kilometre, until the path emerges in the valley bottom. Cross the small river and join the road on the far side for five or six minutes before taking a path uphill to the right. The climb is short, and after skirting the hillside you arrive at **Montalba d'Amelie (543m)**. The hamlet consists of only three or four buildings, including a tiny chapel, and there's a water point beside the road.

Follow the road downhill from Montalba d'Amelie, and cross the bridge over the river. Just beyond the bridge, take a clearly signposted footpath to the right. The climb towards the tiny hamlet of **Can Félix** is steep, sometimes on a rough vehicle track but mostly on a narrow footpath through the trees. After about half an hour, near Can Félix, the gradient lessens; the GR10 is joined here by the HRP. According to one walker I met, if you follow the route of the HRP north for a couple of minutes

Map 88 – Arles-sur-Tech to Las Illas 297

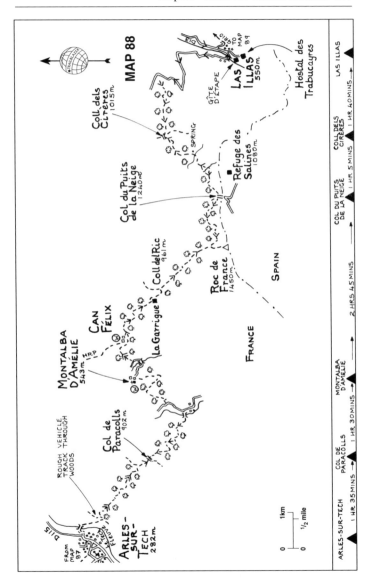

MAP 88

Coll dels Cirères
1015m.

RÍO

TO
MAP
89

GÎTE
D'ÉTAPE

LAS
ILLAS
550m.

Hostal des
Trabucayres

SPRING

Col du Puits
de la Neige
1240m.

Refuge des
Salines
1080m.

Coll del Ric
961m.

Roc de
France
1450m.

SPAIN

La Garrigue

CAN
FÉLIX

MONTALBA
D'AMÉLIE
543m.

HRP

FRANCE

Col de
Paracolls
902m.

ROUGH
VEHICLE
TRACK
THROUGH
WOODS

FROM
MAP
87

D115

FLEUVE

ARLES-
SUR-
TECH
282m.

0   1km

0   ½ mile

ARLES-SUR-TECH →	COL DE PARACOLLS →	MONTALBA D'AMÉLIE →	COL DU PUITS DE LA NEIGE →	COLL DELS CIRÈRES →	LAS ILLAS →
1 HR 35 MINS →	1 HR 30 MINS →	2 HRS 45 MINS →	1 HR 5 MINS →	1 HR 40 MINS →	

Eating out – Pyrenean style

For the walker with a basic knowledge of plants, the Pyrenean woodlands harbour the wherewithal for a delicious meal. I spent a day walking with a Frenchman who really knew his stuff. On the way up through low-bushed slopes we feasted on *myrtilles* (bilberries), and on the way down the opposite hillside we stopped several times to sample *fraises sauvages* (wild strawberries) and *framboises* (raspberries). Passing through the next section of beech wood I was chastised roundly for failing to notice a series of mushrooms that were right next to the path and invited to dinner to share the boxful that we collected.

Mushroom collecting is, of course, a passion on both sides of the border, and if you're walking in the Pyrenees in late summer or early autumn you are likely to find the woods patrolled by locals with large wicker baskets full of fungi. To be a successful collector – and the competition is strong – requires both skill and experience, and I couldn't hope to compete with this depth of knowledge. I did, however, make one vital discovery. The *mûres* (blackberries) along the final section of the GR10 (around Arles-Sur-Tech and Las Illas) are quite the largest and best tasting I've ever come across. Over the period of two days, progress towards the Mediterranean was considerably slowed, not only by the need to feast on blackberries, but the urge to munch the huge *châtaignes* (chestnuts) that lay everywhere.

there's a water point at Can Félix which is not otherwise apparent to those following the GR10.

About an hour after starting the climb, you come to a ruined building, **La Garrigue**. In 1997 this was being rebuilt, but in 2000 there appeared to have been little progress: the building is still a shell, although it does offer a chance of shelter to walkers caught out by the weather. Ten minutes beyond this, you come to the **Coll del Ric (961m)**. Beyond the col, the climb continues to a shoulder where a battered sign points uphill to the **Roc de France**. The GR10 skirts around to the left of the hill top, passing through mature beech woods. Soon the path begins to descend and half an hour beyond the sign for the Roc de France, you arrive at the **Col du Puits de la Neige (1240m)**. The GR10 is clearly signposted, and there's also a sign pointing to an HRP refuge, the ***Refuge des Salines***, which is 25 minutes away to the south-east.

Descend from the col for quarter of an hour, and cross a small rocky gully before climbing again on the far side. Twenty minutes later you pass a **spring** and then briefly join a forestry track. Within a couple of hundred metres, take a footpath to the right, which climbs to the **Col des Cirères (1015m)**. Five minutes' walk south of the col the GR10 begins its descent towards Las Illas. The first 45 minutes is on footpath/vehicle track, and the remaining 45 minutes is on the road.

LAS ILLAS

✉ code 66400

Las Illas is a quiet village, with two places to stay. The *gîte d'étape* (☎ 04 68.83.23.93) is one of the cleanest and most pleasant on the GR10. It costs €8/55F per night to stay here; the building is looked after by Mme Martinez who lives about 50 metres down the road. No food is available.

The *Hostal des Trabucayres* (☎ 04.68.83.07.56) is a friendly bar/restaurant/hotel just up the road from the gîte. Rooms are available from 165F, the food is good, and the terrace is just the place to relax with a cold beer.

LAS ILLAS → COL DE L'OUILLAT   [MAP 89, p301]

The GR10 heads north-east out of Las Illas on the access road (D13), but after less than five minutes it turns right up a small tarmac lane which weaves up the hill to the **Col du Figuier (685m)**. Follow an earthen vehicle track north-eastwards from here as it gently climbs and falls. After $1^1/_2$ hours, you arrive at the **Col de Priourat**; behind the marker stone is a boundary marker – No 565. The track continues downhill, and after some 10-15 minutes, at a sharp left-hand bend, the GR10 departs to the right on a footpath. Many walkers lose their way here, owing to the haphazard route marking: although the last $1^3/_4$ hours along the rough road have been adequately marked, there's one unexpected turning during the morning that is not indicated in any way.

A short while after this, the GR10 rejoins the dusty vehicle track and follows it south-eastwards towards the Fort de Bellegarde, which dominates the little valley. Just below the fort, you pass the remains of the Via Domitia, the road which, with the Via Aurelia, joined Rome to its Iberian conquests. Continue uphill past a small 17th century military cemetery and past the gate of the **Fort de Bellegarde**. The fort, built by Vauban, is open 10.30-12.30 and 14.30-18.30 daily. Entry is €2.50/15F and there are various art exhibitions during July/August/September.

A short way beyond the fort you arrive in **Le Perthus**, a rather grey and unappealing place. If you're planning to stay here you could try *Chez Grand Mère* (☎ 04.68.83.60.96) where double rooms start at €31/200F, or the *Grand Hôtel* (☎ 04.68.83.60,32), where a double room costs €31/200F. Facilities in the town include two food shops, and a Crédit Agricole cash dispenser.

Go north along the road (the N9), and turn right just before the large car park. Pass underneath the **motorway flyover**, and follow the lane uphill for nearly an hour to an old archway over the road near the buildings of **Mas Reste**. One hundred metres beyond the arch, turn uphill through the trees on an old cart track before circling round the hillside to the buildings of **St-Martin-de-l'Albère**. After a day with few pleasant views this is a great place to take a break and look back across the valley.

The GR10 follows the road away from St-Martin-de-l'Albère but soon cuts uphill on a footpath. After several minutes' climbing, it crosses

The évadés

During the Second World War, the mountains to the south-west of Perpignan were extensively used (as were almost all parts of the Pyrenees) to smuggle évadés (escapees) into Spain. George Millar's account of his escape, brings to life the extreme arduousness of such a journey. Millar crossed successfully only on the third attempt; his first attempt having been dogged by bad luck, and his second ruined by an incompetent guide. Finally, led by a wiry old Spaniard, and accompanied by a group of unfit American airmen, it appeared that the end was in sight.

'...we moved on slowly to what he said was the last slope. It was very steep, and the snow was deeper and softer. The four weak Americans were all in grave difficulties. Fritz and I had to divide all that they carried between us...The guide and his assistant did nothing to help. They only got angry, screaming at us and jabbering in fast, incomprehensible Catalan...

[Gable] collapsed finally. Fritz and I tried everything we could think of, praise, vilification, encouragement, massage, wine from the Spaniard's skin, alcohol from Fritz's little bottle. The big man would not move. Tears oozed from his eyes. "Leave me to die, you fellows. I can't go on"'.

What the group had not been told was that even having reached the border, after two nights' walking, there were still many miles to be covered to escape the clutches of the Spanish border guards, who might send them back. Finally, they made it to a small farmhouse, and the guide knocked on the door:

'A thin, nondescript Spaniard came forward, said in French that he was from the British Consulate in Barcelona, and asked us to fill in our particulars, rank, regiment, etcetera, on a paper he carried...' (From *Horned Pigeon*, by George Millar, London 1946).

the road up to the Col de l'Ouillat and runs directly up the spur, at first through trees and then across open grass. Near the top of the spur there's a path junction; the right-hand path takes you up to the Pic Neulos; the **Col de l'Ouillat (936m)** is 20 minutes' walk up the left path. The *Chalet de l'Albère* (☎ 04.68.83.62.20), at the col, has dormitory accommodation for about 20 people, and there are a few private rooms too. A night in the dormitory costs €11/70F, and demi-pension costs €28/180F.

COL DE L'OUILLAT → BANYULS-SUR-MER   [MAP 90, p303]

Climb steeply through the woods behind the gîte d'étape until, after 15-20 minutes, you reach a path junction, with two wooden signs. One sign points back to the gîte while the other points downhill to the right. Confusingly the path to the Pic Neulos is to the left. Five minutes along a level path brings you to the Col des Trois Termes (1100m) where you join the tarmac lane leading up to the **Pic Neulos**. Walk up the road as far as the entrance to the radio installation, where there's a yellow sign: BANYULS-SUR-MER 7H 20. Take the track forking left by the sign to skirt around the edge of the installation and descend through beech trees

Map 89 – Las Illas to Col de L'Ouillat 301

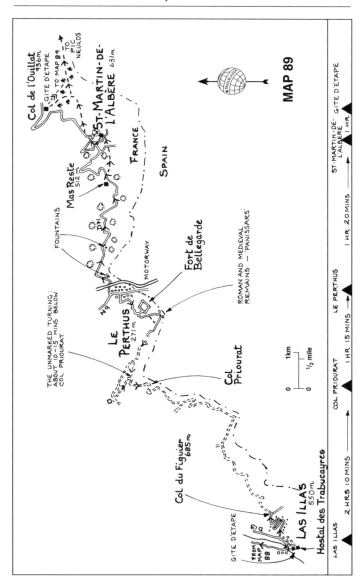

MAP 89

Col de l'Ouillat 936m.
GITE D'ETAPE
TO MAP 89
TO PIC NEULOS

ST-MARTIN-DE-L'ALBÈRE 631m.

FRANCE

SPAIN

Mas Reste 512m.

FOUNTAINS

D13

Fort de Bellegarde

MOTORWAY

THE UNMARKED TURNING; ABOUT 10-15 MINS BELOW COL PRIOURAT

Le Perthus 271m.

N9

ROMAN AND MEDIEVAL REMAINS — PANISSARS'

Col Priourat

0   1km
0   ½ mile

Col du Figuier 685m.

LAS ILLAS 550m.
Hostal des Trabucayres

GITE D'ETAPE

FROM MAP 88

LAS ILLAS ► 2 HRS 10 MINS ► COL PRIOURAT ► 1 HR 15 MINS ► LE PERTHUS ► 1 HR 20 MINS ► ST-MARTIN-DE-L'ALBÈRE GITE D'ETAPE ► 1 HR ►

towards the ridge below. The path passes above a bunker set into the hill-side, near which is a **fountain** – this is the last water point before Banyuls. (The notice says the water is non potable so you should use purifying tablets). Just beyond the fountain, you come to a *refuge/cabane* which can take 10-12 people.

For the next 1-1$\frac{1}{4}$ hours, although some of the paint markings are pretty faded, route finding is simple enough as you just keep going along the ridge. The path climbs and falls over a series of low crests with good views to the north and south. At the top of the **Pic des 4 Termes (1156m)**, follow the pointers for the Pic Sailfort and Col des Gascons. After an hour you arrive at the **Pic Sailfort (981m)**, from which you get the first view of Banyuls itself. When coming down off the Pic Sailfort, be careful to take the correct path; there are several tracks and the GR markers are not initially very prominent. From the rocky outcrop of the Pic you need to follow one which heads due east down the spur. After a steep walk down, you join an almost level footpath which runs along the north side of the ridge to the **Col de Baillaury (438m)**. Cross the vehicle track here and climb briefly on a footpath which soon levels out and leads around the hillside to the **Col des Gascons (386m)**.

From the Col des Gascons, the GR10 joins the road but after only 50-100m down the hill it cuts left down the terraced slopes of the vineyards. The path meets and crosses the road twice more before arriving at the **Col de Llagastera**. The route of the GR10 down to Banyuls is well marked and you soon enter the town near a railway bridge. Walk under the bridge and head eastwards through Banyuls' maze of streets to the seafront.

BANYULS-SUR-MER
✉ code 66650
Banyuls is the archetypal French Mediterranean town – sunny, relaxed and full of holiday-makers. Allow a day here to celebrate your achievement; there's very little to do but eat, drink, swim and sunbathe – wonderful.

Services
Banyuls has most services you could want. There are two **banks**, a **launderette** and plenty of **shops**. There's a large **post office**, and the **tabac** opposite the post office is licensed to change money, a service it provides all week except Sunday afternoons.

If you're looking for a souvenir of your trip, buy a bottle or two of the local wine. It's extremely thick and quite sweet, and tastes rather more like port than wine; it should be drunk chilled as an apéritif.

Where to stay
There is no shortage of places to stay, although only a small selection is given here. One of the smartest is *Hôtel La Pergola* ☆☆ (☎ 04.68.88.02.10) where a double room with a sea view costs €31-75/200-490F; the restaurant looks excellent. *Hôtel Al Fanal* ☆☆ is in the same league; double rooms start at €38/250F – or €46/300F for a room facing the beach. At the budget end of the scale, a good choice is the *Hôtel/Restaurant Canal* ☆ (☎ 04.68.88.00.75, 🖹 04.68.88 13.85) which is on a quiet street just back from the beach; single rooms start at €21/140F. *Camping du Stade* (☎ 04.68.88 31.70) is a fair walk from the sea front, by the sports stadium.

Map 90 – Col de L'Ouillat to Banyuls-sur-Mer   303

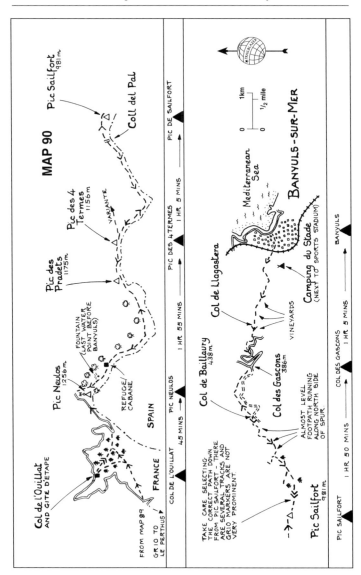

MAP 90

Pic Sailfort
981m

Coll del Pal

Pic des 4
Termes
1156m

VARIANTE

Pic des
Pradets
1175m

FOUNTAIN
(LAST WATER
POINT BEFORE
BANYULS)

Pic Neulos
1256m

REFUGE/
CABANE

SPAIN

FRANCE

Col de l'Ouillat
AND GÎTE D'ÉTAPE

FROM MAP 89

GR10 TO
LE PERTHUS

Mediterranean
Sea

BANYULS-SUR-MER

Camping du Stade
(NEXT TO SPORTS STADIUM)

VINEYARDS

Col de Llagastera

Col de Baillaury
438m

Col des Gascons
386m

ALMOST LEVEL
FOOTPATH RUNNING
ALONG NORTH SIDE
OF SPUR.

TAKE CARE SELECTING
THE CORRECT PATH DOWN
FROM PIC SAILFORT – THERE
ARE SEVERAL TRACKS AND
GR10 MARKERS ARE NOT
VERY PROMINENT

Pic Sailfort
981m

0   1km
0   ½ mille

PIC DE SAILFORT

◄ PIC DES 4 TERMES   1 HR 5 MINS ►

◄ PIC NEULOS   1 HR 55 MINS ►

◄ COL DE L'OUILLAT   45 MINS ►

◄ PIC SAILFORT   1 HR 50 MINS ►

◄ COL DES GASCONS   1 HR 5 MINS ►

◄ BANYULS ►

APPENDIX: FRENCH AND SPANISH

As with travel to any part of the world, time spent learning the local language is well worth while. People instantly become more prepared to help, and to share a joke (even if it happens to at your expense!). In the Pyrenees you can get by without speaking anything other than English but a little effort will open a lot of doors. The following short selection of useful words and phrases in no way replaces the need for a phrase book.

	French	Spanish
Some phrases		
Good morning	*Bonjour*	*Buenos dias*
Good evening/good night	*Bonsoir*	*Buenas noches*
Goodbye	*Au revoir*	*Adiós*
Hi!	*Salut!*	*¡Hola!*
Help!	*Au secours!*	*¡Socorro!*
How are you?	*Comment allez-vous?*	*¿Como esta?*
Well, thank you	*Très bien, merci*	*Bien gracias*
Do you speak English?	*Vous parlez anglais?*	*¿Habla usted inglés?*
I don't understand	*Je ne comprends pas*	*No entiendo*
How much is it?	*C'est combien?*	*Cuánto es?*
General vocabulary		
Bank	*banque* (f)	*banco* (m)
Cash dispenser (ATM)	*distributeur de billets*	*cajero automático*
Post office	*poste* (f)	*oficina de correos* (f)
Rucksack	*sac à dos* (m)	*mochila* (f)
Shop	*magasin* (m)	*tienda* (f)
Today	*aujourd'hui*	*hoy*
Tomorrow	*demain*	*mañana*
Tourist office	*Syndicat d'initiative* (m)	*oficina de turismo* (f)
Directions		
left	*gauche*	*izquierda*
right	*droite*	*derecha*
straight on	*tout droit*	*todo recto*
Where is...?	*Où est...?*	*¿Dónde esta...?*
near	*près*	*cerca*
far	*loin*	*lejos*
Is it far to ...?	*C'est loin pour aller à...?*	*¿A cuánto está ...?*
Trekking		
col	*col* (m)	*collado*(m)
farm	*ferme* (f)	*borda*(f)
hut	*cabane* (f)	*cabaña*(f)
lake	*étang* (m), *lac* (m)	*lago* (m), *estany* (m)
map	*carte* (f)	*mapa* (m)
pass	*pas* (m), *port* (m)	*puerto* (m)
path	*chemin* (m), *sentier* (m)	*senda* (f), *camino* (m)
plateau	*pla* (m)	*meseta* (f)

	French	**Spanish**
shelter	*abri* (m)	*abrigo* (m)
slope	*pente* (f)	*cuesta* (f)
stream	*gave* (m), *ruisseau* (*abbrevrau*) (m) *arroyo* (m)	
summit	*cîme* (f), *sommet* (m)	*cima* (f)
valley	*vallée* (f), *val* (m)	*valle* (m)

Accommodation

Accommodation	*hébergement* (m)	*alojamiento* (m)
Camp-site	*camping* (m)	*camping* (m)
Full (booked out)	*complet*	*completo*
Full board	*pension* (f)	*pensión completa* (f)
Half board	*demi-pension* (f)	*media pensión*
Overnight stay	*nuitée* (f)	*noche* (f)
Room	*chambre* (f)	*habitación* (f)

Food and drink

beer	*bière* (f)	*cerveza* (f)
bill	*addition* (f)	*cuenta* (f)
bread	*pain* (m)	*pan* (m)
breakfast	*petit déjeuner* (m)	*desayuno* (m)
cheese	*fromage* (m)	*queso* (m)
coffee	*café* (m)	*café* (m)
dessert	*dessert* (m)	*postre* (m)
dinner	*repas* (m), *dîner* (m)	*cena* (f)
egg	*oeuf* (m)	*huevo* (m)
fish	*poisson* (m)	*pescado* (m)
lunch	*déjeuner* (m)	*comida* (f)
meat	*viande* (f)	*carne* (f)
milk	*lait* (m)	*leche* (f)
sandwich	*sandwich* (m)	*bocadillo* (m)
snack	*casse-croûte* (m)	*bocado* (m)
tea	*thé* (m)	*té* (m)
vegetables	*légumes* (m)	*verduras* (f)
water	*eau* (f)	*agua* (f)
wine	*vin* (m)	*vino* (m)

Numerals

1	*un/une*	*uno/una*
2	*deux*	*dos*
3	*trois*	*tres*
4	*quatre*	*cuatro*
5	*cinq*	*cinco*
6	*six*	*seis*
7	*sept*	*siete*
8	*huit*	*ocho*
9	*neuf*	*nueve*
10	*dix*	*diez*
11	*onze*	*once*
12	*douze*	*doce*
13	*treize*	*trece*

Numerals (cont)

	French	Spanish
14	*quatorze*	*catorce*
15	*quinze*	*quince*
16	*seize*	*dieciséis*
17	*dix-sept*	*diecisiete*
18	*dix-huit*	*dieciocho*
19	*dix-neuf*	*diecinueve*
20	*vingt*	*veinte*
21	*vingt et un*	*veintiuno*
22	*vingt-deux*	*veintidós*
23	*vingt-trois*	*veintitres*
24	*vingt-quatre*	*veinticuatro*
25	*vingt-cinq*	*veinticinco*
26	*vingt-six*	*veintiseis*
27	*vingt-sept*	*veintisiete*
28	*vingt-huit*	*veintiocho*
29	*vingt-neuf*	*veintinueve*
30	*trente*	*treinta*
40	*quarante*	*cuarenta*
50	*cinquante*	*cincuenta*
60	*soixante*	*sesenta*
70	*soixante-dix*	*setenta*
71	*soixante et onze*	*setentiuno*
75	*soixante-quinze*	*setenticinco*
80	*quatre-vingts*	*ochenta*
90	*quatre-vingt-dix*	*noventa*
95	*quatre-vingt-quinze*	*noventicinco*
100	*cent*	*cien/ciento*
150	*cent-cinquante*	*cien cincuenta*
200	*deux cents*	*doscientos*
300	*trois cents*	*trescientos*
400	*quatre cents*	*cuatrocientos*
500	*cinq cents*	*cincocientos*
600	*six cents*	*seiscientos*
700	*sept cents*	*sietecientos*
800	*huit cents*	*ochocientos*
900	*neuf cents*	*nuevecientos*
1000	*mille*	*mil*
5000	*cinq mille*	*cinco mil*
1,000,000	*un million*	*un millón*

INDEX

Sahara Overland – a route & planning guide
Chris Scott
544 pages, 45 maps, 280B&W & 26 colour photos
ISBN 1 873756 26 7, *1st edition*, £19.99, US$29.95
This new guide covers all aspects Saharan, from acquiring documentation to vehicle choice and preparation; from descriptions of the prehistoric rock art sites of the Libyan Fezzan to the ancient caravan cities of southern Mauritania. How to 'read' sand surfaces, guidance on choosing a reliable guide, using GPS – it's all here along with 35 detailed off-road itineraries covering over 16,000kms in nine countries, from Egypt's Western Desert to Mauritania's Atlantic shore – Morocco, Mauritania, Libya, Mali, Tunisia, Algeria, Niger, Chad, Egypt.

　　*'As addictive as it is informative' **Global Adventure***
　　*'THE essential desert companion for anyone planning a Saharan trip on either two wheels or four.' **Trailbike Magazine***

Japan by Rail　*Ramsey Zarifeh*
320 pages, 40 maps, 30 colour photos
ISBN 1 873756 23 2, *1st edition*, £12.99, US$18.95
With a Japan Railpass, travelling around this country can be surprisingly good value. This guide includes detailed route and planning information, where to stay, where to eat and the most interesting places to stop off along the way. Includes rail maps and town plans.

Australia by Rail　*Colin Taylor*
288 pages, 50 maps, 30 colour photos
ISBN 1 873756 40 2, *4th edition*, £11.99, US$19.95
Previously published as *Australia and New Zealand by Rail*, this guide has been re-researched and expanded to include 50 strip maps covering all rail routes in Australia plus new information for rail travellers.

Trans-Siberian Handbook　*Bryn Thomas*
432 pages, 48 maps, 32 colour photos
ISBN 1 873756 42 9, *5th edition*, £12.99, US$19.95
First edition short-listed for the **Thomas Cook Guide book Awards**. Fifth edition of the most popular guide to the world's longest rail journey. How to arrange a trip, plus a km-by-km guide to the Trans-Siberian, Trans-Manchurian and Trans-Mongolian routes. Fully updated and expanded to include extra information on travelling independently in Russia.

　　*'The Trans-Siberian Handbook is a must.' **The Sunday Times***
　　*'Definitive guide' **Condé Nast Traveler***

Adventure Motorcycling Handbook　*Chris Scott*
288 pages, 28 colour & 100 B&W photos
ISBN 1 873756 37 2, *4th edition*, £12.99, US$19.95
Every red-blooded motorcyclist dreams of making the Big Trip – this comprehensive manual will make that dream a reality. Timbuktu to Kathmandu or Patagonia to Mongolia, whether you're planning your own Big Trip or just enjoy reading about other people's adventures, this book is guaranteed to illuminate, entertain and, above all, inspire.

Trekking in the Moroccan Atlas *Richard Knight*
256 pages, 53 maps, 30 colour photos
ISBN 1 873756 35 6, *1st edition*, £11.99, US$17.95
The Atlas mountains in southern Morocco provide one of the most spectacular hiking destinations in Africa. This new guide includes route descriptions and detailed maps for the best Atlas treks in the Toubkal, M'goun, Sirwa and Jbel Sahro regions. Places to stay, walking times and points of interest are all included, plus town guides to Marrakesh and Ouarzazate.

The Inca Trail, Cuzco & Machu Picchu *Richard Danbury*
256 pages, 32 maps, 24 colour photos
ISBN 1 873756 29 1, *1st edition*, £9.99, US$16.95
The Inca Trail from Cuzco to Machu Picchu is South America's most popular hike. This practical guide includes 20 detailed trail maps, plans of eight Inca sites, plus guides to Cuzco and Machu Picchu.
'Danbury's research is thorough...you need this one'. **The Sunday Times** *'...difficult to put down...This book is essential.'* **International Travel News (USA)**

Trekking in Ladakh *Charlie Loram*
288 pages, 70 maps, 24 colour photos
ISBN 1 873756 30 5, *2nd edition*, £10.99, US$18.95
Since Kashmir became off-limits, foreign visitors to India have been coming to this spectacular Himalayan region in ever-increasing numbers. Fully revised and extended 2nd edition of Charlie Loram's practical guide. Includes 70 detailed walking maps, a Leh city guide plus information on getting to Ladakh.
'Extensive...and well researched'. **Climber Magazine**
'Were it not for this book we might still be blundering about...'
The Independent on Sunday

Trekking in the Everest Region *Jamie McGuinness*
256 pages, 38 maps, 20 colour photos
ISBN 1 873756 17 8, *3rd edition*, £9.95, US$15.95
Third edition of the guide to the world's most famous trekking region. Includes route guides, Kathmandu and getting to Nepal. Written by a professional trek leader.
'The pick of the guides to the area.' **Adventure Travel**

Trekking in Langtang, Helambu & Gosainkund
Jamie McGuinness, 256pp, 35 maps,14 colour photos
ISBN 1 873756 13 5, *1st edition*, £8.95, US$14.95
This third guide in the **Nepal Trekking series** covers the region north of Kathmandu. Comprehensive mapping, where to stay and where to eat along the trails. Written by a professional trek leader.

Trekking in the Annapurna Region *Bryn Thomas*
256 pages, 50 maps, 26 colour photos
ISBN 1 873756 27 5, *3rd edition*, £10.99, US$16.95
Fully revised third edition of the guide to the most popular walking region in the Himalaya.
'Good guides read like a novel and have you packing in no time. Two from Trailblazer Publications which fall into this category are Trekking in the Annapurna Region *and* Silk Route by Rail.' **Today**

Trekking in the Dolomites *Henry Stedman*
256 pages, 52 trail maps, 13 town plans, 30 colour photos
ISBN 1 873756 34 8, *1st edition,* £11.99, US$17.95
The Dolomites region of northern Italy encompasses some of
the most beautiful mountain scenery in Europe. This new guide
features selected routes including Alta Via II, a West-East traverse and other trails. Places to stay, walking times and points
of interest are included, plus detailed guides to Cortina, Bolzano,
Bressanone and 10 other towns. Also includes full colour flora
section and bird identification guide.

❑ OTHER GUIDES FROM TRAILBLAZER PUBLICATIONS

Adventure Motorcycling Handbook	4th edn Jan 2001
Australia by Rail	4th edn out now
Azerbaijan (with excursions to Georgia)	2nd July 2001
The Blues Highway – New Orleans to Chicago	1st edn Aug 2001
China by Rail	2nd edn out late 2001
Inca Trail, Cuzco & Machu Picchu	1st edn out now
Indian Ashram Guide	1st edn late 2001
Istanbul to Cairo Overland	1st edn out now
Japan by Rail	1st edn late 2001
Land's End to John o'Groats	1st edn Dec 2001
Mexico's Yucatan & the Ruta Maya	1st edn Jan 2002
Norway's Arctic Highway	1st edn Jan 2002
Tibet Overland – mountain biking & jeep touring	1st edn Oct 2001
Siberian BAM Guide – rail, rivers & road	2nd edn July 2001
The Silk Roads – a route and planning guide	1st edn Jan 2002
Silk Route by Rail	2nd edn out now
Sahara Overland – a route & planning guide	1st edn out now
Sahara Abenteuerhandbuch (German edition)	1st edn early 2001
Ski Canada – where to ski and snowboard	1st edn out now
Trans-Siberian Handbook	5th edn Jan 2001
Trans-Canada Rail Guide	2nd edn out now
Trekking in the Annapurna Region	3rd edn out now
Trekking in the Everest Region	3rd edn out now
Trekking in Langtang, Gosainkund & Helambu	1st edn out now
Trekking in Corsica	1st edn Dec 2001
Trekking in the Dolomites	1st edn Mar 2001
Trekking in Ladakh	2nd edn out now
Trekking in the Moroccan Atlas	1st edn Jan 2001
Vietnam by Rail	1st edn Dec 2000

For more information about Trailblazer and our expanding range of guides,
for where to find your nearest stockist, for guidebook updates
or for credit card mail order sales (post free worldwide) visit our Web site:

www.trailblazer-guides.com

ROUTE GUIDES FOR THE ADVENTUROUS TRAVELLER

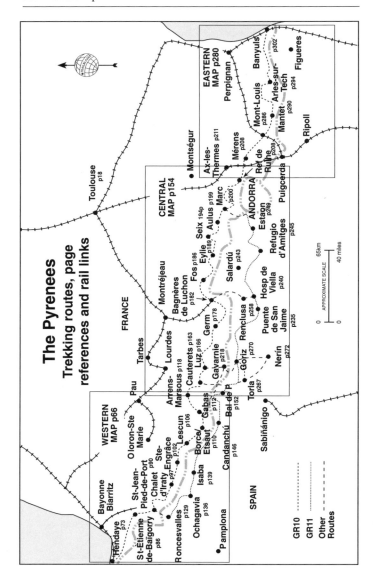

The Pyrenees
Trekking routes, page references and rail links

FRANCE

SPAIN

ANDORRA

Bayonne
Biarritz

Hendaye p73

St-Jean-Pied-de-Port

St-Étienne-de-Baigorry p86

Roncesvalles

Ochagavia p129

Isaba p136

Pamplona

Chalet d'Iraty p97

Ste-Engrâce p102

Lescun p106

Borce Etsaut p110

Candanchú p146

Sabiñánigo

Oloron-Ste-Marie p90

Pau p118

Tarbes

Lourdes

Arrens-Marsous p118

Gabas p112

Bal-de-P p152

Cauterets p163

Luz p166

Gavarnie p218

Torla p267

Nerín p272

Gòriz p270

Germ p178

Reinclusa p258

Puente de San Jaime p235

Hosp de Viella p240

Salardú p243

Bagnères de Luchon p182

Montréjeau

Fos p186

Eylie p189

Aulus p199

Selx 194p

Marc p200

Estaon p249

Refugio d'Amitges p245

Puigcerdà

Ax-les-Thermes p211

Montségur

Mérens p208

Ref de Ruhe p208

Ripoll

Mont-Louis p286

Arles-sur-Tech p290

Mantet p294

Banyuls p302

Figueres p294

Perpignan

Toulouse p18

WESTERN MAP p66

CENTRAL MAP p154

EASTERN MAP p280

APPROXIMATE SCALE

0   65km

0   40 miles

GR10 ....
GR11 ——————
Other Routes – – – –